Blood Moon's
MEDIA BUZZ

Everything You Wanted to Know but Were Afraid to Ask

Darwin Porter & Danforth Prince

WHAT IS BLOOD MOON PRODUCTIONS?

"Blood Moon, in case you don't know, is a publishing house on Staten Island that cranks out Hollywood gossip books, about two or three a year, usually of five- six- or 700-page length, chocked with stories and pictures about people who used to consume the imaginations of the American public, back when we actually had a public imagination. That is, when people were really interested in each other, rather than in Apple 'devices.' In other words back when we had vices, not devices."

—The Huffington Post

www.BloodMoonProductions.com

Challenging the Status Quo's Beliefs about
Celebrity & the Ironies of Fame

Blood Moon's Media Buzz

Within the pages of this book, with the kind permission and
approval of Anita Finley, twenty years of monthly columns
authored by Darwin Porter were resurrected from the archives of
Boomer Times & Senior Life,
South Florida's leading magazine for Seniors

**Darwin Porter
& Danforth Prince**

ISBN 978-1-936003-97-6

Book design, layouts, and editorial services by Danforth Prince.
Unless otherwise stated, all texts are copyright ©2025 Blood Moon Productions, Ltd.
with all rights reserved.
www.BloodMoonProductions.com

The galleys for this book were composed and laid out on Quark Express.
It was manufactured in the USA, and distributed worldwide through
Ingram, Amazon.com, and internet vendors everywhere.

This Book Is Dedicated to Anita Finley

Portraits of a Lady: Anita Finley

Anita is the founder and publisher of the now-defunct *Boomer Times and Senior Life* Magazine, once the premier magazine for seniors in South Florida, a periodical of influence throughout the State, and a generator of massive advertising revenues. Long ago and far away, it was included as a monthly supplement within home deliveries of the *Miami Herald* throughout Dade and Broward Counties, Florida.

A noted gerontologist and a woman of influence, Anita became famous for organizing symposiums that assembled experts on health care, non-traditional methods of healing, and the fine art of generating friendships and acquiring happiness. The discussion groups that evolved from these conclaves genuinely made a difference in the well-being of seniors throughout the state.

This book is an anthology of the editorial materials crafted over the lifespan of her magazine by Darwin Porter and Danforth Prince, Focussing on pop culture and show-biz, they appeared in her magazine at monthly intervals as MEDIA BUZZ.

For permission to replicate them, here, in expanded formats, as a testimonial to the way we were, we thank, honor, and acknowledge her.

FOR MORE THAN TWENTY YEARS, THROUGH HER MAGAZINE AND HER RADIO PROGRAM, ANITA & DARWIN WOKE UP SOUTH FLORIDA

THEY MET AT THE RIGHT TIME—WHEN THE 21ST CENTURY WAS STILL IN DIAPERS.

She had established a popular magazine for senior citizens in South Florida, and shortly before she met Darwin, she had arranged a distribution deal with the Miami Herald.

Issued monthly, Boomer Times was filled with fascinating articles intended to help senior citizens lead happier, healthier, and better lives. Of particular interest were her overviews of current trends in BOOKS and ENTERTAINMENT, subjects which Darwin understood and spoke and wrote about (some even said "obsessed" about) frequently.

But other than the humor, glitter, and flash that Darwin brought to it, Boomer Times for the most part focused on practical subjects of everyday merit, enriched with advice from experts.
Here are some sample headlines Anita's readers witnessed during its evolution:

HOW TO RESOLVE MARRIAGE CONFLICTS CAUSED BY RETIREMENT
TERM Vs. PERMANENT LIFE INSURANCE
THE PROMISE OF MEDICAL BREAKTHROUGH IS NOW!
HOW TO REVERSE BRAIN AGING
NEW BEGINNINGS FOR YOUR FINANCIAL WELL-BEING
DO YOU BANK ON SOCIAL SECURITY FOR YOUR RETIREMENT INCOME?

***

When Anita began to publish columns by Darwin, he was the most widely read author of travel guides in the world. Since 1960, often in partnership with Stanley Mills Haggart (1910-1980), Darwin had written many dozens of travel guides to cities, regions, and countries of Europe, and to states or regions of the U.S. from California to New England. Depending on the assignment and its venue, he had been based, for practical and sometimes whimsical reasons, in venues as far-flung as New York, Los Angeles, London, Paris, and Rome.

***

BUT TIMES WERE CHANGING: Intuitively, and perhaps with a sense of impending doom for "the way it was," Darwin realized early in the New Century that travel guides in the form we knew during our heydays would fade in both popularity and sales. Indeed, as the travel industry's status quo went "Gone With the Wind," he shifted his writing talents to biographies, mostly of Hollywood stars of the Golden Age. He had multiple caches of research data at his disposal—mostly in the form of oral histories he'd been collecting, obsessively, since his early teens.

What did these stories have in common? Each shared a theme that focused on The IRONIES OF FAME. *Boomer Times* provided a venue for the publication of social truths that were too hot for release when they originally unfolded. From this monthly collaboration, **A STAR WAS BORN**: Her name is **Anita Finley,** to whom this book is dedicated.

DID YOU KNOW? THAT IN 2023, ANITA, A GERONTOLOGIST KNOWN FOR HER FORMIDABLE INTERPERSONAL SKILLS, MADE **MARITAL NEWS** AFTER A FAST-PACED LATE-IN-LIFE ROMANCE (AND SUDDEN MARRIAGE) TO ONE OF THE MOST ELIGIBLE BACHELORS IN SOUTH FLORIDA?

AND DID YOU KNOW? THAT IN DECEMBER OF 2025, ANITA ORGANIZED THE WRITING AND THE PUBLICATION OF HER HUSBAND'S MEMOIR, A NOSTALGIC OVERVIEW OF A LIFE OF PUBLIC SERVICE AND MILITARY HONOR (SEE FRONT AND BACK COVERS, BELOW)

BORN AMID THE ROCKS AND CONIFERS OF IDAHO, HE'S FORMER NAVAL COMMANDER JOHN PATRICK DERR. AFTER HIS RETIREMENT FROM ACTIVE DURY IN 1977, HE WORKED FOR TEN YEARS AS THE EMERGENCY MANAGEMENT DIRECTOR OF CHARLOTTE COUNTY, FLORIDA AND ORGANIZED CHARTER SAILS FROM FLORIDA TO THE BRITISH VIRGIN ISLANDS. HE'S PICTURED IN THE LEFT PHOTO, IN 2024 (POST-NUPTIAL), WITH ANITA ON THE DRIVEWAY OF THEIR HOME IN PORT CHARLOTTE, FL. ABOVE, RIGHT, HE'S TAKING CARE OF ACTIVE NAVAL DUTIES IN THE 1960S.

IN THE WAKE OF THEIR WEDDING IN 2023, DOZENS OF ANITA'S FANS NATIONWIDE SAID "**BRAVISSIMA!**" AND SENT HEARTFELT CONGRATULATIONS TO EACH OF THEM.

STARING DOWN A HUNDRED YEARS

A RETIRED U.S. NAVAL OFFICER RECAPS NEARLY A CENTURY OF 'EPISODES'

JOHN P. DERR

RETIRED NAVAL COMMANDER JOHN P. DERR'S OBSERVATIONS ARE CULLED FROM BOTH LIFE ON THE HIGH SEAS AND MANY PLACES ON EARTH, ALL BEGINNING FROM A RURAL LIFESTYLE ON A FARM IN NORTH IDAHO.

ENJOY THIS COLLECTION OF SOUVENIRS, MUSINGS AND REFLECTIONS FROM A 96-YEAR OLD WORLD TRAVELER WHO HAS "BEEN THERE AND DONE THAT."

HE AND HIS WIFE, ANITA FINLEY-DERR, AND THEIR NEW ADDITION, "JP," ALSO KNOWN AS THE "GANG OF THREE," LIVE IN PORT CHARLOTTE, FLORIDA.

Blood Moon proudly defines *Media Buzz* as Volume Twelve in its Magnolia House Series

Contents

Part One
    Boomer Times, which celebrates his inclusion as a monthly columnist, proudly re-introduces **Darwin Porter**   page 1

Part Two: BABY BOOMERS
    Boomers Had it Good That's not the case for Zoomers   page 5
    A Call for Boomer Power   page 7
    Decline & Fall of the Boomers   page 9

Part Three: CONNECTED ZEITGEIST STARS WHO ROCKED
    Elon Musk   page 11
    Stormy Daniels   page 21
    Michael Cohen   page 29

Part Four: CREATIVE MALADIES
    Paul Gauguin   page 33
    William Shakespeare   page 35
    Alan Turing   page 37
    Tennessee Williams, Gore Vidal, and Truman Capote   page 39

Part Four: HOW TO BEHAVE (or not to behave) DURING SEISMIC HISTORIC EVENTS
    Paul Farnes & the Battle of Britain   page 41
    Gudren Himmler Burwitz   page 43
    Lady Jean Campbell   page 45
    Hugh Hefner   page 47
    Howard Hughes   page 51
    Charles Lindbergh   page 53
    Jeremy Meeks   page 55
    Bess Myerson   page 57
    Evaluating the Celebrities of History   page 59
    Gianni Russo   page 61
    Josef Stalin   page 63
    Volodymyr Zielinskyy   page 65

Part Five: THE KENNEDYS

Lem Billings	page 67
Caroline Kennedy Cashes in on Camelot	page 69
Jackie's Affair with RFK	page 71
JFK Jr.	page 73
Joe Kennedy III, Son of Camelot	page 75
THE KENNEDYS: All the Gossip Unfit to Print	page 77
Jackie-O: A Life Beyond Her Wildest Dreams	page 79
Rosemary Kennedy	page 81

Part Six: BY THE DAWN'S EARLY LIGHT

Darwin & Anita's Monthly Spin on Celebrity & Fame	pages 83-206

Part Six of this book has everything You've Ever Wanted to Know about what *Boomer Times* broadcast at monthly intervals "by the dawn's early light" during the final years of the American Century.

Fueled by a near-obsession with the American concept of celebrity and fame, the Porter/Finley *kaffeeklatches* included indiscreet allegations about every star in Golden-Age Hollywood:

Their flash points included **Ingrid Bergman, Gina Lollabrigida, Brigitte Bardot, Humphrey Bogart, Katharine Hepburn, Marlon Brando, Frank Sinatra, Vivien Leigh, Laurence Olivier, Elizabeth Taylor** (and what people were saying about her), **Steve McQueen, The Celluloid Closet, the F.B.I's J. Edgar Hoover & Clyde Tolson, Luscious Lana Turner, Carrie Fisher and Debbie Reynolds, Howard Hughes, The Kennedys, The Reagans, the Clintons, Donald Trump, Playboy's Hugh Hefner, That Terrible Trio of glitterati playwrights (Tennessee Williams, Gore Vidal, & Truman Capote), Rock ("Casting Couch" and "Apollo Incarnate) Hudson, Burt Reynolds, Linda Lovelace and the Legacy of *Deep Throat*, Paul Newman, Kirk Douglas, Peter O'Toole, Zsa Zsa and Eva Gabor, Michael Jackson,** did we say **Donald Trump?, Henry Fonda and his outspoken children, Peter and Jane, Judy Garland and Liza, Mercedes de Acosta and her fashionably *avant-garde* coterie of lesbians, Jackie-O!, Lucille Ball & Desi Arnaz, Marilyn Monroe** (who really killed her?), and a few insights into what motivates Blood Moon Productions and makes its authors tick.

Part Seven: LET US ENTERTAIN YOU

The Canteen Girl, Phyllis Creore	page 207
Fly Me to the Moon	page 209
Joan Rivers	page 211
Oprah Winfrey	page 213

Part Eight: ODDITIES OF EARTH

Celebrity Internet Fraud	page 215
Dumbness of Americans	page 217
Hurricanes	page 219
Is It Incest?	page 221
Return of the Woolley Mammoth	page 223
Medical Oddities of Yesteryear	page 225
Napoléon's Penis	page 227
Nobody Lives Forever: An Overview of Very Old, Very Famous Women	page 229
UFO's	page 231
Victory Gardens	page 233

Part Eight: POLITICS

Hillary Clinton and Her Boy Lover from Outer Space	page 235
Bill & Hillary: So This Is That Thing Called Love	page 237
Doug Emhoff: First Gent in the White House?	page 239
Pete Buttigieg: American's First Self-Defined Gay Cabinet Member	page 240
First Ladies, Part One	page 241
First Ladies: The Hardest Unpaid Job in the World	page 245
Lacerating First Ladies: America's Favorite Blood Sport	page 247
Dolley Madison	page 249
Franklin & Eleanor: Adultery in the White House	page 251
Sandra Lee and Andrew Cuomo	page 253
Emmanuel Macron of France	page 255
Mourning the Destruction of the Ukraine	page 257
Tricia Nixon and Her Many Ironies	page 259
Obama to Africa: "I'll Be Back"	page 261
Silver Tsunamis	page 263
Jackie Speier	page 265
The Man Who Tried to Kill Ronald Reagan	page 267
Justin Trudeau	page 271
Who Was the Worst U.S. President?	page 273

Part Nine: STARRY NIGHTS

James Dean, the 20th Century's OTHER Most Famous Icon	page 275
Extinction of the Movie Star	page 277
Kirk Douglas	page 279
The Casting Couch Triumphs of Rock Hudson	page 281
Rock Hudson's Blackmailer, Phyllis Gates	page 283
The Strange Multi-Cultural Lives of Hedy Lamarr	page 285
Latino and Older Female Actors: "What About Us?"	page 287
Alexander McQueen: *Fashionista* of *Haute* London	page 289
Dina Merrill	page 291
HEEEEEERE's MERV!	page 293
The Cold War Ironies of MM and Nikita Khrushchev	page 295
Mystic Ladies: Mona Lisa and the Statue of Liberty	page 297
Broadway Joe Namath	page 301
Unsinkable Tammy and Princess Leia in Hell	page 303
Jane Russell	page 307
Dear Abby: Twin Sisters Offer Advice to the Lovelorn	page 309

Part Ten: THE WINDSORS

Sarah Ferguson	page 311
God Save the Queen	page 313
Resurrection from the Grave	page 315
Who Is the Biological Father of Prince Harry?	page 317

AUTHORS' BIOS   page 321

PREVIOUS WORKS BY DARWIN PORTER

BIOGRAPHIES

Blood Moon Productions: Its Origins, Its Oeuvre, Its Sources, and Its Legacy
Entertainment About How America Interprets Its Legends, Icons, & Celebrities

Clark Gable, The King of Hollywood
Volume One (1901-1938) of a Three-Part Biography

The Donald: How Did It Happen (The Gathering Storm)

Henry Fonda, He Did It His Way
(Volume One —1905-1960—of a Two-Part Biography)

The Fondas, Henry, Jane, & Peter
(Volume Two—1962-1982—of a Two-Part Biography)

Lucille Ball & Desi Arnaz: They Weren't Lucy & Ricky Ricardo
(Volume One—1911-1960—of a Two-Part Biography)

The Sad & Tragic Ending of Lucille Ball
(Volume Two—1961-1989—of a Two-Part Biography

Marilyn: Don't Even Dream About Tomorrow
(a 2021 revised version of the best-selling Marilyn at Rainbow's End: Sex, Lies, Murder, &
the Great Cover-Up (2012)

The Seductive Sapphic Exploits of Mercedes de Acosta
Hollywood's Greatest Lover

Jacqueline Kennedy Onassis, Her Tumultuous Life & Her Love Affairs

Judy Garland & Liza Minnelli, Too Many Damn Rainbows

Historic Magnolia House: Celebrity & The Ironies of Fame

Glamour, Glitz, & Gossip at Historic Magnolia House

Burt Reynolds, Put the Pedal to the Metal

Kirk Douglas, More Is Never Enough

Playboy's Hugh Hefner, Empire of Skin

Carrie Fisher & Debbie Reynolds,
Princess Leia & Unsinkable Tammy in Hell

Rock Hudson Erotic Fire

Lana Turner, Hearts & Diamonds Take All

Donald Trump, The Man Who Would Be King

James Dean, Tomorrow Never Comes

Bill and Hillary, So This Is That Thing Called Love

Peter O'Toole, Hellraiser, Sexual Outlaw, Irish Rebel

Love Triangle, Ronald Reagan, Jane Wyman, & Nancy Davis

Pink Triangle, The Feuds and Private Lives of Tennessee Williams, Gore Vidal, Truman Capote, and Famous Members of their Entourages.

Those Glamorous Gabors, Bombshells from Budapest

Inside Linda Lovelace's Deep Throat, Degradation, Porno Chic, and the Rise of Feminism

Elizabeth Taylor, There is Nothing Like a Dame

J. Edgar Hoover and Clyde Tolson
Investigating the Sexual Secrets of America's Most Famous Men and Women

Frank Sinatra, The Boudoir Singer. All the Gossip Unfit to Print

The Kennedys, All the Gossip Unfit to Print

The Secret Life of Humphrey Bogart (2003), and
Humphrey Bogart, The Making of a Legend (2010)

Howard Hughes, Hell's Angel

Steve McQueen, King of Cool, Tales of a Lurid Life

Paul Newman, The Man Behind the Baby Blues

Merv Griffin, A Life in the Closet

Brando Unzipped

Katharine the Great, Hepburn, Secrets of a Lifetime Revealed

Jacko, His Rise and Fall, The Social and Sexual History of Michael Jackson

Damn You, Scarlett O'Hara,
The Private Lives of Vivien Leigh and Laurence Olivier

FILM CRITICISM

Blood Moon's 2005 Guide to the Glitter Awards

Blood Moon's 2006 Guide to LGBTQ Film

Blood Moon's 2007 Guide to LGBTQ Film, and

50 Years of Queer Cinema, 500 of the Best LGBTQ Films Ever Made

NON-FICTION

Hollywood Babylon, It's Back!; Hollywood Babylon Strikes Again!; and
Hollywood Babylon with Detours to Gomorrah

An enlarged, new edition of the scandal-soaked anthologies that made Blood Moon famous
Hollywood Remembered: Glamour, Glitz, Triumph, & Tragedy
A Tribute to the Glory Days of Entertainment & the Way We Were

NOVELS

Blood Moon
Hollywood's Silent Closet
Rhinestone Country
Razzle Dazzle
Midnight in Savannah
The Delinquent Heart
The Taste of Steak Tartare
Butterflies in Heat
Marika (a roman à clef based on the life of Marlene Dietrich)
Venus (a roman à clef based on the life of Anaïs Nin)
Sister Rose

BIOGRAPHIES

From Diaghilev to Balanchine, The Saga of Ballerina Tamara Geva
Greta Keller, Germany's Other Lili Marleen
Sophie Tucker, The Last of the Red Hot Mamas
Anne Bancroft, Where Have You Gone, Mrs. Robinson?
(co-authored with Stanley Mills Haggart)
Veronica Lake, The Peek-a-Boo Girl
Running Wild in Babylon, Confessions of a Hollywood Press Agent

HISTORIES

Thurlow Weed, Whig Kingpin
Chester A. Arthur, Gilded Age Coxcomb in the White House
Discover Old America, What's Left of It

TRAVEL GUIDES

MANY EDITIONS AND MANY VARIATIONS OF THE FROMMER GUIDES, THE AMERICAN EXPRESS GUIDES, AND/OR TWA GUIDES, ET ALIA TO:

Andalusia, Andorra, Anguilla, Aruba, Atlanta, Austria, the Azores, The Bahamas, Barbados, the Bavarian Alps, Berlin, Bermuda, Bonaire and Curaçao, Boston, the British Virgin Islands, Budapest, Bulgaria, California, the Canary Islands, the Caribbean and its "Ports of Call," the Cayman Islands, Ceuta, the Channel Islands (UK), Charleston (SC), Corsica, Costa del Sol (Spain), Denmark, Dominica, the Dominican Republic, Edinburgh, England, Estonia, Europe, "Europe by Rail," the Faroe Islands, Finland, Florence, France, Frankfurt, the French Riviera, Geneva, Georgia (USA), Germany, Gibraltar, Glasgow, Granada (Spain), Great Britain, Greenland, Grenada (West Indies), Haiti, Hungary, Iceland, Ireland, Isle of Man, Italy, Jamaica, Key West & the Florida Keys, Las Vegas, Liechtenstein, Lisbon, London, Los Angeles, Madrid, Maine, Malta, Martinique & Guadeloupe, Massachusetts, Melilla, Morocco, Munich, New England, New Orleans, North Carolina, Norway, Paris, Poland, Portugal, Provence, Puerto Rico,

IT WAS THE BEGINNING OF A BEAUTIFUL FRIENDSHIP

Editor's Note: HERE is the text that Boomer Times *used to introduce Darwin as a columnist, several decades ago, back when his byline was new and novel to their readers.*

In 2025, it's so outdated as to be almost quaint. Nonetheless, we replicate it below as a reminder of how his association with Boomer Times began, long ago and far away.

Boomer Times, in His Capacity as a Monthly Columnist, Proudly Introduces

DARWIN PORTER

Blood Moon Productions, in cooperation with *Boomer Times & Senior Life*, is proud to announce the debut of Darwin Porter as a monthly columnist for this magazine. Darwin's link to Florida is strong and affectionate: A graduate of the University of Miami, where he was editor-in-chief of the school paper, and a former Key West bureau chief for *The Miami Herald*, Darwin is well-known as the head writer of "about 50" current editions of *The Frommer Travel Guides*.

Other than travel, Darwin's real journalistic love involves the tricky art of the celebrity interview. He's gifted at coaxing revelations from celebrities about show-biz indiscretions that in many cases have never before seen the light of publication. "After a certain point in their lives, movie celebrities stop caring about whether what they say will have an adverse affect on their career," says Darwin. "They figure, 'what the hell, I'll be dead soon anyway.' And in many cases they want to set the record straight about what really happened during key episodes of their lives and careers."

With impish charm, Porter admits to having conducted "about a thousand" official interviews, and about five times that many "unofficial," less formal conversations with big-name celebrities, snippets from which have made their way into some of his recent biographies. The best of those anecdotes will be wending their way into this column.

Here's **Darwin Porter** during the heyday of his Florida-based rise, as a Bureau Chief, at the *Miami Herald*, to journalistic prominence.

Despite his origins in western North Carolina, his vast European exposure through **The Frommer Guides**, and his half-century residency in New York City, he still defines himself as "a spiritual Floridean," steeped in the ethos of the politics and priorities of the very complicated Sunshine State.

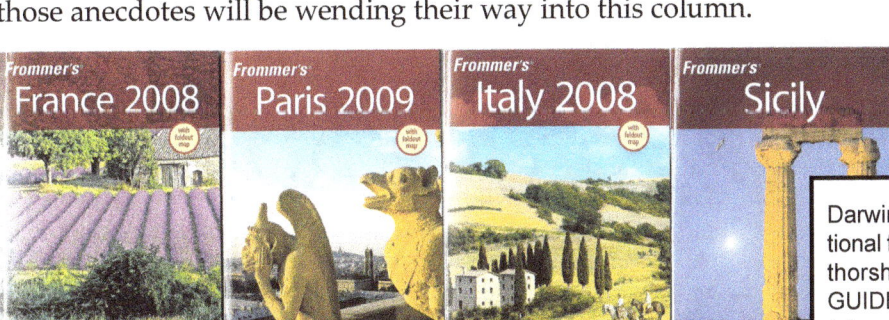

Darwin's grasp of the politics associated with international fame is deep, thorough, and world-class. His authorship of hundreds of editions of THE FROMMER GUIDES took him everywhere and introduced him to (almost) everyone during the 50 years when the celebrity haunts of the world were, indeed, his "beat."

What should readers expect in the weeks to come? Darwin's arsenal of stories will feature, among other revelations, what Ronald Reagan was really up to "between marriages;" **Marlon Brando** as you never knew him; **Bette Davis** in some shocking, surprising jams; **Ingrid Bergman** confiding what really went on between **Bogie** and herself during the making of *Casablanca*; and lots of other good insiderish stuff telling the real stories about everybody from **Elvis Presley** to **Joan Crawford**.

Stay tuned, through upcoming editions of *Boomer Times*, for more about Hollywood from Darwin Porter.

Recent critically acclaimed biographies by Darwin Porter include *The Secret Life of Humphrey Bogart: The Early Years (1899-1931)*; and *Katharine the Great: Secrets of a Lifetime Revealed*, in which relatively unknown aspects of the life of Katharine Hepburn were described and published for the first time. Darwin's most recent release, simultaneously reviewed in March of 2005 by three of London's biggest newspapers (including *The London Times*), is *Howard Hughes: Hell's Angel*, which the *New York Daily News* described as "a book that pulls THE AVIATOR firmly back to earth." Blood Moon plans a September release for Darwin's upcoming memorial to Marlon, *Brando Unzipped*.

Three views of Darwin Porter: *Left and right*: Yesterday, when he was young, and *center photo* from around 2010, being interviewed at home during a televised interview with documentarians from a Japanese television station.

Travel Guides Authored by Darwin Porter

MANY EDITIONS AND MANY VARIATIONS OF *THE FROMMER GUIDES*, *THE AMERICAN EXPRESS GUIDES*, AND/OR *TWA GUIDES*, ET ALIA TO:

Andalusia, Andorra, Anguilla, Aruba, Atlanta, Austria, the Azores, The Bahamas, Barbados, the Bavarian Alps, Berlin, Bermuda, Bonaire and Curaçao, Boston, the British Virgin Islands, Budapest, Bulgaria, California, the Canary Islands, the Caribbean and its "Ports of Call," the Cayman Islands, Ceuta, the Channel Islands (UK), Charleston (SC), Corsica, Costa del Sol (Spain), Denmark, Dominica, the Dominican Republic, Edinburgh, England, Estonia, Europe, "Europe by Rail," the Faroe Islands, Finland, Florence, France, Frankfurt, the French Riviera, Geneva, Georgia (USA), Germany, Gibraltar, Glasgow, Granada (Spain), Great Britain, Greenland, Grenada (West Indies), Haiti, Hungary, Iceland, Ireland, Isle of Man, Italy, Jamaica, Key West & the Florida Keys, Las Vegas, Liechtenstein, Lisbon, London, Los Angeles, Madrid, Maine, Malta, Martinique & Guadeloupe, Massachusetts, Melilla, Morocco, Munich, New England, New Orleans, North Carolina, Norway, Paris, Poland, Portugal, Provence, Puerto Rico, Romania, Rome, Salzburg, San Diego, San Francisco, San Marino, Sardinia, Savannah, Scandinavia, Scotland, Seville, the Shetland Islands, Sicily, St. Martin & Sint Maarten, St. Vincent & the Grenadines, South Carolina, Spain, St. Kitts & Nevis, Sweden, Switzerland, the Turks & Caicos, the U.S.A., the U.S. Virgin Islands, Venice, Vienna and the Danube, Wales, and Zurich.

Entertainment-Industry Overviews by Darwin Porter, a recognized expert in the business of celebrity bios, movie stars, and the ego-driven incentives that make them tick.

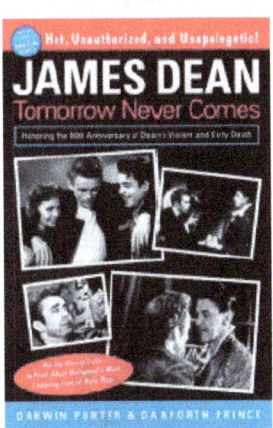

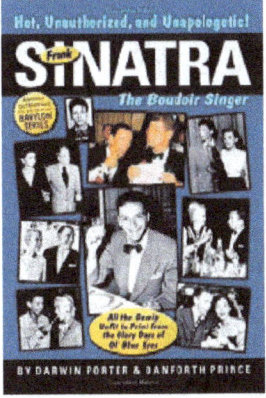

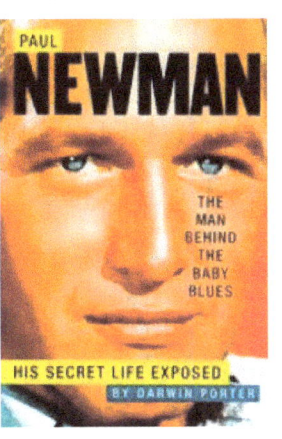

More Entertainment-Industry Overviews by Darwin Porter

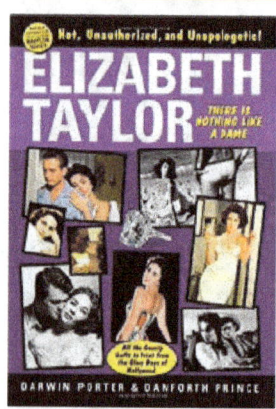

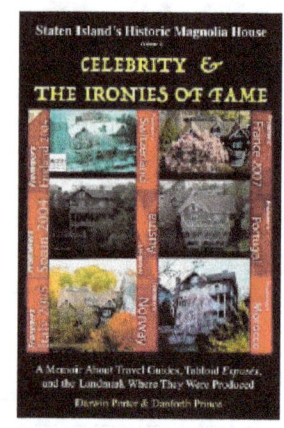

April 2023

WHEREAS BOOMERS HAD IT GOOD, ZOOMERS ARE FACING DISASTER

Fires, Pandemics, Worldwide Starvation, Climate Change, Floods, Crop Failures, Political & Economic Instability

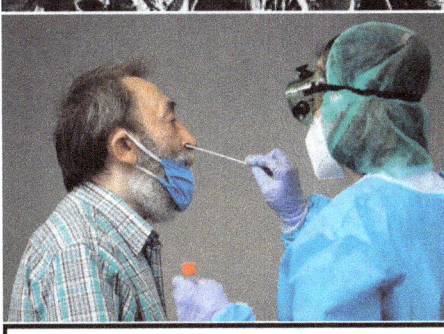

If, as some futurists are predicting, Armageddon is on the way, **Zoomers** might face "oceans of agony" more severe than anything experienced during their lifetimes by **Boomers.**

The long-awaited report from the world's foremost scientists about climate change has been released. The conclusion was that time is running out, and that it is almost too late to avoid a catastrophe, and that people around the world should at least make attempts to lessen the impact.

This startling news was almost buried under the barrage of stories from the besieged Ukraine, now fighting a World War II-style military attack from Russia.

The Intergovernmental Panel on Climate Change is a body of experts from seventy countries which conducted detailed investigations into the massive upcoming crisis. Some 195 governments have already accepted their findings.

A dismal forecast was presented. Beginning in the immediate decades, upheavals affecting billions of lives were forecast: Flooded coastal regions; widespread famine causing millions to starve; the worst wildfires the world has ever known; storms that will destroy miles-long stretches of homes; widespread droughts and massive crop failures.

Once plentiful, drinkable water will become a vital resource. Its scarcity will devastate some 800,000 people, that number eventually swelling to three billion.

Some one million plant and animal species will become extinct before the end of this century. Newer and more dreadful pandemics will devastate the populations of every continent on earth.

Although some of them are already here, of course, the disasters will only get worse. In Kenya recently, a prolonged drought devastated farmlands before bitter cold descended on the land, killing herds of goats and sheep on which Kenyans depend.

The scientific panel concluded that at its present rate, the world will face warming of two to three degrees Celsius, and that when temperatures rise a mere 1.5 degrees Celsius, unimaginably catastrophic events will begin to unfold.

Governments are spending billions right now on humanitarian emergencies, but it's not enough, the panel concluded. Even one of the poorest countries in the world, South Sudan, shelled out $375 million last year after floods left thousands of its people homeless.

On looking back, Baby Boomers born after World War II are said to have lived through the greatest prosperity the world has ever known. There were disasters, of course, like the Vietnam War, but for the most part, it was an era of growth, invention, the greatest artistic Renaissance of all time, and a standard of living never achieved before.

However, the "Zoomers," as Generation Z is called, will not have it so good. As the smartest of them know, "We will face the greatest problems our world has ever seen," as stated by Greg Toulouis, born in 1992.

"Many of us will get married and want a family. However, to prevent overpopulation, it would be better if my wife and I adopted children from the world's homeless, instead of birthing a brood ourselves."

March 2022

AN URGENT CALL FOR BOOMERS TO USE THEIR POLITICAL POWER

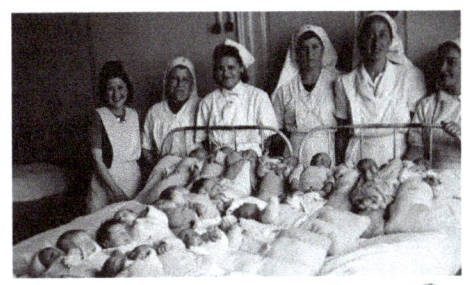

Baby Boomers (upper photo) used their political clout effectively to influence government policies at events that included **Woodstock** (lower photo).

Bill McKibben, America's leading environmentalist, is sending out a clarion call to his fellow Boomers to join the fight to save the planet from devastation by climate changes.

He has organized a group of Boomers known as "The Third Act." Their goal involves establishing branches in every region of the country. Early members include Norman Lear, Jane Fonda, and Senator Bernie Sanders of Vermont.

McKibben's hope involves firing up "the boilers of activism" again, reminding Boomers that in the 1960s and 70s, they radically changed the cultural, social, and political history of America. According to McKibben—who among other duties is a professor at Middlebury College in Vermont—"I think we can do it again."

Before it inevitably passes away from them, vast amounts of political power remains in the hands of Boomers who, along with their aging parents, include 75 million members (and voters) of the U.S. population. In 2020, they formed 44 percent of the U.S. electorate, and they control 70 percent of America's wealth. [That percentage is in vivid contrast to millennials, who control only 5 percent of it.]

"It seems unfair to leave the problems of climate change to today's high schoolers," McKibben says. "Young people are already accusing us of leaving the planet in worse shape than we found it. Of course, we Boomers are closer to the door marked 'exit' than the one labeled 'entrance.' But time remains to bring about change before we go on our way."

"Septuagenarians still hold great political power." McKibben continues. "Joe Biden, for example, is no spring chicken. His 'climate czar,' John Kerry, who once ran for U.S. President, needs far more help than he gets and a lot more resources."

So far, McKibben has written the best book on the dangers of climate change, a best-seller called The End of Nature. His revelations are frightening: "Every day, the extra heat from carbon sent into the atmosphere is the equivalent of five 1945-era Hiroshima bombs. The non-believer need only look at the images on television of massive floods and raging forest fires."

Zeitgeist luminary **Bill McKibben** suggests that if the world gets "saved" from traumas to come, Baby Boomers will have to get politicized and "resist" even more strenuously than they did during the peak of their anti-Vietnam rage.

Scientists tell us that emissions must be cut in half by 2030 or there will be dire consequences. The clock is ticking. Thousands of Boomers are taking climate change seriously, but millions more are needed to pressure Congress and State legislatures.

"Many young people, fearing for their future, are already engaged," McKibben says. "Boomers should join them. It is not a partisan fight. It is an American fight. Remember this—the Arctic is melting, the Amazon degraded, and the oceans heating up. If a chapter of *Third Act (www.ThirdAct.org)* comes to your neighborhood, sign up," McKibben urges. "We need you. Obviously, it's too late to completely stop global warming. The question is, 'Can we stop short of the point where it destroys civilizations?'"

September 2016 — Celebrating 26 Years of PRINT, RADIO & WEB

Boomer Times
& Senior Life

Listen to Boomer Times Radio Shows! Saturdays 5-8am, WSBR 740am

boomertimesfl.com
boomerexpofl.com
cure-symposium.com

Like us on Facebook   Click BoomerTimes YouTube

THE DECLINE AND FALL OF THE BABY BOOMERS
(They're Expected to Expire in 2083)

Futurists who analyze population trends predict that the sputtering out of what's by then left of the Baby Boomers will happen in 2083. That's based on the assumption that Boomers produced in the final year (1964) of what has traditionally defined as the last birth year of the Boomer demographic will have reached the by-now feasible age of 119.

Impossible, you say? No, it's not. In fact, the oldest living American, Sarah Krauss, was born in 1880 when Rutherford B. Hayes was president. She survived when medical practice was, by today's standards, relatively primitive. Men of her era often died of "old age" at 52. Sarah was 28 when she rode in Henry Ford's Model T. During each of America's World Wars, the Stars and Stripes flew from her rooftop. Ironically, she lived to see Bill Clinton, as President, facing impeachment for lying about his affair with Monica Lewinsky.

***

Launched with the "Baby Tsunami" of 1946, Baby Boomers grew up to rule America, and many of them are still in charge. By 2060, however, the Boomers who remain are expected to count for only one percent of the population.

Why? At that time, the number of U.S. citizens 65 and over is expected to spiral to 95 million by 2060. That will put a great burden on Social Security, which is badly funded even today. Unfortunately for them, Generation Z and those to follow will need to take care of an aging population.

The politics of the new generations are already radically different from that of many prominent politicos today. Generation Z will certainly foster new revolutions of their own. It has an ironically powerful message for the Supreme Court: "WE WILL OUTLIVE YOU!"

Since the country's founding, whites have been the dominant power, but within the New America, new rulers, new priorities, and a new kind of language will emerge. The argot of tomorrow will be a pop-derived mixture of Spanish and English, with many tech-age references (some derived from "artificial intelligence") thrown in. These changes will signal radical changes in everything from morality to politics.

Baby Boomers will for the most part have disappeared before additional (major) dysfunctions descend on the planet: Famine, the acquisition of hydrogen bombs by terrorist regimes, climate change, overpopulation, territorial wars, and a continuation of the ongoing extinction of thousands of species of wildlife.

These problems will be left for upcoming generations to solve. We wish them well. These new power brokers will be your great-grandchildren, even your great-great-grandchildren

We, the kings and queens of the Boomer Era will be gone. Long live the kings and queens who replace us.

Upper photo: Emulation of tenderness between a robot and a human based on Artificial Intelligence, and *Lower photo:* **Boomers** in a moment of (hopefully) wise and reflective decline.

The Kings & Queens are Dead, Long Live the Kings and Queens:

Some historians interpret the headline as ""The King cannot die - only the actors who play him." It also implies that the institution of the monarchy never dies, since the reign of the new king begins at the moment of death of his predecessor.

The Illustration depicts the **Death of Saint-Louis**, France's King Louis IX, in 1270. Obviously, Europe and the World continued, frenziedly, without him.

January 2016

Celebrating 26 Years of PRINT, RADIO & WEB

Boomer Times
& Senior Life

babyboomers-seniors.com
boomerexpofl.com   cure-symposium.com

Boomer Times Invites You!

Celebrate the 15th Boomer Expo
Friday, January 22 from 10 to 4
Seminole Hard Rock Hotel & Casino

WIN Over 50 Great Prizes
Fun, Music & Special Exhibitors
Dedicated to our Veterans

Finding Peace When Your Heart Is in Pieces
"Book of the Month"
A Step-by-Step Guide to the Other Side of Grief, Loss, and Pain
PAUL COLEMAN, PsyD

The Brief, Rage-Inducing Reign of an American Co-President

ELON MUSK
The Richest Man in the World

One of the most controversial persons in the world—and also the wealthiest—Elon Musk makes headlines as a polarizing figure. In 2025, he was called "The Co-President of the United States", "The Shadow President", or "The Actual President-Elect."

Many reporters, and much of the public, constantly mention their surprise that "King Trump," as he is sometimes known, is willing to share his throne with this headline grabber.

Opinions of him vary, but on one thing, most of the public agrees. He is, indeed, the richest man in the world. According to *Forbes*, his fortune hovers around $100 billion, his bank vaults growing more stuffed every day. In contrast, certain companies like Tesla (which he owns) will suffer losses in the billions.

Of course, he can't become the real President because he was not born in the United States, as is required by law. Actually, he came into the world on June 28, 1971, in Pretoria, South Africa, a scion of British and Pennsylvania Dutch ancestry. His family wasn't poor, as his father, Errol Musk, was part owner of a Zambian emerald mine. Elon was born into the notorious apartheid era in South Africa.

His childhood was hectic. He always remembered at one point when he was sent to a school in the wilderness that he called "a paramilitary *Lord of the Flies*" horror. Bullying was the rule of the day and boys were goaded into fighting each other over rations. At one point, he was beaten so severely that he had a long hospital stay before recovery.

Upper photo: It's "thumbs up" for **Elon Musk** as he sits proudly aboard Air Force One with President **Donald Trump.** The business tycoon was rumored to have claimed, "It was my millions that bought the office for him."

Of course, the braggart had a motive. He knows Trump will create favorable operation conditions for his many businesses, from SpaceX to Tesla, from Neuralink to X.

He departed from his native land after the end of white rule, settling into Canada. One newsman claimed, "He left South Africa, but Old South Africa never left him."

His arrival in Canada occurred in June of 1989, a season that hardly prepared him for the winters to come. He worked at odd jobs and, for a time at least, as a farmhand in Saskatchewan.

In 1990, he was a student at Queen's University in Ontario, later enrolling in the University of Pennsylvania until 1995.

After that, Silicon Valley in California lured him away.

No one seems to know just how many companies Musk owns. Maybe he can't even keep up with his business empire, since it is expanding so rapidly, and he is so deeply involved in the firing of Federal government workers.

Here are some of his major business ventures:

In May of 2002, Musk became the CEO and Chief Engineer of SpaceX, a space technology company centered in Brownsville, Texas. Since its origin, the company has had great ambitions to launch America into space, aiming for advancement in rocket propulsion, reusable launch vehicles, human spaceflight, and satellite constellation technology. In 2025, it became the world's dominant space launch provider, although it has suffered some major disasters. One of Musk's most am-

In the spring of 2025, **Elon Musk** seemed everywhere, firing Federal employees at a rate never seen before. Who needs cancer research? With dizzying regularity, he was popping in and out of the Oval Office, even dominating cabinet meetings.

bitious goals is to create a "greenhouse" on Mars.

In 2020, SpaceX launched its first crewed flight, becoming the first private company to shoot astronauts into orbit. In 2024, NASA awarded the company an $843 million contract.

In the late spring of 2019, SpaceX also launched the first gib convoy of some 60 satellites, beginning to deploy what would become the world's largest commercial satellite constellation the following year. At present, Starlink has 6,000 satellites (subject to change) in orbit.

Tesla, Inc., in the summer of 2020 was the world's most valuable automaker. It was also the world's most valuable company in terms of market capitalization, exceeding $1 trillion in market capitalization, leading the electric vehicle market with a nearly 20% share.

From its Gigafactory outside Austin, Teas, the company, in 2008, began production of its first car model, the Roadster Sports Car. This was followed by the Model S sedan in 2012; the Model X SUV in 2015, the Model 3 sedan in 2017; and the Model Y crossover in 2020. Tesla Semi Truck went on the market in 2022.

In the fall of 2021, Tesla reached a market capitalization of $1 trillion, the sixth company in U.S. history to reach that lofty goal.

Privately, the company has become involved in lawsuits and controversies involving sexual harassment, labor disputes, accidents, recalls for repairs, safety violations, fraud allegations, dealership disputes, thefts of intellectual property, environmental violations, property damage, and racism.

On October 27, 2022, Musk, in a controversial move, acquired Twitter, for 44 billion. He immediately fired several leading executives, taking over the job of CEO himself. That was followed by his laying off a large portion of the staff, a move that was but a prelude to his firing of government workers.

He was criticized for trying to silence some of his critics by deleting their accounts.

Will the day come when all of us will be brainy? Perhaps, if Elon Musk gets his way. In 2016, he co-founded Neuralink alongside eight scientists and engineers.

Originally, scientists set out to create an electronic brain chip to treat traumatic brain injuries. But its concept has gone far beyond that.

Its current aim is to "intermarry" the human brain with artificial intelligence by creating devices that are embedded in the brain. That means that when our history teacher asks who was First Lady in the White House in 1881, you can immediately answer "Lucretia, wife of James A. Garfield."

On a personal level, Musk has admitted that he has suffered from a number of health issues, constantly suffering from back pain, and that he has also undergone several spine-related surgeries, including a disc replacement. In 2000, he contracted a severe case of malaria while on vacation in his native South Africa.

He also stated that he uses ketamine as prescribed by his doctor for his frequent bouts of depression. In an interview with the *Wall Street Journal*, in 2024, he admitted to taking not only ketamine, but LSD, cocaine, and other drugs recreationally.

While hosting *Saturday Night Live* in 2021, he shocked

Trump and Musk sell Teslas from the lawn of the White House.

"The Donald" became the first U.S. President to hawk car sales. Musk has a chance to be the first trillionaire over the next decade if the sales targets for his electric car company become a reality.

SpaceX ignition at the debut of its fifth flight. SpaceX became the first private company to shoot astronauts into orbit. Millions from NASA helped. The ultimate aim of SpaceX involves establishing a human outpost, (i.e., "colony") on Mars.

As part of a marketing campaign for **Neuralink,** company officials opted to depict Elon Musk, the company's founder and owner, as recipient of one of its "inserted directly into the brain" chips.

the audience (and everyone else in TV Land) by admitting that he has Asperger's Syndrome.

The affliction is more common to men than to women and is estimated to affect about 38 million people globally. It is described as a neurodevelopmental disorder characterized by difficulties with social interaction and nonverbal communication, along with restricted, repetitive patterns of behavior and interests. Suicidal thoughts and behaviors are a serious concern within the autistic population.

The Most Controversial Man in America
Elon Musk's Politics

As a supporter of political parties, Elon Musk has had a checkered past, contributing to both Democratic and Republican candidates over the course of many years.

When he lived in California, he was an independent voter. Since 2022, he has developed Republican flu.

By 2024, he was embracing far-right political agendas, sharing far-fetched conspiracy theories. As such, he has become a polarizing figure, spreading disinformation about Federal spending, immigration, COVID-19, or affirming antisemitic and transphobic charges.

Amazingly, in the past, he supported Barack Obama for President in both 2008 and 2012. He voted for Hillary Clinton in 2016 and for Joe Biden in 2020. *[When Donald J. Trump failed to get re-elected in 2020, he is still charging, year later, that that election was stolen from him.]*

Before voting for Biden, Musk at first supported Andrew Yang, the son of Taiwanese-American immigrants. Yang was described as both a dark horse and a novelty candidate. The following year, Musk bolted from the Democratic Party, defining himself as an Independent.

Before switching his vote to Biden, Musk had a temporary infatuation with the controversial candidacy of Kayne West, the rapper and record producer from Atlanta. One of the most prominent figures in the world of hip-hop, he is one of the best-selling music artists of all time, with more than 160 million records sold. He also has won a staggering 24 Grammy Awards.

West's high-profile marriage to Kim Kardashian (2014-2022) became tabloid fodder. His political positions, particularly about African-Americans, have been extremely controversial. He has drawn widespread condemnations for his anti-Semitic views, and he self-identifies as a Nazi, praising Hitler and the swastika and denying the Holocaust.

By 2022, Musk claimed he would, in the future, support Republican candidates, and late in 2023, he threw his backing to Ron De Santis during his ill-fated bid for the White House.

The controversial governor of Florida opposes gay people and abortion. One of his first acts was to forbid male-to-female transsexuals from participation in girl's or women's sports. He also backed a "Don't Say Gay" law and feuded with Walt Disney Company, an entity he interpreted as too gay-friendly.

De Santis didn't go over with a national audience, so Musk threw his support to the 2024 presidential campaign of former president Donald Trump. As a contribution to his campaign, he put up $290 million, which brought a seat at the table in the White House after Trump was elected.

Giving a Nazi salute, Musk praised the re-election of Trump, claiming "the future of civilization is assured."

In getting rid of "waste" (at least his version of it), Musk fired massive numbers of Federal workers. Initially, he was to work in partnership with Vivek Ramaswamy, born to immigrant parents from India. He had tried unsuccessfully to beat Trump for the 2024 Republican

Musk *(right)* with **Kanye West.** Before supporting Trump, Musk backed Obama, Hillary Clinton, Ron De Santis, and Kanye West, the rapper who praised Hitler and denied the Holocaust

As 2023 came to an end, the ever-changing Musk had thrown his backing to the controversial Florida governor **Ron De Santis.**

His campaign for the White House was an utter failure. During the campaign, both the backer and the candidate took on Walt Disney. Perhaps they felt Mickey Mouse was too friendly with gays and trans people.

presidential nomination. When he gave up on that dream, he switched to supporting Trump, his former rival.

Ramaswamy is also a man of immense wealth, at least $960 million, according to *Forbes*.

A week after the 2024 election, the President-Elect announced that both Musk and Ramaswamy would lead the newly organized Department of Government Efficiency (DOGE). However, Ramaswamy soon dropped out, leaving Musk completely in charge.

Before the election, Musk, in an interview with the right-wing Tucker Carlson, admitted "If Trump loses, I'm fucked!"

Ranting about immigration and supporting "white pride," Musk set about slashing Federal spending, firing thousands and thousands of employees. At one rally, he looked like a maniac, swinging and brandishing a chainsaw, the first such appearance in American politics.

"If I didn't do this, and the United Stated continues on its present path, we will, in fact, become bankrupt."

During his first cabinet meeting in the Oval Office, Musk appeared to be the president instead of Trump. He really wasn't dressed for the job, wearing a black MAGA cap and a T-shirt defining himself as "Tech Support.:"

His ultimate aim, or so he claims, involves reducing the size of more than 400 Federal agencies, including the Department of Education (**Who Needs Education?**) to just 100 branches.

Both Trump and Musk seem to want to cut taxes for the rich at the expense of the poor and middle class. One of Doge's more outrageous claims was that Musk's young task force, led by a shadowy figure nicknamed "Big Balls," had discovered $2.7 trillion in improper Medicaid and Medicare payments to people overseas. The charge was outrageous, but nonetheless, hordes of the misinformed believed it implicitly.

Addressing his joint cabinet members, Trump made his position about Musk clear: "If someone in the room is unhappy with Elon, we'll throw him out."

An editorial in *The New York Daily News* ran this statement: "Musk and his team have delivered chaos, with mass firings and layoffs of probationary employees and others across government agencies, with no rhyme or reason, from FAA workers tasked to overseeing the safety of our nation's nuclear arsenal to those trying to combat the rising bird flu epidemic. Pink slips have been flying from Musk's eager cohorts. They don't care who gets whacked. Sometimes they have to backtrack, as happened with the firing of employees of the World Trade Center Health Program.

How long Musk will remain a Trumpian favorite has dim odds among Las Vegas gamblers;. After all, he is working for a man who made himself famous on the hit television show, *The Apprentice*, by shouting "YOU'RE FIRED!" at losing contestants.

Originally, both Elon Musk and **Vivek Ramaswamy** *(above)* were assigned the task of firing thousands of Federal workers. Before that, Ramaswamy ("with the impossible name") had run for President himself. "Vivek and Elon were like a marriage of Putin and Zelensky," wrote reporter Dwight Davis. "Doomed to fail. Exit Vivek."

Profoundly unphotogenic, his face expressing arrogance, **President Trump** stands silent next to talkative **Musk** *(right)*.

During his short reign as America's un-elected "co-president," Musk became the face of the administration's budget-cutting austerity push.

Waving a chainsaw like a raving maniac, **Musk** promises he'll fire thousands of Federal workers. "Without my efforts, America will go bankrupt, owing trillions."

Trump praised him for "cutting fraud and waste. If you're unhappy with Musk, out you go."

THE ROMANCES & MARRIAGES OF ELON MUSK
Where Love Has Gone

Elon Musk has had a tangled love life with wives or mistresses, and he has fathered at least 14 children, one of whom died of sudden infant death syndrome at the age of 10 weeks.

His first wife was the Canadian author Justine Wilson, born in 1972 in Ontario.

As she grew up, she attended Queen's College in Kingston, Ontario, earning a degree in English literature. Later, she moved to Japan, where she taught English to students who wanted to be bilingual.

Relocating in California, she became an author, her most notable book being *Blood Angel*, published in 2005. She called it "cross-genre fiction."

After courting her for a while, Musk married her in 2000. He would have six children with her, the first dying after only ten weeks.

Despite that, they still wanted to enlarge their family. Using *in vitro* fertilization (IVF), they produced twins in 2004, followed by triplets in 2006. One of their twins became a transsexual, renaming herself Vivian Jenna Wilson, taking her mother's surname. *(There's more about her coming up)*.

Justine later complained, " Elon tried to make me a trophy wife, dismissing my aspirations to become a writer."

On September 13, 2008, she announced that she and Musk were getting a divorce, with shared custody of their offspring.

"What do I think of my former husband?" she was asked by a reporter.

"Definitely an Alpha male."

In the wake of his divorce, Musk began dating the English actress, Tululah Riley, born in Hertfordshire, England, in 1985. They were married in 2010 at Dornock Cathedral in Scotland.

As an actress, she had appeared in several films, notably *Pride and Prejudice* (2005), followed by a number of television credits, such as playing Angela in the first two seasons (2016-2018) of the TV series *Westworld*.

Their marriage was short. Musk and Talulah divorced in March of 2021, only to remarry in 2013. She and Musk lived together with five children from his previous marriage.

[Reporters wrote that Talulah was following in the footsteps of another, more famous actress, Elizabeth Taylor, who married fellow actor Richard Burton, divorcing him but later remarrying him, only to divorce him later for the final time.]

For half a year before the divorce, the estranged couple lived apart as he dated other women.

Riley would later marry actor Thomas Brodie-Sangster in June of 2024 in the English shire of her birth Hertfordshire, England.

Justine Wilson Musk. Is an author who characterized her work as "cross-genre fiction." A Canadian, she later moved to California, where she met and fell in love with Elon Musk. The couple produced six children. One of their sons wanted to become a woman.

Talulah Riley, an English beauty, married the recently divorced Musk in 2010 in Scotland. She was an actress with several film credits. Their first marriage was short and tumultuous. After their divorce, they remarried, but then divorced again.

***

[The year of his divorce, Musk was "pursuing" the actress Amber Heard, although it would be 2017 when they began to indulge in some "heavy dating," according to the gossips of the day. This came in the wake of Heard's widely publicized, even scandalous, divorce from actor Johnny Depp.

A native of Austin, Texas, Heard was born in 1986. Before her marriage to Depp, she was involved in a four-year relationship with the photographer, Tasya van Ree. Heard publicly came "out" in 2010. "I don't label myself one way or another," she confessed to the press. "I have had successful relationships with both men and women. I love who I love. It's the person who matters."

She met and became involved with Depp when they were cast in The Rum Diary (2009). The couple began dating in 2012 and were wed in a civil ceremony in February of 2015.

They divorced in 2016. Charges and counter-charges flew at their divorce, making sensational headlines across America. Originally, she demanded $50,000 a month alimony, but after many court appearances, she settled for $3 million, plus $500,000 to pay her legal bill.

For a while, at least, Elon Musk was "seriously dating" **Amber Heard** *(above right)*, depicted here with the object of her hatred, **Johnny Depp,** during their tormented divorce proceeding of 2016-17. When it ended, it resulted in one of the biggest divorce settlements—in Amber's favor—in California history.

Depp retained his real estate and his 42 vehicles. She told he press that the actor "got off easy," since, according to the property laws of California, "I'm entitled to a half of his treasure trove."

Heard dated Musk for several months in 2017, but they never married. When they broke up, she did not leave a "dump" in Musk's bed, as Depp alleged that she had done in his.

"I was really in love with Amber," Musk told Rolling Stone. "Her leaving me hurt me real bad. Well, she broke up with me more than I broke up with her. That is, I think."]

***

After that, Musk began dating a singer and musician who billed herself as "Grimes." Born in Vancouver in 1988, she had released five studio albums, often focusing on feminist themes, even sci-fi.

The couple had a rocky relationship. She made a number of provocative statements, claiming "not to relate strongly to female gender identity." On a post on Twitter, she claimed, "I vibe in a gender-neutral space so I'm kind of impartial to pronouns." In another post, she stated, "I personally am put off by the word 'woman,' at least as far as I'm concerned."

She also claimed that she has been charged with being a Nazi because she is proud of white culture.

In May of 2020, Grimes gave birth to Musk's son, whom they gave the curious name of "X Æ A=Xii Musk."

The kid was seen by millions in the Oval Office with Trump. Reportedly, he told him, "My dad would make a better President than you."

As the autumn leaves began to fall in 2021, Musk and Grimes became "semi-separated."

"I would probably refer to him as my boyfriend, but we're very fluid." On March 22, she was calling him "My best friend and the love of my life."

In October of 2023, Grimes sued Musk for parental rights and custody of their child. Apparently, they have agreed to a sort of joint custody.

***

A Canadian technology executive and venture capitalist, Shivon Zilis, was born in Canada in 1986. Her father was Canadian, her mother a Punjabi Indian. A graduate of Yale, she was Director of Operations at Musk's Tesla from

Left photo: **Grimes**, during her "brunette period," shown here with **Elon Musk.**

Right photo: The son they produced, for a brief period in 2025, became one of the most famous children of Donald Trump's second administration when the father-son Musk duet arrived in the corridors of power, as displayed in the photo, as something akin to "a working team."

Many Americans found the child adorable until a deeper confusion set in after they became aware of his off-putting, and unpronounceable name: **"X Æ A=Xii Musk."**

2017 to 2019.

She and Musk launched an affair that led to the birth of twins born in 2021 and another child born in 2024.

Zilis told the press that Musk "really wants smart people to have kids, so he encouraged her to get pregnant. If the choice is between an anonymous sperm donor or doing it with the person you admire most in the world, for me that is a pretty fucking easy decision."

***

Ashley St. Claire, author of *Elephants Are Not Birds*, met Musk in 2023 and allegedly started sleeping with him. To complicate his role as a father, she publicly claimed that she gave birth to a son of his. That announcement was made on February 28, 2025, when she took legal action against Musk.

Shivon Zilis seen here with two of the three children fathered by Elon Musk.

Ashley St. Claire also gave birth to another son of Elon Musk

"Two months ago I welcomed a new baby into the world. Elon Musk is the father." She called the baby 'child," not transmitting any information about the child's gender.

Why does Musk have so many sons and daughters? One might ask. Maybe he's following the advice of his father, Errol Musk. "The only reason we are on earth is to reproduce. If I could have another child, I would. I can't see any reason not to."

At least Musk won't have any problem putting food on the table for his kids, or sending them to the best colleges driving custom-made Rolls Royces, or else using his or her chauffeur.

A reporter for the *Daily Mail* wrote: "It's not likely that St. Claire went for Musk because he is so handsome. Perhaps she went for him because he is the richest man in the world."

Vivian Jenna Wilson
The Trans Daughter of Elon Musk

Her father may be the richest man on the planet, but the oldest living child of Elon Musk and Justine Wilson is not speaking to dear ol' dad.

The renamed Vivian Jenna Wilson, born in 2004, might have emerged from the womb as a boy, but at age 16, in 2020, she came out as a trans woman, much to the horror of her wealthy father.

Two years later, a judge allowed her to alter her birth certificate, changing both her gender and her name. She chose to use her mother's surname.

In July of 2024, Musk went public about his daughter's transition from male to female. In an interview about his daughter's sexual conversion, Musk spoke to Jordan Peterson of the *Daily Wire:* "I lost my son, essentially. He is dead, killed by the 'woke mind virus.' I was tricked into signing documents granting my son gender-affirming treatments. To me, he will always be my boy. I was forced to sign the documents because I was told he would commit suicide if I didn't."

On *NBC News*, she disputed her father's claim. "He was not by any means tricked. He knew the full side effects."

Reportedly, she also claimed that as a pre-teen, her father constantly attacked her for being effeminate.

While campaigning for Trump, Musk made an explosive charge: "Neo-Marxists have taken over our colleges and universities. That has infuriated

Vivian Jenna Wilson was born the son of Elon Musk.

me so much that I have vowed to destroy the 'woke mind' virus."

Grimes, the very liberal former mistress of Musk, said, "I support Vivian's transition. She can live her life with her own identity and not play a role forced on her. I'm proud of her for speaking out and wish her a long and happy life with someone she loves…and who loves her back."

Vivian's siblings include her twin, Griffin, along with triplets Kai, Saven, and Domina, plus the youngest arrival, Nevada.

***

Transphobia Sweeps the Nation
(It May Have Led to Trump's Narrow Victory)

Vivian Jenna Wilson as part of a modeling gig in 2025. In March of that same year, she was featured, with full disclosure of her evolution as a transsexual, in *Teen Vogue.*

As any dictator knows, during one's rise to power, its always good to have a group of people to hate. Just ask Hitler. He didn't like Jews.

As strange as it seems, the 2024 presidential election had Donald Trump winning by a narrow margin, which he preferred to define as a mandate. During the closing weeks of the campaign, some $215 million was spent on anti-trans ads, most of them aired at midtime during football games.

A poll showed that some 85% of Americans were against trans people competing in women's sports. Actually, that is hardly a menace, since the percentage of trans athletes competing in sports is only a fraction of one percent.

In some quarters, it was rumored that Elon Musk launched transphobia for personal reasons. He was horrified when one of his daughters, Vivian Jenna Wilson, became a trans woman at the age of 16. She and her father are completely alienated from each other today.

Catering to his bigoted base, Trump has made it abundantly clear: "There are only two sexes: A man and a woman. Nothing in between."

It eventually morphed into a campaign refrain: "Kamala Harris is for trans women. Donald Trump is for you."

In his heyday as a roving bachelor-at-large in Manhattan, Trump could have cared less what sexuality anyone personally endorsed. He lived and moved in a sophisticated world. Obviously, he adopted his anti-gay policies to appeal to his right-wing base. He even made attacks on trans people a main focus of his first State of the Union address, as if this is a major problem facing America and the world in general.

The most extreme right-wingers don't go public with what their private desire is. They speak of it only in their private confabs. They've gone so far as to suggest that the United States should adopt the policy of President Yoweri Museveni of Uganda, a nation in East Africa.

He has cracked down on LGBTQ citizens, signing a law in 2023 demanding life imprisonment for any person engaging in a same-sex relationship. The law also calls for a decade in prison for anyone who even tries to engage in a homosexual act.

Trump wants to remove all trans women from the military, even though they have a distinguished record of serving their country. The trans coterie offers valid services in nursing, special operations, officers, nuclear reactor operators, missile battery commanders. At present, at least until they are forcibly removed, trans people make up only 0.2 percent of the military.

How influential (or how deeply "invested") was **Elon Musk** in the waves of anti-trans protests that swept across the nation in the aftermath of his feud with his trans daughter? Speculation was rife.

One of the biggest accomplishments of Trump and Musk involved preventing trans prison inmates from being allowed to select the underwear of their choice.

Throughout the United States, trans people are under attack, sometimes viciously. To cite one example, take the case of Sam Nordquist, 24, who was discovered upstate in New York in February of 2025. He had been murdered. An African-American from Minnesota, he had been tortured while held in captivity throughout the month of January.

Authorities claimed he faced rape and daily beatings. He was also forced to drink urine and to eat feces. When wounded, bleach was poured on his affliction.

Seven defendants, each of whom had previous arrests, were indicted and charged with first degree murder.

In one of the more ridiculous charges made on the campaign trail in 2024, Trump claimed, "Your son goes to school a boy and comes home a girl."

Trump has been adamant that prisoners must be incarcerated in jails based on their gender at birth, even if they have undergone virginoplasty.

[Virginoplasty is a surgical procedure that results in the construction or re-construction of the vagina. An inversion, pioneered by Georges Burou in a clinic in Morocco in the 1950s, is often performed when a male wants a vagina.

Inversion of the penile skin is the method most often selected to create a "neovagina" by surgeons performing gender-affirming surgery. The inverted penile skin uses inferior pedicle skin for the lining of the "neovagina." The skin is cut to form an appropriately-sized flap. Reports of people seeking vaginoplasty go back to the 2nd Century.]

***

MAYE MUSK
Elon Musk's Mom, in Her 70s, is a Model for the Chinese

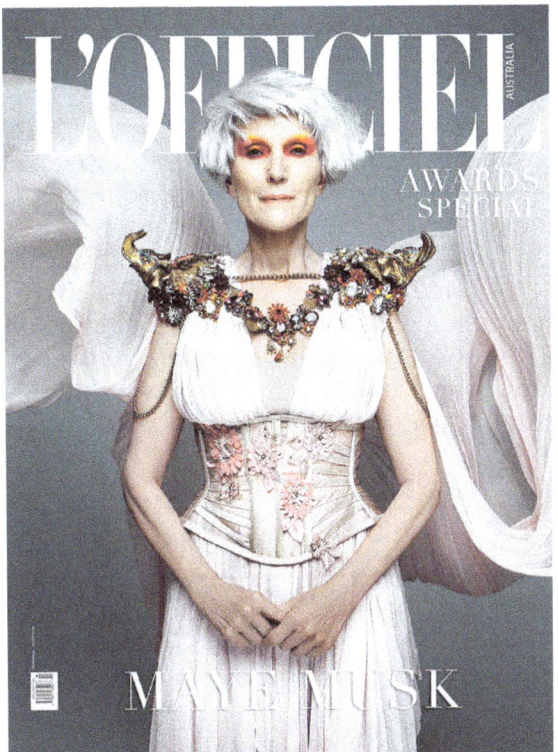

Regardless of what you think of Elon Musk, on one thing, a number of people might agree: Like her or hate her, his mother, Maye Musk, one hell of a woman, will live in history books for birthing one of the most controversial men in American history.

She was born as a twin in Saskatchewan, Canada, in 1948 to Joshua and Wyn Haldeman. She became one of five children, of offspring of a most unusual couple who specialized in everything from ballroom dancing to running a chiropractic practice. When not involved in that, they devoted their days to archaeology.

At the age of two, the family relocated to Pretoria, part of apartheid-era South Africa. As she grew older, she remembered her parents taking her into the Kalahari Desert to search for lost cities—18 of which thrived on the southern edge of the African continent.

"We kids slept outside the tent," she recalled. "We put our sleeping bags over our heads so the hyenas wouldn't eat our faces."

Maye seemed to mature early. With her good looks and slim figure, she became a model, even though she hadn't turned 16. Around this same time, she became only one contest short of winning the title of "Miss South Africa," an all-white beauty and talent contest.

In her late teens, she took up the study of nutrition.

In 1970 she met and married an engineer named Errol Musk Not only did they give birth to Elon the following year but they had another son, Kimbal in 1972, followed by a daughter in 1976.

The family relocated to Canada in 1972, but it evolved into an unhappy move and unhappy marriage. Divorce followed in 1978. Whereas Elon, at 17, and Kimbal went to live with their father, their daughter preferred to stay with Maye.

"I brought my children up like my parents brought us up when we were young—and that is to be independent, kind, honest, considerate, and polite. I taught them to work hard and do good things."

She could never envision at the time that her son would think it "a good thing" to fire millions of Federal workers.

For Elon, life with his father, Errol, turned out to be a mistake. "He should have stayed with Maye," Elon claimed. He complained about his father in the 2017 edition of *Rolling Stone,* and was quite critical of his upbringing.

Errol defended himself, claiming, "I love my children and would readily do whatever for them."

Errol took a second wife, Heide, who already had a four-year-old daughter, Jana Bezuidenhout. The newlyweds would go on to produce two more daughters before they, too, broke up.

As she grew up and wed, Jana's marriage did not work out.

Two views of **Mae Musk** doing her best to "sell" the allure of a dress. The upper photo showcases her as a cover girl for the May, 2021 edition of *L'Officiel Awards Special.*

Seeking comfort, she returned to live with Errol, her stepfather, now single again. He gave an interview in 2018 in *The Sunday Times*. "Jan and I were lonely, lost souls. Once thing led to another—you can call it God's plan or nature's plan."

He fell in love with his stepdaughter and they welcomed a baby girl in 2019. As he told in that interview: "The only thing we are on earth for is to reproduce. If I could have another child, I would. I can't see any reason not to."

Continuing to work as a model, Maye became President of the Consulting Dieticians of Canada. When her children were teenagers, the family moved to California. It was a smart decision. Fame and fortune were on the way as their businesses not only prospered but became gold mines.

In spite of her age, Maye continued to model even during her 70s. In 2022, she posed for the swimsuit edition of *Sports Illustrated*.

China opened its doors to her. Elon already made half of his Tesla cars in China.

Maye not only promoted her bestselling book, *A Woman Makes a Plan,* but modeled to hype Chinese products, endorsing seven brands at once, including makeup products, down jackets, and massage devices. She keeps calling for the U.S. Government to improve its relations with China.

She has also been seen in Kazakhstan and the United Arab Emirates, hoping to create alliances there.

As of this writing, "Elton & Maye" have been seen riding on Air Force One with the President. She also books international lectures. Her topic? "How I raised three amazing children."

Who knows what the situation will be with either Maye or Elon by the time you read this? After all, his President morphed himself into a towering figure thanks to his hit TV show, *The Apprentice,* by shouting, regularly and frequently, "YOU'RE FIRED!"

The Bitter End of a White House Bromance

As was inevitable, the so-called marriage of the co-president (**Elon Mus**k, left) and **Donald Trump** led to a widely publicized divorce. Musk's rise and fall were both pitiful and predictable. By June of 2025, word was flashed around the world that this "bromance" had come to a bitter end in a burst of public insults.

The two mercurial billionaires were not compatible.

Musk attacked Trump's so-called "big, beautiful bill," which would deny health care to millions of Americans. To Trump's fury, Musk referred to the bill as "a disgusting abomination."

Always out for revenge, Trump threatened to cut off billions of dollars in Federal contracts to Musk-owned companies. In retaliation, Musk threatened to support a bill to impeach Trump, and made oblique references to the incendiary nature of the Epstein files.

"I am very disappointed in Elon," Trump said. "I've helped him a lot." He even went so far as to suggest he could have won the presidency without the millions of dollars Musk poured into Trump's bid for the White House.

Musk even suggested that in retaliation, he might finance the rise of another political party which would oppose Trump. Many Republicans, whether it was true or not, publicly claimed that they were horrified at Musk's disrespect of the President.

In retrospect, *The New York Times* claimed that Musk's cutbacks of Federal funds had left a legacy of disease, starvation, and death around the world. The world's richest man had catalyzed the deaths of many of the world's poorest people, especially children.

The Politically Fraught, Legally Stormy Saga of Donald Trump's Penis

STORMY DANIELS

At Last, a Celebrity Stripper Reveals What Americans Want to Know

"The World is Waiting to Hear About His Penis."
—Stormy Daniels

If **Stormy Daniel's** revelations had been limited "merely to infidelities and sex," they might not have traveled far.

But intermingled with the sexual aspects of the brouhaha were election tampering and presidential perjury. Quickly, it became one of the most widely-bruited scandals of the decade.

Here's Stormy, tastefully coiffed and dressed, holding her own and raising temperatures at a news conference during the peak of the scandal.

Stephanie A. Gregory, later known as the porn star Stormy Daniels, was born in Baton Rouge, Louisiana, in March of 1979. In time, she would becme the most famous female porn star in America. Her greatest notoriety would come after her one-night sexual encounter with Donald Trump, then the leading television star of the TV reality series, *The Apprentice.*

Her name, Stormy, came from the first name her father wanted to tab her. Daniels came from Jack Daniels whiskey.

Her childhood was rough: Her father deserted the family after three and a half years, and her mother struggled to pay the bills and put food on the table.

As Stormy remembered it, "The electricity was sometimes turned off because we could not afford to pay the bills. Supper ws sometimes Vienna sausages on Saltines."

"I used to go over to a local McDonald's at closing time. A girlfriend of mine worked there. I might get some hamburgers that were made but not sold."

As a girl growing up, she had no ambition to be a stripper, much less a porn star. She had a dream of becoming a journalist while working in a job answering the phone in a riding stable. There, she developed a love of horses.

Her career goal was derailed when she met a seducer of young girls, who got her a job at the Gold Club, a strip joint in Baton Rouge. She was only 17 at the time. "I watched the other strippers and learned a lot, little knowing that in time, my stripping would morph into my becoming the goddess of porn."

She was lured into appearing in erotic films in 2002 when she was hired by Wicked Pictures. Two years later, after bleaching her hair, she won the Best New Starlet Award from *Adult Video News.*

What Happens in Tahoe Doesn't Necessarily Stay There

(aka, The Donald and the Porn Star)

Mutually trapped on celluloid that was later introduced as evidence in dozens of depositions and court hearings.

Brash, outspoken, and voluptuous, **Stormy Daniels** posed for this publicity photo at *AVN's Adult Entertainment Expo* in Las Vegas in January of 2007. The largest porn-industry sales convention in America, it's been a highly visible staple of midwinter Las Vegas for years.

She appeared with such male performers as Brandon Miller in 2005. By 2015, she would marry him, leading to the birth of a daughter. She divorced him in 2018. In 2022, she married another porn star, Barrett Blade.

Her life would be forever changed when she had a chance encounter with "The Donald," who was being seen on television across the country. In a reality TV series called *The Apprentice,* she was drawn to him because she wanted to make a guest appearance on his hit show.

Her introduction to Trump came one hot summer day in July of 2006. It occurred at a celebrity golf tournament at Lake Tahoe in Nevada. At the time, he was married to Melania Trump, who had given birth to their son Barron four months prior.

Trump seemed captivated by Stormy and genuinely interested in her life, asking many questions. He wanted to know about her use of condoms and a possible fear of sexually transmitted diseases. At last, he turned to the subject she wanted to hear, and that involved her possible appearance on *The Apprentice.* Later, he invited her to dinner that night, suggesting he knew a place where they could order really juicy big steaks.

She agreed to meet him in his hotel suite. Later that night, when she entered the suite, she found him dressed in silk pajamas, hardly an outfit to take her out.

At one point during their chat, she excused herself to go to the bathroom.

When she emerged, she was startled to see him lying on the bed stripped down to his underwear.

Rather nervous, she suggested he might get dressed so they could go out. An experienced woman like herself knew exactly what he had in mind. As she headed for the door, he blocked her, making an odd statement. "This is the only way you're getting out of the trailer park."

"The only way" meant a seduction. With some reluctance, she gave in to him. One might call it an early audition for *The Apprentice.*

"It was in the missionary position, and he did not use a condom, although earlier, he had talked about sexually transmitted diseases. He did not rape me as some reports later claimed when our affair became public. Sex with him was not something I wanted, but I gave in to him."

As she recalled, "I just lay there for about two minutes—maybe two and a half minutes—getting fucked by a guy with Yeti pubes and a dick like the mushroom character in Mario Kart."

***

For those of you who might not have known:

Left photo, below: Here's an AI-generated rendition of a YETI (aka, "Abominable Snowman") "accessorized with bulbous mushrooms, and

Right photo, below: **Here's Toad (aka Kinopio, aka "The Mushroom"),** is a character created by Japanese video game designer Shigeru Miyamoto for Nintendo's **Mario Kart** franchise. Mischievous, irrepressible, and noteworthy for his bulbous headgear, he appears consistently as a supporting character in the franchise.

In the News Flood Generated by Stormy, Mainstream America Got a Peek-a-Boo into the Porn Industry

Thanks to the "Stormy Affair," news junkies who hadn't previously been fixated on porn began to realize that **Miss Daniels** really WAS a big name within her industry.

Upper photo: Fetchingly and straightforwardly, Stormy poses with a *Penthouse* layout wherein she's featured and

Lower photo: the May-June 2018 edition of **Penthouse** features **Stormy** ("She Tells All and Bares All") on a cover that also promotes their "Pet of the Year" (Gina Valentina); and their "Pets of the Month" (Sabina Rouge and Scarlett Sage.)

[EDITOR'S NOTE: As a public response to Miss Daniel's somewhat confusing description of "DJT President's" pubes (see above), columnist Miles Klee, on September 19, 2018, published the following points of view on Medium.com:

Mr. President, There's No Excuse for Yeti Pubes

*When the salacious details of President Trump's nether regions, as described in adult film actress Stormy Daniels' memoir, became a matter of public record, the focus was largely on his dick. The adult film actress likened this "smaller than average" member to Toad, "the mushroom character in Nintendo's **Mario Kart**." This opened the door to a universe of Nintendo jokes, as well as debate regarding broader mushroom-penis resemblances.*

Still, everyone seemed to have a pretty good idea of what she was talking about.

But another phrase from that same passage has attracted slighter attention, while remaining a bit more obscure. Daniels writes that Trump, apart from his unusual unit, was sporting "Yeti pubes." This caused some disgusted and confused speculation. It felt evocative without being all that specific, and people, understandably, had questions.

I choose to follow my own interpretation here: Yeti pubes are, given the nature of the Yeti, an ape-like cryptid (i.e., an animal whose existence is supported only by pseudo-science) said to roam the Himalayan mountain range, by definition unkempt, untrimmed, maybe tangled or densely matted, and likely foul-smelling. Since Daniels opted for "Yeti pubes" over "Sasquatch pubes," I'm also going to assume she also meant to indicate their color — Bigfoot/Sasquatch is traditionally depicted as dark brown, while the Yeti, or Abominable Snowman, is usually thought to be white, to blend in with his frosty environment. Trump turned 60 the year he's alleged to have slept with Daniels, and that's old enough, I presume, to have graying (if not blizzard-white) pubes. There's always a chance she just found "Yeti" more poetic, but let's not get sidetracked.

Miles Klee, is a distinguished social commentarian for, among others, **Rolling Stone**. The article we've replicated here appeared in **Medium.com** back when it was still hot, still permeated with a sense of shame, and still rocking the American electorate.

Knowing all this, I now address the president directly: Sir, you have embarrassed yourself and your country in exposing such a vile pubic bush to a woman you paid to keep quiet about your adulterous tryst in order to keep the affair from the media ahead of a national election. Unlike your freakish salami, the pube situation can be rectified. Are you telling me that someone as vain and wealthy as you doesn't have access to the grooming devices men and women alike use to maintain the hair down there? C'mon.

Length, aside, Mr. President — are you washing your pubes? Because it sounds like they could use a scrub. I know, you probably have a weird phobia of body wash and think it's gay to lather up the ol' crotch nest, but this is really low, even for you. For a narcissist, you don't have much self-respect. As for the carpet not matching the drapes... I don't think any of us could have predicted that. With a golden-orange coiff so notoriously overmanaged and clearly dyed, the relative inattention to pubic style is truly sloppy. This was a porn star 30 years younger than you, dipshit! Guessing you didn't brush the crumbs off your wiry fur-patch from eating chips naked in bed beforehand, either.

Now, back to Stormy's allegations...]

"**There was no foreplay**. During intercourse, his darting tongue pushed in and out of my mouth. I thought he was a terrible kisser. I endured it as he fumbled his dick in me."

After his climax, he lay back on the bed and said, "That's great," he said. "Just great. Oh, you're so beautiful."

Later, in a memoir, Stormy wrote: "The world is waiting to hear about his penis. The expectation is that I will say it's some kind of 'micro-penis.' I am sorry to report that it is not freakishly small. It's smaller than average — below the true average, not the porn average. I did not take out a measuring stick."

"He needs to shave his balls as they are unusually hairy, more so than the rest of him. His hair down there was so much better than what was on his head."

"I could definitely pick his dick out of a lineup. He knows he has a unusual penis. It has a huge mushroom head. Like a toadstool."

She hinted that his seduction of her "may have been the least impressive sex I've ever had."

He suggested they should meet again, "but I was already planning how to get out of his suite."

They would have a further encounter but not for sex.

She learned later that she was not his only sexual encounter at Lake Tahoe that weekend. He also had sex with Karen McDougal, a former *Playboy* playmate.

Stormy claimed, "Seeing Trump again made me feel claustrophobic but I really did want to get on *The Apprentice.*"

***

She next saw Trump on January 17, 2007 at the launch of Trump Vodka. At Les Deux in Hollywood, she attended "a gaggle of wannabe stars, including Kim Kardashian, who was two months away from the release of the sex tape that would make her a star."

Trump told Stormy he had booked a suite at the Beverly Hills Hotel and asked if she'd visit him later that night.

She claimed she was flying out of Los Angeles later that night for a booking she had.

She agreed she'd call on him the next time she was in New York. She did just that, arriving with this young woman named "Yoli." She met Trump on the 26th floor of Trump Tower.

Perhaps to impress Yoli, Stormy told Trump, "You gotta trim those eyebrows of yours. They're out of control. You look like a Muppet.:"

Her next encounter came when Trump sent a limo on March 23, 2007, to pick up Yoli and Stormy to witness the Miss USA Pageant at the Kodak Theater in Los Angeles.

At the pageant, Stormy and Yoli were given good seats in the fifth row. "I met Trump when we went backstage, but other than greeting each other, we did not talk because he was surrounded by people. I gave him my phone number, but we did not get together at that time. He sounded exhausted."

She had a final meeting with Trump on July 29, 2007. She was driven to the Beverly Hills Hotel on Sunset Boulevard. Still hoping to get on *The Apprentice,* she was driven there by Michael ("Moz") Mosny. She'd married him in 2007 and would divorce him two years later.

She met Trump in a bungalow where he called her "Honey Bunch" and ordered a big steak dinner. He still held out the promise that she might get cast on *The Apprentice.* He spent a large part of the evening attacking Rosie O'Donnell.

"To me, that seemed like such an insane tangent," Stormy said.

After the steak, he invited her to sit on the sofa with him watching the documentary *Ocean of Fear: The Worst Shark Attack Ever.*

They were interrupted by a call that came in from Hillary Clinton. From what Stormy could gather, Hillary was facing Barack Obama in seeking the Democratic nomination for President. She seemed to be soliciting Trump's support of her candidacy.

At the end of the call, he turned to Stormy. "I just love Hillary Clinton. She's so damn smart. I'm making another contribution to her campaign, my fourth so far this year. Bill and Hillary showed up at my wedding to Melania."

He told her that a lot of supporters were urging him to run for President one day. "That I will never do," he told her. "I'm having more fun doing what I'm doing now."

When his small fingers wandered to her thigh and began to crawl up her leg, she removed his hand, telling him, "I can't. I'm on my period."

Her last contact with Trump came when he notified her that she could not appear on *The Apprentice.* Roma Downy, the wife of *The Apprentice's* executive producer Mark Burnett, objected to having a porn star on the show.

"I'm sorry, darling," he told her.

That, however, was not the end of the saga of Donald Trump and Stormy Daniels.

***

In 2011, newspapers carried the story that the TV star, Donald Trump, was considering a run for the presidency on the Republican ticket. Stormy Daniels tried to sell the story of Trump's seduction of her to the celebrity magazine *Life & Style* for $15,000. Before publishing the story, the magazine editor contacted the Trump Organization for a response to Stormy's allegations.

From bibles, perfumes, and steaks to sneakers and skyscrapers, Trump has put his name on it, sometimes unsuccessfully.

Here's Donald, who has a reputation for not drinking, in 2007, predicting that his 'T&T' (Trump and Tonic) would quickly surpass Grey Goose as the most popular cocktail in America.

High-cost, gold-etched bottles and branding lawsuits didn't help. By 2011, all U.S. production had stopped.

Here's Stormy in 2007 at the XRCO Award Ceremony with her then-husband, since-divorced **Moz.**

That led to a confrontation with Michael Cohen, Trump's lawyer, who immediately threatened litigation. The editor of *Life & Style* rejected Stormy's allegation.

The same thing happened when she tried to pedal her revelations to the gossip magazine *In Touch Weekly*. Cohen issued the same threat of litigation to *In Touch Weekly* that he'd made to *Life & Style*.

Little did she know at the time, but Cohen would become a dark, dangerous, and sinister figure in her future.

Who was he? Born in Lawrence, New York, in 1966, he was Ashkenazi Jewish, the son of a surgeon who had been a Holocaust survivor. He had graduated from th Thomas M. Cooley Law School in 1991.

He rose quickly in power, becoming Donald Trump's attorney from 2006 to 2018. In time, he was privately referred to as "The Fixer," handling personal problems that arose for Trump. At the time, he also served as Vice President of the Trump Organization and personal counsel to Trump.

He also served as co-president of Trump Entertainment and was a board member of the Eric Trump Foundation, a children's health charity. From 2017 to 2018, he was also deputy finance chairman of the Republican National Committee.

Cohen kept Trump advised of threatened *exposés* by various women from his past, many with information and personal histories considered threatening to his presidential prospects.

In August of 2016, after Trump had announced his run for the presidency, a secret meeting took place among Trump, Cohen, and publisher David Pecker, owner of American Media, Inc. (AMI) and publisher of the *National Enquirer, Weekly World News,* and the *Globe.*

It is said that at the meeting of this notorious trio, a "catch-and-kill" plan was conceived. That is, Pecker would buy stories about Trump's involvement with women and then kill the story, never publishing it. Pecker was said to have paid $150,000 to *Playboy* model Karen McDougal, who'd had a more extended affair with Trump than Stormy's.

On October 7, 2016—only a month before the 2016 Presidential election—a secret tape recording of Trump was released. During normal times, it could have destroyed his presidential run, But Trump had an amazing ability to escape prosecution then and now.

The tape, when released to the public, became known as the "Access Hollywood Tape."

In it, he talked to Billy Bush of his approach to seducing women, not knowing he was being secretly taped.

"I don't even wait. When you're a star, they let you do it. You can do anything, grab 'em by the pussy. You can do anything."

Numerous Republican leaders announced that Trump should drop out of the race. House Speaker Paul Ryan canceled an upcoming political rally with him.

Trump not only survived the release of that tape, but many even more serious charges that lay in his future.

Also, in October 2016, Pecker told Cohen that AMI did not plan to buy and certainly not publish Stormy's revelations. Pecker, or so it was alleged, did not produce any "hush money to squelch the scandal.

On October 26, Cohen paid $130,000 to Stormy, asking her not to reveal Trump's seduction of her. She signed a non-disclosure agreement that Trump did not sign.

"Catch and Kill" **David Pecker** of AMI gets chummy and conspiratorial with **DJT**

When this payment was later disclosed, it was interpreted, legally, as a violation of Federal campaign finance laws.

On February 13, 2017, Cohen had to admit that Stormy's $130,000 had come from his own pocket.

On April 5, Trump lied and said he had "no knowledge" of any such payment. But on April 26, in an about-face, he admitted that Cohen had represented him in the "Stormy Daniels deal."

On May 2, Trump's new lawyer, Rudy Giuliani, said that Trump had reimbursed Cohen for the illegal payment.

On April 9, 2018, FBI agents raided Cohen's office and seized a load of documents, including a record of his payment to Stormy. By August, Cohen pleaded guilty to eight criminal charges, including the illegal payment to Stormy. He claimed that the payment was made "at the direction of a candidate for Federal Office." The court knew that was a reference to Trump. Cohen was disbarred and sentenced to three years in a Federal prison.

News accounts of Stormy's lawsuits against Michael Cohen and Trump had a bleak closure for her.

BLATANTLY POLITICIZED

Sample of a David Pecker/National Enquirer puff piece promoting DJT.

Here is the text of one of them:

Daniels filed three lawsuits against Trump and/or Cohen. In the first lawsuit she argued that the Non-Disclosure Agreement (NDA) was invalid. She won the lawsuit, though it was dismissed after Trump and Cohen agreed not to enforce the NDA. A California court subsequently ordered that Trump pay $44,100 to reimburse her legal fees.

The second lawsuit, in which she argued she was defamed, was dismissed when U.S. district judge James Otero said the tweet in question constitutes "rhetorical hyperbole normally associated with politics and public discourse in the United States that is protected by the First Amendment."

She was ordered to pay $293,000 for attorneys' fees and another $1,000 in sanctions. She was later ordered to repay Trump an additional $121,972, and then later $5,150, in legal fees for failed motions to reduce the initial fee payment.

In the third lawsuit she claimed that Cohen colluded with her previous attorney Keith Davidson against her interests when he negotiated the payment. The lawsuit did not name Trump as a defendant and was settled in May 2019.

While in prison, Cohen wrote a memoir, released in September of 2020. In it, he accused Trump of being "a cheat, a mobster, a liar, a fraud, a bully, a racist, a predator, and a con man."

After Stormy filed her lawsuits, Giuliani verbally attacked her: "Explain to me how she could be damaged. If you're going to sell your body for money, you just don't have a reputation. A woman who sells her body for sexual exploitations, I don't respect."

In 2011, **Daniels** submitted to a polygraph (lie detector) test, which was videotaped for later review. She passed "with flying colors."

Enter…
MICHAEL AVENATTI

In looking back at her life, Stormy might have admitted that two of the biggest mistakes in her life involved letting Donald Trump seduce her and also in hiring Michael Avenatti as her attorney.

Avenatti, born in Sacramento, California, in 1971 into a family of Italian origin, became famous—his critics claimed notorious—when he represented Stormy Daniels in her lawsuits against Trump.

As he grew up, he attended the George Washington University Law School, graduating in 2000, ranking first in his class.

Early in his career, he was linked to many high-profile cases, including a $10 million defamation case against Paris Hilton.

He also helped settle what was called an "idea-theft" lawsuit" against the TV show *The Apprentice* and against producers Mark Burnett and Donald Trump.

Trouble lay ahead. In 2018, Avenatti's law firm was subjected to a $10 million judgment in a U.S. bankruptcy court. He had also defaulted on $440,000 in back taxes, with interest due.

Despite his legal troubles, and starting in 2010, he drove in nearly 35 sportscar races, defying death.

Stormy entered his life in March of 2018 when he filed a lawsuit for her. It sought to invalidate the non-disclosure agreement she'd signed regarding her 2006 affair with Trump. Avenatti also represented Stormy in a defamation suit against Trump.

Avenatti was described as a man "with a refrigerator-sized jaw and an overcaffeinated demeanor. He comes off as a macho protector of Stormy Daniels."

Avenatti beame familiar to Americans when he was a frequent guest on TV shows such as CNN and MSNBC. He also gained a large following on Twitter. There was even talk that he might run for President one day. A Democratic poll put him at No. 15 as a possible candidate.

In early March of 2019, Stormy broke with Avenatti. Later that month, Federal charges were lodged against him. Among one of her accusations was that he had embezzled almost $300,000 from her.

On June 2, 2022, he was sentenced to four years in prison for defrauding her.

Among his other convictions, he was charged with attempting to extort money from Nike, the sports apparel company.

On June 12, 2003, he was sentenced to eleven years for stealing millions from clients. All of this led to his disbarment as a lawyer.

On November 3, 2020, Trump lost the 2020 U.S. Presidential election. In a hostile move never known in the history of the U.S. presidency, he did not show up for the inauguration ceremony of the Democratic candidate, Joe Biden, who had been Obama's Vice President.

Stormy Daniels, at a press conference during her ill-fated alliance with **Michael Avenatti.**

In the wake of all these legal troubles, Stormy received numerous death threats. She even received what she labeled "suspicious substances" in her dressing room. "I've had to hire three full-time bodyguards, calling them my 'dragons.' I also had to take my daughter out of school because of threats against her life, and hire a private tutor for her."

On looking back on her life, Stormy Daniels wrote, "I was struck by the absurdity of my life. I should be living in a trailer park in Louisiana, with six kids and no teeth. I grew up in a house that I should never have escaped, with adults never coming to my aid. I started stripping in high school and still graduated with honors as editor of the school paper. I won the respect of a male-dominated industry as screenwriter and director. And despite everything I did to stay out of it, I ended up in the middle of one of the biggest political scandals in American history."

She continued, "I know that the deck has always been stacked against me, and there is absolutely no reason for me to have made it to where I am, right here talking to you. Except that maybe the universe loves an underdog as much as I do."

"I own my story and the choices I made. They may not be the one you would have me make, but I stand by them."

***

Donald Trump Indicted on 34 Felony Counts

As amazing as it seems, Stormy Daniels, a porn star, will enter history books on the American presidency, thanks to none other than Donald Trump.

In March of 2023, he was indicted for falsifying business accounts by a grand jury in Manhattan. Charges were linked to a "hush money" payment to Stormy during the 2016 presidential election. The case was concluded in January of 2025.

The hush money was to buy Stormy's silence over the one-night sexual encounter they'd shared. With costs related to the illegal transaction included, payments totaled $420,000. Or, as one newspaper reported it, "The most expensive fuck in American history."

Manhattan District Attorney Alvin Bragg accused Trump of falsifying these business records with the intent to commit other crimes. The criminal indictment was the first for a former U.S. President.

On April 3, 2023, Trump traveled from Florida to New York, where he surrendered to the Manhattan District Attorney's Office and was arraigned the next day. He pleaded "not guilty" and stated that he would continue to campaign for the 2024 office of the presidency. He also called the trial a "witch hunt." Or, as one writer put it, "instead of a witch, the DA discovered a warlock."

The trial began on April 15, 2004. By April 30, the disgraced ex-television star became the first U.S. President to be held in criminal contempt of court because of comments he made earlier in the month about individuals involved in the trial.

The prosecution rested on May 20 after listening to the testimony of 20 witnesses about how the hush money was arranged by lawyer Michael Cohen, who was reimbursed via a false retainer agreement. The defense rested on May 21 after calling only two witnesses. Trump's defense team made unsuccessful requests to have the case delayed or dismissed; for presiding Judge Juan Merchan to recuse himself; and for removal of the case to a Federal court.

Trump was convicted on all counts on May 30, becoming the first U.S. President to be convicted of a felony. Following a series of delays and his 2024 presidential election victory, he was sentenced to an unconditional discharge on January 10, 2025. No penalties were cited.

Headlines in London read: CONVICTED FELON BECOMES U.S. PRESIDENT.

During the trial, it was revealed that hush money payments were listed as legal expenses payable to Michael Cohen. Actually, the money was used to reimburse earlier payments that Cohen had made directly to Stormy.

Falsifying business records in the first degree is a felony under New York law. Each count for which Trump was convicted could result in a sentence of up to four years, to be served consecutively, with a maximum sentence of twenty years.

He was permitted to assume the presidency even if he were in prison. The judge might also choose to impose no prison sentence. If he'd gone to prison, the question was, "What would happen to his Secret Service protection?"

On April 3, Trump flew from Palm Beach to New York, where he was alleged to have spent a sleepless night. He was arraigned the next day, as police feared riots in the street.

Judge Merchan refused to allow TV cameramen to broadcast the hearing.

Trump was booked but not handcuffed. However, he was fingerprinted. In the courtroom, he pleaded not guilty to all the felony charges.

[Trump had previously faced a civil lawsuit lodged by E. Jean Carroll, charging sexual assault and defamation.]

Before the trial, a gag order had to be placed on Trump since he was making outrageous statements, even calling Stormy and Cohen "sleaze bags." He attacked Judge Merchan's daughter on social media. Family members of District Attorney Bragg also suffered "savage attacks."

On May 6, Merchan found Trump in contempt of court for the tenth time. Had he been a regular citizen, he could have faced jail time.

After repeated requests for dismissal of the case or removal to a Federal court, a guilty verdict finally came in. One reporter said, "Trump's defense lawyers made enough money for their retirement after all these court filings."

Officials in state and Federal agencies began preparing for a possible incarceration of the disgraced former TV star. Trump's team wanted Merchan to postpone the sentencing hearing until after the election. On September 6, 2024 Merchan postponed the sentencing hearing until November 26.

On January 3, 2005 he set a new sentencing hearing for January10, four days after the Electoral College vote count and ten days before Trump's second inauguration.

On January 10, Trump was sentenced to an unconditional discharge. In other words, he did not have to go to jail. He vowed to have his lawyers appeal his conviction. The judge had allowed him to attend his sentencing via video-conference, stating that it would be impractical to jail a President-Elect of the United States.

The conviction remains on his record.

Some lawyers think he could be re-sentenced for his crimes after he leaves the presidency, but for the time being, he got off lucky, with no prison time. Unlike Michael Cohen, there were no fines and no probation.

MICHAEL COHEN
How Trump's Personal Lawyer Ended Up in Jail

"Donald Trump wishes I was dead"

—Michael Cohen

When he first started testifying in his own defense for the outrages he'd suffered at the hands of THE DONALD, **Michael Cohen's** biggest problem involved earning the credibility, faith, and trust of the American people.

As of this writing, and thanks to his relentless advocacy of his own position on TV and in the press,, most indicators show that he's winning most of his press and PR battles.

For Michael Cohen, being the personal lawyer of Donald Trump from 2006 to 2018 would forever taint his life. So would porn queen Stormy Daniels (*see previous episode*). His link to both of them would ultimately lead to his imprisonment and disbarment as an attorney.

While in prison, he began work on his controversial memoir, *Disloyal*. Published in 2020, it became a *New York Times* Bestseller.

Trump's public language is the most vulgar ever uttered by an American president. But his private language—as revealed within the pages of Cohen's book, might shock the faint of heart.

Cohen's book almost didn't see the sunrise, as government officials desperately tried to bar its publication.

"The idea that Michael Cohen is sitting in solitary confinement in prison because he won't sign papers committing not to publish a book is unfathomable," claimed attorney Alan Dershowitz. "This is the United States of America. We don't send people to solitary confinement because they want to write a book."

A younger, dumber, version of **Michael Cohen** swore that he'd give his life for **Donald Trump**. After his betrayals—and lots of time in prison—he morphed into one of the dozen or so people on whom Trump most wants to wreak vengeance.

The opening lines of the Cohen memoir set the stage for the revelations to come. "The President of the United States wanted me dead. Let me say it the way Donald Trump would: He wouldn't mind if I were dead."

"Trump talked like a mob boss, using language carefully calibrated to convey his desires and demands, while at the same time employing deliberate indirection to insulate himself and avoid actually ordering a hit on his former personal attorney, *confidante*, *consigliere*, and—at least in my heart—adopted son."

These thoughts may have been going through Cohen's head as he traveled one bitter winter morning, February 24, 2019, to testify before both the House of Representatives and the Senate. He alleges in his book that at the time, millions of Americans already knew that the president was a "living lunatic."

Becoming Trump's personal lawyer ultimately sent Cohen into hell's fire, leading to his disgrace and a sentence of three years in a Federal prison and a fine of $50,000. He was also disbarred. His sentence was completed in November of 2021.

Even when Trump was hosting *The Apprentice*, Cohen noticed his disdain for black people. One of the contestants on the show was Dwame Jackson, a brilliant Harvard MBA graduate. Quoted Trump, "There is no way I'm going to let this black fag win."

Trump often expressed his contempt for African Americans. He told Cohen, "Every country run by a black man is a complete shithole."

Cohen had vivid memories of how much Trump detested Barack

According to Cohen, **Trump's** descent into narcissism and tyranny became increasingly obvious during his stewardship ("YOU'RE FIRED") of *The Apprentice.*

Hussein Obama after he won his first election as president. "Trump sort of hissed while pronouncing Obama's middle name."

When Obama came on TV, Cohen claimed that Trump acted like "an enraged Archie Bunker," obviously filled with hatred and contempt for the new President.

He burst into anger when Obama was awarded the Nobel Peace Prize. Later, he would launch a campaign to win that prize for himself. *[As of this writing, he has failed in that goal.]*

When Cohen and Trump watched Obama on television, he would yell, "FUCK HIM!" at the TV set. "He's a fucking phoney. He's not even a fucking American! He was born in Kenya, not Hawaii!"

Cohen watched in awe as Trump broadened his base by enveloping evangelical right-wing Christians. "I think the last time Trump went to church was at the age of seven," Cohen claimed. "As President, he would hawk expensive gold Bibles he'd published. I doubt if he ever read one word of that book."

He did meet with some leading evangelicals, such as Jerry Falwell, Jr., the President of Liberty University. He would enter Cohen's life again in 2015. Then, during a meeting with these so-called devout Christians, Trump listened patiently to their attack on abortion and homosexuality. One leader, who went unidentified, suggested lifetime imprisonment for homosexuality, a policy pursued in Uganda. Trump agreed to run on a campaign of "family values."

Cohen suggested that although Trump didn't give a damn about religion, the evangelicals bought his act and became among his most ardent supporters during presidential elections.

Trump had his own view of these religious fanatics: "Pure horseshit. I can't believe that there are people who actually believe all this crap."

As if he didn't have enough mess on his hands, Cohen even got involved in 2015 with a sexual scandal centered on the religious zealot, Jerry Falwell Jr.

Falwell had reached out to Trump with a request for a personal favor. Falwell confessed that a third party had obtained compromising nude photos of his wife, Becki. Cohen met with the third party. After threats, he agreed to destroy the photos.

Michael Stratford, an education reporter for *Politico*, wrote: "When Falwell and his wife Becki strolled around the campus of Liberty University, they would play a secret game: The middle-age couple would point to students, both young men and women, and imagine what it would be like to have sex with them."

A former student, a member of the school band with the Falwell's son, Trey, claimed that Becki performed oral sex on him when he stayed overnight at the Falwell home. Apparently, her husband watched.

Shortly after Cohen interceded with this student, Falwell became one of the most ardent backers of the *Trump for President* campaign.

Years before his run for President, Trump was a host of both the Miss

In his memoirs, Cohen described "the depths of Trump's hatred' for former president **Barack Obama.**

"Trump would become almost apoplectic" whenever a news clip or photo of him flickered across the media.

Until he grew estranged from (and enraged) by) Trump's betrayal, Cohen "disappeared" many of the jams Trump supporters got involved with. One of them was **Jerry Falwell Jr.**, the homophobic evangelist, shown here with his wife, **Becki.**

Cohen alleges he was instrumental in getting them exonerated from the blackmail plot of a (male) employee they were simultaneously *schtupping*. In the aftermath of his fixing their problem, the Falwells became two of Donald Trump's most fanatical supporters.

In his memoir and in court, **Cohen** has testified that his duties to **Trump** ("Back when I was sycophant-in-chief") involved explaining away, or lying about, Trump's marital infidelities to his wife, **Melania.**

One can't help but wonder whether Melania's (unfortunate) choice of wardrobe, back in October of 2018, during her visit to a children's detention camp, derived from residual rage about Donald's betrayals.

Universe and the Miss USA pageants. After looking over some photographs, he singled out Miss Brazil. "She's fucking gorgeous. Look at that face and that body. Man, I'd like a piece of that."

After Trump married Melania, his third wife, Cohen admitted that one of his duties involved telling lies to her about her husband's extramarital affairs. In a self-confession, Cohen admitted, "My work for the boss was getting him out of one jam after another. It was morally, legally, and ethically repulsive. Also soulless."

The American public didn't need to be told that Trump's favorite daughter was the blonde-haired beauty Ivanka. His other daughter, Tiffany, a product of his second wife, Marla Maples, was viewed as a sort of outcast.

Cohen also claimed that Trump was not overly fond of Jared Kushner, who became his son-in-law following his marriage to Ivanka. He was alleged to be displeased with her conversion to Judaism.

Cohen also weighs in on the competitive tensions that simmer between Trump's daughters, **Tiffany**, *(left)* sometimes a pariah, and the unassailable **Ivanka**, shown on the right in 2025 at the Wailing Wall in Jerusalem.

"Trump tolerates his son-in-law because it seems he's the only one he can really trust.", Cohen said.

Kushner would be called upon "to run the back channel side deals, as they were known."

Of all the Trump children, Donald Jr. is the most belligerent in promoting his father. Yet Cohen revealed that the President held his son in low esteem, even calling him "a hopeless idiot."

Cohen was a key player in Trump's first run for the presidency in 2016. The candidate besieged Cohen with behind-the-scenes tasks that included meeting with David Pecker, the publisher of the *National Enquirer*. He referred to the tabloid mogul as "our go-to bullshit artist."

Sean Hannity, the commentator on Fox, became an avid supporter, whether he believed all the propaganda he broadcast or not.

At home, Cohen did not find either of his children, either his son, Jake, or his daughter, Samantha, to be Trump supporters. His children had been born to his Ukrainian-born wife, Laura Shusterman. Both of his kids were avidly opposed to the Trump presidential run.

Actually, Trump had first seen Samantha when she was only 15. Standing next to him, Cohen had pointed her out within a room filled with other people. Trump then turned to Cohen and said, "I would love some of that."

It was then that Cohen protested, "She's my daughter."

Cohen with his daughter, **Samantha,** in January of 2017 at a Trump inaugural ball.

During his 2016 campaign for the presidency, Cohen came to believe that the candidate could survive almost any challenge, even the *Access Hollywood* tape revealed in a previous episode. In it, Trump had been quoted telling Billy Bush how he grabbed pussies. Cohen nicknamed this as "pussygate."

It seemed amazing how Trump's notorious history of sexual encounters, failed businesses, bankruptcies, and dubious business links didn't prevent him from winning. Often, these scandals were ignored by the average Trump supporter.

That was in total contrast to Hillary Clinton, who had been falsely charged with all sorts of crimes, the most ridiculous of which alleged that she ran a child sex ring out of a pizza parlor in Washington, D.C.

Although in his book he overlooked Trump's "Halloween orange" makeup, Cohen tackled the enduring controversies associated with his hair:

Cohen admits to having arranged with murky, much-contested "catch and kill" setup of Stormy Daniels with AMI president David Pecker.

"The weird hairstyle is the twisted result of a botched scalp surgery and a

complex triple-combover. He underwent a disfiguring hair-implant operation in the 1980s that left unsightly scars on the top of his head. His hair is so long that when it's not piled on top of his head, it hangs down below his shoulder on the right side. The operation that makes it stand involves a ton of hair products and a triple fold. The three-step procedure requires a flop of hair from the back of his head, followed by the flip of the resulting overhang on the back of his pate, and then the flap of his combover on the right side, providing three layers of thinly disguised balding male insecurity."

Wanna know more about Donald and his on-going obsession with his weird hair? **Ask Michael Cohen.**

Campaigning for Trump in front of enthusiastic crowds, Cohen denounced critics who labeled his boss anti-semitic, citing his Jewish son-in-law married to Ivanka. He also claimed that Trump was not a narcissist, although those who watched him on TV disagreed. "He's also been falsely accused of being anti-Hispanic, anti-black, and Islamaphobic. He is not a racist or bigot."

In retrospect, and in reference to his fake and misleading statements, Cohen said, "I gave sycophancy a new definition."

***

It seemed inevitable that the cozy relationship between Trump and Cohen would come to an end. Cohen pleaded guilty to eight counts, including campaign violations and tax and bank fraud. He admitted that at Trump's direction, he had violated campaign finance laws, trying to influence the 2016 election.

In November of 2018, he pleaded guilty of lying to a U.S. Congressional committee about efforts to build a Trump Tower in Moscow.

A jail cell lay in his immediate future.

Early in 2019, Cohen sued the Trump Organization for allegedly failing to reimburse his legal fees. In July of 2023, the parties reached a settlement ahead of a planned trial. In early 2023, Trump sued Cohen for breaching his legal trust. That October, however, he dropped the suit ahead of a planned deposition.

 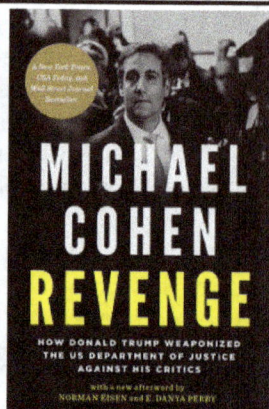

Two books, double the fun: Appropriately entitled memoirs by **Michael Cohen**, each a NY-Times bestseller.

Since then, embittered by his having "taken the fall" for actions and policies inaugurated by Trump himself, Michael Cohen has morphed into one of Donald Trump's most outspoken and implacable enemies, appearing frequently both in court and on news broadcasts to highlight "the sins and illegalities" of "DJT, President."

Michael Cohen with his wife, **Laura Shusterman.**

Creative Malady, February 2020

GAUGUIN
A Child Molester (& Other Scandals)

Provocative issues are being raised about the private lives of painters, actors, musicians, dancers, directors, authors and composers. Should we judge them strictly on their artistic creations, regardless of their morals?

Reputations are being destroyed by revelations about the private lives of certain artists and other creators. Morality tests are being applied to artists of yesterday who are being subjected to a 21st Century perspective of their politics and sexual improprieties.

A study of the private lives of some of the leading figures in world culture would reveal dozens of maladjusted personalities, even demented ones. Examples come to mind: Sigmund Freud, Florence Nightingale, Charles Darwin, Marcel Proust.

Should we no longer read the groundbreaking modernist novels of Céline because he was an anti-Semite? Let's not look too closely into the secret beliefs, recreations, and politics of Cervantes, Richard Wagner, or even Shakespeare.

There is a condition called "Creative Malady," which suggests that great art is often produced by the psychologically damaged. It is said that mental illness, often in the form of a psychoneurosis, can sometimes lead to major success in the production of artwork.

Sir George Pickering, a brilliant septuagenarian physician and author of a book about it (Creative Malady, first published in 1974 and today a widely recommended academic text), claimed that "great work would not have been done, or done in such splendid style, by relatively sober people leading ordinary lives."

Paul Gauguin: a drunkard, a misanthrope, and a maladjusted moral leper...and an artistic genius

Years ago in Key West, Tennessee Williams told me that his plays "stem from my tormented soul, my shattered dreams. I was Blanche Du Bois in *A Streetcar Named Desire*—demented, delusional, self-destructive."

In the past two years, artist Paul Gauguin (1848-1903), that self-professed "savage, exploiter, chauvinist, colonialist," has come under fire for his private life.

Louis-Ferdinand Céline (1894-1961) is credited as one of the greatest novelists in the repertoire of French literature. Sullied by Nazi sympathies and hatred of Jews, his legacy is debated today with something approaching frenzy in academic circles.

Moving to Tahiti in 1891, he became a notorious pedophile, fathering countless children born to girls aged twelve to thirteen. He painted them as dusky, bare-breasted, almond-eyed, mysterious, and dark-skinned beauties. He has also been criticized for promoting racial stereotypes.

Gauguin did not confine his painting to nubile Polynesian maidens. He also painted self-portraits, one of himself as Jesus Christ, another of himself as a de-

By many accounts, **Florence Nightingale** altered forever the mission of nurses—especially in war zones. But some of her contemporaries debated whether her ferocious personality wasn't motivated by more than "just a touch" of mental aberration.

capitated John the Baptist, with a ruby-red glaze of blood on his neck.

Some of his sharpest critics have even demanded that museums and galleries displaying his works cease to do so. Exhibitions of his masterpieces have also been condemned. Yet reproductions of his works decorate thousands of bedrooms. His last painting, "Will You Marry?" sold for $210 million in 2014, the third-highest price ever paid for a painting.

When London's Tate Gallery presented an exhibition of Gauguin's works, many writers were highly critical of its curators for "displaying the art of a child molester." The director at the time, Vicente Todoli, said, "As a person, I might have loathed Gauguin, but as an artist, he is a genius, inspiring future painters such as Picasso and Matisse. When an artist creates something, it no longer belongs to him, but to the world."

As his legacy, Gauguin has inspired novels, operas, even movies such as *Lust for Life* (1956). It starred Kirk Douglas as Vincent Van Gogh, who cut off his ear before being incarcerated in a mental asylum. Anthony Quinn's portrayal of Van Gogh's rough-edged frenemy (Paul Gauguin) brought him an Oscar.

In 1903, the year of Gauguin's death at the age of 54, he said, "No one is good, no one is evil, everybody is both, in the same way and in different ways. It is so small a thing, the life of a man, and yet there is time to do great things."

Two views of 20th century actor **Kirk Douglas** interpreting the role of the maladjusted impressionistic genius **Vincent Van Gogh** in the award-winning biopic, *Lust for Life* (1956).

Some art critics have suggested that Van Gogh's genius lay in being able to actually paint his hallucinations.

DID YOU KNOW that despite the astronomical prices of his art, postmortem, Van Gogh never sold one of his paintings during his lifetime?

"You're mad, bonkers, completely off your head. But I'll tell you a secret. All the best people are."
—Lewis Carroll's Alice in *Alice in Wonderland*

"There is no great genius without a touch of madness"
—**Aristotle**

"Great Art comes from great pain."
—**Kanye West**

"Geniuses don't have a habit of being unbalanced, but they do have a proclivity to it."
—**Craig Wright, PhD.**

It can be argued that each of the five geniuses depicted above (*left to right*, **Miguel de Cervantes, Richard Wagner, Charles Darwin, Sigmund Freud,** and **Tennessee Williams**) suffered from some form of personality disorder...and that each suffered enormously from some kind of mental trauma and/or existential despair. Might their respective forms of despair have contributed to their *oeuvre*?

Creative Malady, June 2015

The Bard
A Mystery Wrapped in an Enigma

Somewhere in the world, 24 hours a day, on some stage, amateur or professional, a play by William Shakespeare (1564-1616) is being performed. Perhaps two hundred years from now, that will also be the case.

Only recently, I saw the brilliantly talented Peter Sarsgaard deliver a crisp, nuanced, and strikingly modern rendition of *Hamlet*. Sporting a hipster suit, he was lucid and emotionally intense in this fascinating revision, bringing a fresh approach to familiar soliloquies.

In a wildly different vein, actor Christian Borle, starring on Broadway in a musical, *Something Rotten!*, portrays Shakespeare more as a rock star than as a writer. In it, the "sacred cow of the theater" (Shakespeare) is skewered, depicted as a crafty and egomaniacal plagiarist. High-stepping actors in 16th century dress with oversized codpieces do the Renaissance drag.

Over the years, I've seen many of the world's greatest actors perform as the stars of *Hamlet*—John Gielgud, Laurence Olivier, Richard Burton, and Peter O'Toole, who called it "the worst play ever written."

Books have been written about Shakespeare, but here's a shocker: We don't know much about him.

What little is known is that his father was a glove-maker, and his mother, Mary Arden, the daughter of a farmer. Both were illiterate. When he was 18, their son, William, married Anne Hathaway, 26, after he got her pregnant.

Their son, Hamnet, died of an unknown disease when he was eleven. Shakespeare never taught either of his two daughters, Susanna and Judith, to read.

He didn't spend a lot of time with Anne. In fact, between 1585 and 1592, he disappears from historical record, at around the time he was denounced as an "upstart crow." There is speculation that during those undocumented years, he traveled on the continent with a male lover and fellow actor, perhaps learning enough about European history for later background in his plays.

He added words or expressions to the English language, such as "wild goose chase" in Romeo and Juliet, or 'foregone conclusion" in Othello. There are at least 80 different ways to spell his last name, including "Shaxbred."

William Shakespeare (1564-1616) is hailed as the greatest writer in the English language and the world's pre-eminent dramatist. His plays have been translated into every major language.

Actor **Peter Sarsgaard** delibers an emotionally intense and lucid **Hamlet.** He seems cranky and angry at the world, prone to fits of sarcasm and petulance and, in his modern interpretations, to an occasional snort of cocaine.

William Herbert, 3rd Earl of Pembroke (1580-1630) was an English nobleman. In 1623, the First Folio of the Bard's plays was dedicated to him.

Actor **Christian Borle** is Shakespeare in *Something Rotten!*, set in 1595.

On Broadway in 2015, it ran for 708 nights, and was nominated for ten Tony Awards.

Henry Wriothesley, 3rd Earl of Southampton (1573-1624), is frequently identified as "The Fair Youth" of Shakespeare's Sonnets.

The question often asked is how did a man with a grammar school education produce such brilliant works and become an unequaled master of the English language. It is suggested that the real authorship of his plays belongs to Francis Bacon, Christopher Marlowe, Edward de Vere, 17th Earl of Oxford, or Queen Elizabeth I herself. The Oxfordian theory is the strongest, but there is no smoking gun—or smoking pen if you will.

Some scholars—without much proof—have claimed that one of the figures portrayed above actually wrote the plays attributed to Shakespeare: *Left to right:* **Francis Bacon, Christopher Marlowe, Edward de Vere,** and **Queen Elizabeth I**

Fake portraits painted in the 18th Century abound, sometimes depicting Shakespeare with a gold earring.

No written contemporary description of his physical appearance survives, and no evidence suggests that he ever sat for a portrait.

The debate over whether he was a homosexual—or not—rages among scholars into the 21st Century.

He never meant for his private sonnets to be published. In his most famous, he is a man writing to another man—"Shall I compare thee to a summer's day?"

When published in 1640, many of the pronouns he used were changed from "he" to "she." The other sonnets are directed to a "dark lady." So it's assumed that the Bard was bisexual. The so-called "Dark Lady of the Sonnets" may have been Amelia Bassano, the musician and poet.

Sonnet 20 defines the male object of his affection "the master-mistress of my passion." Modern readers assume its words express the sentiments of a gay guy in love with a straight man.

The Sonnets are dedicated to a "Mr. W.H.," the "Fair Youth" believed to have been William Herbert, 3rd Earl of Pembroke, whose contemporaries viewed as extremely handsome. It could have been Henry Wriothesley, 3rd Earl of Southampton, to whom Shakespeare dedicated two narrative poems with erotic themes.

The great British actor, Sir Ian McKellen, who has performed Shakespeare since he was a teenager, claimed, "It's obvious he enjoyed sex with both sexes. The mystery of his life makes him even more appealing. What is important is that his words have lasted in the minds of people all over the world for more than 450 years."

Gielgud, Olivier, Burton, O'Toole, and **McKellen,** each interpreting Hamlet, a *de rigeur* role for English actors of their respective heydays.

Creative Malady / January 2020

ALAN TURING
the "Father of Computers"

British historians estimate that the scientific breakthroughs of Alan Turing, a computer scientist (1912-1954), shortened World War II in Europe by two years and saved 14 million lives. To its everlasting shame, Britain persecuted this progenitor of modern computing and, under Victorian laws about homosexuality, forced him to undergo chemical castration. Morbidly depressed, he committed suicide by cyanide on June 7, 1954 at the age of forty-one.

A half-eaten apple was found beside his bed. His method of dying, it has been suggested, came from his favorite fairy tale, Walt Disney's *Snow White & the Seven Dwarfs* (1937), in which the wicked queen immerses an apple in a poisonous brew.

Turing died in obscurity because his remarkable achievements were concealed at the time by the Official Secrets Code of the British government. All that has changed today—in fact, the Bank of England has announced that beginning in 2020, Turing's face will be depicted on the new £50 note.

In 2009, British Prime Minister Gordon Brown apologized "for the appalling way Turing was treated. He deserved so much better."

When President Barack Obama arrived in London, he got it right, praising this code breaker and computer visionary. He hailed Turing, placing him in "the Pantheon of innovators and discoverers from Newton to Darwin, from Einstein to Edison, from Alan Turing to Steve Jobs. Turing's goal was to embody human intelligence into an artificial form—hence, the invention of the computer."

In 2013, the Queen of England issued an official pardon.

In World War II, Turing worked with code breakers at the sprawling estate of Bletchley Park north of London. Here, he cracked the code of Nazi Germany's Enigma machine. Hitler regarded the code as unbreakable, and it remained in use throughout the entire war. That meant that the British knew in advance every major move the Nazis were going to make. Sir Winston Churchill learned that Coventry was going to be bombed but did not order the evacuation of the city, since it would have signaled the Nazis that the Enigma Code had been cracked.

Turing conceived what became known as the Universal Turing Machine, which could perform all sorts of tasks. Sir Winston told FDR of this remarkable achievement, and it was shared with American scientists working on the development of the Manhattan Project.

From that emerged atomic bombs dropped on Japan in the closing days of World War II in the Pacific. Harry S Truman learned that the Japanese planned "to fight to the last man standing" in an invasion of the home islands. He estimated that dropping those bombs, ushering in the Atomic Age, saved the lives of a million and a half American soldiers.

Upper photos show the real-life **Alan Turing** *(left)* wtih a view of one of his early machines.

Lower photo shows how the entertainment industry developed and publicized, as a film, the tragic saga of the maladjusted, relentlessly gauche genius who saved the world.

Here's a replication of **"The Bombe,"** whose moving parts unraveled the code of the Nazi's enigma machine, shortened the course of World War II, and saved millions of lives.

"Turing was a national treasure," said MP John Graham-Cunning, who worked to restore his reputation. "We hounded him to death, but his name will live forever in world history."

In June of 2019—a little late—*The New York Times* finally ran Turing's obituary. In 2014, a film about Turing's life, *The Imitation Game*, was released starring Benedict Cumberbatch.

In the post-war era, during the most intense conflicts of the Cold War, Turing was on the dawn of scientific breakthroughs that would have led to nuclear supremacy as America and Britain faced the menace of the Soviet Union. It's estimated that Turing would have advanced British technology by two decades. But while investigating a routine robbery at Turing's residence, police discovered he was having an affair with a man his own age. In March of 1952, he was convicted of "gross indecency," and, to avoid prison, he submitted to chemical castration. That meant his security clearance was lifted, and he was fired.

On the 100th anniversary of Turing's birth in 2012, posthumous tributes poured in from around the world. Today, statues honor him, wings of buildings are named after him, even bridges and roads. He is acknowledged as "the Father of Computer Science" and also as "the Godfather of All Modern Computers."

Time magazine eventually designated Turing as one of the 100 most important people of the 20th Century. "Everyone who taps at the keyboard, opens a spreadsheet or a word-processing program is working on an incarnation of a Turing machine."

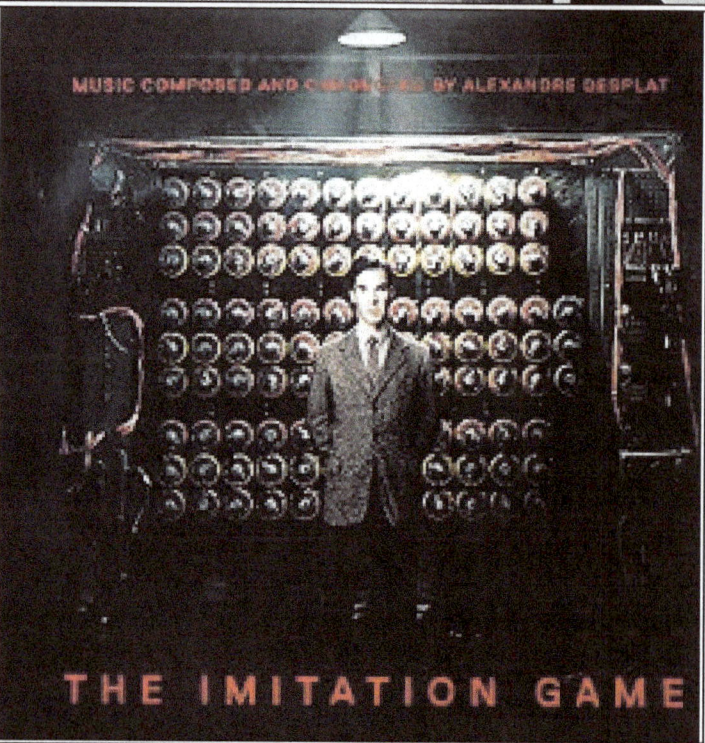

Upper photo: A view of one of Alan Turing's de-coding machines, and *lower photo*, a replica of one of his machines, crafted for the biopic *The Imitation Game*, with **Benedict Cumberbatch** cast as Alan Turing. The film won eight Academy Award nominations.

Photo left: Here's the facade of **Bletchley Park**, site of Alan Turing's de-coding research during World War II. Until Turing's recent "discovery" by new generations of computer enthusiasts, Bletchley Park was slated for demolition. Now, as a museum devoted to the tech victories of the Brits, through Alan Turing against the Nazi menace, it's a thriving museum. It's accessible via an hour's train ride north of London.

Creative Malady, February 2014

AN UNHOLY TRIO

Pink Triangle
Tennessee Williams, Gore Vidal, & Truman Capote
Sexual Outlaws of the Literati

UNHOLY TRIO: Three of postwar America's greatest dramatic writers (*left to right*, **Gore Vidal, Truman Capote,** and **Tennessee Williams**) appear in the only known photo of a shared appearance—in this case on a hot summer's night at a party in Greenwich Village, a few days after the end of World War II.

Ferociously competitive, each was prone to the anguish, excesses and eccentricities of Creative Malady.

The atomic bomb had fallen on the Japanese city of Nagasaki, ending World War II, when three gay writers—Tennessee Williams, Gore Vidal, and Truman Capote—arrived in New York to explode shock waves of their own.

In the post-war era, each of them rose to infamy in the plays, novels, and film scripts they'd create—among them Capote's *Breakfast at Tiffany's*, Tennessee's *A Streetcar Named Desire*, and Vidal's notorious gender-bending *Myra Breckinridge*.

It was not their literary works that shocked audiences, but their scandal-plagued private lives. My latest biography, *Pink Triangle*, explores the secret lives of these three writers, whom I knew intimately over the decades, sharing many of their triumphs and tragedies.

It is not just their story, but the saga of celebrated members of their entourages. What a cast! Tallulah Bankhead, Vivien Leigh, Marilyn Monroe, Marlon Brando, Paul Newman, Elizabeth Taylor, Bette Davis, Katharine Hepburn, Anna Magnani, Burt Lancaster—and the list goes on. Drawn from their drama-filled lives, *Pink Triangle* has a revelation on every page.

In the beginning, Tennessee became friends with both Vidal and Capote, although the latter two became each other's worst enemies, even suing one another for libel.

Tennessee told me, "I liked Gore, but only through the strenuous effort to overlook his conceit. He had studied ballet and was constantly doing pirouettes and flexing his legs. The rest of the time, he attacked Capote."

Tennessee had a more colorful description of Capote: "He speaks with a forked tongue. He's a sodomite's delight, a little monster unleashed from vaginal portals—but charming nevertheless."

Each author was sexually voracious, none more so than Vidal. He claimed that in a style equivalent to the legendary Don Juan, he in time seduced 1,003 men.

In their younger days, their conquests were not just associated with hustlers and wannabee actors, but with major stars—Marlon Brando, James Dean, Montgomery Clift, Rock Hudson, Sal Mineo, Peter Lawford—all of them predictable staples on the list of promiscuous gay or bisexual movie stars of that era. It seemed that every male and female star in Hollywood or on Broadway wanted to appear in a play or screen adaptation by Tennessee.

Both Vidal and Capote had promiscuous mothers, each of them named Nina. Vidal caught his mother "winging low" with Charles Lindbergh, when she wasn't otherwise involved with Time/Life publisher Henry Luce. Simultaneously, Gore's dear old Dad, Eugene Vidal, was

In 2014, newspapers and literary reviews on both sides of the Atlantic paid enormous attention to the release of Darwin Porter's overview of the Pink Triangle's feuds.

One reviewer in London referred to it as "a silken lash we simply cannot get enough of."

"flying high" with Amelia Earhart. In Hollywood, Nina Vidal launched a torrid affair with Clark Gable, wanting him to become her son's stepfather.

In parallel patterns, Truman's mother, Nina Capote seduced everyone from boxing champ Jack Dempsey to Marlene Dietrich.

At various times, Vidal and Jacqueline Bouvier shared the same stepfather, Hugh Auchincloss. In Washington, they became confidants of each other. When she worked as an inquiring photographer for a newspaper, she visited the office of a rising young California politician, Richard M. Nixon. She confessed to Gore, "He made a pass at me."

Sometimes, Jackie and Vidal fell for the same man. Both were balletomanes, each becoming entranced with John Kriza when they saw him perform his folkloric ballet, "Billy the Kid" wearing a white jockstrap and chaps. Later, both of them became romantically involved with the Russian ballet dancer, Rudolf Nureyev.

In Hollywood in the 1950s, Vidal wrote a screenplay for Bette Davis (The Catered Affair, released in 1956). He moved in with an unmarried couple, Joanne Woodward and Paul Newman. He told them that one day he wanted to run for president of the United States. According to Vidal, "If I become president, Joanne agreed to marry me and become my First Lady."

One morning in Key West, Vidal and Tennessee were mapping out a screenplay, Suddenly Last Summer, to star Elizabeth Taylor and Katharine Hepburn. From Palm Beach a call came in from Jackie, who wanted them to drive to Palm Beach to share a late lunch with her husband, then a senator from Massachusetts.

On the way there, Vidal revealed to Tennessee that John F. Kennedy was contemplating a run for the presidency. During the lunch, the quartet bonded, but later Tennessee made a forecast to Vidal: "Jack will never become president. He's too handsome and sophisticated for the American public. But he has some butt on him."

Vidal scolded him. "Tennessee, you can't cruise the future president of the United States."

Capote became the darling of high society, surrounding himself with the rich, the famous, and the infamous. He sailed the Aegean on the yacht of Gianni Agnelli; he sunbathed in Greece in the nude with Aristotle Onassis, and he visited Charlie Chaplin at his home in French-speaking Switzerland. He also became best friends with Babe Paley (voted best dressed woman in America), and her husband, Bill Paley, the chief honcho at CBS. His 1966 "Black and White Ball" at the Plaza Hotel in Manhattan was hailed as "the party of the century."

But in time, he betrayed his friends, painting cruel caricatures of them in the first chapters of his unfinished novel, *Answered Prayers*, published in Esquire. His beautiful swans, as he called his high society ladies, glided away from him, never to return.

Regrettably, Capote and Tennessee fell victims to their own self-destruction, their lives devoured by drugs and alcohol. Tennessee died in 1983, Capote in 1984.

Of the trio, only Vidal lived to a ripe age of 86, dying in 2012, although in his final years, he suffered from dementia.

In Vidal's final assessment, he claimed, "All three of us will resurface even though buried under six feet of earth. We'll be back, perhaps as cannibalistic vegetation sprouting up."

In reference to the trio and the profound influence they exerted on the arts and the American psyche, Orville Prescott, the stodgy critic for *The New York Times*, summed things up differently: "Once you spill mercury from a bottle, you can never brush it all back in."

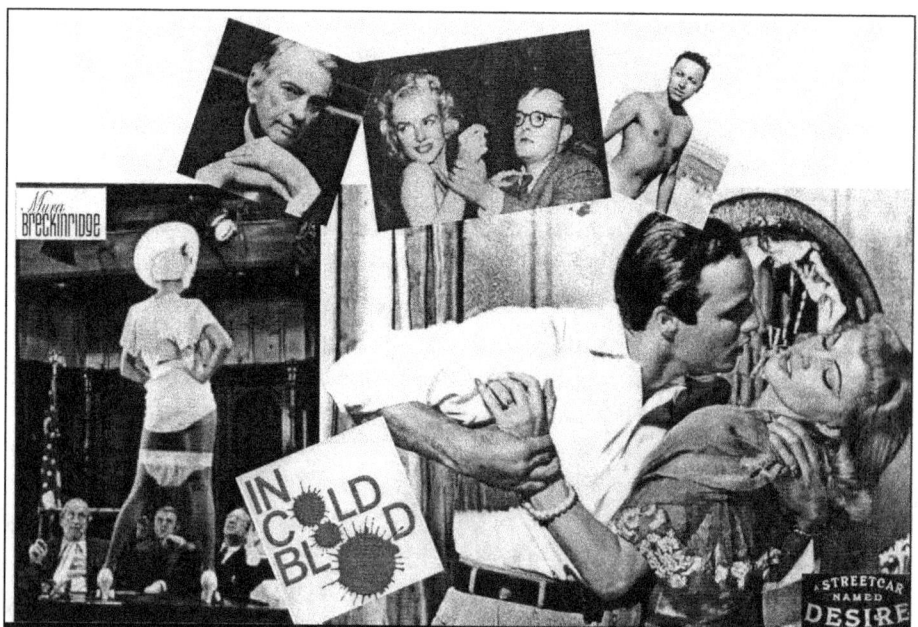

PINK TRIANGLE:
The Feuds and Private Lives of
Tennessee Williams, Gore Vidal, & Truman Capote

by Darwin Porter and Danforth Prince.
From Blood Moon Productions, 2014.

Historic Figures, March 2020

The Battle of Britain
PAUL FARNES
Its Last Ace Fighter Pilot

Nazi Bombers winging their way across the Channel toward Britain in 1940.

Winston Churchill touring the ruined nave of **Coventry Cathedral** during the Battle of Britain.

Dressed to Kill: **Paul Farnes,** Hero fighter pilot of the RAF.

In 1940, as France surrendered to the invading Nazi hordes, the Battle of Britain was about to begin. Hitler called it *Unternehmen Seelöwe* ("Operation Sea Lion"). It was his plan to invade the British Isles, even though Prime Minister Winston Churchill vowed, "We will never surrender."

First, the powerful Luftwaffe launched "The Blitz" with the intention of crippling the Royal Air Force (RAF), which it vastly outnumbered. It lasted from September of 1940 to May of 1941, and included almost nightly bombings of London and England's Channel Ports.

The young pilots of the RAF took to the air, often losing their lives, but they fought bravely to turn the tides of war. Churchill famously said, "Never in the history of human conflict was so much owed by so many to so few."

One of the bravest of these pilots was Paul Farnes, a "hero among heroes." The last living fighter pilot of this historic battle, he died on January 28, 2020 at the age of 101. The world learned of his death on February 10 when it was announced as part of a BBC broadcast.

Farnes was born in England in 1918 in the closing year of World War I. His father, a soldier from Australia, was married at the time with three other children. Farnes' unwed mother died shortly after giving birth. The midwife who had delivered the child adopted and raised him into manhood.

In 1938, as war clouds loomed over Europe, Farnes joined the RAF Volunteer Reserve. Trained as a pilot, he was stationed briefly in France until the British pilots had to return to England after the fall of France.

There, he was stationed in Surrey at the RAF's Kenley Air Base, where he and his comrades awaited attacks from the Luftwaffe.

It came with deadly force. Farnes, among others, took to the air to try to stem the invasion. Whatever Hermann Goering's Luftwaffe sent against Farnes, he fought back in one or another of Britain's dwindling inventories of Hawker Hurricanes and Supermarine Spitfires, fatally hitting Junkers Ju Stuka and Dornier 17 bombers and Messerschmitt fighters. Once, after Farnes shot down a Nazi pilot, the stricken aviator saluted him during his parachute descent into the rough waters of the Channel. Farnes saluted him back.

Paul Farnes, as a lavishly decorated civilian and hotelier, from around the time of his friendship with Darwin Porter.

Many times, Farnes came close to being shot down, but he never wavered, always managing to land back in England, sometimes in a damaged plane.

He rose in rank, becoming a flight lieutenant and squadron leader, At the end of the war, he was a wing commander and later served in Iraq. In 1958, he retired from the RAF.

In civilian life, he ran a small hotel in Worthing, a seaside resort on the English Channel which had been fashionable during the late 18th Century.

When I was writing my first travel guidebook, *Frommer's England*, I checked into Farnes' small hotel for a three-night stay. There, I met its owner, who soon learned that I was a passionate World War II buff. We spend hours that night over beer as he shared details of his RAF adventures. They included service in Malta and North Africa.

By the end of my stay, we had become friends for life. I visited him nearly every year after that, updating my guide. He thanked me for sending him so many American and Canadian visitors.

In 2017, Prince Charles presided over the annual commemoration of the Battle of Britain. Each year, attendance levels of the fighters who were involved declined until Farnes became the only former pilot to show up, representing his comrades and receiving the praise of a grateful prince and a grateful nation.

Charles read from the poem "Ode to Remembrance," by poet Laurence Binyon (1869-1943):

"They went with songs to the battle, they were young.
Straight of limb, true of eyes, steady and aglow.
They were staunch to the end against odds uncounted.
They fell with their faces to the foe."

RAF fighter pilots, racing toward their Hurricanes during the Battle of Britain (1940) prepped and primed for imminent combat with the Luftwaffe

As he choreographs damage assessments and rescue operations from a perch beside Tower Bridge, this member of Britain's air defense team watches, with horror, the firebombings of London.

Members of Britain's Best and Brightest, pose at Whitehall, during the darkest years of World War II, with **Hugh Dowding**, Air Officer Commander of the RAF Fighter Command. Dowding, in the center, is credited, through prudent allocations of planes and scanty resources, with the defeat of Operation Sea Lion.

September 2018

The "Princess of the Third Reich"
GUDRUN HIMMLER BURWITZ
Dies and Fades Into History

Adolph Hitler, in his tawdry dreams of glory, predicted that the Nazis and their Third Reich would last for a thousand years. How wrong he was.

This murderous empire and war machine, of course, dissolved into ashes in April and May of 1945, forcing Germany to surrender to the Allies in the West and to the Soviet forces advancing from the East.

But the final death toll of the Third Reich, so we've learned, was sounded in May of 2018, when news of the death of "The Last Nazi" leaked out.

Dead at 88, she was Gudrun Himmler Burwitz, the daughter of Heinrich Himmler, the Reichsführer and leader of the black-shirted SS. He was also the architect of "The Final Solution," aimed at the extermination of European Jews.

This blonde, pig-tailed little girl—called "Puppi" (German for doll) by her father—was fanatically committed to the mass murderer, whom she labeled "Pappi."

Two views of **Gudrun Himmler** with her notorious father, **Heinrich.** *Upper photo*, at a Nazi rally in 1938; *lower photo*, during a visit with her father (center figure) to Dachau concentration camp, where the family lived in comfort with many servants, in 1941.

Gudrun was cited as the Aryan who was fussed over, and sat on the laps of, more high-ranking Nazis than any other child in the Third Reich. In the upper photo, as a child, she appears on the lap of **Adolf Hitler.**

The lower photo shows her father, **Heinrich Himmler,** a former chicken farmer who morphed into one of the most terrifying figures of Nazi Germany.

At the age of 12, she arrived with him at Dachau, a concentration camp established in 1933, ten miles northwest of Munich. It became the site of 32,000 documented deaths and thousands of undocumented ones.

She wrote in her diary: "We saw everything we could. We saw the beautiful gardens. We saw the pear trees. We saw all the pictures painted by the prisoners. Marvelous. And after we had a lot to eat. It was all very nice."

Gudrun was Himmler's only legitimate child, though he adopted a son later on. He also had two illegitimate children with his mistress/secretary. Gudrun, though, was "the apple of my eye, my beautiful darling" (his words).

Her support for her father never wavered, even during the bleakest of the war years. He remained devoted to Hitler, who called him *der treue Heinrich* (the faithful Heinrich).

Gudrun on holiday with her parents, **Marga and Heinrich,** emulating the Teutonic ideal the Nazis had romanticized. Heinrich, author of plans to exterminate the "undesirables" of Europe, seems to revel in his folkloric *schtick*.

As the war years dragged on, Gudrun attacked Göring, head of the Luftwaffe, as a "fat windbag," and she labeled Goebbels "a narcissistic show-off."

By 1945, Himmler knew that the Nazi regime was collapsing, and he tried to negotiate Germany's surrender to the Allies. Hitler found out and turned on him, ordering his arrest and assassination.

Himmler shaved off his mustache and donned a black eyepatch but was arrested by British forces. He killed himself three days later by biting down on a cyanide capsule concealed in a hollowed-out tooth. Gudrun, however, claimed that the British "murdered my father."

The flamboyant Nazi princess (*Schillernde Nazi-Prinzessin*-a term that was "assigned" to her during the postwar years by the German press), lost her crown and fled to Italy with her mother. She was captured by U.S. troops and brought to Nuremberg for interrogation at the War Crimes Tribunal. A U.S. interrogator said, "Gudrun was a true believer in Nazism, the zealot of zealots, and that made her dangerous. Her name and that of her father will live in infamy."

She married Wulf Burwitz, a right-wing journalist and member of the National Democratic Party.

Until the day Gudrun died, she supported the remaining coterie of Nazis, including Anton Malloth, a former prison guard who beat at least 100 prisoners to death at the Theresienstadt concentration camp. She was a leader in the Nazi coven called *Stille Hilfe* (Silent Aid), funneling money to ex-Nazis such as Martin Sommer, "the Hangman of Buchenwald."

For the rest of her long life, Gudrun remained a dedicated Nazi, expressing only high praise for her father. "I'm proud of him. He was a good and kind man, very loving, a wonderful father."

"Germans should erect monuments to him," she said, "because he tried to make our Fatherland a better place by eliminating undesirables."

"If Hitler had won the war, I might have married the next Führer and become queen of the Third Reich—not just its princess."

Upper photo, from the German National Archives, **youngsters** in the enthusiastic heat of a Nazi adolescence.

Lower photo: Deeply depressed but still fanatically loyal to the Nazi cause, **Gudrun Himmler** in 1954.

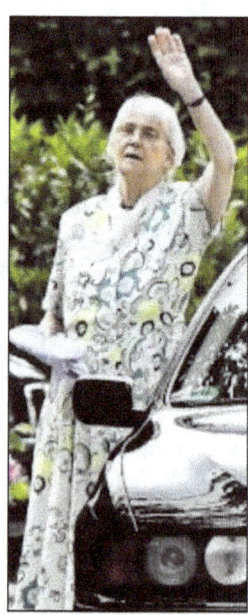

Two views of **Gudrun Himmler** with her mother, **Margaret** (aka **Marga**). *Left photo*: Idyllically sited, with Marga in the height of fashion, still favored by Himmler before he left her for a mistress. *Right photo*: A chastened and deeply depressed Marga, in black, attended by a 16-year-old **Gudrun**, forcefully preserving, even then, the sanctity and heroism of her father.

Death of a Nazi Princess. Gudrun Himmler Burwitz: One of her final goodbyes

October 2021

Her Ladyship
LADY JEANNE CAMPBELL

Seducer of JFK, Nikita Khruschev, Fidel Castro, & more

Three views of **Lady Jeanne Campbell:** *Upper photos*, as a correspondent in the New York office of her grandfather's newspaper, *London's Evening Standard*, and *lower photo*, with husband #1, the volatile, egomaniacal, and abusive American novelist, **Norman Mailer.**

Left Canadian-born news mogul **Max Aitkin (aka Lord Beaverbrook)** was a close but intensely competitive friend and sometimes ally of **Winston Churchill** *(right)*. They appear here together in 1941, one of the darkest years, for Britain, of World War II.

Jeanne Campbell was Beaverbrook's favorite granddaughter. Even her most vocal detractors said her quick wit and formidable social skills derived from him directly.

At my home in Key West, a call came in from my friend, Tennessee Williams. He informed me that one of his closest friends, Lady Jeanne Campbell, would be arriving late the following morning at the airport.

He wondered if I would entertain her for a week, taking her to lunches, introducing her around, showing her the sights, and taking her boating.

"As you know, I'm in my studio until five in the afternoon every day before I'll see anybody," the playwright said.

I was intrigued and anxious to meet her. Since I was a teenager, I'd read about Lady Jeanne Campbell. Staunchly British, she was an actress, socialite, and foreign correspondent for the *London Evening Standard*. Daughter of the 11th Duke of Argyll, and granddaughter of Baron Lord Beaverbrook (the owner of the newspaper she worked for), she was also related to Queen Victoria.

From the moment of her arrival in Key West, she and I bonded, and she soon found out I'd been a reporter the *Miami Herald*.

Although she'd gone to finishing schools, she spoke like a tough newspaperman herself, having learned to survive in what was, back then, largely a man's world.

Actually, Lady Campbell was infamous for her seductions more than for her reporting. As far as it is known, she is the only (known) woman who slept with President Kennedy, Nikita Khrushchev, and Fidel Castro.

She was blunt in her boudoir reviews of this trio of world leaders. "JFK had back pain and lay prone while I did all the work. Nikita was fat and stubby, and "'on-and-ooof, do-it-quick' man with a lot of huffing and puffing. Now take Fidel: He was one of the greatest lovers, an erotic treat for any woman and the best-equipped for action."

She'd had a brief marriage to author Norman Mailer (1962-1963). When Gore Vidal asked her why she'd married such a volatile figure, she replied, "Because I'd never gone to bed with a Jew before."

After their divorce, Mailer struck back at her She became the inspiration for his depiction of "the bitch" in his controversial 1965 novel, *An American Dream*. This book was attacked by critics for its portrayal and treatment of women. The protagonist murders his wife by throwing her over the balcony of a high-rise, then tries to make it appear like a suicide jump.

Before and after Mailer, Lady Campbell had gone through many affairs, with a wide diversity of lovers. What might have been the most prestigious was publisher Henry Luce (1898-1967), the founder of such magazines as Time and Life. Married at the time to Clare Boothe Luce, he was hailed as "the most influential private citizen in America."

During a fling in Jamaica, "I was mad about the boy" (her words). She was referring to author Ian Fleming, the creator of the James Bond spy novels. Columnist Dorothy Kilgallen wrote, "Lady Jeanne Campbell was the obvious inspiration for Fleming's character of 'Pussy Galore,' the *femme fatale* of *Goldfinger*."

Lady Campbell's most notorious affair was in the 1930s with the aristocratic and dashingly handsome politician, Sir Oswald Mosley. At the time, he flamboyantly presided over the pro-Nazi British Union of Fascists. Reviled less than a decade later, in 1940 during the London Blitz, he was imprisoned.

Her most violent affair was with Randolph Churchill (1911-1946), the only son of Sir Winston Churchill. As Noël Coward said, "Randolph was utterly unspoiled by failure."

His wartime wife (1939-1946) had been Pamela Digby, later a prominent fundraiser for Bill Clinton and the Democratic Party.

As Lady Campbell recalled, "Randolph arrived like a thunderbolt in my life and for two months it was a world of liquor, drugs, suicide threats, and a cascade of physical and verbal abuse and money troubles."

"After he tossed all my clothes and two mink coats out of an eighth-floor window of London's Ritz Hotel and gave me a black eye, I fled into the night. 'Randy Randy needed a mother more than a mistress."

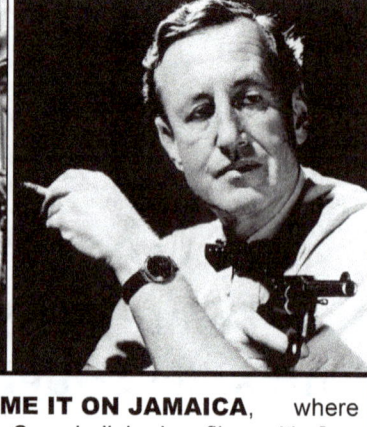

BLAME IT ON JAMAICA, where Lady Campbell had a fling with **Ian Fleming** (above).

Wisely, Ms. Campbell opted not to marry Randolph Churchill...unlike **Pamela Digby Churchill Harriman** (*left photo*), who did. Later a major-league American socialite & key player for Bill Clinton and the Democrats, Digby appears with **Winston Churchill's son, Randolph**, after their (prestigious but disastrous) wedding in 1939.

Physically nondescript, pleasant, and unpretentious, **Lady Jeanne Campbell** became a long-time resident of New York City and an active (and by all accounts, very penitent) member of a Catholic congregation in Greenwich Village. Displayed above are two photos of her, chipper and cheerful, from the 1960s—an obviously very intelligent woman whose opinion was sought after by some of the most influential, brainy, and intimidating men of her era.

The term for someone primarily attracted to people with high IQs or intellectual qualities is **sapiosexual**. One can only wonder whether Lady Campbell might have defined herself as one of them. Here, *left to right*, are some of the power brokers she was said to have become intimate with—if only briefly. *Left to right*, **Fidel Castro, Nikita Khruschev, JFK, Henry Luce,** and **Sir Oswald Moseley**.

November 2017

R.I.P
Hugh Hefner
Founder of the EMPIRE OF SKIN & Avatar of Sybaritic Males

Hugh Hefner, avatar of "the good life", died on September 17, 2017. He's seen here surrounded by Bunnies during the peak years of their novelty and sense of flirtatious chic.

Hugh Hefner, founder of *Playboy* magazine in 1953, passed into immortality on September 27, 2017, at his decaying mansion in Los Angeles. He was 91.

His legacy may live for at least two or three more generations, as he was the sparkplug that helped set off the sexual revolution of the 1960s, changing American attitudes about "the good life" and sex for the rest of the 20th Century and beyond.

For $500, with money borrowed from his mother, he purchased nude photographs of Marilyn Monroe, which she'd posed for back in the days when she was broke and hungry. With Monroe on the cover, the first edition of *Playboy* hit the newsstands—and was an instant hit. If you still have a copy of it in your attic, you can sell it for $25,000 in today's market.

Ironically, in 1992, Hefner paid $75,000 for his remains to rest in the crypt next to Monroe.

Playboy's legion of fans, mostly male, grew, reaching eight million subscribers at its zenith. Along the way, Hefner himself became a cultural warrior, fighting censorship and championing such issues as abortion, gay rights, and the legalization of marijuana.

He became one of the most controversial of all Americans, championed by

In 1946, with his term of duty in the U.S. Army behind him, **Hef** had to find a new gig...one that fit into the volatile flood of post-war consumerism.

The *upper photo,* part of a publicity campaign from **Air Canada**, noted that their flight attendants were delighted by the recent addition of nylon stockings—which had been severely rationed during the war—to their uniforms.

Lower photo: Suddenly, a raft of previously unavailable consumer goods were temptingly presented in bold new ad campaigns from Madison Avenue, sometimes with subliminal sexual overtones. The bold new world of sensual marketing was ripe for a new generation of consumers. Hugh Hefner's daring new conception of manhood, American style, was born.

Hefner's entrepreneurial and advertising genius coincided with the early years of the sexual revolution. Although by later standards of porn and the internet, the carefully coiffed playfulness of the Bunny ethic looks tame, it inspired streams of volatile outrage —-and vast profits for an **EMPIRE OF SKIN** that branched into restaurants, resorts, television, casinos, and an astonishing raft of consumer goods.

It can be argued that Hefner's aesthetic derived from the French in an era when Continental attitudes about undraped beauty were MUCH more relaxed (and realistic) than what was legal in North America. One of his early inspirations was **Brigitte Bardot**, *(photo above)* France's most-watched postwar sex kitten, in *And God Created Woman (Et Dieu Créa la Femme).*

Hefner's legal battles over censorship issues, especially during the Reagan years, became almost epic.

Marilyn, it always comes back to Marilyn.... Here's the cover of Hefner's first issue of *Playboy* in December of 1953, where America's most iconic blonde was featured as its "Sweetheart of the Month."

MM bitterly acknowledged, years later, that she never made a dime in royalties or fees from her role in launching what became one of the most iconic magazines in the world.

millions but with an equal number of attackers, especially feminists who accused him of exploiting women.

Many of the comments after his death were comical, including one by Joseph Fusco of the Bronx: "Is it true that Hefner has been reincarnated as a harem eunuch?"

Vin Morabito of Pennsylvania claimed, "In Hef's honor, pipes resembling the ones he was frequently depicted puffing on shall be flown at full staff on only the most erect of poles."

Hefner was known for his dress code, never wearing underwear, but appearing in sleepwear. During the day, he wore custom-make silk pajamas in "gunfighter black," transitioning to rich colors such as scarlet at night. For company, he put on a smoking jacket.

His admirers were wide-ranging. The Rev. Jesse Jackson praised him as a strong supporter of civil rights, and Larry King hailed him as "The Giant" of free speech and a devotee of the First Amendment.

Our President, Donald Trump, was a great admirer of "Hef," showing up at a Playboy mansion to celebrate the publisher's 80th birthday in 2006 and posing with six bunnies.

Hefner was compared to Citizen Kane, Walt Disney, and F. Scott Fitzgerald's *The Great Gatsby*.

Hefner didn't walk through the 20th Century, he romped through it. Playboy Clubs sprouted up in major cities, and he branched out to open resorts and casinos until his brand faded in recent decades.

The New York State Liquor Authority fought against giving him a license, but by April of 1963, the Playboy Club in Manhattan was the busiest, with 2,700 customers daily, visiting to eat, drink, listen to music, and gaze upon scores of scantily clad young women wearing rabbit ears and bushy tails.

An ardent feminist, Gloria Steinem, went underground, posing as a Playboy Bunny herself to expose Hefner. J. Edgar Hoover, a closeted homosexual, investigated him, and John F. Kennedy became an avid fan.

His fans hope that Hefner is now living in that Playboy mansion in the sky, whereas others have expressed a desire that he burn for eternity in hell's fire.

The outspoken Linda Stasi of the *New York Daily News* came down hard on the Playboy publisher. She denounced him as "living in a world of concubines, a Viagra-fueled fossil in pajamas, who liked bunnies with massive boobs, but not massive brains. His was a case of the Beauty and the Beast, a modern-day Dracula living in a rotting mansion."

Columnist Ross Douthat delivered a most scathing denunciation, calling Hefner "the father of sex addiction, a pretentious huckster, a lecherous low-brow Peter Pan,

Playboy aficionados watched with wry amusement how being featured as a centerfold could break or make, quickly, a girl's career.

In the early years of Playboy, models returning to their home towns were likely to be shunned and shamed.

All that changed toward the end of the Playboy saga, as pros like **Joan Collins** *(upper photo)* and **Madonna** *(lower photo)*, gloried in and celebrated the rebirth of their careers thanks to the centerfold exposure of some of their skin, sometimes tasteful, sometimes not.

a flesh peddler, a leech-like feeder of our vices with custom-tailored erotica that was misogynist, a leering predator, a devotee of priapic senility, a wicked and destructive American, and, finally, a desperate member of Prospero's Court with a Red Death at the door."

But thousands upon thousands of men who grew up in the 1960s and 70s had nothing but praise for Hef. Paul Bacon, a typical fan, noted that he combined photos of nude women with in-depth articles by Gore Vidal, Norman Mailer, and even Jimmy Carter who admitted to having "adultery in my heart."

Bacon said, "Hefner led free speech battles, fighting all the way to the Supreme Court after the post office refused to deliver Playboy to its subscribers."

Before departing his earthly paradise, the avatar of sybaritic male pleasure had a final word of advice: "Life is too short to be living someone else's dream."

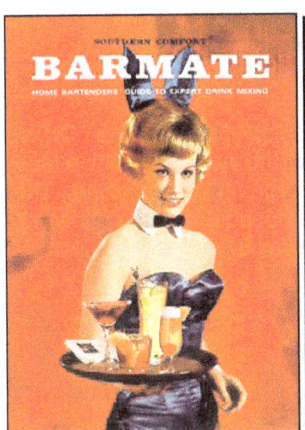    

IN RETROSPECT, IT ALL SEEMS RATHER TAME.

Photos above, *left to right*.

1) As a publishing venture, *Playboy* released a flood of ancillary "how to" guides and manuals that usually generated profits. Here's a publication listing about a hundred high-octane cocktails carefully engineered for Bunnies or wannabees.

2) The respected feminist, **Gloria Steinem**, widely publicized the fact that for a brief period, she "went undercover" into the lion's den of macho, outfitting herself as a Bunny in one of the Playboy clubs, doing "Bunny dips" as part of her service rituals and collecting research notes. Here's **Steinem**, self-satirizing, in a publicity photo for *Show* magazine, where her sensationalist two-part "exposé" ("A Bunny's Tale") first appeared in 1963.

3) In 1985, **Kirstie Alley** replicated the on-site "training" of Gloria Steinem in a made-for-TV movie, *A Bunny's Tale*. Here she is, **Kirstie Alley, portraying Steinem portraying a bunny** in a lion's den of male chauvinism, circa 1963.

Hefner's eccentric and sometimes reclusive lifestyle quirks were widely publicized, eventually becoming woven into the myths and legends associated with the Playboy Mansions.

He's seen *above, left*, on the cover of *People* magazine (a magazine which, ironically, he didn't happen to own) with his then-girlfriend, **Barbi Benton**.

One of his most enduring girlfriends, she was known for multiple appearances in *Playboy* and for a relationship with him that lasted from 1969 to 1976. According to *Playboy* lore, she met him on the set of "Playboy After Dark" in 1968 when he was 42 and she was 18.

Right photo: **Early Hefner**, personifying "the good life" aboard a TWA flight to some place glam with then-girlfriend **Cynthia Maddox**. A cartoon editor for *Playboy*, she appeared in five photospreads of his magazine. Hef's pre-eminent romantic relationship of the early Sixties, she was a *Playboy* receptionist and secretary who became his trusted Assistant Cartoon Editor.

According to an interview in *Playboy*, "I was crazy about Cynthia," Hef admitted, noting that they shared consuming interests in art and classic movies. "And," said Cynthia, "we absolutely agreed on cartoons." What they didn't agree on was marriage, and when it appeared that it wasn't in the cards, Cynthia left.

And then there was **THAT NOTORIOUS GROTTO** at the Playboy Mansion in L.A.

The water was warm, the lighting was dim, there were a LOT of receational drugs, and—in theory at least—"What happened in the Grotto remained in the Grotto." Cameras and cellphones were discouraged...we think. But LOTS of celebrities are said to have migrated in and out. Such was the stuff of Pre-Aids L.A. at "The Bunny Club."

 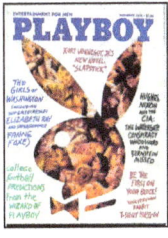 

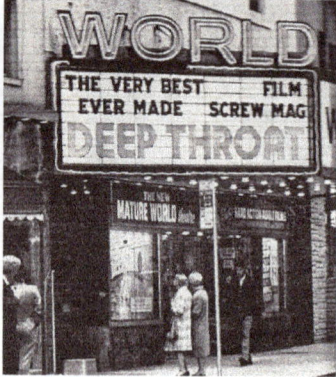

Decades before his death, sales of his magazine and business at his Bunny Clubs, had greatly declined. The magazine's decline was credited (or blamed) on competitors who included **Bob Guccione**, publisher of the more explicit **Penthouse** magazine, and the harder-core films such as *Deep Throat*, whose fan base reached into the millions.

And then there was Hef's fifth and final marriage, to **Mrs. Crystal Hefner**, the lass on the cover of the July 2011 edition (*see above*) of his iconic, but by then, less profitable magazine. The internet with its widely available amateur porn, and the lessening of literate readers who "read Playboy for its articles" had, like Hef himself, greatly diminished.

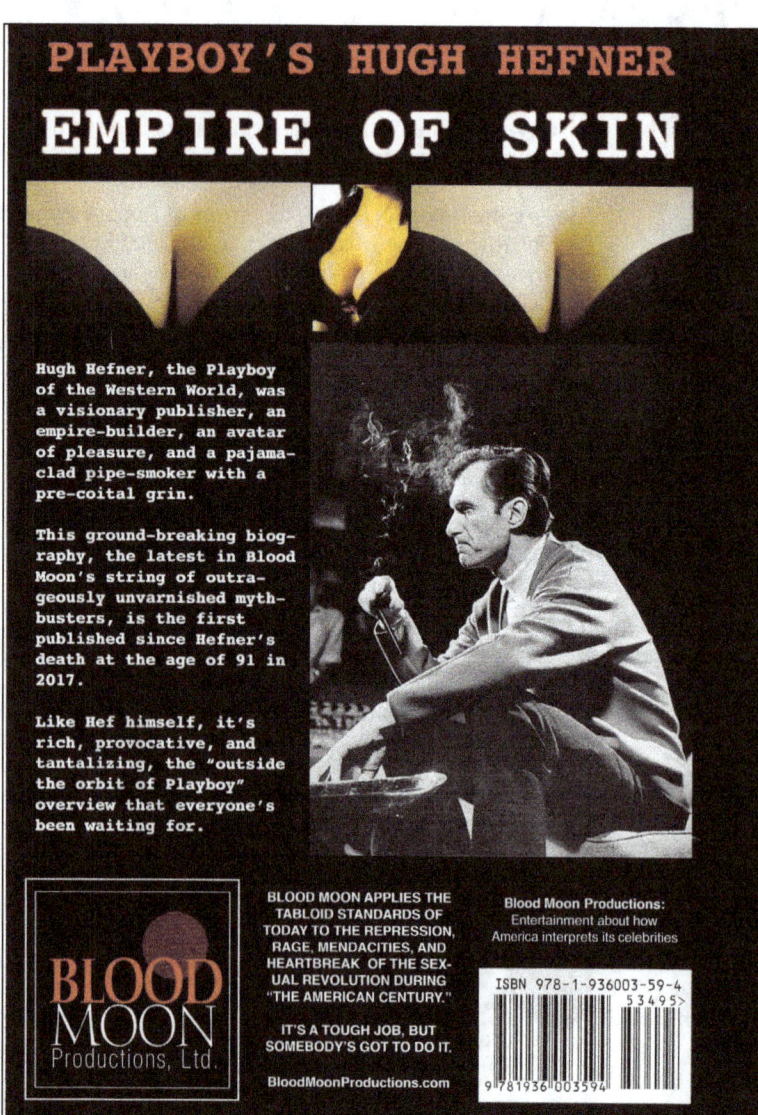

DID YOU KNOW? That in 2017, within a few months of his death, that we (i.e. **Darwin Porter and Danforth Prince at Blood Moon Productions**) published the first postmortem biography of **Hugh Hefner**?

Most of the information included in this preview derived from the information revealed within its pages. Happy Reading. **R.I.P Hef.**

October 2010

CELEBRITY IMPOSTORS
De-Bunking Conspiracies Associated with the Cadaver of Howard Hughes

Six views of the elusive, enigmatic, and eventually insane **Howard Hughes**.

When a great or infamous man dies under mysterious circumstances, there is often bizarre speculation about his demise that can last for decades. "Elvis" was recently seen in a Sioux City shopping mart buying peanut butter and bananas for white bread sandwiches. Other conspiracies cite that Hitler is still alive and was just spotted in Argentina.

Other hoaxes (or self-delusions) have been associated with Amelia Earhart. In 1959, during my long-ago tenure as bureau chief for *The Miami Herald* in Key West, I was sent to Big Pine Key to interview a woman who insisted that she, indeed, was the aviatrix most sources claim has been missing since July 2, 1937.

The real Earhart disappeared during a circumnavigational flight of the globe. She was last heard from somewhere near tiny Howland Island in the Pacific.

The woman I interviewed had some convincing evidence that she might have been "the real deal." But she flunked three questions I'd carefully constructed, the answers of which would be known to the real Amelia Earhart.

The latest "ghost" to return from the dead is Howard Hughes, the famed aviator and mogul who once owned RKO Studios. *[In the 2004 biopic,* The Aviator, *Leonardo DiCaprio played a skewed and not-very-convincing version of Hughes.]*

A recent book *Boxes: The Secret Life of Howard Hughes*, authored by Douglas Wellman, describes a (nonexistent) conspiracy foisted on the world by Hughes himself. Wellman's unconvincing premise claims that Hughes swapped places with a mentally incompetent geriatric whom he stashed away at the Desert Inn in Las Vegas (and later in The Bahamas) while he (the REAL Howard Hughes) lived incognito, in self-imposed isolation until he was 96, eventually faking his own death. According to Boxes, the tycoon assumed the identity of one Verner (Nik) Nicely, who spent a lot of time wandering in the Alabama woods without any clothes on. Wellman goes on to maintain that the half-crazed tycoon eventually married a woman named Eva McLelland (now deceased) in the Panama Canal Zone in 1970, that their union lasted

On July 14, 1938, after his record-setting round-the-world flight, **Howard Hughes**, with his four-man crew, was hailed as a national hero by NYC mayor **Fiorello LaGuardia**,

Hughes (central figure, in a dark suit) appears here in front of City Hall after a tickertape parade.

Two views of the REAL **Amelia Earhart**, *lower photo* with First Lady **Eleanor Roosevelt**.

Howard Hughes Dies at 70 On Flight to Texas Hospital

Billionaire Was Flying From Acapulco With Undisclosed Illness

By JAMES P. STERBA
Special to The New York Times
HOUSTON, April 5—Howard R. Hughes died today as mysteriously as he had lived. The reclusive 70-year-old billionaire was on the way from Acapulco, Mexico, to the Meth-

In ways that evoke rumors associated with the deaths of Adolf Hitler, Elvis, and Amelia Earhart, the death of **Howard Hughes** led to widespread attribution of conspiracy theories

until his death in 2001. and that she lived in constant terror of having to uproot her life and "re-disappear" with him whenever he was threatened with exposure, or "capture," by either the FBI, the Mob, or the IRS.

[Eva, by the way, defined herself as an Elizabeth Taylor look-alike. Having seen a photo of her snapped in 1970, I determined she looked as much like Dame Elizabeth as Carol Burnett.]

My warning about this and other celebrity fakes? "Be careful," I've always said. Many of their claims are ego-driven or "for profit," without merit, and in some cases, deranged.

***

Decades of my own life were spent researching a biography called *Howard Hughes: Hell's Angel.* Hailed as the most insightful overview of his film producing years ever published, with special emphasis on his hit-and-miss relations with other Hollywood players, it was recently reprinted, since interest in the billionaire aviator and movie mogul never dies.

In 1976 the corpse of the feeble and aged wreck of a once-powerful industrialist. aviator, and movie mogul, former Playboy of the Western World, was lying in a hospital-style bed within a $2,000-a-night penthouse in the Acapulco Princess Hotel in Mexico. Until moments before his death, the frail body, riddled with needles, was fading fast, suffering from dehydration and malnutrition.

While he was still breathing, Hughes was examined by Dr. Lawrence Chaffin, who had helped him survive his almost-fatal plane crash over Beverly Hills in 1946, and who had administered to him ever since. He was also examined by his chief physician, Dr. Wilbur Thain. Both doctors who knew Hughes intimately insisted that their patient was the real Howard Hughes.

Hughes died at 10 o'clock on the morning of April 5, 1976 and was placed on a private plane flying to his native Houston. Rumors surfaced even at the time that the actual Hughes had been murdered in 1968 in Las Vegas and that the corpse flown into Texas was an impostor.

Hughes' ailing aunt, Annette Lummis, got the rumor mill spinning again when she claimed that the cadaver was not her nephew. She'd last seen him in 1938.

As for Nik Nicely, that nudist resurrected by Boxes's overview of Hughes' final days, we'd call him a nutbag. We will believe the claims of Wellman's book "when pigs learn to fly," as the saying goes.

Winner of several literary awards, and favorably reviewed by some of the biggest newspapers in the U.S. and U.K., **Darwin Porter's biography of Howard Hughes** was defined by *Boomer Times* as its **BOOK OF THE YEAR** shortly after its inaugural release in 2005.

February 2012

The Dark, Extra-Marital Secrets of
Charles A. Lindbergh

The other night I watched the Billy Wilder film, *The Spirit of St. Louis* (1957), which I had not seen since I was in college. It starred the lovable James Stewart as the celebrated aviator, Charles A. Lindbergh, who entered the history books in 1927 when he flew his single-engine airplane, *The Spirit of St.Louis*, nonstop from New York 's Long Island to Le Bourget in Paris. His achievement stunned the world, as thousands in Paris turned out to greet this genuine hero.

He made very different headlines once again in 1932, when the world learned that his infant baby, Charles A. Lindbergh, Jr., had been kidnapped from the family 's home in New Jersey, during a caper that was referred to in the press as "The Crime of the Century."

The world mourned with Charles and his wife, Anne Morrow, when their beloved boy was found dead. Four years later, in 1936, an unemployed carpenter, Bruno Hauptmann, was arrested, tried, convicted, and electrocuted for the crime.

At that point, Lindbergh was viewed as one of the most sympathetic figures in America, but his story hardly ended there. Between 1936 and 1938, he made several trips to Nazi Germany, where he was warmly received at the invitation of the Luftwaffe's Hermann Goering.

During one of them, Lindbergh referred to the Luftwaffe as "the greatest air force on earth" and asserted that "Hitler is a great man who has done much for the German race." He shocked Americans by saying "I have discovered in Germany a sense of decency and values far ahead of our own."

He also delivered an anti-Semitic attack, accusing the American Jew of "being the chief agitator in urging the United States into a European war." Then, Goring awarded him the Commander Cross of the German Eagle.

Back in America as late as 1940, Lindbergh was the chief spokesman for the America First Committee, urging the country to stay out of the war. Of course, after the attack on Pearl Harbor, that argument faded into history.

FDR denounced the aviator as a "defeatist and appeaser," which prompted Lindbergh to resign his commission in the U.S. Army Air Corps. He redeemed himself in 1944 in the Pacific when , as a civilian, he flew 50 bomber raids on

Upper photo: In 1927, after he piloted a single-engine airplane nonstop across the Atlantic, **Charles Lindbergh** instantly became the most famous person in the world. A shy and self-effacing introvert from the farmlands of Minnesota, he's seen here beside his aircraft, *The Spirit of St. Louis.* It had a name guaranteed to endear it to both the Americans and the French.

Lower photo: He experienced a level of fame on a global scale that no one had encountered before or since. eclipsing the fame associated with the first walk on the moon.

After mobs greeted him at Le Bourget airport in Paris, he was feted **on the streets of the United States** by hundreds of thousands of people, all each of them frantically trying to catch a glimpse of their hero. Many who knew him well cite the floods of adulation as mentally debilitating.

Here's his wife, **Anne Morrow Lindbergh,** holding their newborn son, **Charles Lindbergh Jr.**

A few years later, the child was kidnapped from their home in New Jersey, sparking one of the most widespread (and eventually, controversial) manhunts in investigative history.

The aftermath of that nationally publicized crime was said to have soured their marriage, intensified Lindbergh's sense of isolation, and added fuel to many of Lindbergh's personal and political eccentricities.

Japanese-held posts. He won the praise of General Douglas MacArthur.

Lindbergh's fascination with Germany, however, continued during the post-war years. One night at a dinner party in Munich, when I was researching a *Frommer* travel guide, I met Rudolf Schroeck, who revealed to me a shocking secret. He was working on a book called *The Double Life of Charles A. Lindbergh*. He made the stunning revelation that Lindbergh was the head of, and maintained, three separate families in Germany in addition to his wife, Anne Morrow Lindbergh, and their five surviving children (Jon, Land Morrow, Anne Spencer, Scott, and Reeve) in America.

The aviator visited his three German mistresses and their children between five and seven times a year from 1957 until he died in 1974. Two of his mistresses were sisters, Brigitte and Marietta Hesshaimer, who lived in the small Bavarian town of Geretsried, south of Munich.

With Brigitte, he fathered three children: Dyrk (born 1958), Astrid (1960), and David (1967). The children did not know he was a famous aviator, since during the course of his exposure to them, he used the alias of "Careau Kent."

Lindbergh was also the father of Marietta's two sons—Vago (born 1960), and Christophe (1966). None of his offspring knew that their father was an international aviation hero until Astrid read a feature story in a German magazine about his exploits.

An East Prussian aristocrat, known only as "Valeska," had introduced the Hesshaimer sisters to Lindbergh. "Valeska" had functioned as Lindbergh's private secretary in Europe. With him, she had a son in 1959 and a daughter in 1961. At one time, all three mistresses had lived together in the same apartment in Rome until they discovered that he was involved with each of them. On his death bed in August of 1974, Lindbergh begged those closest to him not to reveal the secret of his four "wives," only one of whom, of course, was legitimate.

Reeve, the younger daughter of the American branch of the Lindbergh family, finally discovered the truth about her hero father's secret German families. Her shock and horror has appeared in a memoir called *Forward From Here, Leaving Middle Age and Other Unexpected Adventures*.

After reading about Lindbergh's secret file, J. Edgar Hoover, shortly before his own death in 1972, scribbled: "He called himself a Lutheran, but with all those wives, he should have been a Mormon."

Perhaps one day, Hollywood will make a true biopic about this amazing man and how he managed to fall in love with four different women and have children he deeply cared for with all of them.

Lindbergh being presented with a Nazi medal by Field Marshal **Hermann Goering** on behalf of Adolf Hitler in 1938.

Lindbergh addresses a rally **of America First**, a vehemently isolationist, and then very influential, group of voters committed to America's isolation from foreign wars.

The Japanese bombing of Pearl Harbor effectively squashed the power of the America Firsters as the U.S. declared war on both the Empire of Japan and Nazi Germany.

Lindbergh *(above, right)* appears here with **Brigitte Hessheimer,** mother of three of his "extra-marital" children. Unknown (or only vaguely suspected) to his wife, Anne Morrow Lindbergh, Lindbergh established romantic relationships with **Brigitte,** her sister, **Mariette,** and with **"Valeska"** his private secretary from East Prussia.

With them, collectively—and in addition to the children he sired with his wife—he fathered seven children, all of them born between 1958 and 1967. His detractors defined it as one of the most deeply engrained cases of betrayal and subterfuge many of of them had ever heard of.

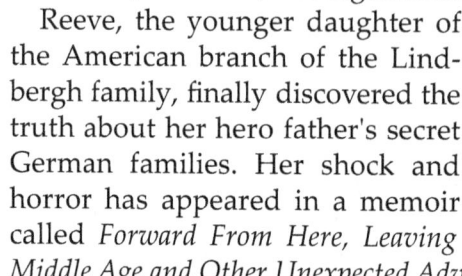

Photo, right: **James Stewart,** in his film portrayal of Charles Lindbergh *(The Spirit of St. Louis; 1957),* gazes wistfully from a window of a Hollywood mockup of an airplane once hailed as the most famous and celebrated flying machine in the world.

August 2017

JEREMY MEEKS

From the Slammer to the Glamour

"The Sexiest Man Alive"

Left photo: Whereas the mug shot of **Jeremy Meeks** snapped in Compton, California, never "took off" on social media, the **center photo,** taken several years later in Stockton, California, made him an international *cause celebre* and fashion icon.

Whereas many applauded his rehabilitation and escape from a life of crime, others mocked and trivialized it with "editorials" like the one displayed on the right.

[Editor's note: Details in this drama were accurate at the time of publication in August of 2017. But life changes.]

Police mug shots of Frank Sinatra, Nick Nolte, Rory Calhoun, and Mel Gibson did little for their careers. But the mug shot of California-born Jeremy Meeks has propelled him into international stardom, fame, fortune, and glamour, as thousands of women across the planet hail him as "The Sexiest Man Alive."

The mug shot showcased his piercing blue eyes with a teardrop tattoo cascading from one of them. Artfully unshaven, he has closely cropped hair, a perfect nose, chiseled cheekbones, and full, sensual lips "made for kissing" (his words).

His mug shot went viral, reaching 2 million Instagram followers around the world.

Although F. Scott Fitzgerald wrote, "There are no second acts in American lives," Ronald Reagan and Jeremy Meeks have proven just how wrong the novelist was.

Meeks got off to a rough start: His mother, Katherine Angier, was a heroin addict, his father serving a life sentence in prison. As a young boy, he became a member of the Northern Crips Gang.

In 2002, Meeks was sentenced to two years for grand theft. Three years later, in April of 2005, he was charged with identity

FASHION HYPE: Jeremy Meeks, as imagined by **Steven Klein** for the cover of *Man About Town*. He's sporting the kinds of gang-member tattoos that, under recent mandates from Donald Trump's ICE brigade, would get him forcibly deported to El Salvador whether he was a U.S. citizen or not.

Tucked in and around Meeks' *haute mode* posturings are Instagram tributes to his "rescue," through luck and love, from his former predicaments. *Upper photo* references his religious foundation, *lower photo*, his son.

theft and arrested again. His third arrest, based on a charge of illegal gun possession, was in June of 2014. That was the arrest associated with his mug shot, now going viral worldwide.

Released from prison at the age of 33, the "hot felon" was besieged with hundreds of offers, some of which are unprintable. For eight years, he'd been married to Melissa Meeks, 38, with whom he'd had a son. (She has two other children.) But he filed a court brief citing "irreconcilable differences" and split.

She posted on Instagram: "It's just me against the world, baby," adding a hashtag: "Still I rise."

Talent agent Jim Jordan, who searches the world for the most beautiful men and women, took Meeks on as a client.

Within weeks, Philipp Plein, the celebrated German fashion designer with shops around the world, hired him to showcase his ready-to-wear fashion. He launched Meeks, who became an overnight sensation, in September of 2016 at New York Fashion Week as a runway model.

"Let's face it," Plein said. "Clothing brands are searching for people who aren't just models, but characters who have a story to tell. Many good girls always fall in love with bad boys."

Since his debut, Meeks has been seen walking the runways of the world. *Forbes*, the magazine of the super-rich, has even profiled him, along with Bill Gates and Donald Trump.

Today, Meeks drives a $250,000 sports car and lives in a lavish mansion.

Dressed in a Kappa tracksuit during Milan's recent Fashion Week, he said, "I'm not a model. I do modeling, but I want to be a movie star and record music. There is no limit as to what I can do."

He was recently seen huddling with director/producer Lee Daniels, who turns out such feature films as *Monster's Ball* and *Precious*, and the hit TV series, *Empire*.

In May, Meeks was a sensation at the annual Cannes Film Festival, and was seen hanging out with Leonardo DiCaprio, Nicole Kidman, Dustin Hoffman, and Paris Hilton.

His date was Nicki Minaj, the Trinidad-born rapper, singer, and model, who recently had a record-breaking seven single hits on *Billboard*'s chart. *The New York Times* called her "the most influential female rapper of all time."

Steven Klein, one of the world's greatest photographers, flew to California to "shoot" the blue-eyed bandit for the upcoming spring issue of *Man About Town*, the British magazine hailed as the progenitor of all of today's men's magazines. Klein photographs such stars as Madonna, Brad Pitt, and Lady Gaga.

Meeks flew to London to be *fêted* at various events, but when he got there, guards from the British police refused his entry into the U.K., and escorted him to the next plane flying to New York. That action led Royal-Watchers to conclude that despite his growing fame, it's unlikely that he'll be invited to Buckingham Palace for tea with Elizabeth II.

Currently, Meeks is having a torrid affair with Chloe Green, the super-rich daughter of British billionaire, Sir Philip Green. He's the owner of Topshop, a string of 500 worldwide shops specializing in high fashion. Tabloids screamed, "Chloe's Romancing a Jailbird!"

Scantily clad, the romantic duo was photographed aboard a spectacular yacht she'd rented for $145,000 a week for a cruise through the Mediterranean. To take up with Meeks, she dumped her beau, Robert, son of the legendary fashion designer, Roberto Cavalli.

Where does he want to go next? The Fashion industry's newest favorite model, Meeks wants to visit Africa, which he calls "My Motherland. I want to explore the culture and life there, and I want young African men to look at me and know that all dreams are possible."

Jailhouse rock, jailhouse chic. Is that crack he's smoking?

  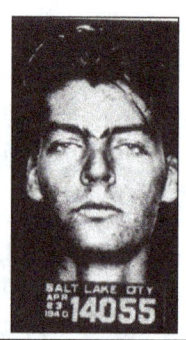  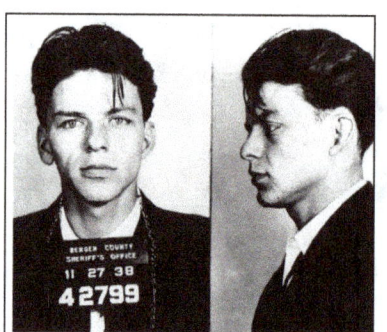

Whereas Jeremy Meeks is hardly the first celebrity (or "pre-celebrity") to be arrested and mug shot, he's one of the very few to have profited from it so instantly.

Left to right, above, each in situations to which they reacted, years later, either defiantly, with shame, or with humor, are **Jane Fonda, Nick Nolte, Rory Calhoun, Steve McQueen,** and **Frank Sinatra.**

May 2013

BESS MYERSON
Whatever Happened to the Satirically Self-Described "Queen of the Jews"?

Two views of **Bess Myerson**, left photo, as a powerhouse "phenomenon of nature," and *right photo*, in the immediate aftermath of her (ultimately disappointing) "elevation:" from Miss NYC to Miss America in 1945.

For the latter half of the 20th Century, the beautiful, smart, sophisticated, but also tragic Bess Myerson was a household name in America.

The Bronx-born brunette burst onto the scene in 1945, as World War II was ending. She was the first Jewish woman to win the Miss America pageant. This was a great propaganda victory for the victorious United States. A Jewish woman was crowned queen as horrifying newsreels of Nazi concentration camps were shown around the world. It was also learned that some six million Jews had been murdered in such death camps as Auschwitz.

In contrast, partly because of its honoring of Myerson, America seemed a beacon of tolerance and diversity. Later that turned out not to be the case. It was learned that pageant officials had urged Myerson to use a pseudonym that "didn't sound so Jewish." Her reign as Miss America was marred by anti-Semitism, as depicted in the Gregory Peck, Oscar-winning film, *Gentleman's Agreement* (1947).

Many commercial sponsors of the pageant withdrew their endorsements. Humiliated, Myerson abandoned her crown long before her reign ended. In her retreat, she sardonically referred to herself as "The Queen of the Jews," a label that stuck to her.

"I'm like a phoenix, rising from the ashes," she said, as she set about in the 1950s and '60s to become a famous TV personality. Her widest exposure unfolded between 1958 and 1967, when she was a TV panelist on I've Got a Secret, a syndicated game show seen by millions.

In the 60s, she entered politics, becoming Commissioner of Consumer Affairs under New York Mayor John Lindsay, later serving as Commissioner of Cultural Affairs under Mayor Ed Koch, whose death earlier this year at the age of 88 brought Myerson back into the spotlight.

"I have a special quality," **Bess Myerson** once informed New York magazine. "I am larger than life." A close associate and aide to NYC mayor **Ed Koch,** she appears here during her campaign for the Democratic nomination to the U.S. Senate. (She lost the primarty to Elizabeth Holtzman, who lost to Alfonse d'Amato.)

Throughout most of their association, she never dismissed speculation that marriage might be in their future while helping to dispel insinuations that Mr. Koch, a bachelor, was gay

During the earlier part of Koch's term, from 1977 to 1989, the bachelor mayor used Myerson more or less as his First Lady at Gracie Mansion. His political enemies accused him of using her as a "beard" covering his closeted homosexuality. In his race for mayor against Mario Cuomo, New York was plastered with signs—**VOTE FOR CUOMO, NOT THE HOMO**.

In a tolerant city, the feisty Koch swept to victory anyway, with Myerson at his side. When asked about his sexual orientation, he told reporters, "F—k off!"

Myerson was endlessly photographed with Koch at all kinds of events. "I'm outraged that people are saying I'm here to dispel rumors that Ed is gay," she told the tabloids.

Myerson herself had survived two stormy marriages, one to Allan Wayne, CEO of a doll manufacturing company. An alcoholic, Wayne was said to have beaten her during their hellish ten-year marriage. Her second marrage to Arnold Grant, a wealthy entertainment lawyer, was also stormy.

He allegedly attacked her low-class background; she'd been born into the Sholem Aleichem Housing Project in the Bronx, the daughter of a housepainter. Grant discovered love letters and diaries relaying details of her affairs with other men.

She and the handsome mayor, John Lindsay, were rumored to have been lovers. Frank Sinatra was among the dozens of men who sought her favors. "Men go after me," she said, "and I choose among them."

The real "Bess Mess," as the tabloids defined it, emerged when she fell hard for a rich sewer contractor, Andy Capasso, 21 years her junior. Their affair became a labyrinthine tale of lust, greed, lies, and betrayal. Capasso's wife, Nancy, learned of the affair and filed for divorce. She was granted a $2 million settlement and awarded $1,850 a week in child support and maintenance.

Myerson used her influence with Judge Hortense Gabel by hiring her 34-year-old daughter, Sokhreet, as her personal assistant, after 50 other potential employers turned the woman down. Judge Gabel then reduced Capasso's alimony to only $680 a week.

Soon after the judge's ruling, Myerson fired Sokhreet, claiming, "She makes me crazy."

Myerson was indicted for using her influence, but later acquitted. Koch dropped her. "Bess has fallen from grace," he said. "I'm amazed at what she did." Her friends claimed, "She did it for love."

Myerson's life began to fall apart. In 1974, she had to endure ovarian cancer and grueling chemotherapy.

Rudy Giuliani, then a U.S. attorney, investigated Capasso, who had been awarded a $54 million construction contract with the City of New York. It was learned that he'd lavished extravagant gifts on Myerson, including a $41,000 Mercedes. He was subsequently indicted and convicted of income tax evasion for failing to pay nearly a million dollars in taxes. He was sentenced to prison for four years.

On May 27, 1988, Myerson was visiting him at the Allenwood Detention Center. After exiting from the prison, she was arrested for shoplifting several valuable items from Hills Department Store in South Williamsport, Pennsylvania. She pleaded guilty and paid a fine.

After that, she disappeared from the radar screen. In the wake of Koch's death, a search began to find out what happened to her. The former beauty queen, nearing her 90th birthday in July, was discovered living in a luxurious condo in Santa Monica, overlooking the Pacific. The once-elegant, stunning brunette was suffering from dementia, Reportedly, she was not aware that her widely publicized friend of yesterday, "America's Mayor," (Koch), had died.

She died on December 14, 2014, in Santa Monica. The press did not learn of her death until three weeks later, when it was confirmed by the Los Angeles Coroner's Office. She was interred in Santa Monica's Woodlawn Memorial Cemetery.

Myerson appears here at NYC's Gracie Mansion in 1974 wearing a green satin dress with a brocade coat during an exposition of Israeli fashions

The former Miss America of 1945, once described as "the best-looking broad on the city scene," had aged well. She fulfilled the feminist dream of a single, successful, and independent career woman. As such, she captured the eye and heart of **Andy Capasso**. They appear here together on the cover of a destructive exposé in *People* Magazine. He had been born in the year Myerson strolled down the runway in Atlantic City in bathing suit and high heels.

Capasso, an ex-laborer by now involved in sewer contracting for New York City, had seven cars, five homes, a net worth of between $12 million and $15 million, and a wife, Nancy. **Myerson's** association with him, and accusations of influencing a court decision in his favor, eventually led to her downfall.

October 2017

Re-Evaluating the Celebrities of History

and Re-Naming U.S. Monuments Accordingly

It began with calls to remove a statue of Robert E. Lee, the leader of the Confederate armies, that stood in Charlottesville, Virginia. Since the violence there in August, the debate over monuments and public images has swept north to New York and across the country to California.

Columnist Ted Wrobeski wrote: "Trying to erase history is a slippery slope. Where does it end? As if taking down statues can rub hate out of people's heart."

It emerges that seemingly no historical figure is without a few skeletons buried in his closet, even men who are celebrated for their remarkable achievements.

Christopher Columbus is hailed as the Italian explorer who "discovered" the New World. But when he landed on the Caribbean island of Hispaniola (now shared by Haiti and the Dominican Republic), he captured and enslaved indigenous tribes.

Los Angeles has become the first large American city to cancel Columbus Day, enraging Italian Americans. New York has seen violent protests about the landmark statue of the explorer in Columbus Circle in Manhattan. Some African Americans want to take his statue down and replace it with one dedicated to Malcolm X.

A growing movement wants to remove the image of Andrew Jackson (president from 1829 to 1837) from the twenty-dollar bill. In 1830, he signed the Indian Removal Act, initiating a virulent campaign to eradicate Native Americans.

No figure seems safe, not even Thomas Jefferson, the principal author of the Declaration of Independence. In some quarters, he's denounced as a "slave-holding pedophile," because of his affair with a teenage mulatto, Sally Hemings.

George Washington, too, has come under fire because he owned slaves. One congressman even advocated the renaming of Washington, D.C.

Abraham Lincoln is almost universally honored as the president who freed the slaves. However, according to some scholars, he wanted to ship these freed people back to their native Africa, but was talked out of it.

General Ulysses S. Grant (1869-77), has also come under fire by issuing an order in 1862 to expel all Jews from three states whose territory he controlled.

There are those who want to rename the city and state of New York because its namesake, the Duke of York, was involved in the slave trade.

Woodrow Wilson (U.S. President from 1913 to 1921) was an avowed white supremacist. The former president was once the head of Princeton University, which has monuments and a build-

> Armed conflicts, and Civil Wars in particular, evoke some of the most painful collective memories in any nation's history.
>
> Such is the case for Americans, split as they sometimes are, in their evaluations of the legacies of "celebrity statesmen'—lightning rods of ingrained belief patterns.
>
> Here are photos of **Robert E. Lee** *(left)* and **Abraham Lincoln.** Opinions have varied widely as new points of view have thundered recently through the national consciousness: —Were they **Saints or Sinners?** The controversies have changed the landmarks of some American cities.

> The "controversy quotients" for **Christopher Columbus** *(left photo)* and **Andrew Jackson** *(right)* are even higher.

ing honoring him. Protests have demanded that his name be erased because he called black people and women voters "disgusting creatures."

His favorite film was D.W. Griffith's *The Birth of a Nation* (1915), which glorified the KKK.

For decades, there have been protests against Margaret Mitchell's book and the spinoff 1939 movie, *Gone With the Wind*. Already, Memphis has canceled its annual showing of the film about the Civil War on the grounds that it presented the slave-owning South in a nostalgic and even romantic light.

Is there no hero, male or female, who can pass the smell test? Some congressmen have suggested that a U.S. military base be named after Audie Murphy, the most decorated American soldier of World War II. But as an oft-cited symbol of a Great American Hero, he comes with baggage and more than a few real and symbolic problems.

He was born to a sharecropper in Texas, who soon deserted his family. Young Murphy had to drop out of school in the fifth grade and learn to shoot a rifle while hunting wild game in the forest to feed his impoverished family.

After Pearl Harbor, he tried to enlist, but was rejected by both the Navy and the Marines. The Army accepted him, and he became a virtual "Nazi Killing Machine," during the invasion of Sicily, and later, landing on the beaches of Anzio, fighting in the liberation of Rome, and for his role in the Allied invasion of southern France. For his astonishing record, he received every known award for valor the U.S. can bestow.

When he returned to America, Hollywood tapped him as a movie star, although he was never a very good actor. He appeared in 40 feature films from 1948 to 1969, none more notable that *Red Badge of Courage* (1951), based on Stephen Crane's Civil War novel.

Murphy also starred in *To Hell and Back* (1955), based on his own World War II memoirs But mostly, he was cast in rather lackluster westerns.

In 1949, he married his co-star, Wanda Hendrix, of Jacksonville, but the union lasted only a few months. On several occasions, he held her at gunpoint, threatening to blow off her head.

He suffered from post-traumatic stress disorder, and was abusive and violent. Sleeping with a loaded gun under his pillow, he sometimes woke up in the middle of the night, firing at imaginary enemies.

His last movie was the aptly named *A Time for Dying*, which had not been released at the time of his death on May 28, 1971. He was a passenger in a private plane which crashed into the Brush Mountains of Virginia.

He was buried with full military honors at Arlington National Cemetery, the ceremony attended by George H.W. Bush, who was the U.S. ambassador to the United Nations at the time.

Today, Murphy's grave site is the second most-visited at Arlington, the first being the tomb of John F. Kennedy.

One of the trickiest historical figures of the "re-evaluation game" is **Audie Murphy**, the lavishly decorated "killing machine" of World War II. Son of a (mostly absent) Texas sharecropper, Audie quit school in the fifth grade to pick cotton for $1 a day. and learned to shoot by killing rabbits and game for his otherwise impoverished mother and siblings.

The *left photo* shows him as the most-decorated enlisted man in U.S. military history. The *right photo* shows a movie poster for his mostly lackluster performances in a mediocre medley of mostly Westerns.

Tragically, Murphy's life was neither happy nor "normal" in the years that followed the celebrity foisted upon him as a wartime "death cyborg." Plagued with PTSD, nightmares, financial problems, and episodes of out-of-control violence, he died in an airplane accident in 1971.

REST IN PEACE AUDIE MURPHY (1925-1971).

April 2019

"Hollywood Godfather" Impersonator
GIANNI RUSSO
Writes a Tell-All Exposé

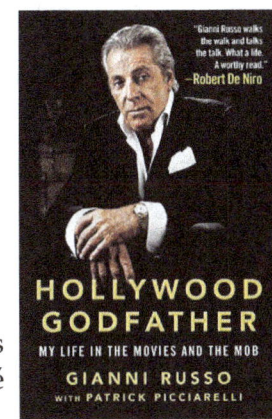

Gianni Russo, an actor and singer best known for his role as Carlo Rizzi in The Godfather (1972), has written a tell-all exposé called *Hollywood Godfather: My Life in the Movies and the Mob*.

In this over-the-top memoir, he spares no one, with tantalizing behind-the-scene stories that include Marilyn Monroe and JFK.

At the age of seven in Manhattan's "Little Italy," Russo contracted polio and spent the next five years in a state ward. After his release, he sold pencils in front of the Waldorf-Astoria.

Left photo: The front cover of a bio written by **Gianni Russo,** mob-member-turned-actor-turned-author. It relays his convoluted but colorful meanderings from street urchin to co-star in a series of mob-related castings that paired him, at his most visible, with **Marlon Brando** (right photo). That 1972 blockbuster went on to launch a series and several franchises.

Hollywood wits have described Russo's movie career as one of the most blatant examples of an actor willfully being type-cast in the history of Hollywood.

There, he met mob boss Frank Costello, known as "The Prime Minister of the Underworld."

"Mr. Costello always gave me a fiver," Russo said.

The gangster admired the boy's spunk, and, as he grew older, hired him to deliver packets of cash for pay-offs in New Orleans, Las Vegas, and Los Angeles. That led to Russo's introduction to some of America's most notorious gangsters and a coven of stars, even political figures.

A handsome man, with startling white teeth and a perma-tan, he appeared in Brioni suits. For a decade, he had an affair with Dionne Warwick and flings with such stars as Zsa Zsa Gabor and Liza Minnelli. With Judy's daughter, he indulged in a "three-way" with a beautiful Las Vegas showgirl.

His special goddess was Marilyn Monroe, whom he met when he was only sixteen, and she was thirty-three. "She was the best lover," he claimed. "She wanted to please you." His on-and-off affair with her continued for the next four years.

Russo was assigned to look after Senator John F. Kennedy during one of his trips to Las Vegas. JFK was the guest of Jack Entratter. Known as "Mr. Entertainment," he ran the iconic Sands Hotel with its Copacabana night club, where Frank Sinatra often was the star attraction.

On the grounds was a luxurious villa where JFK stayed.

Juliet Prowse, a singer and dancer from South Africa, would in time be known for her affairs with both Sinatra and Elvis Presley.

A liaison was arranged between her and JFK. "The Senator wore a thirty-pound metal back brace, and at one point I saw him doing a line of coke off Prowse's stomach," Russo said. "The Senator told me it eased his back pain."

In August of 1962, Russo was a guest of the CalNeva Lodge and Casino on the border of California and Nevada, opening onto Lake Tahoe. Sinatra became one of the owners, and mob boss Sam Giancana was a silent partner.

Two views of **Gianni Russo's** portrayal of Carlo Rizzi, a deadbeat groom to a Mafia Princess (*portrayed by* **Talia Shire**) in the original (1972) version of *The Godfather*. As a transgressive ne'er-do-well and wife-beater, yes, he gets whacked.

Right before her death, Marilyn spent her last weekend there. Giancana had learned that both brothers, JFK and RFK, were flying in for a secret weekend, ostensibly for a "three-way" with Marilyn.

Giancana had arranged for hidden cameras to be installed in the suite to capture the action. With the porno film, he was hoping to blackmail RFK who, as attorney general, was pursuing the mob.

Something came up, and the brothers had to cancel.

Stylish Dalliances: Russo purports sexual intimacies with the South Africa-born dancer, **Juliet Prowse** (left photo) and with (right photo), everyone's favorite Hungarian, **Zsa Zsa Gabor**, the *Bombshell from Budapest.*

Adding to Russo's "credibility quotient" as a bona-fide mobster, he cites early mentoring from **Frank Costello** (left photo) Don of the Genovese crime family, depicted here testifying before the Kefauver Committee in the early 1950s.

He also cites a close association with **Jack Entratter,** (aka **"Mr. Entertainment')** Manager/Promoter of The Sands in Las Vegas virtually from its debut. He's seen here in a photo-op with an over-medicated Marilyn Monroe.

Left photo: In 2020, **Istituto per le Opere di Religione** (aka **The Vatican Bank)** had about a hundred employees, 15,000 clients, and cared for 5 billion Euros of client assets, of which 3.3 billion Euros were assets managed for 3rd parties or under custody.

Right photo: Polish-born **John-Paul II,** in 1978, became the first non-Italian Pope in 400 years. Formerly the Archbishop of Krakow, he played a decisive role in influencing world opinion against the Soviet Union during its breakup. Nine years after his death in 2005, he was canonized as a saint.

Coming unhinged, Marilyn threatened to call a press conference, exposing both the Kennedy brothers and Sam Giancana. She died unexpectedly on August 5, 1962. Murder or suicide? The debate continues…

Russo held RFK responsible for arranging her murder, but more reliable sources claimed that Giancana arranged her death for her having threatened to expose him.

In 1971, Russo mediated a dispute between the producers of *The Godfather* (1972) and mob boss Joe Colombo, who was threatening to shut down production, claiming that the film slandered Italian-Americans.

As a reward, he was cast in the movie as Carlo Rizzi, who marries Don Corleone's daughter.

Russo is a back-stabbing wife-beating thug, and is beaten up by Corleone's son, Sonny, as portrayed by James Caan. Russo ends up with a piano wire for a necklace, coming to a grisly end.

"The star of the movie, Marlon Brando, didn't want me in the picture. I got in his face and threatened him."

Russo said, "I'll cut your f---ing heart out, you mother-f---er. I'm part of this picture, whether you like it or not, c----sucker!"

"I won Brando over by fixing him up with a girl who, on a scale of one to ten, was a twelve," Russo said.

From such an unlikely beginning, he and Brando became friends.

His role in The Godfather led to Russo appearing in some 46 more movies. They included *Goodnight My Love* (1972); *Laserblast* (1978); *Chances Are* (1989); *The Freshman* (1990); *Super Mario Bros.* (1993); *Any Given Sunday* (1999); and *Seabiscuit* (2003).

"Perhaps my most exciting job was delivering bundles of cash to the bank of Vatican City," Russo said. "I met Pope John Paul II."

Russo owned a Las Vegas restaurant that was popular with Sinatra and the mob. Over the course of his life, he successfully defeated 23 Federal criminal indictments on charges stemming from his alleged organized crime associations.

In 1968, he killed a member of the Medellin drug cartel, who was harassing a female patron. The drug dealer lunged toward him with a broken wine bottle, and Russo fatally shot him. The case was ruled a justifiable homicide.

Today, Russo still likes to belt out a Sinatra song, especially with the words "I did it my way."

He says, "I've known five U.S. Presidents, every Mafia boss like John Gotti, and three Popes. I'm like a cockroach. You can't kill me."

The "Wild Women" Spawned by JOSEPH STALIN.

They Preferred Life in the USA

The Russian dictator, Josef Stalin, must be spinning in his grave. One of history's most notorious mass murderers, his iron grip over the Soviet Union lasted from 1929 to 1953.

His only daughter, Svetlana, defected to the United States, and her only surviving child has been recently exposed in the media for her spectacularly bizarre life in Oregon.

How could this have happened?

Svetlana Alliluyeva, born in 1926, was the youngest child of "Uncle Joe," as the Western media called him during World War II, and his second wife, Nadezhda Alliluyeva. As a girl, Svetlana was said to be the only person who could melt her father's cold-blooded, murderous heart. She lived like a princess in the Kremlin, and he often carried her around in his arms, as she dutifully kissed him, as noted by Sir Winston Churchill on a visit.

His daughter revealed many personal details about Stalin, who stood only five feet, six inches. Harry S Truman called him "The Little Squirt." He liked having his portraits painted, but if an artist made him look diminutive, he had him executed.

He had deep pock marks on his face from smallpox as a child, and his left hand and arm were withered.

He was fond of Western cowboy movies and Charlie Chaplin comedies. Based on his fear of flying, he opted to travel by train to Yalta for the 1945 meeting with Roosevelt and Churchill.

In addition to Svetlana, Stalin had two sons, the first of whom was born to his first wife, Ekaterina Svanidze, the second, Vasiliy, to his second wife. Although a distinguished airman in World War II, Visiliy died from alcoholism in 1962.

Yakov's life was more tragic. His father treated him so brutally, he attempted suicide with a pistol, but survived. "You can't even shoot straight," his father said when he recovered. As a soldier in the Red Army, he was captured by the Nazis. Stalin refused to make a deal for his return. Later, he committed suicide by running into an electrified fence at Sachsenhausen concentration camp.

Growing up, Svetlana viewed her father as a hero, crediting him, along with Churchill and Roosevelt, for defeating the Nazis and winning the war. Then one night, her mother told her about all the atrocities her father had committed, and she never felt the same about him again. She spent the rest of her life trying to escape his legacy and chalking up what her enemies (and even her friends) described politely as a series of "dysfunctions."

"I felt like I had been born on the same level as a daughter of Hitler."

Although Stalin loved his daughter, he rarely approved of her choice of lovers and endorsed only one of her husbands. At 16, she fell in love with Aleksei Kapler, a Jewish Soviet filmmaker who was 40. He was shipped off to Vorkuta near the Arctic Circle.

Svetlana with her father, Soviet dictator **Josef Stalin**, in the late 1930s.

Baby Svetlana with her mother, **Nadezhda Alliluyeva,** the second wife of Josef Stalin.

After an argument with her husband in November of 1932, she fatally shot herself.

The following year, she married Grigory Morozov, a fellow student at Moscow University, but Stalin refused to meet him. A son, Iosif, was born in 1945, but the couple divorced in 1947. For a few months in 1949, she was married to Yuri Zhdanov, the son of Stalin's right-hand man, Andrei Zhdanov, and they had a daughter, Yekaterina.

In 1967, Svetlana stunned the world when she entered the U.S. Embassy in New Delhi and asked for political asylum. Eventually, it was granted, and she lived on Long Island for some time, guarded by the Secret Service because of death threats from the KGB. She left her son and daughter behind in the Soviet Union.

During a visit to Arizona, although she was reported to be destitute, she had made $2.5 million for her autobiographical memoir, *Twenty Letters to a Friend*. There, she met and married William Wesley Peters, an architect and acolyte of Frank Lloyd Wright. A daughter, Olga, was born in 1971, but the couple divorced two years later.

In 1978, she became a U.S. citizen. [Olga was already a citizen, having been born in the United States.] The mother and daughter moved to Cambridge (UK) in 1982, and two years later, she returned to Russia, denouncing the Western democracies. She settled in Tblisi, Georgia, the homeland of her father and one of the few regions in the former Soviet Union where his memory is, in some quarters, still celebrated. But she eventually feuded with Stalin's relatives and, in 1986, returned to the United States.

Svetlana's dysfunctionality became increasingly obvious as the years passed. She then moved back to England, where she became a British citizen, but then returned to the United States in 2009, where she was issued a permanent visa. She remained in the U.S. until her death in 2011 from colon cancer.

Olga seemed to disappear from the radar screen. But she was discovered living in Oregon, age 44, under the name of "Chrese Evans." A Buddhist, she runs an antique store there.

Her dress is often exotic enough to make Lady Gaga blush. She paraded through the tabloids recently outfitted like "Tank Girl," a 1980s punk-inspired British comic strip character. Her hair was bleached blonde and close-cropped, and she wore a tank top exposing her midriff and a pistol tucked into her hot pants. She had a cigarette dangling from her overly painted red lips and wore excessive eye shadow and mascara. Her black hosiery was torn, and over her shoulder, she'd slung a gun belt with a rifle in her left hand. Her mother had called her "As American as apple pie," but no one in his or her right mind would ever realistically have arrived at that conclusion. One of her many lurid tattoos read, "Mamma's Girl."

In brief, she was very, very far removed from any fantasy her infamous grandfather, Josef Stalin, would have even been able to conceptualize.

As for her emotionally troubled mother, Olga said, "Svetlana and I were very close. A super duo."

In college, she had studied tax law and accounting. She had eventually been offered a job at the IRS investigating tax cheats, but she turned it down, preferring to go into business for herself.

She did not provide any details of her personal life, except to say, "I like to make Borscht from scratch."

"I don't forgive my grandfather for anything," she said. "He was a murderous tyrant."

She did share her favorite Russian New Year's wish: "May you never forget what is worth remembering, nor remember what is best forgotten."

Left photo: **Svetlana** with her daughter (Josef Stalin's granddaughter), **Olga Evans**, in 1979.

Right photo: **Olga** (renamed **Chrese**) **Evans** in 2016.

Editor's Note: This background article on Zelenskyy appeared in Boomer Times in February of 2023. As we go to press, the future of Ukraine remains uncertain

VOLODYMYR ZELENSKYY

A Brave Jewish Man Takes on the Russian Empire

Actor, comedian, and TV producer turned statesman: **Volodymyr Zelenskyy.**

His thwarted, very dangerous, and megalomaniacal enemy, Russian dictator and genocidist **Vladimir Putin.**

Those mass murderers, Adolf Hitler and Josef Stalin, could never have imagined that a heroic Jewish man, Volodymyr Zelenskyy, now the President of Ukraine, would have rallied his meager and under-equipped Army, in 2022, to take on the forces of Russia after it invaded. But such was the case months after Zelenskyy became president.

Before assuming office and becoming a war hero, he had been a comedian and actor on TV and in films. From 2015 until his election as president in 2019, he had starred in a TV series whose name translates as Servant of the People. In it, he played the President of Ukraine. At the end of the series' filming, he decided to become the real President, running for that office and winning 75% of the popular vote.

He was born in 1978 to Jewish parents, and his first language was Russian. Of course,, he soon learned Ukrainian and later, English.

As a young boy, he became familiar with the tormented history of his country, the poorest in Europe. During World War II, six million of his people had died, 1.5 million of them Jews. Four of his ancestors died in the Holocaust, and his great-grandparents were murdered by Nazi soldiers who also burned down their home.

Throughout most of his life, he advocated peace with Russia. He formed a comedy troupe, Kvartal 95, and toured Russia, playing in local theaters. Even when Putin annexed Crimea in February of 2014, Zelenskyy announced that he would not retaliate. But Putin didn't stop there, masking his involvement in a proxy war that virtually devastated the Donbas region in the southeastern corner of Ukraine, on the border of Russia.

Paris 2019, brinksmanship at one of te most high-profile assemblages of European power of the 21st Century: *Left to right:* **Volodymyr Zelenskyy, Angela Merkel** of Germany, **Emmanuel Macron** of France, and **Vladimir Putin.**

Constructive, happy, and supportive vibes with good personal chemistry: **Zelenskyy** with then-U.S. President **Joe Biden.**

It soon became obvious that Putin coveted all of the Ukraine, not just the Donbas region. His sycophantic advisors assured him that that Ukraine would surrender after a focused three-day attack by Russia's (corrosively corrupted but still very dangerous) invading forces.

To the horror of NATO, some of whose members bordered Ukraine, during the pre-dawn hours of February 24, 2022, the Russian Army attacked and invaded Ukraine.

Zelenskyy vowed to fight back, pleading with the Western democracies, especially the United States, to send aid and equipment. NATO countries responded, too, sending weapons and experts to train the Ukrainians in how to use them.

A snag (later evolving into a major political scandal) came in July of 2019, when then- President Donald Trump threated to hold back $250 million in (Congressionally approved) aid unless Zelenskyy provided incriminating evidence of Hunter Biden's business dealings in the Ukraine. The international press, for the most part "horrified," defined Trump's interference as a "shake-down." Some of them accused Trump of collusion with the Russians.

The matter was eventually resolved, with huge embarrassment to Trump (who was impeached for his interference) and his entourage. Today, thanks to the Biden administration, the United States is now the major supplier of money, medical aid, and military equipment to the beleaguered Ukraine. [As of now, many Republicans want to radically cut back the flow of funds.]

Time magazine has defined Zelenskyy—now hailed as the world's leading Freedom Fighter—as its Man of the Year. In vivid contrast, the latest Gallup polls cite Putin as the most hated world leader on the planet.

If there's any comfort at all within Zelenskyy's life, it's the precious time he spends with his devoted wife, Olena Kiyashko, whom he married in 2003 during the peak of his TV and media years, and his loving son and daughter.

Destructive, unhappy, chaotic, and confusing, with horrible strategic and military outcomes: **Zelenskyy** in the Oval Office with an sarcastic, hectoring, and unsupportive **Donald Trump.**

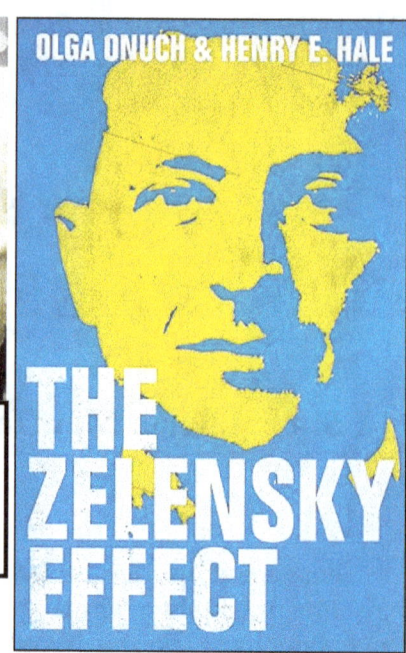

Historians assert that it's difficult to understand the turmoil of 2022 in Eastern Europe without understanding **Volodymr Zelenskyy.**

The authors of this newly "in vogue' biography assert that what makes Zelenskyy extraordinary in war is his very ordinariness as a Ukrainian—and his fervent commitment to the integrity of his nation.

Historians compare **Zelenskyy's** effectiveness in wartime, and his ability to boost the morale of his people, to that of Winston Churchill during the darkest years of World War II. Here's Zelenskyy in the immediate aftermath of a Russian bombardment, the symbol of Ukrainian resistance.

Staunch spokesperson for the Ukrainian cause: Zelenskyy's wife, **Olena Kiyashko,** as she appeared on the cover of the July 2022 edition of *Vogue*.

JFK's "First Friend"

KIRK LEMOYNE BILLINGS

Two views of **Lem Billings** in 1962, a resident of, and posing on, the north lawn of the White House. During JFK's occupancy of the White House, Lem came and went as he wanted to, as he had his own bedroom. On most nights, he slept next to Jack, tending his every need, as he was often in a back brace. The Secret Service referred to Lem as "First Friend." Behind his back, some members called Lem "JFK's second wife."

It is said that Pennsylvania-born Kirk LeMoyne Billings—affectionately called "Lem"—fell in love with John F. Kennedy ("Jack") as they showered together at the Choate School for Boys in 1933. The bond formed during their first week in school would last a lifetime.

To the other boys at the prep school, they became "Jack & Lem." The friendship lasted until the gunfire at Dallas—and beyond—until Lem died on May 28, 1981. Jackie told friends that Lem had died of a "broken heart—he never got over losing Jack that awful day."

Jack (left) with **Lem** in Palm Beach, buttressed by the approval of friends and family

That the friendship even lasted beyond the first week at prep school was amazing in itself. Lem confessed to Jack that he was a homosexual and wanted their friendship to be sexual. To Lem's ever-lasting regret, Jack had to tell him that he was "hopelessly heterosexual."

What private compromise the two young men reached may never be known. At first Jack didn't believe Lem was really gay, thinking instead that he might be experiencing a harmless infatuation. How wrong he was. At one point Jack decided that both he and Lem were going to lose their virginity at the same time and to the same woman. Taking a train to New York, the teenagers headed for a whorehouse in Harlem filled with black hookers. Jack went upstairs first, returning thirty minutes later to tell Lem "the dirty deed is done—you're on, boy."

Lem was gone for only 15 minutes, during which time he sat in a chair after giving the prostitute $20 to keep quiet.

On a summer vacation in 1937, **Jack Kennedy** (left) toured Europe with his "best friend for life," **Lem Billings**, a homosexual in love with Jack. Jack told him, "I'm hopelessly straight. If you can stay with me and love me through all my affairs, then welcome aboard."

"I'm willing to put up with anything to be beside you," Lem claimed.

As a consequence of his first exposure to sex, Jack came down with a bad case of gonorrhea, whereas Lem remained in the best of health, infuriating Jack.

Lem was handsome, athletic, and popular, Jack the skinny kid in ill health. But each boy filled some fundamental need in the other. Biographer David Pitts summed up the relationship like this: "When Jack met Lem, he found someone who idolized him, who was always there when he needed him, and who cared about him in a profound way. Lem offered unconditional love and boosted Jack's confidence and self-esteem at a time when it counted."

Lem Billings (left) with **"baby RFK"** and **teenaged JFK** in Palm Beach.

Jack invited Lem to Hyannis to meet the family in the summer of 1934. They shared the same room, but Jack had trouble adjusting to Lem's snoring. By 1937 they were touring Europe together sharing small beds in cheap boarding houses, although Jack himself could have afforded the best.

It was during that European sojourn that Lem decided to devote the rest of his life to Jack, forsaking any other romance he might have had. Lem would be there through the vagaries of one of the most famous lives of the 20th century—the hospitals, the disappointments, the triumphs, and, yes, the endless parade of women. Teddy Kennedy called it "a bond of perfect trust and understanding that served them all their lives."

As painful as it must have been for Lem, he arranged liaisons with the Hollywood actresses that Jack, like his father before him, craved. Frank Sinatra and Peter Lawford arranged details of the affair with Marilyn Monroe, but Lem was there setting up assignations with Joan Crawford, Susan Hayward, Audrey Hepburn, Jayne Mansfield, Lee Remick, and countless others. With no help from Lem, Marlene Dietrich managed to seduce the teenage Jack, as she had his father before him. Jack bragged about it so much that Lem eventually told him to "zip it up."

At Jack's wedding to Jacqueline Bouvier, Bobby Kennedy told friends, "Jack is taking on another wife." From their home in Georgetown to the White House, Jackie had to cope with Lem. She complained to Senator George Smathers of Florida: "Just one weekend, I'd like to have my husband to myself." But in time she learned to appreciate Lem and admire his devotion to Jack. At times Jack was in such pain that Lem had to bathe and massage him, even put on his shoes and socks. Author Gore Vidal referred to Lem as "Jack's slave for life."

When not fretting about Lem, Jackie also complained to Smathers that she had to cope with her husband's constant womanizing."

"No one was off limits to Jack," Smathers said. "Your wife, your sister, even your mother."

Jackie often had to compete with Lem for Jack's attention. "Lem would throw a tizzy fit if he felt Jack was ignoring him," Smathers said. "Lem was assigned a permanent bedroom at the White House, and he would barge into the Oval Office and demand Jack's attention even if Khrushchev were on the hot line threatening to rain nuclear bombs down upon the east coast of America."

Here, at Hyannis Port in 1955, the affection shared by **Lem Billings** (left) and **JFK** had continued to flourish.

Jacqueline told her sister, Lee Radziwill, "I realized that mariage to Jack meant having to accept Lem, who was like a hungry puppy hanging around for a crumb tossed from his master."

For their summer vacation in 1937, **JFK** (left) toured through Europe with **Lem**, sharing a bed at night. Jack confessed that he was hopelessly heterosexual, but Lem was always welcomed to enjoy him below the belt. "Well, come aboard if you can accept those terms." Lem told him, "I'm in for the duration, and I'm willing to put up with anything to keep you in my life."

"In **Lem Billings** (right), Jack had a devoted slave for life. Lem would make any sacrifice for Jack. He worshipped him He even bathed him and put on his underwear. Jackie slept in a separate room."

"If this isn't love, what would you call it?" **Gore Vidal** asked when he saw this candid shot of **JFK** (top) and **Lem** at play.

December 2013

CAROLINE KENNEDY

CASHING IN ON CAMELOT
(AKA "CAROLINE'S CAM-A-SCHLOCK"

Here's a triple take of **Caroline Kennedy Schlossberg,** based on her reprimand (and plea for silence) of the press corps before her wedding walk down the aisle with Ed Schlossberg in 1986.

As other guardians of Jackie-O's legacy have died off, (including John F. Kennedy Jr.) **Caroline**—to an increasing degree—has grown more deeply entrenched...and reaped stupendous profits from that legacy's not-always-particularly tasteful disposal.

Once again, Caroline Kennedy is frontpage tabloid fodder around the world in the wake of the 50th anniversary of her father's assassination in Dallas (November, 1963), and in that same month (2013), her appointment as America's first female ambassador to Japan.

Newsreel footage of young Caroline at her father's funeral and growing up in the White House has generated some 150 film and TV events.

Her regal and triumphant arrival in a horse-drawn carriage at the Imperial Palace in Tokyo to present her credentials to Emperor Akhito were flashed around the world. Thousands of Japanese hailed her as the "Princess of Camelot."

In contrast, details of her private life have generated unwanted publicity for her. Reportedly, her husband, Ed Schlossberg, 68, opposed her going to Tokyo. Her 27-year-old marriage is constantly reported as "doomed," whether it is or not.

Her children, Jack and Tatiana Schlossberg, appear to be ideal kids. Talking heads on TV claim that the handsome, intelligent, and charming Jack may take up the Kennedy banner and run for president one day. Jackie had wanted that for her own son, John F. Kennedy, Jr., but he died in that 1999 plane crash, going down into the sea with his wife and her sister.

Jackie never saw a political future for her daughter, worrying instead about her marriage prospects. She constantly harangued Caroline for putting on too much weight. Once in a Paris restaurant, she got into a fight with Caroline. Jackie was overheard lecturing her, "You're much too fat. No dessert. No man will ever want to marry you."

Jackie became almost obsessive about keeping her daughter's weight down. In the early 1970s, police found marijuana growing in Jackie's backyard in Hyannis Port, and Caroline was blamed. Jackie handled that calmly, but in contrast, she became enraged when she found two pounds of Mr. Chow's barbecued ribs charged to Caroline. She canceled her credit card. As a local reporter noted, "Jackie doesn't mind the grass

Noblesse Oblige: Here's **"Princess Caroline,"** as snapped by a photographer in the early 60s. The most-adulated female child of her era, she steals the show as she leaves, in her wake, her father—then the most powerful man in the world—holding her doll.

(Right photo). In this 1990 press photo, a bored, zaftig and *blasé* **Caroline** *(right)* waits with her **Uncle Ted** and her famous mother, **Jacqueline,** for the unveiling of a statue in her late father's honor.

Today, Caroline exerts rigorous control over the legal and editorial issues associated with her parent's legacies...and a growing reputation for profiting from it.

as much as Caroline's grazing," referring, of course, to both the marijuana and her daughter's consumption of fattening foods.

Of course, Caroline today, with $400 million in the bank, would have no trouble finding an eligible bachelor regardless of how many pounds she gains. Jackie's former stepdaughter, Christina Onassis, the *zaftig* (and frequently depressed) heiress to her father's shipping fortune, had no trouble attracting lovers or husbands, everyone from Warren Beatty to JFK Jr. himself.

Unlike her parents, whose love affairs have generated international headlines, Caroline has remained free of sexual scandals. What has generated bad media coverage for Caroline involves her selling off the artifacts of Camelot. Blaring headlines have labeled her as "GREEDY CAROLINE, CAROLINE THE HUCKSTER!, and MISTRESS OF CAME-SCHLOCK!"

Shortly before her installation in Japan, Caroline garnered $45 million by selling some land adjacent to her mother's former vacation retreat on Martha's Vineyard.

Her sale of Camelot's artifacts began right after her mother's death in 1994, when she orchestrated America's most infamous "yard sale," defying the objections of her brother. It became the most profitable yard sale in American history, netting Caroline some $35 million. Among other items, she sold a $150 foot stool for $35,000; a $900 lamp for $49,000, and a hat box (without the hat) for a windfall $32,000. Two of her father's former rocking chairs went for nearly a million dollars each.

Parallel to the dramas unspinning within the Jackie-O contingent were the high-camp tragedies permeating the OTHER side of the Jackie-Ari wars.

Here's Caroline Kennedy's embittered counterpart, **Christina Onassis**, daughter of the Greek billionaire **Aristotle Onassis** *(right)* in the years before he married Caroline's "impossibly famous" and expensive-to-maintain mother.

Deeply depressed, Christina, who died at the age of 37 in Buenos Aires of a heart attack in 1988, had a LOT to say about Jackie-O and her "crude, self-involved, self-righteous, manipulative, and avaricious" daughter.

Even the doors to Jackie's dressing room in the White House, which had been removed, complete with their hinges, and hauled away with her when Jackie moved out, were sold to an unknown bidder (price not revealed).

Her most outrageous yard sale occurred in 2005 when she offered worthless household items, including unused toilet paper from Jackie's Manhattan apartment and seven empty pickle jars (three of them chipped). Old magazines were hawked, along with wicker baskets, a rubber doorstop, and even a $5 sugar bowl that netted an outrageous $7,500.

The callousness of the sale incensed Caroline's aunt, Eunice Kennedy Shriver, who appeared and purchased many of the items as a means of protecting Jackie's privacy. "She would have been outraged by this sale," Eunice claimed.

Caroline has also been attacked for making approximately $5 million through her "shameless" publishing ventures, which have been the work of other authors. For example, her name was on the book jacket, but inside was a collection of thirteen essays by other writers. In another book, she cashed in by publishing a collection of poems by other poets, asserting that these poems were "mother's favorites."

In 2012, as part of the most controversial of her marketing schemes, Caroline released the tapes her mother made in 1964, just months after her husband's assassination. Jackie's instructions were to keep the tapes in a vault at the JFK Library for fifty years after her own death. Caroline waited just 17 years.

In Tokyo, as U.S. ambassador, Caroline has been hailed as a unifying element of America's reconciliation with Japan. Ironically, JFK became a war hero when a Japanese destroyer sank his PT-109 boat and he rescued his men.

In her first public announcement since taking the post, Caroline stood tough, siding with Japan in its dispute with China over a rocky archipelago positioned between the two countries. She endorsed the United States' symbolic maneuver of flying two U.S. B-52 bombers over the contested zone, challenging China's claim that it was their airspace.

That move earned Caroline millions of Japanese fans. A poll in a Tokyo newspaper named her "most admired American woman."

Every one of Caroline's appearances there is treated like a royal event. Or, as an aging newspaper editor recalled, "I haven't seen such adulation since Marilyn Monroe, the former mistress of President Kennedy, arrived on our shores."

ALL IN THE FAMILY

JACKIE-O'S "Post JFK" Love Affair with

HIS BROTHER, BOBBY

In part because of their fame and their shared "consumer demand" for women—lots of them—everyone always compared (dressed and undressed) the "Kennedy Brothers Three."

Above, left to right: **JFK, RFK,** and **Teddy.**

A long dormant affair between two of America's most admired people—only whispered about in the heyday of its passion—is now facing massive exposure. More details are being revealed about the love affair of Robert Kennedy, then Attorney General, and his recently widowed sister-in-law, Jackie Bouvier Kennedy.

A hot film script entitled *Triangle* is being shopped around in Hollywood. It's based on Robert's love affair with Jackie and also on his sexual involvement with Marilyn Monroe (his brother's former mistress).

Not only that, but C. David Heymann, one of America's best-known celebrity biographers, who has spent years chronicling the private lives of the Kennedys, is writing a book about the RFK/JBK affair. Renowned historian Burton Hersh is gaining nationwide publicity with the release of his new book, *Bobby and J. Edgar.* Basing his account on recently released FBI files, Hersh documents how the former FBI chief, Hoover, relentlessly spied on the private life of RFK, his avowed enemy.

Bobby was always bedazzled by Jackie, claimed Coates Redman, a close friend of Ethel Kennedy, the mother of RFK's eight children. Perhaps it was inevitable that Jackie and Robert came together. After all, they were the two people who most loved the assassinated President.

In the wake of his brother's death, Robert began spending nearly every evening at Jackie's Georgetown house at 3017 N. Street, which had become Washington's number one tourist attraction. Apparently, they spent hours talking in front of her fireplace. Eventually, Robert started spending the entire night with Jackie, leaving Ethel alone with the children.

As a family, the Kennedy's were large, larger-than-life, and boisterous.

After JFK's assassination, his brothers stepped to the forefront to comfort and protect the shattered nerves of Jacqueline. In the *upper photo*, they present a united front after the assassination, honoring the memory of the dead president.

As the formal mourning ended, **RFK** and **Jacqueline,** depicted together in the *lower photo* facing news cameras—remained spiritually and according to many, romantically bonded.

Jackie's close friend, Nancy Dickerson, said, "After Dallas, no one would have believed that Saint Jackie and Saint Bobby were sleeping together, even though they made it obvious. It would have been considered sacrilege. But Jackie and Bobby were definitely having an affair."

Nancy overstated the case that no one would believe it. At the time, Jackie and Robert were two of the most carefully watched people in earth. Dozens of people learned of their affair, but the press did not report on it. In those days, the press wasn't even writing about the numerous affairs of JFK, including his involvement with the late Marilyn Monroe.

Peter Lawford, Robert's brother-in-law, was one of the first to break the news. He told his wife, Patricia Kennedy Lawford, that "With Jackie, Bobby is now filling in for Jack in all departments."

Jackie and Robert began to show up everywhere together. When Jackie flew to New York, the hotel staff at the Carlyle reported that he shared Jackie's suite. She even went with him when he called on Herbert Hoover in his suite at the Waldorf Towers. It was so obvious to the ex-president that they were in love that he wisely cautioned them that the nation would be shocked to learn of such a liaison.

On the Caribbean island of Antigua, at Bunny Mellon's hilltop villa, a maid serving breakfast reported coming upon Jackie and Robert in bed together in the nude.

"Jackie relied on Bobby for everything, and he adored her," said his close friend Chuck Spalding. He was aware that the Kennedy brothers often passed women on to each other. Bobby had "taken over" the affair with Marilyn after the President had broken off the relationship. Even their father, Joseph Kennedy, passed on women to his sons—or vice versa. Marlene Dietrich was an example of such "an exchange."

Author Truman Capote, a confidant of Jackie's said, "She and Bobby carried on like teenagers even in public. I used to sit with them at Le Club in New York. They were holding hands, kissing, and dancing as close as two leaves stuck together in a storm They were lovebirds in every respect. Bobby was crazy about Jackie. Jackie confided to me that Bobby was thinking of ditching Ethel and marrying her."

Not just Capote, but more and more people kept coming upon Jackie and Bobby "sightings." Bruck Balding, an investment counselor on Long Island, found his two famous guests locked in a passionate embrace when he entered his stables one morning.

On a Pepsi corporate jet, with a host of celebrities, Jackie and Bobby flew to Keene, New Hampshire, for a week of skiing. Ethel was not invited. "Bobby hovered over Jackie," Sammy Davis, Jr. claimed. "It was like he owned her. I had a drink with them in their suite late one night. Jackie was dressed in a beautiful silk robe, but Bobby was walking around in his underwear."

It was a complicated time, with a lot of fast-moving parts: Two views of **RFK and Jackie, post-JFK.** Tongues wagged. To them, it didn't seem to matter.

The affair continued even after Jackie moved to New York into a luxurious apartment on Fifth Avenue. RFK's driver, "Jim," reported that he often dropped his boss off at the apartment around ten o'clock every evening, picking him up the following morning.

The lovers flew to Palm Beach and the Kennedy compound for a holiday. Socialite Mary Harrington reported that from her third-floor window she could look out onto the Kennedy property. "One morning, I saw Jackie sunbathing on the grass," she said. "She had on a black bikini bottom, but no top. Bobby emerged from the house in white swim trunks and knelt down beside her. He kissed her passionately and fondled her breast with one hand. With the other, he felt between her legs outside her bikini. Later, with a towel thrown around her bare breasts, Jackie disappeared inside the house with Bobby."

Author Gore Vidal, who was distantly related to Jackie, saw the affair in a rather cynical light. "I suspect that the one person Jackie ever loved, if indeed she was capable of such an emotion, was Bobby Kennedy. As Lee [*a reference to her sister, Lee Radziwill*] had gone to bed with Jack, symmetry required her to do so with Bobby."

It was Jackie who broke off the sexual involvement, although their close friendship would continue until Robert's death. He proposed marriage to her, promising he'd divorce Ethel and give her custody of the children. Knowing how much Robert wanted to be president, Jackie turned down his offer as an attempt to protect his political future, urging him to return to Ethel and his children.

Peter Lawford claimed that Robert came to him after the rejection. "He took it really bad. He cried all night and into the next day. I didn't know he was capable of such tears, because he could be pretty stoic."

The actor did not condemn the affair, and later said, "After Jack died, Jackie threatened suicide on more than one occasion, although she couldn't stand the thought of leaving her children alone in the world. But she came close to killing herself. Her love affair with Bobby may have saved her life."

For Jackie, lightning struck twice and tragically. At 3:45am on June 6, 1968, she received an urgent call from London, from her sister, Lee Radziwill, She'd been up all night watching the results of the California primary, which Robert had won in his quest for the presidency.

"Jackie," she said. "Bobby's been shot. It just happened."

There was a long silence on the phone, and then a blood-curdling scream. "No, it can't have happened!" Jackie shouted into her receiver. "The only two men I've ever loved. Shot!" Then she slammed down the phone.

JFK JR.
People Magazine's Sexiest Man Alive

The 20th Anniversary of the death of the charismatic John F. Kennedy, Jr. did not pass without notice. A new book is out, a film is in pre-production, and many papers ran commemorative stories, some of them *exposés*. Old conspiracies were brought back, suggesting that his ill-fated plane might have been tampered with by enemies of the Kennedy clan.

My publisher, Danforth Prince, and I are currently at work on a script for a podcast for American Media, Inc. on the charmed but tragic life of the handsome young man. America fell in love with him when, at the age of three, he gave that final salute to the horse-drawn casket of his assassinated father in 1963.

The aim of the podcast, as it was for Marilyn Monroe, is to introduce iconic figures of the 20th Century to a new generation. Polls have shown that JFK Jr. is not recognized by many young people today.

Four Friends, a new book by William D. Cohan, devotes its pages to four classmates at Andover, each a reckless youth taking death-defying chances with their young lives, all of them ending up dead—not just JFK Jr., but also William Daniel, the grandson of Harry Truman.

Although one of the most publicized figures on the planet, much of JFK Jr.'s private life played out in secret. Such was the case with his affair with Christina Onassis. She was eighteen, and he was only eight when they met at the wedding of her father, Aristotle Onassis, and his mother, Jacqueline Kennedy, in Greece.

Looks, charm, charisma, pizzazz...and a family legacy that's priceless. Here's **JFK Jr.** with his mother, **Jackie-O**, ready for prime time and camera ready.

After living through the turmoil of that ill-fated union, Christine and JFK Jr. met again at Studio 54 in Manhattan one sultry summer night in 1982 when she spotted him dancing there with Andy Warhol (of all people).

He dumped the artist to take up with the heiress, retiring to her suite later that night, where he spent the next few days. Back in Greece, she told friends, "He's all grown up now, a hunk and a half."

In London, Princess Diana had long expressed an interest in meeting "America's Prince," as she phrased it, as she seemed no longer charmed by England's Prince Charles.

She set up a liaison with JFK Jr.

One of the most iconic photos of the JFK administration show JFK Sr. at work in the Oval Office with **John John** partially (and adorably) concealed beneath the Resolute Desk. America fell in love....instantly.

After the disappearance of their plane, media was filled with testimonials from trainers, teachers, and friends about **JFK Jr.'s "adrenaline addiction."** Many described a man who took unnecessary chances as a means of feeling "completely aware and com-pletely alive." In the case of his final con-scious moments alive, and the rotten decisions he made en route, his wife and her sister died as part of the gig.

when she flew into New York, and he spent the evening with her at her $3,200-a-night suite at Manhattan's Carlyle Hotel.

As gossip reached London, a wag said, "Maybe the Princess thinks he'll become President of the United States one day, and she can marry him and be First Lady, since it's unlikely she'll ever be Queen of England."

JFK's other high-profile affairs included liaisons with Madonna, a candidate opposed by Jacqueline Kennedy, who also was against her son becoming an actor. She sent him to law school instead.

He dated such actresses as Julia Roberts, Sarah Jessica Parker, Sharon Stone, and model Cindy Crawford, and had a six-year affair with Daryl Hannah.

On September 21, 1996, off the coast of Georgia, he married the elegant fashion expert, Carolyn Bessette. The union soured after only a few months, and the couple began secretly seeing others. Carolyn resumed her affair with supermodel Michael Bergin, who posed for his own brand of revealing underwear and later wrote a confessional about their affair.

JFK Jr. had more than one mistress and was with one of them for his final night in New York, after he secretly slipped into the Stanhope Hotel.

On July 16, 1999, JFK Jr. took the controls of his Piper Saratoga light aircraft winging into the sky as the sun was going down over Fairfield, New Jersey. His passengers in the rear included his wife Carolyn, and her sister, Lauren Bessette. They were flying to a wedding in Hyannis Port in Massachusetts.

Navy divers discovered their bodies on July 21. The National Transportation Safety Board blamed the air crash on "pilot error."

According to the long-range dynastic plans of the Kennedys, JFK Jr. was to run for president in 2016 at the age of 56. Had he lived, he, not Hillary Clinton, might have faced the Republican challenger Donald Trump.

In this case, history probably needed a rewrite.

Christina Onassis in 1978. After the death of her father, Aristotle Onassis, she lamented, "Now I've got to pay off the whore," a reference to her stepmother, Jacqueline Kennedy Onassis.

Had JFK Jr. lived, he'd have been a politically viable 56 years old during the 2016 Presidential election—old enough to have replaced Hillary as the Democratic candidate against "The Tangerine Terror." Might he indeed, have won? Such are the ironies (and regrets) of hindsight and of "WHAT IF's?"

Pulchritude, notoriety, and fame, all wrapped up into an adrenaline-soaked smorgasbord of *Ooooh-la-la*. Objects of Junior's affection, *Left to right:* **Madonna, Diana Spencer, Sarah Jessica Parker, Julia Roberts,** and **Cindy Crawford.**

The press followed the "heir apparent's" ins and outs with slavish devotion. Jackie-O "only occasionally" got involved...But when she did (as in, a forceful "disrecommendation: of Madonna, she made herself very very clear.

[Editor's Note: This column ran in Boomer Times in 2017, during the first Presidential administration of Donald Trump. True and valid at the time, it is now historic. We've included it in this retrospective of Boomer Times features as "A Remembrance of Things Past."]

JOE KENNEDY III
The Last of the Still Viable, Still-Electable Sons of Camelot

Joe Kennedy III—The best, brightest, and most electorally viable Kennedy left within a once-formidable, now much-diminished arsenal of relatives.

Could it be that we'll live to see another Kennedy sitting in the Oval Office at 1600 Pennsylvania Avenue? That is entirely possible and is being privately mulled over in the corridors of power in secret Democratic confabs.

Of course, there have been attempts by other Kennedys to follow in the footsteps of their beloved John F. Kennedy, who was assassinated in Dallas in November of 1963. The best chance the Democrats ever had to replace him came in 1968 when Senator Bobby Kennedy was ahead in the race for the White House. After he won the California Primary, an assassin's bullet in Los Angeles took him down.

Another brother, Teddy, seriously eyed a run in 1980 against the sitting president, Jimmy Carter. But the drowning of Mary Jo Kopechne in 1969 on Chappaquiddick lingered on in the voters' minds.

It was no secret that Jacqueline Kennedy Onassis diverted the acting ambitions of her charismatic son, John F. Kennedy Jr., and was grooming "America's Prince" to run for president in the 21st Century. Neither of them would live to greet the New Millennium.

After the assassinations of JFK and his brother, RFK, the demise of the Kennedy's took a giant step forward in 1969.

Then, as noted nationwide in this frontpage news story, **Teddy Kennedy**, their younger brother, was embarrassingly implicated in the drowning of a campaign aide, **Mary Jo Kopechne,** (aka "one of the "Boiler Room Girls') one dark, drunken night on Martha's Vineyard. Although he staggered on for several more decades as "The Lion of the Senate," his presidential dreams (and credibility) never fully recovered.

Here's Joe Kennedy's confused and spectacularly unpopular uncle, **Robert Kennedy Jr.,** Donald Trump's bumbling and unqualified choice as Secretary of Health & Human Services.

An self-admitted heroin addict for decades and an almost sociopathic denier of scientific research associated with vaccines, he has done more to tarnish the Kennedy legacy than any other member of the once-much-admired, once easy-to-elect clan.

Hope blooms eternal. Today, the spotlight on "The Sons of Camelot" burns more brightly on the head of Joe Kennedy III than on any of the other young Kennedys. Many other would-be hopefuls, including Robert Kennedy Jr. [Donald Trump's much-disliked and deeply mistrusted Secretary of Health and Human Services], Michael Kennedy, and William Kennedy Smith, became mired in drug addiction, alcoholism, and various sex scandals, including a rape charge.

[For the record, Trump's cabinet pick, the very controversial Robert Kennedy Jr., is Joe Kennedy III's unsavory uncle.]

In contrast to the history of his aberrant (and emotionally unstable) uncle, Joe III's record, both public and private, is almost too good to be true. He's handsome, charismatic, intelligent, and has spent his adult life helping the unfortunate. One of his credits includes a campaign to protect them from mortgage foreclosures after the economic meltdown of 2008.

No other U.S. representative has his distinguished ancestral links. He is the grandson of Bobby Kennedy, a great-nephew of JFK and Teddy, and the great-grandson of Joseph P. Kennedy, founder of the dynasty, whose name he carries today.

Born on October 4, 1980, Joe III has a twin brother, Matt. Unlike his parents, Joseph II and Sheila, who divorced in 1991, Joe III has been happily married to his former classmate, Lauren Anne Birchfield, since 2012.

Although he descended from some heavy boozing Irishmen, Joe III at Harvard was nicknamed "The Milkman." When he went bar hopping with his teammates, he ordered glasses of milk

As a member of the Peace Corps, he spent two years in the Dominican Republic, where he became fluent in Spanish. What an asset if he ever ran for President in a nation where Spanish is the second language.

In 2012, he ran for Congress from the 4th District in Massachusetts, winning 90 percent of the Democratic primary vote, and 61 percent in the November election. When he ran again in 2014, he was unopposed in the primary and general election. In 2016, he defeated his Republican challenger by 40 points.

Today, he's one of the most active members of Congress, flying to Afghanistan or trying to save Health Care. In that, he is aided by his wife, a health policy lawyer.

If he decides to run in four, or more likely in eight years, he'll face formidable challengers on the right. As the Republican party's heir apparent, Vice President Mike Pence is wooing donors, even though he denies it. Senator Tom Cotton of Arkansas and Senator Ben Sasse of Nebraska have been stomping through the summer cornfields of Iowa. Ohio Governor John Kasich has signaled he might run in 2020 even if Donald Trump attempts a renomination.

As the world knows, Democrats ran a woman, Hillary Clinton, for president in 2016. Many GOP power brokers are focusing on another woman, Nikki Haley, former governor of South Carolina and the current U.S. ambassador to the United Nation. The senator from Massachusetts, Elizabeth Warren, might be her possible Democratic challenger.

A New York pollster, Marshall Miller, said, "The men haven't done such a good job of it. Why not give a woman a chance?

William Kennedy Smith some of Jean Kennedy Smith and Stephen Edward Smith, is known for being charged with rape in a nationally publicized 1991 trial that ended with his acquittal. Some detractors said that that was thanks, in part, to the intervention of his very famous uncle, Teddy Kennedy.

Although his chances of being elected to a high-visibility post are dimmer than he might have hoped for, he has, to a large degree, "rehabilitated" himself through a medical career. At least some of it focused on the outlawing, internationally, of land mines and the medical rehabilitation of their victims.

"It's been a helluva long time" Kennedy detractors are saying, "since **Ethel and Bobby** *(i.e. Ethel Skakel Kennedy and RFK)* produced 11 children."

It was widely assumed at the time that at least some of them might have carried on the clan's fabled reputation for easy electability and much-applauded public service.

Since then, however, that worn-out belief is seriously out of date. Ethel's detractors, including Jacqueline Kennedy herself, made occasional snide comments about how Ethel remained constantly and unapologetically pregnant "almost constantly" for decades.

Since then, the only viable Kennedy remaining a guiding light on the national scene is their nephew, Joseph Kennedy III, the featured centerpiece of this episode.

Boomer Times' column of August 2011

THE KENNEDYS:
The Scandalous Saga of a Family Consumed by Its Own Passions

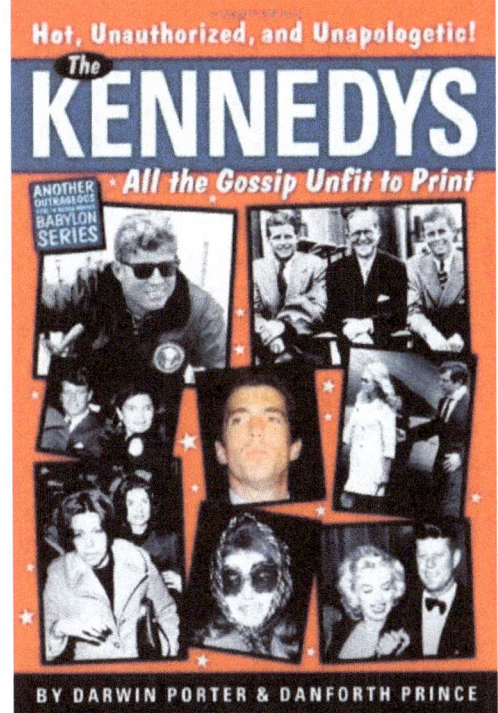

Loaded with glitter, gossip, and gore, my latest biography, co-authored with Danforth Prince, is a heavily illustrated look at *The Kennedys*, published on the 50th anniversary of their ascension to power. It's a scandal-soaked compendium of the vanities, gaffes, mendacities, and indiscretions of the first "true movie stars," as they were labeled by Hollywood, ever to occupy the White House.

Amid today's intense media scrutiny, their brazen indiscretions would have demolished their myth after just a few months in the public eye. But back in the early 60s, based on an almost stupefying sense of entitlement, they re-created the mythical Kingdom of Camelot and got the world to believe the fantasy. There was a lot of "rot" in Camelot, but what fun it was until its panache and chivalry evolved into personal and national tragedies that rivaled any Greek drama. Incidentally, JFK hated that song, "Camelot."

After the dust of decades has settled, it's time to revisit what really went on with the politicians who shaped so much of our culture. In 2011, we know a lot more about each of the Kennedys than we did in 1961. Following the death of Teddy Kennedy in 2009, we learned even more, perhaps some of it hard to digest. New revelations, some of them based on declassified FBI reports and a private diary Teddy carelessly left aboard an airplane, have made most of those dusty and archaic Kennedy books in your library hopelessly out of date.

Millions of people are aware of at least some of the details associated with JFK's romantic dalliance with screen goddess Marilyn Monroe, the "Happy Birthday, Mr. President" Lady. Thousands of Americans know that when the president dumped her, she shared her sexual charms with Bobby Kennedy. Far fewer people know that after Bobby, too, abandoned her, she launched a torrid affair with the youngest and perhaps most tormented of the Kennedy brothers, Teddy.

And it will come as a surprise to many to learn that JFK sustained a brief early fling with Marilyn in 1946, back when she was a struggling starlet. Four years later, JFK's father, Ambassador Joseph P. Kennedy, Sr., also succumbed to her charms when he was introduced to her by director John Huston on the set of the *film noir, The Asphalt Jungle*.

That's not all: Rumors persisted for decades that not only did Marilyn "inherit" Teddy, but so did Jackie.

In the 1950s, as president of the student body at the University of Miami (and later as a Bureau Chief for the *Miami Herald*), **Darwin Porter** seen in the *two photos, right*, managed to successfully maneuver his way around the jagged meanderings of Florida politics.

His mentor at the time was Florida Senator **George (aka"Gorgeous George") Smathers,** a close and intimate "bordello buddy" of JFK.

Smathers eventually "enrolled" Darwin as a cooperative and collaborative witness to many of his "secrets."

In the *photo left*, **JFK and Smathers** share side-by-side seats at The Orange Bowl.

When Robert Kennedy abandoned his affair with Jackie in anticipation of his bid for the presidency in 1968, Teddy picked up the slack. It was hardly a secret that he had long coveted his brother's widow. As Jackie told her friend and confidant, author Truman Capote, "I'm in love with two men at same time, both Bobby and Teddy." Teddy--looking after protecting her financial interests--became her confidant, protector and lover during the course of her turbulent marriage to the Greek shipping tycoon, Aristotle Onassis.

Our Kennedy saga unfolds like the fast-paced drama it was. One revelation is piled onto another, with meticulous attention to the how, when, and why. Among hundreds of others, they include the first detailed report of JFK's first marriage to Durie Malcolm, the Palm Beach socialite; the president's affair with the late goddess, Elizabeth Taylor; JFK Jr.'s brief fling with Princess Diana; Onassis' pursuit of beautiful young boys and his attraction to transgendered cross-dressers; Jackie's affairs with both Warren Beatty and Marlon Brando; and Grace Kelly's burning desire to become First Lady in Washington instead of Princess of a small principality on the French Riviera. The beat goes on.

Despite accusations that we were motivated by desires to topple the Kennedy clan's myth from its pedestal, we are not immune to their charm and panache. I've been obsessively covering the Kennedy saga since the late 1950s, when I was editor of *The Miami Hurricane,* the University of Miami's student newspaper, organizing political favors for then-Senator George Smathers, a "bordello buddy" of the then-junior Senator from Massachusetts, JFK.

Warning to readers: Caroline Kennedy, today's most motivated "Keeper of the Kennedy flame," won't like this book. But critics in Hollywood have already cast their vote of approval. This title has already won a literary award for biography from the 2011 Hollywood Book Festival.

Jackie's competitive sister, **Lee Radziwill**, became indiscreet with *Über-bitch* **Truman Capote**. They're seen here at Truman's "Party of the Century" in 1966.

WHEN DIVAS with a history of *schtupping* JFK CLASH: Her Serene Highness **Grace Kelly** met for lunch with **Jackie and the President** at the White House. It didn't go well. Read about it here.

THE KENNEDYS, All the Gossip Unfit to Print,
by Darwin Porter and Danforth Prince. From Blood Moon Productions. Hardcover, 456 pages, with hundreds of photos.

WHO KNEW AT THE TIME? The tragedies and glory that the Kennedys would attain during the (sometimes brief) lifetime of its members? *Left to right,* as collectively photographed in 1931: **Rosemary, Joseph Jr., Kathleen** (later, the Marchioness of Hartington), **Patricia** (later, Mrs. Peter Lawford), **Rose, Joseph Sr., Jean, Eunice, John** (*aka* President JFK), and **Bobby** (*aka* Attorney General RFK). **THE KENNEDYS,** spearheaded by **Darwin Porter,** tells it all...unauthorized, unapologetic. and true.

BOOK RELEASE NEWS
as it appeared in Boomer Times in 2014

Jacqueline Kennedy Onassis: A Life Beyond Her Wildest Dreams

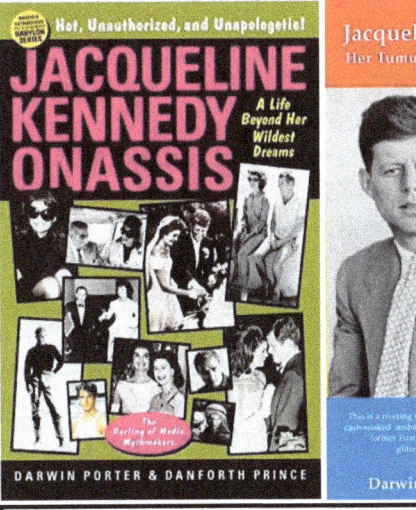

This award-winning book's first edition *(left photo)* was released, with lots of media commentary, in 2014. It was re-released, with different cover art *(right photo)*, in 2021.

Jacqueline Kennedy Onassis was a mystery wrapped in an enigma. Although the most publicized woman in the world at mid-20th century, she had defied her would-be chroniclers from exposing what was behind that black widow's veil that captured the imagination of the world in November of 1963 in the wake of JFK's assassination in Dallas.

Jacqueline hated the nickname "Jackie" or her designation as First Lady. ("It sounds like a race horse.") She spent much of her life trying to suppress revelations about herself, even suing some of those who tried. Yet she remains an enduring figure in history, and a worthy subject for scrutiny.

On the 20th anniversary of her death, I'm taking a crack at her life story, believing that even a mystery this convoluted can be solved. It took me only fifty years to gather all this information.

As the chief writer of The Frommer Travel Guidebook series, I followed directly in her footsteps to India, to Pakistan, to Haiti, to Palm Beach, to California, to Newport (Rhode Island), to Boston, to Hyannis Port, to Greece, to London, to Paris, to the French Riviera, to Rome, to Washington, and especially to New York.

In this, my latest biography, I explore beyond the myths to try to understand one of the most famous, revered (or reviled), and most talked-about women who ever lived.

Images from which legends are made: Jackie, grieving, and in consultation with her priest at JFK's funeral

Although not that close to many women, Jacqueline adored men, and attracted some of the most powerful or alluring members of that species to her side. Those included her final lover, the much married diamond merchant, the rather portly Maurice Tempelsman, who had the savvy to take $20 million from her and leverage it, through investments, into $200 million.

A distant relative, author Gore Vidal, once said, "Jack, Jackie, and I were priapic." Of course, her own sexual conquests hardly matched the debauchery of those two gentlemen who, like Caligula, were known for their voracious sexual appetites. Pursued by some of the most desirable men on the planet, Jacqueline told her sister, Lee Radziwill, "I never could resist temptation."

She loved gossip, especially Hollywood gossip, and was fascinated by male movie stars. Over the course of many years, some famous actors were invited into her boudoir, including her special favorite, William Holden, along with Paul Newman, Gregory Peck, Warren Beatty, Richard Burton (star of her favorite musical, Camelot), Frank Sinatra, and Marlon Brando.

Teenaged Jackie with her notorious father, mentor, and role model, **Black Jack Bouvier.**

She hardly limited herself to screen idols, attracting a distinguished and widely diverse coterie of suitors. These included the roguish cartoonist, Charles Addams, who created the Addams Family. (Perhaps Jackie was his Morticia?); Fiat czar Gianni Agnelli; heart surgeon Christiaan Barnard; Lord Harlech, poet Robert Lowell; Franklin D. Roosevelt; politician Roswell Gilpatric (Jacqueline was cited as "the other woman" in his wife's divorce petition); and columnist Peter Hamill, whom she stole from the arms of her rival, Shirley MacLaine.

Some of her romances escaped radar detection, including her involvement with Pierre Trudeau, Prime Minister of Canada. In his search for the First Lady of Canada, he wavered between Jacqueline and Barbra Streisand, eventually choosing neither of them.

Perhaps her most emotional entanglements were with her brother-in-law, Bobby Kennedy, a liaison that developed in the aftermath of JFK's assassination. When Bobby was also assassinated in 1968, she directed her love to Teddy, interpreting him as the torch carrier of Camelot.

Jacqueline wasn't close to that many women, and often maintained feuds with some of her chief rivals for JFK's affection. The most famous of these included Grace Kelly, Elizabeth Taylor, and, most notoriously, Marilyn Monroe. She was always pained by Audrey Hepburn, whom JFK had originally wanted to marry.

As might be expected, my biography includes many insights into that "grizzled satrap," Aristotle Onassis. Scandalous spins on Jacqueline's marriage to the shipping tycoon are revealed in all their fascinating horror as she slowly discovered his "perversions." After his first beating of her, he informed her that "All Greek men beat their women. It's a token of their love."

Perhaps the most shocking of all was the love-hate relationship his son, Alexander, had with Jackie. He denounced her as a gold-digger, yet was physically attracted to her. He had long cherished "this thing for older women," as exemplified by his love affair with the notorious Fiona Campbell-Walter Thyssen Bornemisza.

A buyer at Barnes & Noble told me that in readers' quest for a compelling summer read, I'll be competing with another recently released book about a First Lady, Ida Saxon McKinley, wife of President William McKinley *[in office 1897-1901]*. Like Jacqueline and Martha Washington, Ida was one of the richest First Ladies in U.S. history. An epileptic, she was confined to bed throughout most of her husband's presidency, during which time she crocheted 3,500 slippers. But despite their glaringly obvious differences, Ida and Jacqueline did have something in common: Both of their husbands were assassinated.

Jacqueline Kennedy leaves the chapel with her new husband, **Aristotle Onassis**, after their October 20, 1968 Greek Orthodox wedding on the island of Skorpios.

Rose Kennedy commented, "Jackie is one of the world's most expensive women to maintain, and Onassis has one of the world's greatest fortunes."

Jacqueline Kennedy Onassis, A Life Beyond Her Wildest Dreams,
**Darwin Porter and Danforth Prince,
from Blood Moon Productions,**
Softcover, 700 pages, with photos.

**Jackie-O. The most iconic woman of her era.
Jacqueline Bouvier Kennedy Onassis
1929-1994
Rest in Peace**

ROSEMARY
The Tragedy Behind "The Dirty Little Secret" of the Kennedy Family

She was the first daughter of one of America's greatest political dynasties. But after being presented at the Court of St. James's in London in 1938, when her father, Joseph P. Kennedy, was U.S. Ambassador, she more or less disappeared from public view. For decades, a "cover up" ensued.

In 2016, the story of Rosemary Kennedy, third child of Joseph and Rose Kennedy, born on September 13, 1918, will get its greatest media exposure to date.

First there is the new book out, *Rosemary—the Hidden Kennedy Daughter*, by Kate Clifford Larson. And in Hollywood, a documentary film is in the pre-production for what is hoped will be a TV special. It will include film footage of this tragic daughter who was, shrouded with shame, hidden away like a madwoman in a Victorian novel.

She had the misfortune of being born into one of America's most competitive families. Joe Kennedy not only incited envy from other families, but he encouraged sibling-on-sibling rivalry among his children. He was also grooming Joe Jr. to run for president one day, with his younger brother, Jack, regarded as the family weakling—at least until Rosemary was born.

To a Kennedy, weakness was not acceptable. In 1934, the handsome young Joe Jr. visited Nazi Germany. He wrote a chilling letter back to his father, praising Hitler's sterilization policy: "It's a great thing and will do away with many of the disgusting specimens of men."

In 1938, Rosemary, the most beautiful of the Kennedy daughters, was presented to the Queen of England. With her flirtatious nature, she was attracting many beaux from the English aristocracy who wanted to marry into a wealthy American family. *(In this case, much of the loot had come from bootlegging and the movies.)*

With war clouds looming over England, Rosemary was shipped back to America, where it became increasingly evident that she couldn't keep up with the reading and writing skills of the rest of the Kennedy clan. She had been born dyslexic.

Her problems might have been based on a specific moment related to her birth: Dr. Good, the family physician, had brought Joe Jr. and Jack into the world. When Rose was ready to give birth to her first daughter, the doctor was not immediately available, and ordered his nurse to hold Rose's legs together until he got there, since he would get a much higher fee if present.

Consequently, the emerging infant was trapped in the birth canal for two excruciating hours until the doctor arrived. She was not getting enough oxygen, which no doubt caused her to be born mentally impaired.

Matriarch **Rose Kennedy** (center, top) holding year-old **Rosemary**, flanked by **Joe, Jr.**, (left) and **baby JFK** (right).

Rosemary Kennedy

Left to right: **Rosemary, JFK, Eunice, Joe, Jr.,** & **Kathleen** at Hyannis Port, summer of 1925.

Back in Massachusetts, in 1939, Rosemary's behavior became erratic, and she was said to wander off at night. Joe feared an unwanted pregnancy, which could bring disgrace to his family's political aspirations.

In November of 1941, on the eve of America's entry into World War II, he made a fateful decision. Acting alone, he ordered the doctors at St. Elizabeth's Hospital in Washington, D.C. to perform a dangerous prefrontal lobotomy.

The surgeons entered her brain through the upper portion of her eye socket, asking her to recite songs as they cut nerve endings to her brain. Within minutes, she was silenced, almost permanently so.

Returned to Hyannis Port, Rosemary was said to explode in violent eruptions. Joe sent her away to St. Coletta's School in Jefferson, Wisconsin, where nuns would take care of her. He ordered his brood never to speak of her again. If a reporter inquired, the story was that she was in a hospital in Wisconsin suffering from spinal meningitis.

Joe would never see his daughter again, and Rose would wait twenty years before paying her a visit. When she did arrive in Wisconsin, and Rosemary recognized her mother, she began to scream in rage.

The nuns heard Rose say, "Oh, Rosie, what have we done to you?"

Rosemary's saga was given an ironic twist in 1961 when Joe, in Palm Beach, suffered a massive stroke. Rose and her children watched as the patriarch, who was once ruthless and powerful, entered the dim twilight of his life. His condition mirrored Rosemary's, as he suffered partial facial paralysis, as well as a partially crippled body, a tendency to drool, and an inability to speak intelligibly. For five decades, he'd ferociously concealed what he called the Kennedy family's "dirty little secret." Now, his own pitiful condition made frontpage news around the world.

Joe Kennedy Sr., age 81, released his last breath on November 18, 1969, just five days before the sixth anniversary of the assassination of his son in Dallas in 1963.

In 1995, Rose, a shadow of her former self, died at the age of 104. A decade later, Rosemary would pass on at the age of 86, with her siblings Eunice, Jean, Patricia, and Ted at her side.

In time, Eunice and her brother, the Senator, would become passionate champions of persons suffering from disabilities.

At the Court of Saint James's in 1938, the wife of the new American ambassador to Britain, **Rose Kennedy** *(center)* joined her daughters **Kathleen** *(left)* and **Rosemary** *(right)* during their presentation to then-King George VI and Queen Elizabeth (aka the Queen Mother, aka Elizabeth Bowes-Lyon). It was in the aftermath of the traumatic abdication of King Edward VIII in 1936.

Both sisters ended tragically. **Kathleen,** designated "debutante of 1938," eventually married the Marquess of Hartington, heir apparent to the 10th Duke of Devonshire. Four months after their wedding, he was killed on the battlefields of Belgium. In 1948, Kathleen, too, by then associated with a different partner, was killed in an airplane crash.

Rosemary went on to be lobotomized in a decision which her parents regretted till the end of their respective lives. In its aftermath, she remained permanently institutionalized for decades.

The procedure was an immediate and obvious failure. One of the nurses who was present at the surgery was so traumatized by its outcome that she was said to have quit the medical profession entirely

OTHER VOICES OTHER ROOMS
Joe Sr. and **Rose Kennedy** *(both of them on the far right)* appear here with eight of their nine children in 1934. **Rosemary** is the fourth from the right. Obviously missing from the photo is Joe Kennedy Jr., who was alive at the time, but who died on the battlefields of Europe in 1944.

DARWIN & ANITA's MEDIA MAGIC,
ONCE A MONTH, FOR DECADES, BY THE DAWN'S EARLY LIGHT

How, every 4th Saturday, for decades, Anita Finley would
"**Celebrity Kaffeeklatsch**" with Darwin, either on the radio or on YouTube to an early morning "congregation" of listeners throughout South Florida.
Danforth Prince was privy to the HOW, WHAT, and WHY of those early-morning conversations, and elaborates on them in the chapter that follows.

Over the course of several decades, Saturdays-usually the first of any given month-were noted as the scheduled date for Darwin Porter's once-a-month live interviews with Anita Finley (aka "The Voice of Senior South Florida"), president and executive producer of *Boomer Times & Senior Life.*

Their monthly "conversations" began at 5am and rambled on for at least an hour, after which both Darwin and Anita would retreat, exhausted, after "blowing their respective loads" on shared (and whippersnapping) tirades about cultural issues of importance to their respective fan bases.

As a bemused but detached observer of this ritual, every designated Saturday, regardless of what had happened the previous (Friday) night, I'd awaken at dawn, tune my radio (or computer) on to "the wavelength that mattered" for an earful of whatever the Finley/Porter collaboration had unearthed, of interest, as dawn's rosy light gleamed.

The book ideas and cultural overviews they discussed were up-close-and-relevant to the national landscape of the minute, each dovetailing with Blood Moon's (and Darwin's) books in progress. Regardless of whatever formal announcements we released later, to other, bigger, periodicals (the *Daily Mail* and the *New York Post* come to mind), Anita got (and distributed) the news first. Years later, Darwin still credits her with venues that sharpened his ability to encapsulate, in speakeasy jargon, the show-biz exposés he was laboring over at the time.

Examples include his biographical treatments of THE KENNEDYS and THE CLINTONS; MARILYN, the brunette ("LA LIZ") who competed with her for headlines; VIVIEN LEIGH and HER HEATHCLIFF; bad boy SINATRA and his "even badder" frenemies PETER O'TOOLE and "Noble Tool" MARLON.

My point is that regardless of the icon Darwin animatedly discussed with Anita that month, she was invariably the first to announce it to the media landscape at large, and to coach him through an articulation of its relevance. Her style evoked the flashiest days of Merv Griffin: For example, she heralded the debut of each of her interviews with something akin to "*HEEEEERE'S DARWIN!*"

Larger outlets tended to follow her lead and amplify the stories she broke. Anita, [*"bless her," we said at the time*] invariably emerged as the "news hound" who broke them first, faithfully transmitting them through the dim early morning light to fans throughout South Florida.

The pages that follow are loosely "transcribed' from interviews Anita conducted with Darwin when his books were new and defiantly edgy. Each of her interviews shaped Darwin's ability to articulate his brand during the heady pre-release· days of his prolific backlist.

We present the meatiest aspects of those interviews in the pages that follow as testimonials to the *zeitgeist* skills and communications savvy of Anita Finley.

Who Is **Danforth Prince?**

A graduate of Hamilton College and a native of Easton and Bethlehem, Pennsylvania, he's the president and founder (in 1996) of the Georgia Literary Association, of the Porter and Prince Corporation, and of **Blood Moon Productions**, the most prolific publisher of celebrity biographies in the world.

According to Prince, "Blood Moon provides the luxurious illusion that a reader is a perpetual guest at some gossipy dinner party populated with brilliant but occasionally self-delusional figures from bygone eras of the American Experience. Our success at salvaging, documenting, and articulating the (till now) orally transmitted histories of the Entertainment Industry—in ways that have never been seen before—is one of the most distinctive aspects of our backlist. That effervescent sense of novelty always crackled whenever "D&A" charged , full tilt, into South Florida's early dawn.

CELEBRITY and the IRONIES OF FAME

HOW DECADES AS THE MOST VISIBLE AND PROLIFIC WRITERS AT THE FROMMER GUIDES TURNED DARWIN PORTER AND DANFORTH PRINCE INTO CELEBRITY-CHASING ADVENTURERS ON LOCATION IN EUROPE, CALIFORNIA, THE CARIBBEAN, AND THE WORLD AT LARGE

The point we want to make in this introduction is that before Blood Moon Productions ever existed, its writers devoted themselves to the research and production of many titles within the world-renowned **FROMMER TRAVEL GUIDES**

The venue was unique. As their designated representatives to most of Europe, the Caribbean, and large swaths of the USA, we saw the world, experienced its cultural and aesthetic wonders, worked hard, and had a fabulous time.

But in 2013, the party ended. After a recession and radical changes in how Americans opted to educate itself about their travel tastes and options, the Frommer guides were curtailed, sold and re-sold (multiple times) and endured radical reductions of their budgets and titles. **A way of life had ended. Inevitably, we had already seen the beginning of the end. (Who could have possibly missed it?) As such, we had already begun the (painful) process of "re-formatting' our research headquarters (historic Magnolia House in Staten Island) and morphing it into the headquarters of a bold new publishing venue with a unique, "celebrity-centric" mission statement....i.e., Blood Moon Productions.**

Our Ongoing Obsession with the American Concept of Celebrity and Fame

Even during the heyday of the postwar travel industry, we'd been consistently fascinated by the concept of celebrity and fame in America. And *(full disclosure)*, we had occasionally used our niche at Frommer as a vehicle (or disguise) for the meeting and greeting of celebrities. Tourist authorities in Sweden, Italy, and/or France cooperated with requests we made for introductions to, for example, **Ingrid Bergman, Gina Lollabrigida, and Brigitte Bardot** (among many others) each of whom were willing to be identified with "the best and brightest" of their respective cultural scenes.

So when the Frommer guides as we had known them collapsed, we "fell" into a celebrity-indulgent cocoon whose foundations had already been more or less defined and established.

Here, then, as laid out within the pages of this book, is the story of what happened AFTER the travel party ended, AFTER the Frommer Guides imploded, and when we, as the "keeper of the secrets" and writers of most of the Frommer series were forced to pursue other venues.

As such, we present, through this book, a History (or Biography) of the publishing venture we built, sweated, and labored over AFTER THE BEGINNING OF OUR END at the Frommer Guides, during the tumultuous final years of "The American Century."

It's been a helluva story. Throughout our administration of Blood Moon's experimental saga, we've showcased an alternative (counterculture) spin on the Entertainment industry that would never have been endorsed by Hollywood overseers of previous decades. Here lies the heart—and it's been a helluva ride.

Darwin Porter

Danforth Prince

What were some of the topics that broke Dawn's Early Light, long ago and far away, over the coral-studded landscapes of South Florida?

Among many others, it was

HUMPHREY BOGART

like no one had ever talked or written about him before.

The Secret Life of Humphrey Bogart
The Early Years (1899 - 1931)
Darwin Porter

This myth-shattering biography gives a controversial CLOSEUP of a young, hot and Humpy Bogart pre-Casablanca, pre-Bacall, pre-African Queen Revealing for the first time what was under the trench coat of history's most famous movie star

Darwin Porter's myth-shattering biography (the first of a two-part set) gives a controversial CLOSEUP of a young, hot, and humpy Bogart, pre-*Casablanca,* pre-Bacall, pre-*African Queen*, revealing for the first time what was really under the trench-coat of history's most famous movie star.

Learn what America's most visible male star was doing during his mysterious early years on Broadway and in Hollywood at the dawn of the Talkies--details that Bogie worked hard to suppress during his later years with Bacall.

The subject of more than 80 radio interviews by its author, and widely covered by both the tabloids and the mainstream press, it's based on never-before-published memoirs, letters, diaries, and interviews from men and women who either loved Bogie or who wanted him to burn in hell. No wonder Bogie, in later life, usually avoided talking about his early years.

Serialized in three parts by Britain's *Mail on Sunday*, it demonstrates that Hollywood's Golden Age stars were human, highly sexed, and at least when they were with other Hollywood insiders, remarkably indiscreet.

WHAT THE CRITICS SAID

"This biography has had us pondering as to how to handle its revelations within a town so protective of its own...This biography of Bogart's early years is exceptionally well written."
—JOHN AUSTIN, *HOLLYWOOD INSIDE*

"In this new biography, we learn about how Bogart struggled for stardom in the anything goes era of the Roaring 20s."
—*THE GLOBE*

"Porter's book uncovers scandals within the entertainment industry of the 1920s and 1930s, when publicists from the movie studios deliberately twisted and suppressed inconvenient details about the lives of their emerging stars."
—*TURNER CLASSIC MOVIE NEWS*

"We can only hope that Darwin Porter doesn't run into Lauren Bacall in a dark alley!"
—SALON.COM

HOW THE TABLOIDS HUMPED FOR BLOOD MOON'S PAIRED OVERVIEWS OF BOGIE

In the early stages of its publishing life, Blood Moon's frenemies sometimes rebuked it for "Courting and Romancing" the Tabloids. But the humping paid off. The Daily Mail and its weekend counterpart, The Mail on Sunday, along with the National Enquirer, The Globe, The Examiner, The New York Daily News, and publications across Europe all delivered SCADS of early publicity. We've replicated some of the coverage that the press lavished on our double-volumed release of revelations about "Hunky Humpy" Bogart.

HERE'S THE SECOND OF DARWIN PORTER'S
TWO-VOLUME SET OF BOOKS ABOUT BOGIE

HUMPHREY BOGART
THE MAKING OF A LEGEND
BY DARWIN PORTER

Startling New Information about Golden Age Hollywood that Readers Had Never Seen Before

Whereas Humphrey Bogart is always at the top of any list of the Entertainment Industry's most famous actors, very little is known about how he clawed his way to stardom from Broadway to Hollywood during Prohibition and the Jazz Age.

This radical expansion of one of Darwin Porter's pioneering biographies begins with Bogart's origins as the child of wealthy (morphine-addicted) parents in New York City, then examines the scandals, love affairs, breakthrough successes, and failures that launched Bogart on the road to becoming an American icon. Drawn from original interviews with friends and foes who knew a lot about what lay beneath his trenchcoat, this exposé covers Bogart's life from his birth in 1899 till his marriage to Lauren Bacall in 1945. It includes details about behind-the-scenes dramas associated with three mysterious marriages, and films such as *The Petrified Forest, The Maltese Falcon, High Sierra,* and *Casablanca.* Read all about the debut and formative years of the actor who influenced many generations of filmgoers, laying Bogie's life bare in a style you've come to expect from Darwin Porter. Exposed with all their juicy details is what Bogie never told his fourth wife, Lauren Bacall, herself a screen legend.

This revelatory book is based on dusty unpublished memoirs, letters, diaries, and often personal interviews from the women—and the men—who adored him. There are also shocking allegations from colleagues, former friends, and jilted lovers who wanted the screen icon to burn in hell. All this and more, much more, in Darwin Porter's exposé of Bogie's startling secret life.

Bogie (left photo) with three relatively unknown wives, *left to right,* **Helen Mencken, Mary Philips,** and **Mayo Methot.**

And then, focus moved from Bogart toward
KATHARINE HEPBURN, *and the conversation instantly changed.*

You already know about what *Kate Remembered*, because there are a LOT of "deferential and obsequious whitewashes" already in print.

BUT HERE AT LAST IS AN UNVARNISHED ACCOUNT OF WHAT KATHARINE HEPBURN DESPERATELY WANTED TO FORGET

KATHARINE THE GREAT
A LIFETIME OF SECRETS REVEALED

DARWIN PORTER

Foreword Magazine's Book of the Year Award Finalist

Katharine Hepburn was the most obsessively secretive actress in Hollywood.

Her androgynous, pan-sexual appeal usually went over big with movie audiences--until those disastrous flops when it didn't. This book tells the how and why of Kate Hepburn's most closely guarded secrets.

There's a carload of other biographies about Hepburn that eiher got the facts wrong or whitewashed them to the point where there's almost been a consistent act of academic sabotage.

But here at last is a biography that isn't afraid to wrestle with the outrageous ego and ferociously guarded privacy of Hollywood's most mysterious *Über-diva*:

Katharine Hepburn.

Katharine Hepburn was Hollywood's most successful, most eccentric, and most phobically secretive actress.

Here's the OTHER side of her life, exposed at last.

A gossippy tell-all that fans of Old Hollywood find fascinating.

Last year, Darwin Porter dumped The Secret Life of Humphrey Bogart on us, and we lapped up every sentence of it, despite some doubt about its veracity…His avowed sources were there, reliable and substantiated, amassed over several years and guarded until such time that the subjects had shed these mortal coils. Now, once again, the author draws upon his vast storehouse of notes and quotes regarding the movie stars of an earlier period—notes and quotes that could never be published in the time of the good old, bad old days of studio fiefdom, when damage contral was the name of the game.
This time out, Katharine Hepburn is the subject, …and the inner workings of a studio (RKO in the early 30s) in that period are relished."

--Conrad J. Doerr in Palm Springs' BOTTOM LINE

Darwin Porter's biography of Katharine Hepburn cannot be lightly dismissed or ignored. Connoisseurs of her life would do well to seek it out as a forbidden supplement" — *The Sunday Times (London)*

"Behind the scenes of her movies, Katharine Hepburn played the temptress to as many women as she did men, ranted and raved with her co-stars and directors, and broke into her neighbors' homes for fun. And somehow, she managed to keep all of it out of the press. As they say, *Katharine the Great* is hard to put down."
—*The Dallas Voice*

"The door to Hepburn's closet has finally been opened. This is the most honest and least apologetic biography of Hollywood's most ferociously private actress ever written."

—*Boomer Times /Senior Life*

BRANDO UNZIPPED

Darwin Porter

This "entertainingly outrageous" (FRONTIERS MAGAZINE) biography provides a definitive, blow-by-blow description of the "hot, provocative, and barely under control drama" that was the life of America's most famous Postwar actor.

The same animalistic intensity Marlon Brando brought to the role of Stanley Kowalski in *A Streetcar Named Desire* lives again within these pages, based on unpublished material gathered over a lifetime of research. The blue jeans made famous by Brando In. Streetcar are unzipped in this richly anecdotal, "warts-and-all" biography of the greatest film actor of the 20th Century.

Within its pages, veteran Hollywood reporter Darwin Porter paints an extraordinarily detailed portrait of Brando, particularly about his early years, that is as blunt, uncompromising, and X-rated as the man himself.
From the male sex symbol of the 1950s to an overweight slob and tabloid scandal at his century's end, Brando was filmdom's most original star. Women wanted him, and certain men also desired him. He was willing to share his charms—he called it "my noble tool"—with his admirers.

A self-admitted bisexual, he seduced more women and the occasional man than any other actor in the history of Hollywood. His trail of conquest led from the A-list boudoirs of New York to similar padded enclaves in Hollywood and eventually to the backwaters of the South Pacific.

His secret meetings with Hollywood legends such as Greta Garbo and Cary Grant are told with frankness, as are his so-called "mercy fucks" with such stellar lights as Joan Crawford, Bette Davis and even John Gielgud. To Brando's bedroom came not just the famous, but the unknown pickups, including "almost every Japanese woman associated with the film Sayonara."

Revealed for the first time are the intimate details of his troubled but enduring love affair with the doomed Marilyn Monroe, to whom he was both confidant and lover. But was he also her husband? Was their "marriage" really legal?

One of the most poignant episodes revolves around his brief but evocative affair with the mentally disturbed Vivien Leigh, the Blanche DuBois to his Stanley In *A Streetcar Named Desire.*

Marlon's Men
as reviewed by
London's *Gay Times*

"He was considered one of the most dynamic and imposing actors of his generation, but as author Darwin Porter finds, it wasn't just the acting world that Marlon Brando conquered...It was the actors, too."

> "Marlon Brando understood sexual liberation long before the rest of us. Here, as interpreted by Darwin Porter, is a portrait of Hollywood's most seductive bad boy, as you never could have dreamed."
>
> —George Mills

The roles Brando lived off-screen were even more provocative than those he created in his films. Through his life paraded an array of luminaries, including some of the most famous women of the 20th century. An aging Marlene Dietrich seduced him when he was just emerging into manhood. Brando bedded Grace Kelly on the night both of them won Oscars. He also impressed a widowed Jacqueline Kennedy with his charms. At Brando's peak, his list of lovers read like a Who's Who of the cultured elite: Rita Hayworth, Leonard Bernstein, Noel Coward, Laurence Olivier, Shelley Winters, Gloria Vanderbilt, Tyrone Power, Hedy Lamarr, Anna Magnani, Tallulah Bankhead, Rock Hudson, Ingrid Bergman, and Doris Duke (at the time, the world's richest woman.)

The decade-long passion Tennessee Williams maintained for Brando is explored, beginning one night on a lonely beach in Provincetown during World War II. Also revealed for the first time are his tortured relationships and love affairs with his two chief rivals, Montgomery Clift and James Dean.

Personal family tragedy is also documented in pictures, including Brando's incestuous relationship with his teenage daughter, Cheyenne, who committed suicide in 1995. Also explored is Christian Brando's murder of Cheyenne's boyfriend, Dag Drollet.

If Marlon had not existed, no novelist could have conjured up such a towering, larger-than-life creature.

WHAT THE CRITICS SAID ABOUT BRANDO UNZIPPED

"Lurid, raunchy, perceptive, and certainly worth reading...One of the ten best show-biz biographies of 2006."
—*The Sunday Times (London)*

"**Yummy**. An irresistably flamboyant romp of a read."
—*Books to Watch Out For*

"Astonishing. An extraordinarily detailed portrait of Brando that's as blunt, uncompromising, and X-rated as the man himself."
—*Women's Weekly*

"This shocking new book is sparking a major reassessment of Brando's legacy as one of Hollywood's most macho lotharios."
—*Daily Express (London)*

"As author Darwin Porter finds, it wasn't just the acting world Marlon Brando conquered. It was the actors, too."
—*Gay Times (London)*

"*Brando Unzipped* is the definitive gossip guide to the late, great actor's life."
—*The New York Daily News*

FRANK SINATRA
THE BOUDOIR SINGER
All the Gossip Unfit to Print from the Glory Days of Ol' Blue Eyes

Frank Sinatra's career spanned more than half a century, earning him millions of fans. His influence on popular music in the 20th century was unsurpassed. Because of the fame and the widespread media coverage, he attracted, you might think that there were no stones left unturned in one of the most heavily chronicled lives of any entertainer.

But Darwin Porter, America's leading celebrity chronicler of Golden Age Hollywood, manages to turn over more than a few boulders in Sinatra's secret garden. After all, Sinatra lived in an era when "inconvenient truths" were conveniently (and systematically) buried.

Porter has virtually stalked Sinatra since 1955, when, as a teenage journalist-in-the-making, they met at the home of Miss Sophie Tucker, "Queen of Miami Beach."

Co-authored with Danforth Prince, Frank Sinatra, The Boudoir Singer is the latest in Blood Moon's Babylon Series. It answers many mysterious questions that have puzzled the public for decades.

In his research, Porter drew upon a treasure trove of both celebrity contacts and dialogues with so-called "little people" (room service waiters, bartenders, Las Vegas call girls, etc.) who surrounded Sinatra throughout his life.

The "Stranger in the Night" international icon had it all--fame, untold riches, stunningly beautiful women, the world for a playground. "That's Life" was lived not in the sun, but in shadows. Pleasure became debauchery, mood swings turned violent, joy brought pain, triumphs tragedy. Within the pages of this book, one of the most controversial and elusive figures of the 20th century emerges as "The Man Behind the Myth."

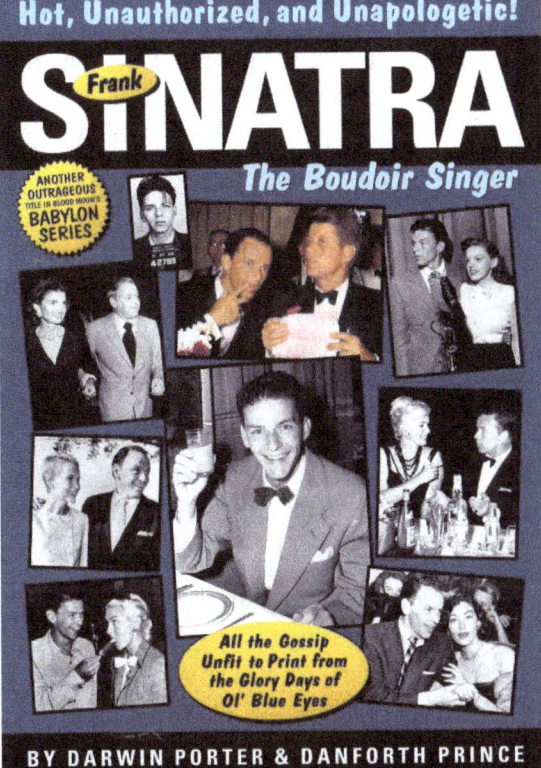

Who, exactly, was this mercurial, enigmatic man? For this compendium of show-biz scandal, Darwin Porter, former bureau chief and entertainment columnist for *The Miami Herald*, drew upon a treasure trove of celebrity contacts he accumulated over the years. This award-winning tell-all has everything you ever wanted to know about Sinatra—and more.

"You name 'em, he's had 'em—Lana Turner, Jackie Kennedy, Gloria Vanderbilt, Natalie Wood, Lee Remick, Lee Radziwill, Janet Leigh, Kim Novak, Shirley MacLaine, Judy Garland, Zsa Zsa Gabor, Angie Dickenson. I'm leaving out 2,000 other women."

--Dean Martin

There are dozens of other stars Frank seduced, some of them unknown to Dean, but all of them are explored within the pages of this book. They include the pinup queen Bettie Page, June Allyson, Joan Crawford, Ingrid Bergman, Betty Grable, Eva Gabor, Hedy Lamarr, Linda Lovelace (of Deep Throat fame), Marilyn Chambers (of Behind the Green Door fame), Rita Hayworth, Jo Stafford, Peggy Lee, Billie Holiday, Lena Horne, Grace Kelly, Juliet Prowse, plus many prostitutes, waitresses, starlets, singers, and women from all occupations and stations of life.

PORTER'S DISCOVERIES REVEAL THAT THERE IS STILL MUCH TO TELL ABOUT OLD BLUE EYES:

• His secret affairs with two First Ladies occupying The White House. These trysts were conducted when **John F. Kennedy** or **Ronald Reagan** were out of town.
• The night a drunken Sinatra almost ordered the "execution"" of **Elvis Presley**.
• His little-known affair with **Elizabeth Taylor** and their agreement to abort their child.
• A discovery by Sinatra that led to his booting of **Sammy Davis Jr**. and **Peter Lawford** from the Rat Pack.
• His 11th hour negotiations to prevent the marriage of **Grace Kelly** to **Prince Rainier** of Monaco. Sinatra wanted her to marry him instead.
• His long, torturous affair with **Judy Garland**—"We kept each other from committing suicide," he said.
• The sultry brunette, **Judith Campbell Exner**, that Sinatra shared with both JFK and mob boss **Sam Giancana**.
• The role of Sinatra as White House pimp, delivering a string of Hollywood goddesses to the bedside of the president.
• How Sinatra planned to marry **Marilyn Monroe** but called it off at the last minute. Even so, he prevented her from presiding over a press conference that could have destroyed the Kennedys' dynasty. He also investigated the murder of Monroe and concluded who did it.
• What really happened that night Sinatra arrived unexpectedly at his Palm Springs compound and discovered **Lana Turner with Ava Gardner**. What made him kick both of these glamour girls out into the night?

Frank Sinatra, The Boudoir Singer, reveals exactly what the Chairman of the Board meant when he sang that he did it "My Way." Thanks to the publication of this book, many of Ol' Blue Eyes' fans will never be able to look at their idol in quite the same way ever again.

"When Sinatra dies, they'll donate his zipper to the Smithsonian." —Dean Martin

"F-R-A-N-K-I-E-E-E-E-E! Take my virginity!," screamed a bobby-soxer in midtown Manhattan in 1943

*"Every time I sing a song, I'm actually making love on stage.
Call me 'The Boudoir Singer.'"* —Frank Sinatra

"He was no Joe DiMaggio in bed" said Marilyn Monroe.

"*Mais oui!* The Mercedes-Benz of men!" said Marlene Dietrich.

"A complete shit!" claimed Lauren Bacall when he dumped her at the aisle.

"Our problems were never in bed," said Ava Gardner, his greatest love. "We were always great in bed: 10 pounds of Frank, 110 pounds of cock."

"He's the most fascinating man in the world. Don't stick your hand in his cage." —Tommy Dorsey

DAMN YOU, SCARLETT O'HARA
THE PRIVATE LIFES OF LAURENCE OLIVIER AND VIVIEN LEIGH

Darwin Porter and Roy Moseley

This book tears away the velvet curtain previously draped over the reputations of this famous team, exposing with searing insights the depths of their sexual excess and interpersonal anguish. Some of the most iconic figures of the 20th century move through chapters that highlight a revelation on every page.

HOT, SHOCKING, METICULOUSLY RESEARCHED, AND WINNER OF FOUR DISTINGUISHED LITERARY AWARDS SINCE ITS CONTROVERSIAL RELEASE IN FEBRUARY OF 2011.

Here, for the first time, is a biography that raises the curtain on the secret lives of (Lord) **Laurence Olivier**, known for his interpretation of the brooding and tormented Heathcliff of Emily Brontë's *Wuthering Heights,* and **Vivien Leigh,** who immortalized herself with her Oscar-winning portrayals of Scarlett O'Hara in Margaret Mitchell's *Gone With the Wind,* and as Blanche DuBois in Tennessee Williams' *A Streetcar Named Desire.*

Even though the spotlight shone on this famous pair throughout most of their tabloid-fueled careers, much of what went on behind the velvet curtain remained hidden from view until the publication of this ground-breaking biography. The PRIVATE LIVES (to borrow a phrase from their gossipy contemporary, Noël Coward) of this famous couple are exposed with searing insights into their sexual excess and personal anguish.

Dashing and "impossibly handsome," Laurence Olivier was pursued by some of the most dazzling luminaries, male and female, of the movie and theater worlds. The influential theatrical producer David Lewis asserted, "He would have slept with anyone." That included Richard Burton, who fell madly in love with him, as did Noël Coward. Lord Olivier's promiscuous, emotionally disturbed wife (Viv to her lovers) led a tumultuous off-the-record life whose paramours ranged from the A-list to men she picked up off the street. None of the brilliant roles depicted by Lord and Lady Olivier, on stage or on screen, ever matched the power and drama of personal dramas which wavered between Wagnerian opera and Greek tragedy. *Damn You, Scarlett O'Hara* is the definitive and most revelatory portrait ever published of the most talented and tormented actor and actress of the 20th century.

Darwin Porter is the co-author of this seminal work. Winner of numerous awards for his headline-generating biographies, he has shed new light on Marlon Brando, Steve McQueen, Paul Newman, Katharine Hepburn, Humphrey Bogart, Merv Griffin, Michael Jackson, and Howard Hughes.

Roy Moseley, this book's other co-author, maintained a decades-long association with the famous couple, nurturing them through their tumultuous triumphs, emotional breakdowns, and streams of suppressed scandal.

This award-winning book has received accolades from the following:
San Francisco Book Festival 2011, Honorable Mention for Biography
Paris Book Festival 2011, Winner, BEST BIOGRAPHY
New York Book Festival 2011, Honorable Mention for Biography
Beach Book Festival 2011, Grand Prize Winner for BEST SUMMER READING of 2011

THERE IS NOTHING LIKE A DAME
"BRUNETTES ARE BETTER, AND BRUNETTES HAVE MORE FUN,"

says Danforth Prince, President of Blood Moon Productions, about the release, this week, of his company's hot new biography of Hollywood's ultimate brunette, Elizabeth Taylor.

It's the publishing industry's most comprehensve overview of scandals associated with the world's most famous (brunette) movie star. ELIZABETH TAYLOR, with detailed descriptions of incidents that the Über-Goddess would NEVER have tolerated during her lifetime

WHAT A DAME!

Her enemies described her as the Serpent of the Nile. WE think, however, that she was an Uber-Diva and Mega-Celebrity who redefined hedonism and pop culture in America.

IT'S ALL HERE

Sympathetic but shocking—a richly detailed roster of revelations and insights into LA LIZ and her ongoing role within America's Entertainment Industry during the peak of its muscle and power.

Her scandals—and a lot more—are exposed in a saga that's both sympathetic and shocking. This book contains enough irony, drama, and detail to fascinate anyone who's ever been intrigued with the lore and legend of the 20th Century's most notorious *femme fatale*. **All of them are included within this ode to a great Dame and a fabulous movie star.**

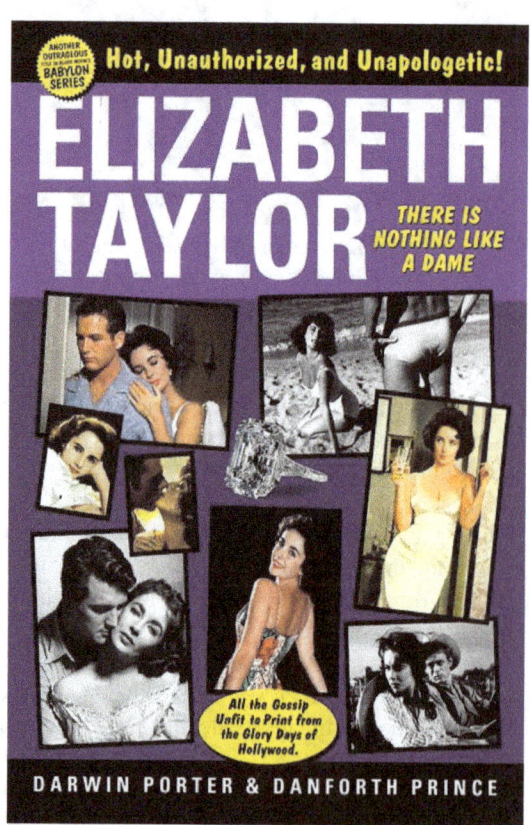

"BEFORE THEY WITHER, ELIZABETH TAYLOR'S BREASTS WILL TOPPLE EMPIRES."
—RICHARD BURTON

THE SAGA OF ELIZABETH TAYLOR AND HER HUSBANDS would fill at least one volume alone without ever going into a preview of her fabled film career.

Her first husband, Nicky Hilton, always claimed, "I took the virginity of Elizabeth when I became her first husband."

But did he? In Darwin Porter's ***There Is Nothing Like a Dame,*** it's clear that Elizabeth had some sexual encounters when illegally young. Perhaps not a penetration, but some very heavy "petting."

After her divorce from the philandering Hilton hotel heir, she married the English actor Michael Wilding, who had a bisexual past, notably a long affair with actor Stewart Granger.

Her next husband was the doomed Mike Todd, a showman and producer who was once known as "The Third Mr. Joan Blondell."

His tragic death in an airplane crash (she was supposed to have been aboard that flight) sent her into a deep depression.

She was (emotionally) rescued by his best friend, Eddie Fisher, who was married at the time to Debbie Reynolds. Messily, he divorced her to marry Elizabeth, causing a nation-wide scandal, one of many that Elizabeth would create during the course of her tabloid-fueled career.

More scandal was on the way: Elizabeth as Cleopatra, the title role in the 1963 blockbuster with that name, met Burton, cast in that film as Marc Antony. Both of them were married (to other players) at the time. Nonetheless, they, "vibed," fell in love, and launched an affair that generated scandal-soaked headlines (they continued in one form or another for almost a decade), around the world. Eventually, after their respective divorces, they got married.

Burton and Taylor would go on to make a number of other movies together, including their most memorable, Edward Albee's *Who's Afraid of Virginia Woolf?* For that, Elizabeth won a Best Actress Oscar. Previously, she had been awarded the Oscar for *BUtterfield 8* in which she played a prostitute.

Other Burton/Taylor co-starring vehicles included *The V.I.P.s* in 1964, *The Sandpiper* in 1966, *The Taming of the Shrew* in 1967, and *Doctor Faustus* in 1968.

They also co-starred in *Boom!* In 1968. That drama had first appeared on Broadway as *The Milk Train Doesn't Stop Here Anymore,* starring Tallulah Bankhead with (of all actors) Tab Hunter.

In Key West, its author, playwright Tennessee Williams, admitted to Darwin Porter, "I am horrified at both the performance of Tallulah and Hunter in the play and equally horrified at Elizabeth and Richard tackling my drama. He was far too old for the part."

Regardless of the age she was at the time, "Diamond Liz" certainly captured the imagination of the world. As a child, she began to attract media attention when she starred in *National Velvet* (1944). Rung by rung, she climbed the Hollywood ladder to superstardom.

She married and divorced Burton twice. Later, she was seen as the submissive, unhappy, and overweight wife of Senator John Warner of Virginia. Finally, in an unfortunate union, she wed a truck driver, Larry Fortensky, a marriage that was doomed almost from the beginning.

"Chances are," said Danforth Prince, co-author of Blood Moon's biography of Elizabeth, "The world will never see the likes of Dame Taylor again. She, along with the legend of Cleopatra, will thrive in the world's imagination for decades to come."

EVERYBODY
(INCLUDING ELIZABETH TAYLOR)
HAD A POINT OF VIEW ABOUT ELIZABETH TAYLOR

"She is one of the most misunderstood and underestimated people of our time."

—**Truman Capote**

"Nobody on earth is better company than Elizabeth Taylor, more lively, more fun, and more of a three-ring circus. When I began seeing her, she was fifty-five and better than ever. The year was 1986. She had divorced Senator John Warner and shed all that weight that John Belushi lampooned on Saturday Night Live. For Elizabeth, looking great was the best revenge."

—**George Hamilton** in *Don't Mind If I Do*

"She was a femme fatale. I was an homme fatale. We made a fatal combination. She told me she wanted to marry me, but she was still a struggling actress at the time. I told her she couldn't afford me."

—**Porfirio Rubirosa** to Elsa Maxwell

"Let's face it: My life seems to lack dignity."

—**Elizabeth Taylor**

"Elizabeth was a committed wife—at least for the first week."

—**Lana Turner**

"Elizabeth's favorite pastime was celebrity gossip. Her definition of celebrity included royalty, world leaders, writers, artists, and musicians, and the occasional Greek billionaire. She needed gossip as fuel to shock at dinner parties. She had to know who was sleeping with whom, who was great in bed, and who was not, and who was well hung. The gay secretaries were especially good at collecting that necessary information, especially Richard Hanley, whose years at MGM had made him a sexpert on the entire film industry."

—**Vicky Tiel**, It's All About the Dress

"I lied about being a virgin on my wedding night. Actually, my first sexual experience was giving John Derek a blow-job when I'd just learned to walk, which is only a slight exaggeration. I was very, very young at the time, and he was a child molester."

—**Elizabeth Taylor** at a dinner party in Gstaad in 1968

"Elizabeth should have acquired more jewelry and fewer husbands. But who am I to cast 'stones,' dah-link?"

—**Zsa Zsa Gabor**

"That Krupp diamond is far too vulgar to wear in public."

—**Princess Margaret**

"After Elizabeth and I smelled each other out, we became two fast friends. Bitches in heat recognize each other."

—**Laurence Harvey**

"My troubles all started because I have a woman's body and a child's emotions."

—**Elizabeth Taylor**

"I was torn in my loyalties between two goddesses—Bessie May and Pussy."

—**Monty Clift**, using his nicknames for Elizabeth Taylor and Marilyn Monroe

"I called Elizabeth Taylor and told her that Monty Clift was being held a prisoner in his apartment in New York. He got involved with this dangerous hustler. He's bringing in guys who want to fuck Monty and charging them a hundred dollars a lay. You've got to come and rescue him."

—**Truman Capote** in Key West

"What is this, a memory test?"

—**Elizabeth Taylor**, responding to the justice of the peace at her wedding to Larry Fortensky when he asked her the names of her former husbands.

"You know, an actress can learn to hate Elizabeth Taylor."

—**Patricia Neal**

"I often fucked actors who liked to fuck each other—Peter Lawford, Monty Clift (well, I tried at least), Rock Hudson, James Dean, Paul Newman. Or, actors who other actors wanted to fuck—namely George Hamilton, Robert Wagner...do we have all night?"

—**Elizabeth Taylor**

"No raise. Now get out. You're such a whore."

—MGM's casting director **Benny Thau** to Elizabeth Taylor after denying her request for a pay raise

"Burt Lancaster raped me that night back in April of 1961 after we'd won our joint Oscars for BUtterfield 8 and Elmer Gantry. Well, it wasn't rape exactly, but a gal can pretend, can't she?"

—**Elizabeth Taylor** in 1975

"Elizabeth Taylor got to sample my noble tool when we made Reflections in a Golden Eye together. Burton found out and was seriously pissed off, probably because I didn't fuck the sod himself."

—**Marlon Brando** to Carlo Fiore

"Drugs have become a crutch. I wouldn't take them just when I was in pain. I needed oblivion, escape...I was hooked on Percodan and of course, I could drink everybody under the table. I had a hollow leg. My capacity to consume was terrifying. I didn't even realize I was an alcoholic."

—**Elizabeth Taylor**

"I guess in time all of us fucked her. I know Sammy did. So did Frank. So did Peter, a long time ago. Joey Bishop was the only one who didn't join the rat race."

—**Dean Martin** about Elizabeth Taylor

"What did you expect me to do—sleep alone?"

—**Elizabeth Taylor** to Hedda Hopper

"The trouble with Elizabeth Taylor is that she always envied my sex appeal. She just didn't have it, and I did."

—**Marilyn Monroe** to Clark Gable

"I have written a sequel to The Wizard of Oz about a 60-year-old Dorothy returning to Oz and I'm talking to Elizabeth Taylor about starring in it. She told me she wants to play the role, and she would be perfect for it."

—**Rod Steiger,** 1998

"Yes, it's true. On that infamous night I recited the Gettyburg Address at the Lincoln Memorial wearing nothing but a mink coat. Ask Halston. He was the designer who dressed me."

—**Elizabeth Taylor**

"In this Age of Vulgarity, marked by such minor matters as war and poverty, it gets harder every day to scale the heights of true vulgarity. But given some loose millions, it can be done—and, worse, admired."

—**The New York Times** on the Taylor/Burton roadshow

"I know I'm vulgar, but would you have me any other way?"

—**Elizabeth Taylor**

"Does it matter what Maureen Stapleton weighs? Why the hell does it matter what I weigh? It's nobody's damn business what I weigh, but talking about it seems to be a national pastime. And that pisses me off!"

—**Elizabeth Taylor**

"I visited her in London in the hospital when she had that trachotomy. She had what looked like a silver dollar in her throat. I couldn't figure out what held it in place, and it surprised me she wasn't bleeding or oozing. A few nights later, I went out with Eddie Fisher. The next afternoon, Elizabeth told me that Eddie thought I was trying to make a pass at him. At that moment, she played a trick on me and yanked at the plug in her throat, spurting out champagne—I'd brought her a magnum of Don Perignon—all over the hospital room. I thought I was going to pass out."

—**Truman Capote**

"After I married Mike Todd, he invited Eddie Fisher into our bedroom and pulled the sheet off me, exposing my nude body to Eddie. I think he really wanted a ménage à trois. There are those who say we had one."

—**Elizabeth Taylor**

"She had the face of an angel and the morals of a truck driver. We'd make love three, four, five times a day. We'd make love in the swimming pool, on Mexican beaches, under waterfalls, in the back seat of a limousine on the way home from a party. There was nothing more erotic than a moonlit beach and Elizabeth Taylor."

—**Eddie Fisher**

"Did I seduce Mike Todd's son and Peter Lawford's son? I wouldn't put it past me."

—**Elizabeth Taylor**

"I think Elizabeth is having an affair with Sammy Davis, Jr., but she dismisses the notion, joking that 'just over five foot tall' Sammy couldn't reach that high."

—**Richard Burton**

"Do you want to know some people I screwed that most people don't know about? Ardeshir Zahedi, the Iranian ambassador to the United States. Would you believe that Swedish boxer, Ingemar Johansson? Ronald Reagan, Errol Flynn, John and Bobby (guess who?), Prince Aly Khan."

—**Elizabeth Taylor,** overheard by the author in 1961, in a bar in Portofino

"If you leave me I shall have to kill myself. I love you. There is no life without you."

—**Richard Burton** during his second divorce proceedings from Elizabeth Taylor.

"I hung up the phone after Mike Todd told me he was in love with Elizabeth Taylor. I had been...taken. When I wasn't looking, I was delivered the knockout punch. I felt jilted. I should have seen it coming. He fell in love too fast. Like that phone call from Moscow to Marlene Dietrich when she was still big news. Like that circus act when he got Marilyn Monroe to ride the pink elephant at Madison Square Garden. And now Elizabeth Taylor beckoning with her little pinkie."

—**Evelyn Keyes** in her memoir, *Scarlett O'Hara's Little Sister*

"In May of 2000, I was critically ill with pneumonia and had a near death experience. I was on the other side, like in a tunnel, and I was with Mike Todd. I held onto him and he said, 'You have to go back now. You have things to do and I will be here.' I wanted to stay with Mike. He was my one true love."

—**Elizabeth Taylor**

"Elizabeth Taylor was the last of the great glamour stars. She was the longest running soap opera in history, and represented all the allure and tragedy that attracts people to Hollywood."

—British director **Michael Winner**

"I'm old and I'm tired and I've represented everyone from that cunt Bette Davis to Elizabeth Taylor and Richard Burton. Everyone wants to know my secrets. Okay, I'm dying and out of harm's way now, so I'll tell you a few —Burton said he liked to fuck Fisher's ass better than he did Elizabeth's. She screwed Ronald Reagan, John F. Kennedy, Bobby Kennedy. Tallulah Bankhead masturbated Elizabeth at the dinner table one night. Marilyn Monroe went down on her one night in Las Vegas. Elvis Presley fucked Elizabeth and wanted to do a movie with her. She had a three-way with Monty Clift and Marlon Brando. And I'm only just getting wound up."

—Talent Agent **Robert Lantz**

"I get pissed off with all the talk of the great love story of my husband Richard Burton and Elizabeth Taylor. Yes, they were in love, but they divorced twice. That means their marriages didn't work. I'm still very bitter about the torch Richard carried for that woman."

—Richard Burton's widow, **Sally Hay,** in 2011

"Richard Burton fucked me long before he did the honors with you."

—**Noël Coward** to Elizabeth Taylor on the set of *Boom!*

"I knew she would be devastated, shattered by the death of Burton, but I didn't expect her to become completely hysterical. I could not get her to stop crying. She was completely out of control. I realized how deeply tied she was to this man, how vital a role he played in her life. And I realized I could never have that special place in her heart she keeps for Burton. For me, the romance was over, and I told Elizabeth that."

—**Victor Luna**, Mexican Attorney

"We have been fighting and have been fighting for over a year now over anything and everything. I dread it at night when she has had her shots of drugs and is only semi-articulate. When she moans and groans in agony, I simply become bored. What is more frightening is she has become bored with everything in life. I have always been a heavy drinker, but now I'm drinking twice as much. The upshoot will be that I'll die of drink while she'll go on blithely in her half-world."

—**Richard Burton** in his diary, 1969

"Being with Elizabeth Taylor is like sticking an eggbeater in your brain. I loved her, and I think she loved me. But on the practical level, she was not the woman I needed in my life. With her, there was a great deal of maintenance. This is not a woman who gets up in the morning and fixes breakfast. By the time she comes downstairs for breakfast, it's time for dinner. Her life is built completely around Elizabeth, and she needs a man to service her life 24/7."

—**Robert Wagner**

"In our last chat, I told Elizabeth that getting old is really shit. She said, 'It certainly is. It certainly is, Debbie. This is really tough. I'm really trying to hang in there.'"

—**Debbie Reynolds** in 2011

"She told me that there had never been a time in her life when she wasn't famous."

—**Barbara Walters**

"We just stopped communicating. Why was every guy she befriended gay?"

—**Larry Fortensky**

"'Stay with me,' Elizabeth said. Curling up close, spoon fashion, I wrapped my arms around her and looked at the room I found myself in. A woman's bedroom. So inviting. So frightening."

—**Frank Langella**, in his memoirs

"I'm called a scarlet woman. That's wrong. I'm positively purple."

—**Elizabeth Taylor**

"I can't write an honest version of my own memoirs, because if I did, too many people would sue me."

—**Elizabeth Taylor**

"She was a great broad."

—**Whoopi Goldberg**, commenting on the death of Elizabeth Taylor

What did STEVE McQUEEN really have to do to make it in Show Biz? Finally--A COOL Biography that was too HOT to be published during the lifetime of its subject.

KING of COOL — TALES OF A LURID LIFE

This book is potentially dangerous for middle-aged men."

—The Sunday Times (London)

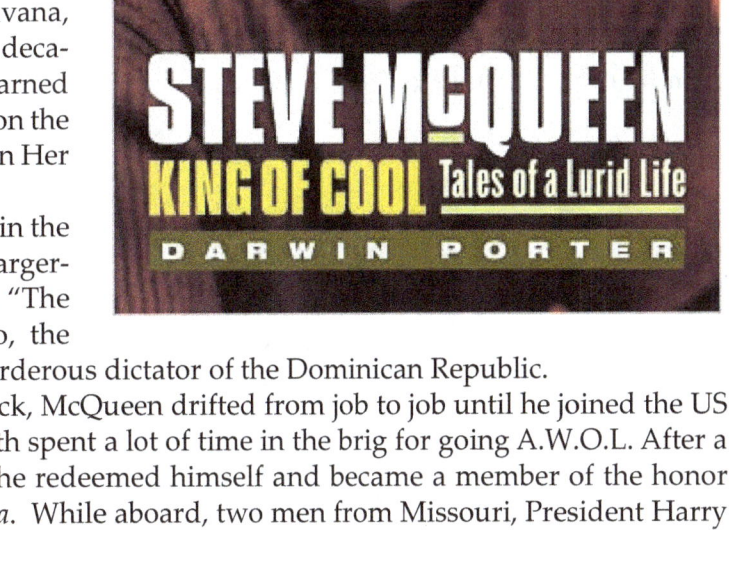

The drama of Steve McQueen's life far surpassed any that he portrayed on screen. Abandoned by his father (a stunt pilot), he followed in the footsteps of his beautiful mother, a prostitute, a sordid drama that led to an Oedipal fling.

As a young boy, he was brutally molested by one of his "stepfathers," who forced him into work as a child prostitute along Santa Monica Boulevard, a situation which led to his brutal gang rape.

As a teenager, he worked in bordellos in Havana, Santo Domingo, and Port Arthur, Texas. In Havana's decadent heyday, during the years before Castro, Steve earned a living through appearances on camera in porn, and on the sage in an erotic revue, his skit entitled, "The Cream in Her Coffee."

Long before he became the top box office star in the world, he was intimately involved with legendary, larger-than-life figures. They included Porfirio Rubirosa, "The Playboy of the Western World," and Flor de Oro, the nymphomaniacal daughter of Rafael Trujillo, the murderous dictator of the Dominican Republic.

After stints as a carnival barker and lumberjack, McQueen drifted from job to job until he joined the US Marine Corps. During his service, the rebellious youth spent a lot of time in the brig for going A.W.O.L. After a heroic maneuver in Arctic waters to save his crew, he redeemed himself and became a member of the honor guard aboard the U.S. presidential yacht, *USS Sequoia*. While aboard, two men from Missouri, President Harry S Truman and McQueen played serious poker.

Returning to New York after his tour of duty, McQueen hustled rich homosexuals in Greenwich Village, clients he secretly hated. In a tux borrowed from Rubirosa, he became a "Gentleman for Rent," the toy boy/escort of visiting Hollywood stars who included Lana Turner, Joan Crawford, and Marlene Dietrich.

After dozens of near misses, Hollywood stardom finally came. When it did, the abused became the abuser. "I live for myself," McQueen said, "and I answer to nobody. And the last thing I ever want is to fall in love with a broad." In spite of that pronouncement, he fell for a broad, the beautiful dancer/actress Neile Adams, who was on her way to stardom until her new husband systematically de-railed her career.

Marriage did not stop McQueen's string of seductions that earned him an almost mythical status as a pansexual Love Machine. He began a long-term affair with Frank Sinatra's former wife, sultry Ava Gardner, and one by one knocked off the leading ladies of his day, including Shelley Winters, Natalie Wood, Judy Garland, blonde bombshell Mamie Van Doren, and beautiful Tuesday Weld. Along the way, he found time for a tryst with Marilyn Monroe.

Publicly, he insisted that he loathed homosexuals, yet he sometimes went to bed with them, especially if they were bikers or race car drivers. He had a tumultuous sexual relationship with James Dean, and a longer love/hate affair with Paul Newman. Other sexual liaisons developed with Peter Lawford, Sal Mineo, Rock Hudson, Chuck Connors, and George Peppard.

Detailed for the first time is McQueen's involvement in a three-way relationship with the doomed hairdresser, Jay Sebring, and the beautiful Sharon Tate, wife of director Roman Polanski. Both Tate and Sebring would eventually be murdered by Charles Manson's sociopaths. McQueen himself was high on Manson's "death list," but he avoided mutilation on that fateful night in favor of a spontaneous encounter with a prostitute.

McQueen lived life at top speed, like the machines he raced so famously. His early death remains a source of lurid speculation, all of it explored within this pioneering biography by celebrity chronicler Darwin Porter.

With its publication, the result of years of research by the author who UNZIPPED Marlon Brando and Paul Newman, and who brought BABYLON BACK TO HOLLYWOOD, untold stories are exposed. Within its pages, "McQueen's Unreachable Star" comes back to earth.

McQUEEN: Screen hero, Rebel. Sexual Outlaw. Megastar. Loner. Male hustler. Street kid. Gigolo. Restless husband. Mysterious recluse. Brutal yet tender. Savage. And in the words of Jacqueline Bisset, "a beautiful, beautiful man."

WHAT STEVE McQUEEN THOUGHT OF HIMSELF AND WHAT OTHERS HAD TO SAY

"Steve lost his virginity to me when we were in reform school together. He fucked me and turned me gay for life. I was the youngest member of a gang that stole cars."
--Buster Lang

"I knew Steve McQueen in our early days. We were friends for a while. He shared a secret with me. His favorite form of having sex was with another man in bed with his girl. He watched as the guy went first and then it was Steve's turn. He preferred sloppy seconds, because he liked to enter a girl when she was still warm. He offered me a chance to share his bed with a dame, but I politely thanked him for the offer before turning it down."
--Paul Newman

"Steve liked to fuck blondes, but he married brunettes. I was wife No. One. He always came home after a night of sexual conquests. He boasted to me of his seductions."
--Neile Adams, dancer/actress

"I once interviewed McQueen on location. Amazingly, he agreed to pose frontally nude for me. I think he was a little bit drugged. Years later, I sent that eight-by-ten to Darwin Porter when we were working on a book about Laurence Olivier and Vivien Leigh. I don't know if he'll ever dare publish it."
--Author Roy Moseley

"I am a real man. I want my wife barefoot, pregnant, and in the kitchen while I play around."
--Steve McQueen

"The thing about my husband, Steve McQueen, is that he didn't like the women in his life to have balls,"
--Ali McGraw

"Steve probably set a world record for getting laid in flight in the toilet of an airplane."
--Elmer Valentine, a close friend

"She'll probably deny it, but I once fucked Barbra Streisand."
--Steve McQueen

"Steve always boasted that he had sex with all his female leading ladies. Like Ann-Margret, Jacqueline Bisset, Faye Dunaway, Barbara Leigh, and others. Frankly, I think he missed one or two."
--Neile Adams

"I was screwing Sharon Tate around the same time she was murdered by the Charles Manson gang. In fact, I was heading for that same party the night of the mass murders. On the way, I met this hot number and took her to bed, missing the party. You might say that pick-up saved my life. What a break for me."
--Steve McQueen

It's Blood Moon's *Babylon Series*

Outrageous overviews of exhibitionism, sexuality, and sin as filtered through 85 years of Hollywood indiscretion.

HERE'S VOLUME ONE OF THREE
HOLLYWOOD BABYLON IT'S BACK!

"From the Golden Age of beautiful bombshells and handsome hunks to today's sleaziest, most corrupt, and most deliciously indecorous hotties, this is the hottest compilation of inter-generational scandal in the history of Hollywood.

As they were unfolding, these stories were known only within Hollywood's most decadent cliques. But all of that changed with the release of this series.

Dishing with abandon, the authors spare no one—especially not the dead. Marilyn Monroe had an affair with Ronald Reagan. Marilyn also had a tryst with Joan Crawford but refused to make it an ongoing affair. James Dean showed a disconcerting interest in a 12-year-old boy in the early 1950s. Lucille Ball launched herself into show business as a hooker, and her husband Desi Arnaz had a fling with Cesar Romero. Cary Grant had an incestuous relationship with his stepson, Lance Reventlow. And this, by the way, is only the tip of the iceberg."

—**Rush & Molloy, The NY Daily News**

"The American movie industry is always eager for the spotlight if the close-up is flattering and good for business. But Hollywood may get more than it bargained for with **Hollywood Babylon's** compendium of stories, rumors, and myths. Virtually every page features one kind of train wreck or another, usually accompanied by spectacularly lurid photographs. Darwin Porter and Danforth Prince provide a hair-raising list of compromises and strategically granted sexual favors as proof that some stars will do anything for a part. Try as you might, you won't be able to stop turning the pages. In revealing so many facts previously under wraps, this book, in fact, raises the question of how much more remains hidden."

—**Shelf Awareness/ Bookselling News**

"These books will set the graves of Hollywood's cemeteries spinning"
—**Daily Express**

Hollywood Babylon-It's Back!
Darwin Porter and Danforth Prince

HERE'S THE PROFOUNDLY OUTRAGEOUS VOLUME TWO OF THREE-PART SERIES
HOLLYWOOD BABYLON STRIKES AGAIN!

"You know, everyone thinks Hollywood is a cesspool of epic proportions today, but please! It's always been that way. And if you love smutty celebrity dirt as much as I do (and if you don't, what's wrong with you? Ya got morals or something?), then have I got a book for you!"
—**The Hollywood Offender**

*"Despite Babylon's many explicit photos, the real meat (haha, you see what I did there?) of the book is the stories of old Hollywood that further prove that the whole place needs to be wiped out by an act of God. How crazy and depraved was Hollywood back then? Hold onto your f****** hat."*
—**from blogsite I Don't Like You in that Way (HOLLYWOOD IS INSANE)**

"This is the best classic scandal bible on Hollywood ever published. And believe me, I;'ve read hundreds...It's a must for anyone who's ever been to the movies or watched TV."
—**David Hartnell**

"The reader is truly spoiled for choice when selecting the high (or low) points in HBIB, but the standout chapters involve Lucille Ball (who was apparently aptly named in her pre-Desi days), Bette Davis (who may very well have caused the delayed death of her second husband by clobbering him with a lamp), Ava Gardner (who enjoyed hanging out with hookers—just to talk. Really), Cary Grant and heiress Barbara Hutton (and Barbara's son Lance and Cary...), and Nick Adams ('60s TV star whose suicide might have been arranged by the Memphis Mafia. I'm already contemplating what Porter and Prince could have planned for future volumes."
—**The Pride Edition of Seattle Gay News, June 20, 2008**

*"It's the more outragious accusations from this book that linger in the mind: That James Dean was having it off with a 12-year-old boy, Cary Grant was f****** his stepson. Nick Adams was murdered because he was writing a tell-all autobiography, Errol Flynn raped his son Sean, Marcello Mastroianni was regularly blown by Pope Paul VI. Lucille Ball was a hooker, and (sadly) Tony Randall was a self-loathing 'faggot.' This is one hell of a gossip bible."*
—**Barry Lowe in SX News** (Australia)

Winner of the Los Angeles Book Festival's Best Nonfiction Title of 2010,

and the New England Book Festival's Best Anthology for 2010.

HERE'S VOLUME THREE OF AN AWARD-WINNING THREE-PART SERIES

HOLLYWOOD BABYLON WITH DETOURS TO GOMORRAH

OUT OF THE CELLULOID CLOSET—HOMOSEXUALITY IN THE MOVIES

Hip, Funny, & Informative.

DID YOU KNOW? That before the worldwide breakout of Covid, Blood Moon launched what was envisioned as an ongoing series of guidebooks to gay & lesbian film, replete with special features, gossip about "When Divas Clash," insights into intra-industry *brouhahas*, AND the Blood Moon Awards.

Winner of the New England Book Festival's Best GLBT Title of 2010, and winner of coveted nominations from Foreword Magazine for its Book of the Year (Performing Arts), from the Benjamin Franklin Awards for "Best GLBT nonfiction title." It also won an Honorable Mention from the Hollywood Book Festival.

Volume One (published 2006)
ISBN 978-0-9748118-4-0

Volume Two (published 2007)
ISBN 978-0-9748118-7-1

The Collector's Edition
An indispensible sourcebook.
ISBN 978-0-9748118-9-5

WHAT THE CRITICS SAID

"Authoritative, exhaustive, and essential, it's the queer girl's and queer boy's one-stop resource for what to add to their feature-film queues. The film synopses and the snippets of critic's reviews are reason enough to keep this annual compendium of cinematic information close to the DVD player. But the extras--including the special features and the Blood Moon Awards--are butter on the popcorn."
—*Richard LaBonte, Books to Watch Out For*

"**Blood Moon's Guide to Gay and Lesbian Film** is like having access to a feverishly compiled queer film fan's private scrapbook. Each edition is a snapshot of where we are in Hollywood now. It's also a lot of fun..."
— *Gay Times (London)*

"Startling. It documents everything from the mainstream to the obscure, detailing dozens of queer films from the last few years."
—*HX (New York)*

"Includes everything fabu in the previous years' movies. An essential guide for both the casual viewer and the hard-core movie watching homo."
—*Bay Windows (Boston)*

"From feisty Blood Moon Productions, this big, lively guidebook of (mostly) recent gay and gayish films is not meant to be a dust-collecting reference book covering the history of GLBT films. Instead, it's an annual running commentary on what's new and what's going on in gay filmmaking."
—*Mandate*

MORE ABOUT
50 Years of Queer Cinema
500 of the Best GLBTQ Films Ever Made
(See Previous Page)

It's a comprehensive paperback designed as a reference source for private homes & libraries. 534 pages, with film reviews, gossip, special features, insider dish, and hundreds of photos. **ISBN 978-0-9748118-9-5**

AN INDISPENSIBLE REFERENCE SOURCE FOR FILMS ABOUT

The Love that Dare Not Speak Its Name

As late as 1958, homosexuality couldn't even be mentioned in a movie, as proven by the elaborate lengths the producers of Tennessee Williams' swampy Cat on a Hot Tin Roof took to evade the obvious fact that its hero, Paul Newman, was playing it gay. And in spite of the elaborate lengths its producers took to camouflage its lavender aspects, in-the-know viewers during the late 50s realized all along that Joe E. Brown was fully aware that Jack Lemmon wasn't a biological female ("nobody's perfect!") in Some Like it Hot (1959).

That kind of baroque subterfuge ended abruptly in 1960, when cinema emerged from its celluloid closet. With the release of Boys in the Band in 1970, gay cinema had come of age. It was queer and here to stay. Decades later came Brokeback Mountain, Transamerica, and Milk.

This comprehensive anthology documents it all, bringing into focus a sweeping rundown of cinema's most intriguing Gay, Lesbian, Bisexual, Transgendered, and "Queer Questioning" films that deserves a home next to the DVD player as well as on the reference shelves of public libraries. Crucial to the viability of this book is the fact that new DVD releases have made these films available to new generations of viewers for the first time since their original release.

More than just a dusty library reference, this book shamelessly spills 50 quasi-closeted years of Hollywood secrets—all of them in glorious technicolor.

"In the Internet age, where every movie, queer or otherwise, is blogged about somewhere, a hefty print compendium of film facts and pointed opinion might seem anachronistic. But flipping through well-reasoned pages of commentary is so satisfying. Add to 'that physical thrill the charm of analysis that is sometimes sassy and always smart, and this filtered survey of short reviews is a must for queer-film fans.

"In part one, Porter and Prince provide a succinct "A to Z romp" through 500 films, with quick plot summaries and on-point critical assessments, each film summed up with a pithy headline: *Yossi & Jagger* is "Macho Israeli Soldiers Make Love, Not War."

"The films surveyed in part two are quirkier fare, 160 "less publicized" effort , including—no lie—*Karl Rove, I Love You*, in which gay actor Dan Butler falls for 'George W. Bush's Turd Blossom."

"Essays on **Derek Jarman, Tennessee Williams, Andy Warhol, Jack Wrangler, Joe Gage** and others—and on how *The Front Runner* never got made—round out this indispensable survey of gay-interest cinema."

—RICHARD LABONTE, BOOK MARKS/QSYNDICATE

Corruption, Mendacity, & Punitive Hanky Panky from within the FBI

J. Edgar Hoover & Clyde Tolson

Investigating the Sexual Secrets of America's Most Famous Men and Women

Darwin Porter

Criminal Activities and Voyeuristic Mania from America's Chief Law-Enforcement Officer

It was 1928. Into FBI Director **J. Edgar Hoover**'s Office walked a job applicant. **Clyde Tolson**, fresh from America's Corn Belt. He was handsome, macho, well-built, and soft-spoken. Later, he'd be called "the Gary Cooper of the FBI."

Hoover sat up and took immediate notice of Tolson's commanding presence, especially his piercing black eyes. After an hour of chatting with Tolson, Hoover proclaimed, "Our bureau needs more men like you."

When Hoover invited Tolson to his home for dinner that night, the meal would mark the beginning of thousands served over the next forty years. Before the rooster crowed, Hoover had been nicknamed "Speed," and Tolson was called "Junior." In public, of course, Tolson referred to Hoover as "The Boss."

But as Tolson, one drunken night, told their "fag hag," **Ethel Merman**: "When we go home and shut the door, I'm the boss."

For their sexual amusement, but often for blackmail purposes, Junior and Speed became intimately familiar with the obscene files of the FBI. Illegal wiretaps and hidden microphones were used to destroy their enemies.

"Hoover ruled as the head of America's Gestapo," claimed an angry **Harry S Truman**. Through nine different presidents, Hoover kept his job, even blackmailing **Dwight D. Eisenhower**.

The files he accumulated on "my worst enemy," **Eleanor Roosevelt**, silenced her opposition to him. As time went by, Hoover and Tolson opened a celebrity version of Pandora's box, learning the darkest secrets of **Errol Flynn** (was he a Nazi?), **Marilyn Monroe, Elvis Presley**, the **Kennedys, Marlon Brando, Rock Hudson**, and especially **Martin Luther King, Jr.**, among countless others.

"For decades, America has been in the grip of two homosexual lovers," **Lyndon B. Johnson** told his pal, **Florida Senator George Smathers**. "And there's not a God damn thing I can do about it. He's got us by the *cojones*, and he'll never let go."

For nearly half a century, this peculiarly private man, who carefully guarded his own dark secrets, held virtually unchecked public power. He manipulated every president from **FDR** (*"Sometime, J. Edgar, we'll catch you with your pants down"*) to **Richard Nixon**. He used illegal wiretaps and hidden microphones to destroy anyone who opposed him. And just for fun, he and bedmate Clyde Tolson investigated America's greatest entertainers, including **Marilyn Monroe** and **Elvis Presley**; its greatest scientists (including **Albert Einstein**), and its greated civil rights leaders.

Darwin Porter's saga of power and corruption has a revelation on every page—cross dressing, gay parties, sexual indiscretions, hustlers for sale, alliances with the Mafia, and criminal activity by the nation's chief law enforcer.

It's all here, with chilling details about the abuse of power on the dark side of the American saga.
But mostly it's the decades-long love story of America's two most powerful men who could tell presidents "how to skip rope." (Hoover's words.)

Darwin Porter has been fascinated by J. Edgar Hoover, the Justice Department, and the American concept of fame since he worked as an entertainment columnist for **The Miami Herald**. *Since then, he's evolved into one of the most acclaimed celebrity biographers in the world.*

LANA TURNER

The Sweater Girl, Celluloid Venus, Sex Nymph to the G.I.s who won World War II, and Hollywood's OTHER Most Notorious Blonde

Beautiful and Bad,
Her Full Story Has Never Been Told. UNTIL NOW!

Lana Turner was the most scandalous, most copied, and most gossiped-about actress in Hollywood. When her abusive Mafia lover was murdered in her house, every newspaper in the Free World described the murky dramas with something approaching hysteria.

Blood Moon's salacious but empathetic new biography exposes the public and private dramas of the girl who changed the American definition of what it REALLY means to be a blonde.

Here's how CALIFORNIA BOOKWATCH and THE MIDWEST BOOK REVIEW described the mega-celebrity as revealed in this book:

"Lana Turner: Hearts and Diamonds Take All belongs on the shelves of any collection strong in movie star biographies in general and Hollywood evolution in particular, and represents no lightweight production, appearing on the 20th anniversary of Lana Turner's death to provide a weighty survey packed with new information about her life.

"One would think that just about everything to be known about The Sweater Girl would have already appeared in print, but it should be noted that Lana Turner: Hearts and Diamonds Take All offers many new revelations not just about Turner, but about the movie industry in the aftermath of World War II.

"From Lana's introduction of a new brand of covert sexuality in women's movies to her scandalous romances among the stars, her extreme promiscuity, her search for love, and her notorious flings - even her involvement in murder - are all probed in a revealing account of glamour and movie industry relationships that bring Turner and her times to life.

"Some of the greatest scandals in Hollywood history are intricately detailed on these pages, making this much more than another survey of her life and times, and a 'must have' pick for any collection strong in Hollywood history in general, gossip and scandals and the real stories behind them, and Lana Turner's tumultuous career, in particular."

LANA TURNER, Hearts & Diamonds Take All
Winner of the coveted "Best Biography" Award from the San Francisco Book Festival

Darwin Porter and Danforth Prince

Carrie Fisher & Debbie Reynolds
Princess Leia & Unsinkable Tammy in Hell

It's history's first comprehensive, unauthorized overview of one of the greatest mother-daughter acts in showbiz history, Debbie Reynolds ("hard as nails and with more balls than any five guys I've ever known") and her talented, often traumatized daughter, Carrie Fisher ("one of the smartest, hippest chicks in Hollywood"). Evolving for decades under the unrelenting glare of public scrutiny, each became a world-class symbol of the social and cinematic tastes that prevailed during their heydays as celebrity icons in Hollywood.

It's a scandalous saga of the ferociously loyal relationship of the "boop-boop-a-doop" girl with her intergalactic STAR WARS daughter, and their iron-willed, "true grit" battles to out-race changing tastes in Hollywood.

Loaded with revelations about "who was doing what to whom" during the final gasps of Golden Age Hollywood, it's an All-American story about the price of glamour, career-related pain, family anguish, romantic betrayals, lingering guilt, and the volcanic shifts that affected a scrappy, mother-daughter team—and everyone else who ever loved the movies.

"Feeling misunderstood by the younger (female) members of your gene pool? This is the Hollywood exposé every grandmother should give to her granddaughter, a roadmap like Debbie Reynolds might have offered to Billie Lourd."

—Marnie O'Toole

"Hold onto your hats, the "bad boys" of Blood Moon Productions are back. This time, they have an exhaustively researched and highly readable account of the greatest mother-daughter act in the history of show business: Debbie Reynolds and Carrie (Princess Leia) Fisher. If celebrity gossip and inside dirt is your secret desire, check it out. This is a fabulous book that we heartily recommend. It will not disappoint. We rate it worthy of four stars."

—MAJ Glenn MacDonald, U.S. Army Reserve (Retired), © MilitaryCorruption.com

"How is a 1950s-era movie star, (TAMMY) supposed to cope with her postmodern, substance-abusing daughter (PRINCESS LEIA), the rebellious, high-octane byproduct of Rock 'n Roll, Free Love, and postwar Hollywood's most scandal-soaked marriage? Read about it here, in Blood Moon's unauthorized double exposé about how Hollywood's toughest (and savviest) mother-daughter team maneuvered their way through shifting definitions of fame, reconciliation, and fortune."

—Donna McSorley

Winner of the coveted "Best Biography" Award from the 2018
New York Book Festival

Carrie Fisher & Debbie Reynolds,
Unsinkable Tammy & Princess Leia in Hell

Darwin Porter & Danforth Prince

THIS IS WHAT HAPPENS WHEN A DEMENTED BILLIONAIRE LANDS IN HOLLYWOOD

This biography reveals inside details about his destructive and usually scandalous associations with other Hollywood players.

HOWARD HUGHES, HELL'S ANGEL

Darwin Porter

Thanks in part to THE AVIATOR, the world already knows about Howard Hughes's filming of *Hell's Angels*, his links to blonde goddess Jean Harlow, his trans-global flight, his obsessive tinkering with *The Outlaw*, the bra he designed for Jane Russell, and the Senate investigations associated with his Spruce Goose. Many readers know about his long hair and fingernails, his drug addictions, his obsessive-compulsive disorders, and his role as America's first billionaire.

This, however, is a journey into the private and shadowy world of Howard Hughes, revealing for the first time the inside details about destructive and usually scandalous associations with other Hollywood players.

It's an astonishing tale of outrageous fortune, unbounded ambition, and tragic greed, the signs of which were already visible during Hughes's years as a teenager. It's the story of a man whom most of America celebrated, at least briefly, as a genuine hero and a man whom many of his former associates loved to vilify.

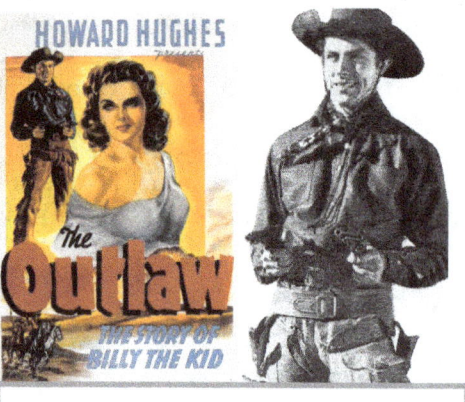

Contrary to popular Hollywood legend, producer Howard Hughes did not seduce **Jane Russell** during the making of the controversial *The Outlaw*. Instead, he ordered **Jack Beutel**, cast as Billy the Kid, to join him in bed.

Howard Hughes lavished gifts and introduced a **young Robert Taylor**, *depicted above*, to a life of flying high in airplanes, sailing yachts, and "being devoured" in bed.

Billie Dove *(photo, left)* the grandest silent screen diva of her era, became his lover...until she gave him syphilis

Winner of a respected literary award from the Los Angeles Book Festival, this is an astonishing tale of outrageous fortune, unbouonded ambition, and tragic greed.

Hughes led a life of almost unprecedented debauchery, at least for his era. This biography documents that corruption and the A-list legends who collaborated. Hughes's sexual and emotional odyssey is described frankly and even graphically, without apologies to the faint of heart. Throughout the unimaginable changes that affected America between Hughes's birth in 1905 and the sinister circumstances of his death in 1976, this biography gives an insider's perspective about what money can buy—and what it can't.

Hughes emerges as the 20th century's greatest Lothario, with origins that included a devouring and incestuous mother, an indulgent but absent father, and seductions of the greatest all-star cast of lovers—male and female—ever assembled into a single lifetime.

Hughes feverishly seduced some of the world's greatest women, but in this epic biography, he is also dragged kicking and screaming out of the closet. As his pimp, Johnny Meyer, once said, "Bossman was an equal opportunity seducer. The gender of his victim didn't matter. He had just one requirement: Beauty."

Howard was involved, sometimes pivotally, in Hollywood murders whose victims included Paul Bern (Jean Harlow's tragic husband), Thelma Todd ("Hot Toddy") and David Bacon, publicized as "the handsomest man in Hollywood." There were peripheral involvements with the mysterious deaths of as many as four or five lesser luminaries too.

Thanks in part to these revelations, the canon of Hollywood legend will never be the same. The author's rundown on the relationship of Hughes with Cary Grant, Tyrone Power, Ava Gardner, Bette Davis, and Katharine Hepburn challenges virtually everything that has ever been filmed or written about those famous figures.

This is an intimate, carefully authenticated account of a great but bizarre American life, often drawn from courtiers who factored in some way into Hughes's empire. From his reckless pursuit of love as a rich teenager to his final days as a demented and decaying fossil, he tasted the best and worst of the century he occupied. Along the way, he changed the world of aviation and entertainment forever.

Darwin Porter's biography is a tribute to a flawed but majestic American icon. As one critic said, "If Howard Hughes did not exist, no one would dare invent him. His life would defy a novelist."

Set amid descriptions of the unimaginable changes that affected America between Hughes's birth in 1905 and his death in 1976, this book gives an insider's perspective about what money can buy--and what it can't.

"The Aviator flew both ways. Porter's biography presents new allegations about Hughes' shady dealings with some of the biggest names of the 20th century"
—*New York Daily News*

"Darwin Porter's access to film industry insiders and other Hughes confidants supplied him with the resources he needed to create a portrait of Hughes that both corroborates what other Hughes biographies have divulged, and go them one better." —*Foreword Magazine*

"Thanks to this bio of Howard Hughes, we'll never be able to look at the old pinups in quite the same way again."
—*The Times* **(London)**

Blood Moon has been cited as "dauntingly prolific," with a knack for multiple children.

So with that in mind, let's talk about Twins, Triplets, and (GASP) Quintets.

We've already released many of them, and yes, they're still in print. Others (including two associated with Clark Gable and two associated with Gary Cooper are on their way.

Expect a lot from in years to come from Blood Moon Productions.. It will be worth the wait.

    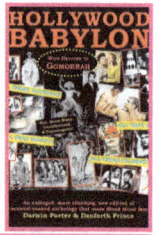   

LUCY X2
(I.E., THE RICARDOS, INCLUDING DESI

A JUICY TRIPTYCH OF BABYLONS

TRIPLE-PLAY GUIDES TO LGBTQ FILMS

  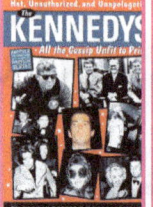    

OUR DOUBLE DOSE OF DONALD MEANS DOUBLE THE FUN!

GOMORRAH ON THE POTOMAC
(A ROLLICKING PRESIDENTIAL QUINTET)

THE FONDAS:
TRIPLE EXPOSURE IN TWO VOLUMES

THE FACE OF BLOODY AND BEAUTIFUL THINGS TO COME
ALREADY WRITTEN, WITH EDITORIAL COMPLETION BEGINNING IN SIX MONTHS AND EXTENDING OVER INTO A PERIOD OF TWO YEARS,

 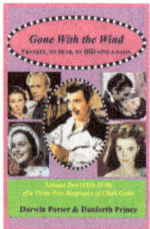    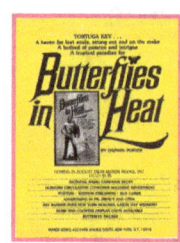 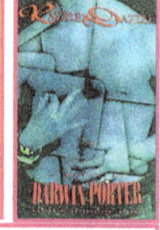

A THREE-VOLUME CELEBRATION
OF CLARK GABLE

A DOUBLE-WHAMMIED
EDITORIAL ROLL IN THE HAY WITH
"HIGH NOON IN HELL" GARY COOPER

AND LEST WE FORGET,
FROM LONG AGO
AND FAR AWAY:
BUTTERFLIES IN HEAT,
A CULT CLASSIC, WITH
ITS SOUTH FLORIDA SEQUEL,
RAZZLE-DAZZLE.

THE KENNEDYS

ALL THE GOSSIP UNFIT TO PRINT

A Staggering Compendium of Indiscretions Associated With Seven Key Players in the Kennedy Clan; A Cornucopia of Relatively Unknown but Carefully Documented Scandals from the Golden Age of Camelot. Jaw-dropping, a myth-shattering overview of a family consumed by its own passions.

Darwin Porter & Danforth Prince

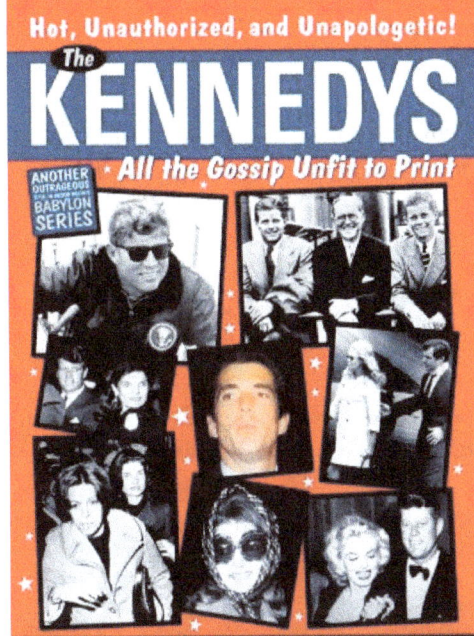

"The great enemy of truth is very often not the deliberate, contrived, and dishonest, but the myth--persistent, persuasive, and unrealistic."
--President John F. Kennedy

THE PUBLIC HAS CONSISTENTLY VOTED JFK as America's most popular president. This Prince Charming and his fairytale princess, Jacqueline, presided over the mythical kingdom of Camelot.

But did they really dwell there? Didn't they actually inhabit a house of tragedy and doom that shimmered with more glamour than that of any other First Family in White House history?

In observance of the 50th anniversary of JFK's ascension to power in 1961, Blood Moon celebrates its gossipy involvement in sixty years of Kennedy-watching by raking over every rock, compiling an overview of the clan's staggering compendium of indiscretions, some of them percolating since the 1920s. Within these pages is the ultimate lowdown about what was really going on during the ascendency, reign, and decline of this horny tribe.

The Kennedys lived by their own code--Tomorrow Will Never Come. Until the aftermath of their tragic ends, there was never a secret that charm, a bribe, and a threat couldn't conceal. Information that was once closely guarded has been revealed by deathbed confessions. Also, the release of heretofore suppressed FBI documents have put new spins on those tired, oft-repeated myths.

*****

Charismatic and dazzling, JFK became the first "political movie star," the master image maker of his generation. His second marriage (her first) to the beautiful débutante, Jacqueline Lee Bouvier, made her, at least for a few shining moments, the most famous woman of her time, the most pursued and written about, the most photographed.

During his administration, JFK held the world's fate in his hands, supervising tensions that came breathtakingly close to nuclear holocaust. Fighting a self-destructive streak, chronic illness, and personal demons, he at least appeared triumphant, his facade supported with a sometimes horrified collaboration from both the media and the Secret Service. Until the very end, he won public adulation and votes, thanks to a promise of a better future until an assassin (or assassins) swept him from the Promised Land.

The power behind the throne--brash, ambitious, and ruthless--Joseph P. Kennedy ("Papa Joe") schemed and maneuvered to establish a political dynasty. He launched a Golden Age for the Kennedys that ran off a bridge on a moonless, alcohol-sodden night on Martha's Vineyard. What really happened? The public never knew the whole story--until now. During the inquest and the eventfully promiscuous years that followed, Teddy became a media star in his own right.

Bobby: Attorney General and hero to millions. Was he a good man who saw wrong and tried to right it, or a manipulative bully who lusted equally after both his sister-in-law and Marilyn Monroe, and who colluded unsuccessfully with the Mafia?

John-John: Despite their bitter differences, Jack and Jackie spawned an American Adonis, John F. Kennedy Jr., People Magazine's "Sexiest Man Alive." Had he not defied multiple warnings aboard that small aircraft that fateful stormy night, he might have sought and won the American presidency in 2008.

After JFK's death, Jackie transferred her sexual lust to Bobby and then on to Teddy, despite her marriage at the time to "that shipping tycoon." Aristotle Onassis was not only a womanizer like JFK, but a cross dresser and a (very rich) closeted homosexual. As for Marilyn Monroe, she didn't just seduce JFK she maintained affairs with Papa Joe, Bobby, and Teddy as well. These are just some of the lurid details revealed in the pages within.

Here in all its glitter and gore is the inside story of the Kennedys, revelation by revelation—the hushed-up feuds, the hidden scandals, the love affairs, the awesome power they wielded and sometimes abused, the inevitable heartbreaks. Throughout these pages emerges an understanding of the cruel price demanded by power and fame.

As literary critic John McFarland said about Blood Moon's The Kennedys: "Amazing. jaw-dropping, and mightily delicious. A feast for all Kennedy gawkers in a myth-shattering *exposé* of a family consumed by its own passions."

THE KENNEDYS ALWAYS ELICITED CONTROVERSY.

HERE'S HOW THEY WERE REVIEWED BY SOME OF THEIR CONTEMPORARIES:

"JFK was a lout, a cad, a boor, an oaf, a schemer, a liar, a blackmailer, and a reckless gambler with the nation's security, its integrity and its institutions. Kennedy was a man thoroughly out of control, thoroughly out of his depth, and maybe thoroughly out of his mind. Kennedy wasn't just a hoodlum Prince of Camelot, he was the incarnation of Sodom and Gomorrah."

Seymour Hersh, *The Dark Side of Camelot*

"During the Thousand Days, Kennedy arrogantly and irresponsibly violated his covenant with the people. While saying and doing appropriate things in the public light, he acted covertly in ways that seriously demeaned himself and his office. With the appointment of his brother as attorney general, he tried to found a political dynasty, abhorred by the founding fathers. The metaphor of Camelot, after all, is ultimately un-American and undemocratic, conjuring up images of crowns and dashing young princes and noble birth."

Professor Thomas Reeves

"Kennedy did not have incisiveness and he was out of his depth where he was. I hate to say this because I know it's going to be misunderstood, but his reputation is greater because of the tragedy of his death than it would have been if he had lived out two terms. He did not seem to me to be in any sense a great man."

Dean Acheson, former Secretary of State

"Jack told me he wasn't through with a girl till he'd have her three ways."

Traphes Bryant, Veteran White House staff member

"I found the president very penetrating."

Marilyn Monroe

"He never said a word of importance in the Senate and never did a thing."

Lyndon B. Johnson

"Why should I go back? What good would it do?"

John F. Kennedy on the stillbirth of his child in 1956 when he was sailing the Mediterranean with a boatload of females.

"My good buddy, John (Kennedy) was married to socialite Durie Malcolm. I knew her too. Old Joe had the marriage records in Palm Beach destroyed."

Senator George Smathers

"Joe Kennedy was one of the biggest crooks who ever lived."

Mob boss Sam Giancana

"Listen, honey, if it wasn't for me, your boyfriend wouldn't even be in the White House."

Sam Giancana to Judith Campbell Exner

"Maybe Marilyn, had she lived, her back stooped from osteoporosis, munching carrot sticks and sipping Dom Perignon, would sink into her sofa one autumn evening, slide in one of those tapes made-for TV movies and smile at just how wrong the filmmakers had gotten it all. Still, she might have mused, it made a lovely story."

David Marshall

"I never had Addison's disease."

John F. Kennedy

"That's a lie—he looked like a spavined hunchback."

Lyndon B. Johnson

"The dog will keep biting you if you only cut off its tail. You must cut off the dog's head."

Carlos Marcello, mob chief of New Orleans who controlled Texas, vowing revenge when JFK had him deported and dropped in a Guatemala jungle.

"A vulgar slut, a publicity seeker, an egomaniac, a self-promoter, a vicious bitch, an unbalanced drug addict, an alcoholic whore, a dime-a-dance floozie."

Jacqueline Kennedy on Marilyn Monroe

"Bobby Kennedy was human. He liked to drink and he liked young women. He indulged that liking when he traveled—and he had to travel a great deal."

Historian Arthur Schlesinger

"Sex to Jack Kennedy was like another cup of coffee, or maybe dessert. For this Kennedy, evidently, sex was not to be confused with love."

Journalist Nancy Dickerson

"The Kennedy story is about people who broke the rules, and were ultimately broken by them."

Christopher Lawford

"God, I hate Camelot. I've begged Jackie to tell them to play something else, but it's like talking to a goddamn brick wall."

John F. Kennedy, on the Marine String Orchestra playing at the White House.

"The point is, you've got to live every day like it's your last day on Earth. That's what I'm doing."

John F. Kennedy

"I don't think there are any men who are faithful to their wives. Men are such a combination of good and bad."

Jacqueline Kennedy Onassis

"Joe Kennedy represented the height of vulgarity. He was horny—that's all he was."

Columnist Doris Lilly

"JFK was one of the great cunt men of all time—except for me."

Jerry Lewis

"Jack always had his mind between his legs."

Lady May Lawford

"Kennedy was the frequent recipient of nonreciprocal fellatio from longtime close friend LeMoyne Billings."

Mart Martin

"Is it not possible to be an effective president of the United States without necessarily being personally virtuous?"

Alice Leavenbrook

"John F. Kennedy was the most overrated public figure in American history."

American Heritage

"According to our poll, John F. Kennedy was the most popular president in U.S. history—75% rate him good to great, 30% wish he were still president."

Newsweek

"Lifting us beyond our capacities, he gave the country back to its best self, wiping away the world's impression of an old nation of old men, weary, played out, fearful of the future; he taught mankind that the process of rediscovering America was not over. He transformed the American spirit."

Arthur Schlesinger Jr.

"I'm afraid he's going to grow up to be a fruit."

Jacqueline Kennedy, discussing JFK Jr.

"We want winners. We don't want losers around here."

Joseph P. Kennedy Sr., to his sons

"I don't think Jack Kennedy was a ladies' man. He always felt they were a useful thing to have when you wanted them, but when you didn't want them, put them back."

Charles Houghton, JFK's roommate at Harvard

"Well, JFK Jr. is kinda naïve, like a young boy."

Madonna

"In the brief time Jack had, he touched our hearts with fire, and the glow from that fire still lights the world."

Senator Ted Kennedy

"Granny-O, they called her in the later years. She had become the dowager First Lady, the last American Queen, editing books, escorting the Clintons on a cruise. People had long since stopped gossiping about whether she knew of Jack's infidelities, if Warren Beatty had once been a beau. It didn't matter. She was a survivor. It was almost impossible to separate her from the myth of Camelot. After all, she actually invented it. In the end, she liberated herself from the Kennedys and became the last real Kennedy--glamorous, desirable, mythic."

Reggie Nadelson, describing Jacqueline Kennedy Onassis

"If there's anything I'd hate in a son-in-law, it's an actor. And if there's anything I think I'd hate more than an actor as a son-in-law, it's an English actor."

Joseph P. Kennedy to his daughter, Patricia, about her upcoming marriage to Peter Lawford

"The old man [Joseph P. Kennedy] had an eye out for every woman that walked. In the Kennedys' sense of morality, that was all right."

Fashion designer Oleg Cassini

"Women keep calling to invite me to dinner, and I keep turning them down."

John F. Kennedy Jr.

"The greatest twenty seconds of my life."

Angie Dickinson, describing JFK

"Jack lost his virginity when he was seventeen years old in a Harlem whorehouse to a black prostitute."

LeMoyne Billings, JFK's homosexual friend

"Jackie related to men by flirting with them. She loved to have male admirers around her, including FDR Jr. She used to tease Franklin. She was horrid. She was so dreamy that he'd be floating on air. I didn't realize it myself at the time, but that was simply Jackie's style with men."

Suzanne Roosevelt

"When John F. Kennedy Jr. was named by People Magazine as The Sexiest Man Alive, he was subjected to merciless ribbing from his friends, which he endured graciously. Eager to poke fun at himself, John went to one Halloween party as 'The Golden Boy' clad only in a loincloth and gold glitter. He attended another bash as Michelangelo's David, wearing something akin to a fig leaf."

Author Christopher Andersen

"Peter Lawford was not a model father. With his children he was, I always felt, essentially ill at ease. He considered them more Kennedy than Lawford—or at any rate they had been, in his opinion, 'brainwashed' to be. He worried about what other Kennedy family members told them about him. He was humiliated to the point of hysteria by the rumors and writings and mouthing that he had 'pimped' for Jack and Bobby Kennedy with Marilyn Monroe and that he had been instrumental in helping to speed her death. He felt it all made him look like a 'court fool' he said to me."

Author Lawrence J. Quirk

"If all the stories about JFK's women are to be believed, as president he turned the White House into a Deer Park, like the Sun King at Versailles. He was like Nietzsche's rope-dancer. In the end, the danger line became a death line. Like Jack, Ted was drawn to danger but more in his private than his public life. He had Jack's attitude toward women: To triumph as often as possible, but to keep from yielding his heart and commitment. They both had difficulty in relating with any emotional depth to a woman, or seeing her as other than a sex object and a field for conquest."

Max Lerner

"Ari [Aristotle Onassis] told me that Teddy Kennedy was just like his brother Jack. He wanted me to organize a party to welcome him to Greece. I was instructed to round up some good-looking broads."

Johnny Meyer, pimp to Onassis

"Ari [Aristotle Onassis] was able to keep his growing intimacy with Jackie a secret for a very long time. Rumors that she'd taken up with Bobby after Jack's death were believable...and even understandable. But the American public just could not believe that she'd tumble for a beast like Ari. It was truly the mating of The Beauty and The Beast."

JFK aide David Powers

"People keep telling me I can be a great man. I'd rather be a good one."

John F. Kennedy, Jr.

"Marilyn would tell me breathlessly about Jack, though she never mentioned Bobby. Most of the stories involved how sexually obsessed Jack was with her, how many times and where they made love, from the suites at the Plaza in New York to broom closets at the Sands. I knew how horny Jack was, so nothing she said surprised me, except her belief in his promises that he would leave Jackie and that she would be his First Lady for his second term. That guy would say anything to score."

George Jacobs, valet to Frank Sinatra

LOVE TRIANGLE
Ronald Reagan, Jane Wyman, & Nancy Davis

HOW MUCH DO YOU REALLY KNOW ABOUT THE REAGANS?

THIS BOOK TELLS EVERYTHING ABOUT THE SHOW-BIZ SCANDALS THEY DESPERATELY WANTED TO FORGET.

Unique in the history of publishing, this scandalous TRIPLE BIOGRAPHY focuses on the Hollywood indiscretions of former U.S. president Ronald Reagan and his two wives. A proud and Presidential addition to Blood Moon's Babylon series, it digs deep into what these three young and attractive movie stars were doing decades before two of them took over the Free World.

As reviewed by Diane Donovan, Senior Reviewer at the California Bookwatch section of the Midwest Book Review: "Love Triangle: Ronald Reagan, Jane Wyman & Nancy Davis may find its way onto many a Republican Reagan fan's reading shelf; but those who expect another Reagan celebration will be surprised: this is lurid Hollywood exposé writing at its best, and outlines the truths surrounding one of the most provocative industry scandals in the world.

"There are already so many biographies of the Reagans on the market that one might expect similar mile-markers from this: be prepared for shock and awe; because Love Triangle doesn't take your ordinary approach to biography and describes a love triangle that eventually bumped a major Hollywood movie star from the possibility of being First Lady and replaced her with a lesser-known Grade B actress (Nancy Davis).

"From politics and betrayal to romance, infidelity, and sordid affairs, Love Triangle is a steamy, eye-opening story that blows the lid off of the Reagan illusion to raise eyebrows on both sides of the big screen.

"Black and white photos liberally pepper an account of the careers of all three and the lasting shock of their stormy relationships in a delightful pursuit especially recommended for any who relish Hollywood gossip."

In 2015, LOVE TRIANGLE, Blood Moon Productions' overview of the early dramas associated with Ronald Reagan's scandal-soaked career in Hollywood, was designated by the Awards Committee of the HOLLYWOOD BOOK FESTIVAL as Runner-Up to Best Biography of the Year.

LOVE TRIANGLE:
Ronald Reagan, Jane Wyman, & Nancy Davis

Darwin Porter & Danforth Prince

> RONALD REAGAN WAS THE FIRST U.S. PRESIDENT TO TRIUMPH OVER WHAT HAD BEEN CONSIDERED, PRIOR TO HIS ELECTION, AN INSURMOUNTABLE STIGMA: HE WAS A DIVORCÉ WHO HAD BEEN MARRIED TWICE.
>
> THIS IS THE STORY OF THE LOVE TRIANGLE WHOSE COMBATANTS ARE FEATURED BELOW.
>
> ## HERE'S WHAT HOLLYWOOD AND D.C. INSIDERS SAID ABOUT THE REAGANS:

"He's about as good in bed as he is on the screen." —Jane Wyman

"During every picture, I developed Leading-Lady-Itis." —Ronald Reagan

"This would never have happened if Hollywood had given him better parts." —Lauren Bacall, on the eve of President Reagan's Inauguration

"Clark Gable turned her down. So Nancy had to settle for Reagan." —Adolphe Menjou

"Jane Wyman fell for Rock Hudson, then learned he was gay." —Peter Lawford

"Nancy Davis was one of those girls whose phone number was handed around a lot." —Anne Edwards

***

"*Love Triangle* is that rare animal: A book that appeals both to the devotees and the detractors of Ronald Reagan. There's not a page in this large, monumentally researched work that doesn't contain a gold nugget of insider Hollywood revelation, some of which might shock the faint of heart."

"All the dish is here on star Jane Wyman and starlet Nancy Reagan, too, those naughty ladies from the good (bad) days of Golden Age Tinseltown. Back then, secrets were to be covered up, not exposed as they are so blatantly today when personal communications, not meant for public viewing, lead off the night news, thanks to some hacker."

—Florence Gavin, *Dirty Laundry*

SCENES FROM THE LIFE OF AN AMERICAN PRESIDENT

"Back in Dixon, Illinois, a rich older woman wanted me to be her kept boy. But I had other plans. I headed for Hollywood."

"Talk about getting your ass beat. When I returned to my *alma mater*, Eureka College, in 1947, my TKE frat brothers left me with red buns."

"If there's one thing I liked to do, it was playing Cowboys and Indians."

"Here, I'm ready to scalp a few, although Barbara Stanwyck (*right*, his co-star in *Cattle Queen of Montana; 1954*) preferred to shoot them down off their horses."

"*(Above)* In 1955, John Payne and I made *Tennessee's Partner*. People in Hollywood always claimed that Jane had this thing for Payne."

"Here, he and I take a break and absorb some sun. You decide which of us is the hottie."

(Above) "Okay, so Jack Warner had fired me and I had to make a living. Here I am in Las Vegas with the slapstick Honey Brothers. It was burlesque, but I insisted that the showgals wear pasties."

(Above) "At Eureka College, they wouldn't let me on the baseball team. I showed them."

"Here, as Governor of California, I threw out the first ball of the 1972 World Series at Oakland."

(Above) Michigan governor George Romney (yes, Mitt's father) watches as Reagan fails to flip a jelly bean into his mouth. The setting was the Governors' Conference in Washington, D.C., on March 17, 1967.

(Above) Running for Governor of California in 1966, Reagan on horseback waves his cowboy hat in San Jose during Mexican Independence Day. He told friends, "Sacramento is the first act before I gallop off to the White House."

(Above) "When Nancy and I arrived in Sacramento, we realized that that Victorian monstrosity of a governor's mansion was a damn fire trap. We moved out. Here I am, carrying our dishes."

During his Governorship, the Reagans' housing dilemma was solved by rich friends, who bought them an elegant home in an exclusive suburb of Sacramento.

(Above) "Here, I am at my ranch in California on a foggy day, August 13, 1981."

"Whereas Hitler danced a jig at the fall of France, I'm tossing my leg into the air after signing the largest tax reduction and spending control bill in American history."

(Left) "Forget Milton Berle! That Liz from across the pond could wow them with her jokes about the heavy rains of California."

On March 10, 1983, Queen Elizabeth II visited the flooded Reagan spread, **Rancho del Cielo.**

Nancy told the press, "Thank god she didn't spend the night! Our guest bedroom could house a Munchkin or two from *The Wizard of Oz*. And Ronnie used to say, 'If you sat down on the can, your legs stuck out the door.'"

(Left) "At my ranch in California, I drove my Jeep to clear some dead limbs from my property."

"In Washington, I set out to clear deadwood from the government."

(Above) Reagan shook the hand of John F. Kennedy, Jr., as Caroline Kennedy looks on. It was their first visit to the White House since the Presidential regime of Richard Nixon in 1973. Reagan told the handsome young man, "I believe I'm shaking the hand of a future President of the United States."

After JFK Jr. departed, Reagan told Nancy, "I hope my prediction never comes true."

(Above) A former First Lady, Jacqueline Kennedy Onassis *(on the right)*, greets a presiding First Lady, Nancy, as a smiling and indulgent President Reagan looks on. The June 25, 1985 rendezvous occurred in Boston at a fund-raiser for the John F. Kennedy Presidential Library.

Later, Reagan told his aide, Donald Regan, "I first met Jackie in Hollywood in the late 1950s, when she was screwing my best friend, Bill Holden."

(Above) Reagan and Nancy dig into the earth at a ground-breaking ceremony for the Ronald Reagan Presidential Library and Museum in Simi Valley, California, on November 21, 1988.

Again, Reagan was fast with a quip, telling reporters, "Nancy learned the use of a shovel by scooping up horse shit on my ranch in Malibu."

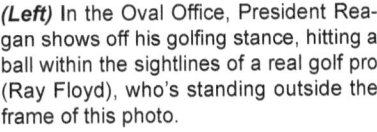

(Left) In the Oval Office, President Reagan shows off his golfing stance, hitting a ball within the sightlines of a real golf pro (Ray Floyd), who's standing outside the frame of this photo.

When this photo was published on June 24, 1986, golf pros thought Reagan's pose was "effeminate."

When he heard that, Reagan, always fast with a quip, told aides, "They don't know the half of it. In private, I give the best pansy imitation in the history of the Presidency."

(Above) Reagan and Nancy appear to be admiring a sculpted replica of a Komodo Dragon presented to them in Bali in May of 1986.

His shirt was a gift from the Indonesian people. As he later quipped, "The only thing louder was the mouth of Jimmy Carter."

(Left) President Reagan welcomes the Iron Lady of Britain, Margaret Thatcher, to Camp David on November 6, 1986. There was press speculation that he had always been drawn to strong-willed women. "Take his two wives or his mother, Nelle, as an example," wrote one reporter.

Another had a different view. "I think Mrs. Thatcher had the hots for him."

(Left) President Reagan certainly earned his place in the sun in American history. But was it good for his nose? Apparently not.

In August of 1987, he appeared at a press briefing in the Old Executive Office Building in Washington. He'd just had surgery on his nose for cancer.

(Above) In January of 1989, after eight years residency in the White House, President Reagan and Nancy bid farewell to their assembled well-wishers at Washington's Andrews Air Force base, before a plane hauled them away to their retirement in California. The occasion caused them to shed tears.

When Reagan was later asked about it, he said, "Richard Nixon in his farewell address also shed tears—and so did his wife, Pat. But Dick and I were tearing up for very different reasons during our exit from the White House."

BILL & HILLARY
So This Is That Thing Called Love

Confused about how to interpret their raucous pasts?
This uncensored tale about a love affair that changed the course of politics and the planet is of compelling interest to anyone involved in the slugfests and incendiary wars of THE CLINTONS.

This is both a biography of the Clintons and a political *exposé*; a detailed, weighty exploration that traces the couple's social and political evolution, from how each entered the political arena to their White House years under Bill Clinton's presidency, and the sometimes hysterical over-reactions of their enemies.

***

Shortly after its release in December of 2015, it received a literary award *(Runner-up to Best Biography of the Year)* from the New England Book Festival.

Was There a Vast, Right-Wing Conspiracy?

Reactions to Bonnie & Clyde's Invasion of Washington

"It became well known during the Clinton years that while the president was a 'certified' sleazeball, the most evil partner of this Bonnie and Clyde duo was Hillary. She is the *consigliore* of the couple, the one who executes (pun intended) their dastardly plans and deeds."
—*Larry Klayman*

"When Hillary Clinton spoke of a vast right-wing conspiracy determined to bring down the president, many people dismissed the idea. Yet, if the First Lady's accusation was exaggerated, the facts that have since emerged point toward a covert and often concerted effort by Bill Clinton's enemies—abetted by his own reckless behavior—which led inexorably to impeachment. Clinton's foes launched a cascade of well-financed attacks that undermined American democracy and nearly destroyed the Clinton presidency."
—*Joe Conaston & Gene Lyons*

"I saw it all—the violent arguments, the back-hall scheming, the empire-building, the backstabbing, the cynical posturing, the raw ambition, and the last-minute flip-flops that somehow produced real accomplishments, but also set in motion an almost tragic series of events that placed the president's fate in the hands of the Senate."
—*George Stephanopoulos*

"Who is Hillary? High-powered lawyer or re-invented cookie-baking wife and mother? Trusted helpmate to her hubby, or the one who pulls the strings? Human computer or warm, caring person? Proud spirit or suffering wife, betrayed by Bill's marital infidelities?"
—*Judith Warner*

"When it comes to lipstick, I say the brighter. Besides, being the mother of Bill and Roger, I'm known for my weird hair, heavy makeup and colors, and my penchant for playing the horses."
—*Virginia Clinton Kelley*

"We were the only game in town. A Southern babe, a Rhodes scholar presidential candidate, a compelling wife, tabloid sex, lies, an audiotape—how could you care about another candidate?"
—*James Carville on the 1992 presidential race*

"The story of the Clinton presidency has always been the story of a marriage. Their relationship is both supportive and destructive. Hillary is addicted to Bill, and he desperately depends on her to bring him back again from the political dead."
—*Gail Sheehy*

"The Clinton years might seem like a long national nightmare of scandal, sleaze, and ruthless acquisition of power. Hillary herself is the link from the excesses of the Watergate staff to the Whitewater fiasco to abuses of executive power and obstruction of justice. But now it is her turn. The Clinton era is far from over, and Hillary's ambitions are far from satisfied."
—*Clinton hater Barbara Olson,
whose hijacked plane crashed into the Pentagon*

"That stain on Monica Lewinsky's blue dress distracted the FBI and other security forces from recognizing the imminent attack of 9/11."
—*Hillary Clinton*

"The Clinton family had long-standing ties to the notorious Dixie Mafia. Billions of dollars of cocaine, cash, and weapons passed through Arkansas in the 1980s with the full knowledge of Bill and Hillary. During their reign, Arkansas was nothing less than a narco-state, with tiny banks in backwoods Arkansas laundering more cash than the big banks of New York City."
—*Victor Thorn*

"No public figure in contemporary life has elicited more polarized reactions than Hillary Rodham Clinton, the first presidential spouse who pursued a major policy-making role. The beleaguered First Lady has been a heroine and a role model for her feminist allies—and, to her conservative foes, a malevolent, power-mad shrew. Is she Bill Clinton's greatest asset, or his greatest liability?"
—*David Brock*

"In spite of Paula Jones' allegations about a peculiar bend in President Clinton's penis, in terms of size, shape, direction, whatever the devious mind wants to concoct, he is a normal man."
—*Clinton Attorney Bob Bennett on CBS*

"Hillary Clinton directs a coven of brutally correct women who want to rule over us. Her regiment of hardened militant feminists include lesbians, sex perverts, child molester advocates, Christian haters, and the most doctrinaire of communists. If she becomes president, will she go on to usher in a frightening new Millennium?"
—*Texe Marrs*

"I worked for both Bill Clinton and George W. Bush on the White House staff. President Clinton had his faults, but Bush wasn't perfect. During the worst nights, he used to chase imaginary flies with a fly swatter, running up and down the corridors of the White House until Laura restrained him."

—*an anonymous White House aide*

"Bill and Hillary Clinton left the White House under a cloud, dogged by sordid sexual scandals, a series of highly compromising investigations, and last-minute pardons that won bipartisan condemnation. Even many Democrats were glad to see them go. Yet within just a few years, Bill had secured a reputation as a global humanitarian and Democratic Party Elder Statesman, and Hillary was running for president."

—*Daniel Halper*

"I was singing in nightclubs, wearing very sexy outfits and gowns, a very independent and liberated woman. I was the Madonna of my day in Little Rock. Bill Clinton was the love of my life."

—*Gennifer Flowers*

"Bill Clinton is a womanizing, Elvis-loving, non-inhaling, truth-shading, war-protesting, draft-dodging, abortion protecting, gay-promoting, gun-hating Baby Boomer from hell."

—*George H.W. Bush*

"Brad Pitt is too good looking to play me in a movie of my life. George Clooney is at least more my size. He's good looking, you know. You could put bulbous things on his nose and could do makeup with him."

—*Bill Clinton*

"I don't think you should conclude that Bill Clinton has done anything to merit this hatred, other than be a symbol of everything some people fear and despise about the modern world. These are tales from the fundamentalist apocrypha. He's been accused of everything but devil worship."

—*Gene Lyons, The Arkansas Democrat-Gazette*

"In America now, paranoia runs deep, and the Clinton crazies' influence taps into that climate. Nearly half the population believes that the C.I.A. was involved in the assassination of President Kennedy; one in ten adults thinks the moon landing was a hoax. People seem to want to believe the worst about the Clintons. They don't trust the networks, the newspapers, or the government."

—*Philip Weiss, The New York Times*

PLAYBOY'S HUGH HEFNER
EMPIRE OF SKIN

THE COMPREHENSIVE, UNAUTHORIZED *EXPOSÉ* THAT EVERY SURVIVOR OF THE SEXUAL REVOLUTION WILL WANT TO READ
DARWIN PORTER & DANFORTH PRINCE

Hugh Hefner, the most iconic Playboy in human history, was a visionary, an empire-builder, and a pajama-clad pipe-smoker with a pre-coital grin.

In 1953, he published his first edition of *Playboy* with money borrowed from his puritanical, Nebraska-born mother. Marilyn Monroe appeared on the cover, with her nude calendar inside.

Rebelling against his strict upbringing, he lost his virginity at the age of 22.

His magazine, punctuated with nudes and studded with articles by major literary figures, reached its zenith at eight million readers. As a "tasteful pornographer," Hef became a cultural warrior, fighting government censorship all the way to the U.S. Supreme Court. As the years and his notoriety progressed, he became an advocate of abortion, LGBT equality, and the legalization of marijuana. Eventually, he engaged in "pubic wars" with Bob Guccione, the flamboyant founder of *Penthouse,* which cut into Hef's sales.

Lauded by millions of avid readers, he was denounced as "the father of sex addiction," "a huckster," "a lecherous low-brow feeder of our vices," "a misogynist," and, near the end of his life, "a symbol of priapic senility."

During his heyday, some of the biggest male stars in Hollywood, including Warren Beatty, Sammy Davis, Jr., Mick Jagger, and Jack Nicholson, came to frolic behind Hef's guarded walls, stripping nude in the hot tub grotto before sampling the rotating beds upstairs. Even a future U.S. president came to call. "Donald Trump had an appreciation of Bunny tail," Hef said.

Hefner's last Viagra-fueled marriage was to a beautiful blonde, Crystal Harris, 60 years his junior. "There's nothing wrong in a man marrying a girl who could be his great-granddaughter," he was famously quoted as saying.

This ground-breaking biography, the latest in Blood Moon's string of outrageously unvarnished myth-busters, was the first published since Hefner's death at the age of 91 in 2017. It's a provocative saga, rich in tantalizing, often shocking detail. Not recommended for the sanctimonious or the faint of heart, and loaded with ironic, little-known details about the trendsetter's epic challenges and the solutions he devised.

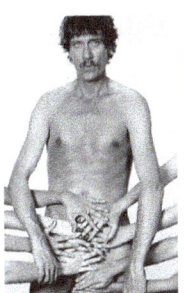

From Blood Moon, To the Memory of Players Passed

Inserted below is what we placed on the opening pages of *Playboy's Hugh Hefner, Empire of Skin* when it was released in 2018

We extend special thanks to the Playboys and Playmates who contributed to the Sexual Revolution that altered bedtime in America, and to those who stumbled, fell, failed, or died during the pursuit of their hopes and dreams. May all of them Rest in Peace

This bunny, who's ready for her closeup, wants to improve literacy, liberate America, find love, guarantee happiness, and pay tribute to her friends and lovers from other times and other places.

Hugh Hefner was an Army veteran and illustrator who had trouble adjusting to the censorship strictures of the early 1950s. He recognized how ready Americans were for variations in how they could entertain themselves in bed.

Blood Moon's *Empire of Skin* reveals how his empire got built, and the implications it carried for the generations that followed.

Contents

PUBLISHING MOGUL
HUGH HEFNER
as a horny teenager

PROLOGUE

CHAPTER ONE
   BEFORE LAUNCHING AMERICA'S SEXUAL REVOLUTION
   "The World's Swingingest Bachelor" is born on a windy afternoon in Chicago, joins the Army, survives boot camp, dates "Victory Girls," and dreams of becoming a cartoonist and illustrator.

CHAPTER TWO
   ORGIASTIC & AVAILABLE, AS AN ARMY VET & SWINGER IN POSTWAR CHICAGO, HEF RUNS WILD, ORGANIZING ORGIES AND MAKING STAG FILMS.
   In his search for a job, he's repeatedly rejected or trivialized. He launches the first edition of *Playboy* in December of 1953 with a nude Marilyn Monroe as its centerfold

CHAPTER THREE
   HEFNER MEETS "THE PLAYBOY OF CHICAGO," THE ULTIMATELY MOST INFLUENTIAL MEMBER OF HIS ADMINISTRATION, VICTOR LOWNES.
   Inspired by postwar Europe and its permissive censorship codes, Hef and his team define the Playboy aesthetic, building a brand, adding cartoons, editorials, artwork, lifestyle tips, and merchandising. Janet Pilgrim! Bettie Page! Gina Lollobrigida! Sophia Loren! Dating, orgies, and sex before AIDS. Bunny hops. Playmates of the month. Censorship and suppression from the U.S. postal authorities.

CHAPTER FOUR
   PLAYBOY RIDES THE WAVES OF LITERARY CHIC: HEF AND THE AVANT-GARDE AMERICAN LITERATI. ENTRENCHING THE VISION, FINDING A VOICE
   Playboy's success spawns a host of ferocious competitors smirking, leering, and trading, with varying degrees of vulgarity, on the female torso. Privately, Hef directs a porn flick co-starring Jayne Mansfield and her husband, Mr. Universe, Mickey Hargitay.

CHAPTER FIVE
   IT'S A *PLAYBOY* WORLD: EVERYONE WANTS TO BE ONE, AND EVERYONE WANTS AN INVITATION TO THE MANSION IN CHICAGO. THE PLAYBOY BUNNY BECOMES AN INTERNATIONAL ICON OF SEXUAL LIBERATION.
   Free at last from the "shackles of marriage," Hef launches one affair after another with the Playmate of his choice. Interactions and photo-maneuvers with Brigitte Bardot, Anita Ekberg, Frank Sinatra, Lenny Bruce, and Ella Fitzgerald. As a promotion for his magazine and its lifestyle image, he launches a late-night TV talk show (*Playboy Penthouse*) and stages the greatest three days of Jazz in the history of Chicago.

CHAPTER SIX
   MARKETING TO A NEW BREED OF MALE CONSUMERS, HEF LAUNCHES THE PLAYBOY CLUBS! ITS PROTOTYPE IN CHICAGO BECOMES THE BUSIEST NIGHTCLUB IN THE WORLD. CENSORSHIP ISSUES, BOURGEOIS OUTRAGE AND CONDEMNATION.
   After he runs nude pictures of Jayne Mansfield, the Chicago Police invade his bedroom and haul "Mr. Playboy" off to jail. Hef interacts with the Rat Pack, competing with Sinatra for the affections of the same women. Famous women maneuver for tasteful presentations of their undraped charms in *Playboy*. *Sex and the Single Girl*, a "lifestyle changer" from the editor of *Cosmopolitan*, fuels the flames of the sexual revolution.

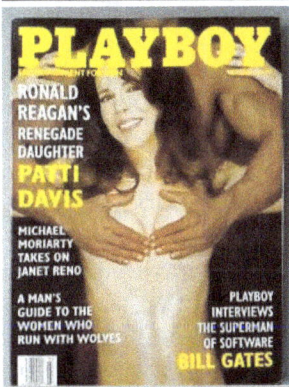

Former First Daughter **PATTI DAVIS**, daughter of Ronald and Nancy Reagan, horrified her parents, in her (some said, "vengeful") appearance as one of Hefner's topless cover girls.

CHAPTER SEVEN
   PLAYBOY MORPHS, DIVERSIFIES, AND PROMOTES HEF'S PHILOSOPHY AS A MANUAL FOR THE GOOD LIFE.
   Feminists target Hefner as a chauvinistic demon, launch labor strikes to liberate Bunnies, and maneuver "undercover" to expose their "exploitation." Fingering Hef as destructive to American values, government officials persecute Hef and his associates. Stressed out from

business and legal conflicts, his Mansion's growing reputation as a "mecca of hip," and all those freeloading celebrities, Hef survives on a diet of Pepsi and dexedrine.

CHAPTER EIGHT
BUNNY FEVER. HEF'S PLAYBOY CLUBS AND RESORTS MULTIPLY AND THRIVE
"The Brand" is reinforced with new locations in Boston, Kansas City, San Francisco, Lake Geneva (Wisconsin), Great Gorge (New Jersey), Tokyo, Osaka, and many others. The most iconic of "the Bond Girls" (Ursula Andress) poses as a centerfold. Celebrities (Joe Namath, Burt Reynolds) get permanently associated with *Playboy* in the eyes of consumers, and "The Playboy Interview" becomes a standard fixture in the culture wars of the fast-changing 60s. Hef launches an updated version (*Playboy After Dark*) of his late-night TV series, battles with feminists and "irrational chicks," and integrates his roster of undraped centerfolds.

CHAPTER NINE
HEF'S SHANGRI-LA. THE PLAYBOY MANSION IN L.A. BECOMES A BRANDING TOOL AND AN ORGY SITE FOR FILM STARS.
Migrating between Chicago and Los Angeles, and navigating his way through internal corporate politics, Hef takes Playboy public in a nationwide stock offering. Love hurts (aka, "Bunnies can bite"). Show-biz maneuverings from Barbi Benton, Roman Polanski, and the Rolling Stones. Fun and games in the Grotto. The rise and fall of *Oui*, "Spectorsky's Last Hurrah," and how Hef and Victor Lownes "played chess" for the future of the casino trade.

CHAPTER TEN
CONFRONTED WITH MORE EXPLICIT EROTIC STYLES FROM *PENTHOUSE*, *SCREW*, AND *HUSTLER*, HEF JOINS IN "THE PUBIC WARS," FOR CONTROL OF THE NATION'S LOVE AFFAIR WITH SKIN MAGS.
Linda Lovelace, riding high on her unexpected porn celebrity, gets Deep and Throaty at the Playboy Mansion. In a murky sting operation linked to official efforts to curtail pornography and the drug trade, Bobbie Arnstein, Hef's chief assistant, commits suicide. Sex, drugs, and celebrity at the Playboy Mansion (West) become notoriously and famously interconnected. Christie Hefner becomes "Hare Apparent," chief cost cutter, and chairperson of Playboy's board of directors. Interludes with Jimmy Carter, David Bowie, porn king John C. Holmes, and a raft of Bunnies who "kiss and tell." Casino-license horrors for Playboy operations in Atlantic City and London.

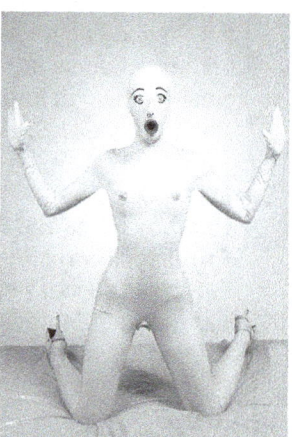

CHAPTER ELEVEN
HUGH HEFNER'S HOLY WAR WITH THE U.S. PRESIDENT. HOW RONALD AND NANCY REAGAN, BOLSTERED BY THE JUSTICE DEPARTMENT AND SIMULTANEOUSLY WITH MILITANT FEMINISTS, TRIED TO DESTROY *PLAYBOY*.
Bye-Bye Bunnies! It's the end of an era when *Playboy* gets downsized and reconfigured, and re-examined. *Playboy TV* competes for a share of the growing market for explicit erotica. Dorothy Stratten's murder and its publicity challenges. Carrie Leigh and her palimony suit. Sexual Politics: Jessica Hahn, featured in *Playboy* as a centerfold, reinforces embarassments for the religious right. Hef marries Kimberley Conrad—his "second time around"—and produces two sons.

CHAPTER TWELVE
HEF'S TWILIGHT, "THE RUNAWAY BRIDE" (CRYSTAL) AND MARRIAGE NO. 3.
FAMOUS AND NAKED: HEF'S PORTFOLIO OF CELEBRITY NUDES FEATURED IN *PLAYBOY* (JOAN COLLINS! PATTI DAVIS! ANNA NICOLE SMITH! DREW BARRYMORE! NANCY SINATRA! FARRAH FAWCETT! PAMELA ANDERSON!) SUDDENLY BECAME SOUGHT-AFTER, SHAME-FREE, AND PROFITABLE.
More presidential politics: *Playboy* spread-eagles the "white trash" scandals of the Clinton administration. Girlfriends Three (i.e., "The Girls Next Door), More "Kiss and Tell" (Kendra! Holly! Bridget! Isabella! Jill Ann! Suzen! Stephanie! Girls Girls Girls!) *exposés*. Passing the torch (Cooper!) and Hef's legacy ("We've come a long way, baby!") becomes part of the history books

PINK TRIANGLE

The Feuds and Private Lives of Tennessee Williams, Gore Vidal, Truman Capote, & Famous Members of their Entourages

Darwin Porter & Danforth Prince

In the aftermath of World War II, during the latter half of "The American Century," when literacy was higher and where more people discussed contemporary books and theater than they do today, three men, each a homosexual, rose from obscurity to positions of spectacular literary fame.

Collectively, they changed America's tastes in entertainment, expanded the boundaries of censorship, and redefined "The Golden Age of Postwar American Literature."

They paid a high price for their success. Their ferociously competitive personalities and private lives—frequently referenced in the tabloids, in literary journals, and on TV—eventually became more widely reviewed than their writings.

There were many witnesses to the sometimes bitchy dynamics of this infamous trio. Their habit of pulling other famous people into their slugfests invariably drew explosive media coverage and rivers of gossip among insiders on Broadway, in Hollywood, and among the jaded *cognoscenti* worldwide.

Darwin Porter, the senior co-author of this anthology of scandal, began recording its information when—as the youthful Bureau Chief for *The Miami Herald* in Tennessee Williams' home town of Key West—he began asking questions, taking notes, and dreaming of the day when his overview of the "Lavender Literati" could become public.

With the publication of this book, Blood Moon has made history's first attempt to compile an overview of this brilliant trio into a coherent whole. **The Triangle it illuminates is Pink, its references are literate and sexy, its gossip is captivating, and its meat is raw, juicy, and bloody, indeed.**

With this book, we proudly present, as a documentation of another, more literate era, *The Pink Triangle*, and through it, an insight into the awesome personal histories of **Tennessee Williams, Truman Capote, and Gore Vidal.**

It's Triangular, It's Literate, It's Hot, and It's Pink

This book, the only one of its kind, reveals the backlot intrigues associated with the literary and script-writing enfants terribles of America's entertainment community during the mid-20th century.

It exposes their bitchfests, their slugfests, and their relationships with the glitterati—Marilyn Monroe, Brando, the Oliviers, the Paleys, U.S. Presidents, a gaggle of other movie stars, millionaires, and international *débauchés*.

This is for anyone who's interested in the formerly concealed scandals of Hollywood and Broadway, and the values and pretentions of both the literary community and the entertainment industry.

"A banquet... If PINK TRIANGLE had not been written for us, we would have had to research and type it all up for ourselves...Pink Triangle is nearly seven hundred pages of the most entertaining histrionics ever sliced, spiced, heated, and serviced up to the reading public. Everything that Blood Moon has done before pales in comparison. Given the fact that the subjects of the book themselves were nearly delusional on the subject of themselves (to say nothing of each other) it is hard to find fault. Add to this the intertwined jungle that was the relationship among Williams, Capote, and Vidal, of the times they vied for things they loved most—especially attention—and the times they enthralled each other and the world, [Pink Triangle is] the perfect antidote to the Polar Vortex."
—**Vinton McCabe** in the *NY JOURNAL OF BOOKS*

"Full disclosure: I have been a friend and follower of Blood Moon Productions' tomes for years, and always marveled at the amount of information in their books—it's staggering. The index alone to Pink Triangle runs to 21 pages—and the scale of names in it runs like a Who's Who of American social, cultural and political life through much of the 20th century."
—**Perry Brass** in *The Huffington Post*

"We Brits are not spared the Porter/Prince silken lash either. PINK TRIANGLE's research is, quite frankly, breathtaking. PINK TRIANGLE will fascinate you for many weeks to come. Once you have made the initial titillating dip, the day will seem dull without it."
—**Jeffery Taylor** in *The Sunday Express (UK)*

Photos above, left to right: **#1 Truman Capote,** sharpening his nails for catfights to come; **#2 Vidal, Capote, and Williams,** gathered together in a NYC apartment in the aftermath of World War II; **#3 Darwin Porter,** then Key West bureau chief for The Miami Herald, monitoring the slugfests of the Terrible Trio; and **#4 Tennessee Williams** on the front porch of his home in Key West, entertaining **Gore Vidal**.

In Pink Triangle, celebrity *spinmeister* **Darwin Porter,** after years of intimate familiarity with the three most notorious writers in America, comes clean with an overview of their ferocious battles for fame, literary supremacy, and better boyfriends. Based on years of dialogue with each of them, this book reveals how **Myra Breckinridge, In Cold Blood,** took a ride *A Streetcar Named Desire*.

THEY CALLED HIM "THE ROCK."

ROCK HUDSON

EROTIC FIRE

Darwin Porter & Danforth Prince

IN THE DYING DAYS OF HOLLYWOOD'S GOLDEN AGE, ROCK HUDSON WAS THE MOST CELEBRATED PHALLIC SYMBOL AND LUST OBJECT IN AMERICA. THIS BOOK DESCRIBES HIS RISE, FALL, AND THE INDUSTRY THAT CREATED HIM.

"THE INCARNATION OF APOLLO"

As the 20th Century reached its midpoint, there was no leading man as popular as Rock Hudson in both comedy and drama. For seven consecutive years (1957-1964), he was one of the Top Ten Stars of the year.

He repeatedly beat out all "the bubblegum boys," such as blonde Tab Hunter or blonder Troy Donahue, at the box office, not just in the United States, but around the world.

For raw masculinity, he was a walking mass of testosterone. He fitted into that leading man category occupied by Clark Gable, Burt Lancaster, and Robert Mitchum. Women by the millions wanted him, and men wanted to be like him. Other men just wanted him.

Just released from the Navy, the muscled, 6'4" hunk, then known as Roy Fitzgerald, arrived in Hollywood with a clear understanding of what he wanted: "I don't want to be an actor…I want to be a movie star! And I don't give a damn how many casting couches I have to lie on!"

To that end, between gigs as a truck driver, he donned very tight, faded jeans and seductively stationed himself near the entrances to Warners and Universal. Eventually, he was "discovered."

Almost from the moment he set foot in Tinseltown, young Rock set off an "erotic fire" that blazed all the way to the Hollywood Hills. He was given such appellations as "Hollywood's Sexiest Man" and "The Reincarnation of

Apollo." Columnist James Bacon said, "If Hollywood ever makes a film called *Adonis,* it should star Rock Hudson."

Always after the new boy in town, Joan Crawford was the first diva to lure him into her boudoir, later pronouncing him "a cross between Gary Cooper and Robert Taylor." Others followed, including a drunken Judy Garland and a very young Marilyn Monroe. His affair with Elizabeth Taylor, his co-star in *Giant* (1956), developed into a life-long friendship.

Also during the production of *Giant*, his affair with James Dean turned sour. While making two soap opera dramas with Rock, Jane Wyman, the ex-Mrs. Ronald Reagan, wanted to marry Rock. His most bizarre seductions ranged from Tallulah Bankhead to Liberace.

The matinee idols of yesterday also wanted him—Tyrone Power, Errol Flynn, Robert Taylor, Jeff Chandler, Tony Curtis. Rock also seduced many of the emerging young stars of the 1950s: Marlon Brando, Monty Clift, Jeffrey Hunter, Troy Donahue, Steve McQueen, and Tony Perkins.

Early in his career, he was assigned roles in a string of B-pictures, playing handsome Apaches, easy-on-the-eyes sea captains, and "Ordinary Joes" whose charm moviegoers remembered way beyond the limited scale of his roles. Meanwhile, power players in Hollywood clamored for him up close and personal, too.

Stardom finally arrived based on a performance opposite Jane Wyman in that tear-jerking melodrama, *Magnificent Obsession* (1954).

Three eventful years later, his status as one of the most popular (and most consistently profitable) actors in Hollywood was reinforced, based on his co-starring performance opposite Doris Day in the spectacularly successful *Pillow Talk* (1959). Together, as a captivating duo, they went on to appear together in other "artfully campy" battles of the sexes.

Compiled as a memorial for the 30th anniversary of his death, *Rock Hudson Erotic Fire* is based on dozens of face-to-face interviews with Rock Hudson's friends, co-conspirators, and enemies. Researched over a period of a half century, it reveals the secretive actor's complete, never-before-told story within a context of scandal-soaked and historic ironies, many of which have never been fully explored—until now.

Although maligned by the media because of the stigmas associated with his AIDS-related death, Rock showed inner courage and manly grace as he lay dying. "This is my shining hour," he told his closest friends, as the media rushed to "Out" him as a "celebrity bisexual" who'd been stricken by the then-stigmatizing scourge.

Today, beloved by hordes of cultish fans and film buffs around the world, Rock Hudson is the often misunderstood (until now) Golden Icon of a glamourous bygone era.

> **Rock Hudson** charmed every casting director in Hollywood (and movie-goers throughout America) as the mega-star they most wanted to share PILLOW TALK with. This book describes his rise and fall, and how he handled himself as a closeted but promiscuous bisexual during an age when EVERYBODY tried to throw him onto a casting couch.
>
> In 2017, the year of its release, it was designated as winner ("BEST BIOGRAPHY") at two of the Golden State's most prestigious literary competitions, the Northern California and the Southern California Book Festivals.
>
> It was also favorably reviewed by the *Midwestern Book Review, California Book Watch, KNEWS RADIO, the New York Journal of Books,* and the most popular Seniors' magazine in Florida, *BOOMER TIMES.*

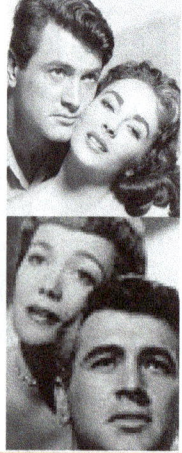

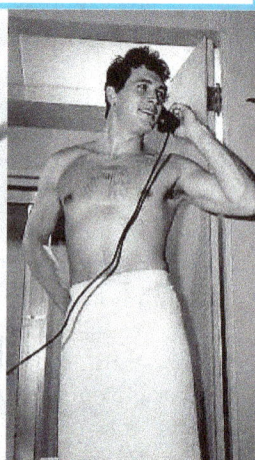

Roy Fitzgerald, movie-star handsome and almost ready to Rock.

Pansexual and promiscuous, Rock Hudson managed to perform, again and again and again, both onscreen and in private. Read all about his rise and fall, and the industry in which, for a while at least, he thrived.

BURT REYNOLDS

How a Nude Centerfold Sex Symbol Seduced Hollywood

Darwin Porter & Danforth Prince

BURT REYNOLDS
Put the Pedal to the Metal:
How a Nude Centerfold Sex Symbol Seduced Hollywood

Leading Ladies & Box Office Smashes from a Good Ol' Boy

Another Outrageous Celebrity Exposé by Darwin Porter & Danforth Prince

In the 1970s and '80s, Georgia-born **BURT REYNOLDS** —the highest-grossing movie star of his era— represented a new breed of movie star.

Charming and relentlessly macho, he was a good old Southern boy who made hearts throb and audiences laugh. He was Burt Reynolds, a football hero and a guy you might have shared some jokes with in a redneck bar. After an impressive but tormented career, rivers of negative publicity, a self-admitted history of bad choices, and a spectacular fall from Hollywood grace, he died in Jupiter, Florida, at the age of 82 in September of 2018.

For five years, both in terms of earnings and popularity, he was the number one box office star in the world. *Smokey and the Bandit* (1977) became the biggest-grossing car-chase film of all time. As he put it, perhaps as a means of bolstering his image, "I like nothing better than making love to some of the most beautiful women in the world." Perhaps he was referring to his romantic and sexual involvements with dozens of celebrities from New Hollywood. More unusual dalliances occurred with Marilyn Monroe, whom he once picked up on his way to the Actors Studio in New York City. Love with another VIP came in the form of that "Sweetheart of the G.I.s," Dinah Shore, sparking chatter. "I appreciate older women," he once said in a moment of self-revelation. According to Sally Field, "Burt still lives in my heart." But then she expressed relief that, because of his recent death, he never read what she'd said about him in her memoir.

Men liked him too: He played poker with Frank Sinatra; shared boozy nights with John Wayne; intercepted a "pass" from closeted Spencer Tracy; talked "penis size" with Mark Wahlberg; went "wench-hunting" with Johnny Carson; and threatened to kill Marlon Brando, to whom his appearance was often compared. He also hung out with Bette Davis. ("I always had a thing for her.")

His least happy (some said "most poisonous") marriage—to Loni Anderson—was rife with dramas played out more in the tabloids than in the boudoir. According to Reynolds, "She's vain, she's a rotten mother, she sleeps around, and she spent all my money."

This biography—the first comprehensive overview of the "redneck icon" ever published—reveals the joys and sorrows of a movie star who thrived in, but who was then almost buried by the pressures and insecurities of the New Hollywood. A tribute to "truck stop" America, it's about the accelerated life of a courageous spirit who "Put His Pedal to the Metal" with humor, high jinx, and pizzazz. He predicted his own death: "Soon, I'll be racing a hotrod in Valhalla in my cowboy hat and a pair of aviators." On his tombstone, he wanted it writ: "He was not the best actor in the world, but he was the best Burt Reynolds in the world."

INSIDE LINDA LOVELACE'S DEEP THROAT

DEGRADATION, PORNO CHIC, AND THE RISE OF FEMINISM

DARWIN PORTER

The most comprehensive biography ever written of an adult entertainment star, her tormented relationship with Hollywood's underbelly, and how she changed forever the world's perceptions about censorship, sexual behavior patterns, and pornography.

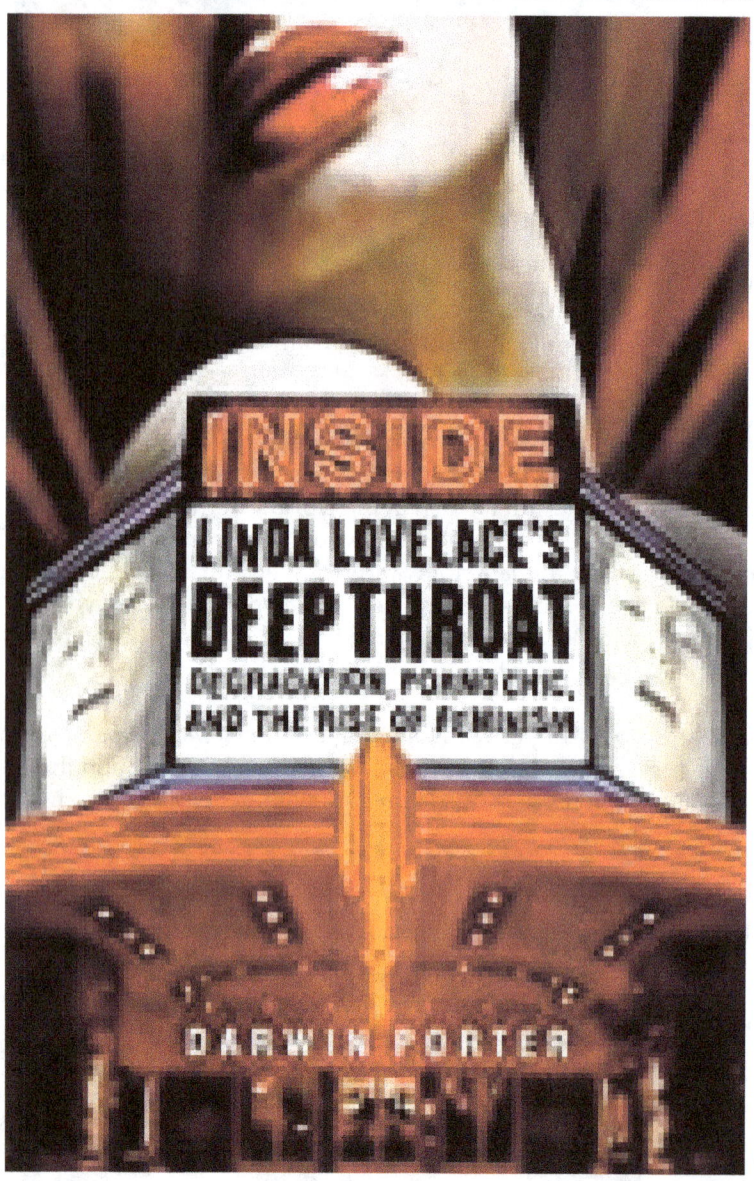

THE BEACH BOOK FESTIVAL'S Grand Prize Winner for **BEST SUMMER READING** of 2013.

RUNNER-UP TO "BEST BIOGRAPHY OF 2013"
—THE LOS ANGELES BOOK FESTIVAL

Darwin Porter, author of more than FORTY critically acclaimed celebrity exposés of behind-the-scenes intrigue in the entertainment industry, was deeply involved in the Linda Lovelace saga as it unfolded in the 70s, interviewing many of the players, and raising money for the legal defense of the film's co-star, Harry Reems. In this book, emphasizing her role as an unlikely celebrity interacting with other celebrities, he brings inside information and a never-before-published revelation to almost every page.   *"This book drew me in..How could it not?"* Coco Papy, Bookslut.

WHO WAS LINDA LOVELACE?

A SEX-CRAZED NYMPHOMANIC? OR A TRAGIC VICTIM OF RAPE AND ABUSE?

"Deep Throat, strange as it may seem, changed America's sexual attitudes more than anything since the first Kinsey Report in 1948. It altered the lives of everyone associated with it. It super-charged the feminist movement. It gave the Mafia its most lucrative business since Prohibition. And it changed the nation's views on obscenity forever."
—Journalist **Joe Bob Briggs**

"Somebody told me that the two best-known names of 1973 were Henry Kissinger and Linda Lovelace. We each made notable breakthroughs: The distinguished Mr. Kissinger helped open the doors to Red China and Russia. I opened my throat for all the world to enjoy...I've learned to do things with my mouth and my vagina that few women anywhere can ever hope to achieve."
—**Linda Lovelace**

"Norman Mailer and I had a competitive relationship. Frankly, he wanted to be Hemingway but never made it. He always had to top one of my stories. One night at a party in Brooklyn, he told me that he came home, woke up his wife, and bragged to her that he had just fucked a black drag queen. He also told me that one night he hired Linda Lovelace, who brought him to three climaxes without removing his penis from her throat. Oh, that Norman."
—Author **Gore Vidal**

"My initiation into prostitution was a gang rape by five men, arranged by Chuck Traynor. It was the turning point in my life. He threatened to shoot me with the pistol if I didn't go through with it. I had never experienced anal sex before, and it ripped me apart. They treated me like an inflatable plastic doll, picking me up and moving me here and there. They spread my legs this way and that, shoving their things at me and into me. They were playing musical chairs with parts of my body. I had never been so frightened, disgraced, and humiliated in my life. I felt like garbage."
—**Linda Lovelace**

"The biggest status symbol this year is to have your cock sucked by Linda Lovelace. You guys had better book a date with her, or else you'll no longer be the Kings of Cool."
—**Sammy Davis, Jr.**, to fellow Rat Packers at the Sands Hotel in Las Vegas in February, 1973

"Sammy Davis, Jr. was subject to bouts of debauchery and dissipation that nearly wrecked his life and threatened to compromise his career. For instance, he spent periods of his life hanging out with the denizens of the hard-core porn industry and with practitioners of Satanism. He even suggested marriage to Linda Lovelace when she was at the height of her career, cruising Hollywood and Las Vegas as a sex toy for the very rich and famous."
—**Gerald Early**, from *The Sammy Davis, Jr. Reader*

"I have met stars who were my idols when I was little—Elvis Presley, Warren Beatty, Hugh Hefner, Elizabeth Taylor, Ann-Margret, and Frank Sinatra—and I've been keeping a diary."
—**Linda Lovelace**

"Steve McQueen's seduction of Linda Boreman marked a turning point in her life. Upon the sensational release of Deep Throat, she became the reigning Queen of Porn. Not only that, she became the 'party favor' [her words] to movie stars, sports figures, one U.S. senator, and one vice president of the United States. In all, she estimated that she performed fellatio on more than fifty household names who range from Frank Sinatra to Joe DiMaggio, from Elvis Presley to Desi Arnaz, from Marlon Brando to Johnny Carson."

—Columnist **James Bacon** at a stag roast for Ed McMahon in Palm Springs, 1978

"The reason I attended a showing of Deep Throat in Los Angeles was because I suspected that Desi had had a fling with her. Frankly, I wanted to see the girl's technique. I didn't want to lose Gary Morton the way I'd lost Desi. After I saw the movie, I knew I could never top her. You see, I have this gag reflex."

—**Lucille Ball** to Ethel Merman

"I went to see Deep Throat at a movie theater on Duval Street in Key West. I don't know what all the excitement is about. I can swallow bigger cocks than that."

—**Truman Capote** to Tennessee Williams

"I was the Queen of Porn and John C. Holmes was the King of Porn and known for his 13½ inch penis. A private film collector offered me $5,000 on a bet, claiming that he knew for sure I couldn't swallow the whole thing. He paid Holmes $1,000 and I won the $5,000. Yes, indeed, I did it! Down to the last inch. That was a private film. Porn collectors should try to find a copy of Exotic French Fantasies if they want to see John and me together."

—**Linda Lovelace**

"Linda Lovelace has the air of fresh carnality, the air of thoroughly debauched innocence, the sense of a woman exploring the limits of sexual expression and feeling. Linda Lovelace is the girl next door grown up into a shameless woman."

—**Kenneth Turan** and **Stephen F. Zito** in their book, Sinema

"Linda kept staying at my house, and I was having sex with the three or four other girls living with me. We had a giant waterbed, and Linda just sort of became one of the girls on the giant waterbed. She now says that the orgies went on there were actually setups for hooker deals, and that she hated that. She said I'd beat her up if she didn't do it, but that was bullshit. Everybody just got stoned and partied."

—**Chuck Traynor** in The Other Hollywood

"Giving more head, she became frantic—her tongue and lips were everywhere. Then I felt the muscles in the back of her throat opening up. Her head lowered over me. Suddenly, I could feel my cock go right into her throat. I couldn't believe she ate the whole thing. My cock and balls and half my pubic bush were all engulfed in that cavernous, deep throat of hers."

—**Harry Reems**, co-star of Deep Throat

"Throughout most of the 1970s, I was used as a sex toy in New York, Las Vegas, Palm Springs, and Hollywood. I was treated like a cheap whore. Once I'd satisfied a client, I was shown the door. Dozens of celebrities—mostly men, but also Katharine Hepburn—wanted to date me. For the most part, they requested only one thing. My specialty."

—**Linda Lovelace** in a speech before feminists in Denver, 1984

"Imagine: A major adult star like Linda Lovelace in a bestiality movie. It was very graphic. Linda is indeed having sex with the dog in nearly every position one can imagine in a porn flick. Bestiality is illegal in most states now, so one must take care to view it. It was made in a time when things were more liberal."

—**Csmineatlast's** online review of *Dogfucker*

"In a memoir, I wrote about a famous movie star and his son who did all sorts of perverted things at the same time with me. My publisher wouldn't let me reveal their names. But I can tell you who they were. Paul Newman and his son, Scott. Okay, Newman does a lot for charity, and I give him credit for that, but he's not so squeaky clean. He can get down and dirty. I've gone to bed with enough Hollywood stars to know that their image is one thing, reality the other."

—**Linda Lovelace**

"All of us do that kind of stuff—but not all of us want to be on camera."

—**Shirley MacLaine**, after viewing *Deep Throat*

"If you're having a male sexual experience, after you have your orgasm, your next impulse is not to bend down and look over and watch someone's scrotum pounding against someone's shaved beaver or whatever."

—**Jack Nicholson** during an interview with *Screw* magazine regarding his viewing of *Deep Throat*

"By the time I got around to sampling the specialty of Linda Lovelace, her throat was too loose. I turned the bitch over and fucked her in the ass. She was real tight."

—Gangster **Mickey Cohen** to Liz Renay

"Linda Lovelace said she was forced into sex. Like hell she was. She couldn't get enough of me. She wore me out, and I'm what is known as a sex maniac."

—Actor **Forrest Tucker** to John Wayne at a health club in Los Angeles

"My husband, Chuck Traynor, beat me physically. I literally became a prisoner. I was not allowed out of his sight, not even to use the bathroom, where he watched me through a hole in the door. He slept on top of me at night; he listened to my phone calls with a .45 automatic eight pointed at me."

—**Linda Lovelace**

"This is the woman who never took responsibility for her own choices, but instead blamed everything that happened to her in her life on porn."

—Adult film actress **Gloria Leonard**

"Teddy Kennedy rented Linda Lovelace's deep throat for one night. She was taken to this house in Palm Springs. I heard about it, but I didn't personally arrange it. Sammy Davis did the honors."

—**Chuck Traynor**

"Does Dick Nixon look like a man who has ever gone down on a woman? If he had, or if he could, I bet the country would be different."

—**Linda Lovelace**

"In her book, Ordeal, Linda left out a number of incidents involving Hugh Hefner and his Playboy Mansion in Los Angeles, even though they were newsworthy incidents about sex and celebrities."

—**Gloria Steinem**

[Note: We at Blood Moon do not share Linda's restraint. Her heavily censored allegations are published for the first time in this book]

"Good riddance to trash. She was a good cocksucker. She was a piece of shit. Her book, Ordeal, was a lying piece of crap. She was a hooker, a scumbag, a lying trollop. I'm glad Chuck Traynor taught her to suck cock. I dropped several ejaculations down her throat. I want to do a final load, so that when she goes to hell, my sperm will go with her."

—**Al Goldstein**, in his epitaph to Linda Lovelace in 2002

"It was really hard and kind of terrifying playing Linda Lovelace. The director gave me some liberties, but I had to play someone who existed in history, someone who had quite an established reputation for something very extreme. I don't have to say what that specialty is, since millions of people saw her do it."

—**Amanda Seyfried**, star of the biopic *Lovelace*

"The movie, Lovelace, stars Amanda Seyfried as Linda Lovelace. It also stars Hollywood favorite James Franco as a young Hugh Hefner, who also seduced Lovelace. Sarah Jessica Parker plays the feminist Gloria Steinem. Demi Moore had to drop out of the role during her split with Ashton Kutchner and his cheating heart. Lindsay Lohan was to play Lovelace, but was fired after her repeated bouts in court."

Advance publicity associated with *Lovelace* (the film)

Peace at Last / Rest in Peace
Linda Boreman Lovelace Marchiano (1949-2002)

COITUS INTERRUPTUS:
LINDA LOVELACE EXPOSED
HOW A PUBLISHING DREAM OF THE LATE 1980S DEVELOPED STREP THROAT

(A message from this book's publisher)

The degradations, celebrity liaisons, court trials, and legal anguish of Linda Lovelace have never been given a detailed accounting, in spite of the publication of her quartet of ghost-written "memoirs": *Inside Linda Lovelace* (Pinnacle Books, 1973); *The Intimate Diary of Linda Lovelace* (Pinnacle Books, 1974); *Ordeal* (Bell Publishing Company, 1980), and *Out of Bondage* (Lyle Stuart, 1986). Although each of these blunt and earthy memoirs purported to be full and candid assessments of the tragic star's career, they described only the tail of the elephant, not the beast itself.

Had circumstances been different way back in 1988, a more complete and unbiased "book of record," or something reasonably equivalent, might have been marketed with klieg lights and fanfare. There was, in fact, a burning ambition among some people back then to produce a block-busting and uncensored overview of the remarkable life of an unlikely woman who, because of her starring role in history's most famous porn film, became a cultural icon of the 20th century.

Then something went terribly wrong...

LINDA BOREMAN LOVELACE MARCHIANO
52 YEARS AFTER THE RELEASE OF HER INFAMOUS MOVIE, HER STORY IS STILL BEING TOLD

In the late 1980s, the concept for a potentially best-selling memoir unfolded within the high-pressure Manhattan office of what was at the time one of the hottest literary agencies in the world, Jay Garon-Brooke Associates. Jay Garon, the company's abrasive and occasionally brilliant president, was the most sought-after literary agent in America for authors with celebrity sagas to peddle. Garon's previous triumphs had included the development and packaging of Hedy Lamarr's graphically controversial *Ecstasy*, and scandalous overviews of such stars as Bette Davis. **Garon**, who was a close personal friend of both **Darwin Porter** (author of this book) and the most feared and hated lawyer in America (**Roy Cohn**), would go on to launch the career of the best-selling novelist **John Grisham**.

Sixteen years after the release, in 1972, of *Deep Throat*, Garon proposed a tell-all autobiography of Linda Lovelace, which would not only list the names of the movie stars she'd seduced, but would give intimate, graphic details of their performances in bed. The very successful *Here Comes Harry Reems*, written by the actor who had co-starred with Linda in Deep Throat—released by Pinnacle Books in 1975—was cited as a good omen for the potential success of the Lovelace project.

By now a world-famous figure in her own right, Linda was bursting with revelations harvested from years as a celebrity whose sexual specialty was widely discussed, widely visible, and available for hire. Even the name of the low-budget porn movie she'd starred in had transcended the standards of modesty, having been adopted by the mainstream media as the code name for an (otherwise anonymous) key witness during Richard Nixon's Watergate scandal.

Sammy Davis, Jr., had even been credited with suggesting to his fellow Rat Packers, including Frank Sinatra, that "you're not cool until you've sampled Linda's specialty."

During the development phase of the Lovelace project, the first question addressed by Garon's team was, "Would Linda's story be believed?" Both Lyle Stuart, publisher of her previous memoir, and Garon himself had already subjected her to lie detector tests, which she had successfully passed.

Based on a subjective quirk, Linda refused to be interviewed by Garon's male research team. She preferred instead to deliver her ideas to Reba-Anne Howard, who had briefly trained as a psychologist in Austin, Texas, and who had some vague previous connection to Linda. Present at many of the editorial meetings, with access to the project's notes and ongoing discussions, was Garon's client and frequent dining companion, Darwin Porter, author of this book.

At this point in the project's development, no one had designated who would actually author the as-yet-unwritten book. Garon had asked one of his most successful clients, author James Leo Herlihy, if he would work with Linda on the project. Previously, Herlihy had enjoyed a hit with an ultimately famous book he had written, one that centered on male prostitution,

Midnight Cowboy. It was later adapted into a film, the first X-rated movie ever to win an Oscar as Best Picture of the Year in 1969. Herlihy, after interviewing Linda and after reading the Lovelace material, rejected Garon's offer, citing her as "too sleazy for me."

Even without a designated author, a sales proposal was bashed together for what promised to be Lovelace's most comprehensive and controversial memoir, tentatively entitled *Linda Lovelace Exposed.*

Garon's team distributed the proposal throughout New York's publishing community. It received positive and potentially lucrative responses from more than thirty publishers. For a brief moment, the concept of *Linda Lovelace Exposed* showed a frenzied promise of being something that major publishing houses would want to promote.

Then something went terribly wrong: Lyle Stuart's publishing group, attacked for statements she had made in the Lovelace memoir he had printed in 1986 (*Out of Bondage*), was hit with two crippling libel suits.

When news of these lawsuits became public, the Garon/Lovelace book project died overnight. "Despite its potential for enormous sales, the fear of additional lawsuits almost guaranteed that no publisher would ever touch it," Garon claimed.

Fascinated by the project and by Linda's scandalous and almost heart-breaking story, Darwin Porter paid Ms. Howard for her research and acquired the rights to the still-unfocused project for authorship at some undetermined future date.

Porter was partly motivated by a sense of political outrage. He had been horrified when *Deep Throat*'s co-star, Harry Reems, the only actor ever prosecuted by the government for obscenity on film, was threatened with a jail term because of his role in the movie. Porter became a key player in raising money among celebrities for the actor's defense.

Deep Throat, both the movie and its legend, never died. More than 40 years after its inaugural release, it's still for sale or rent in at least 170 countries. Now, with the renewal of interest in Linda Lovelace and with her configuration as the subject of an upcoming A-list movie, Blood Moon decided that the time had come to release her complete story without any of the censorship or legal dangers imposed in the past. Her revelations from the late 1980s, enhanced by numerous eyewitnesses to her life and legend, was at last unleashed upon the public.

As of this writing, very few of the movie stars who enjoyed intimate contact with Linda are still alive—and although the full details of their association with her are not laid out within this book, they know who they are.

Danforth Prince
President & Founder,
Blood Moon Productions

THE LEGACY OF *DEEP THROAT*

"There is a disconnect between the freedom of expression that *Deep Throat* promised and what actually transpired. Now we have total liberation of sexual things, but we also have the Patriot Act. We never made the connection between sexual speech and political speech. Sex today has nothing to do with revolution anymore. It's about capitalism and protecting little profit centers."

—Novelist **Erica Jong**

"I was in Toronto recently, and the city is like being in middle America. And you've got very hot, young 18- to 20-year old girls with tongue studs, and they are simply publicly advertising that they are interested in and capable of giving you really good oral sex if you're interested. And that's not even designed to be shocking. We owe it all to Linda Lovelace."

—**Brian Grazer**, producer of *Apollo 13* and *How the Grinch Stole Christmas*

PAUL NEWMAN, THE MAN BEHIND THE BABY BLUES
HIS SECRET LIFE EXPOSED

DARWIN PORTER

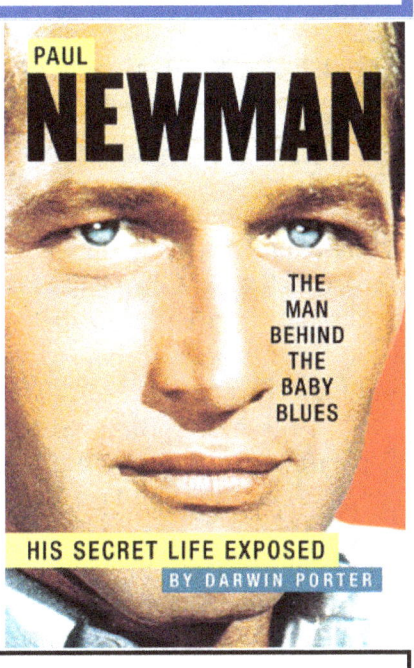

"*Paul Newman had just as many on-location affairs as the rest of us, and he was just as bisexual as I was. But whereas I was always getting caught with my pants down, he managed to do it in the dark with not a paparazzo in sight. He might have bedded Marilyn Monroe or Elizabeth Taylor the night before, but he always managed to show up for breakfast with Joanne Woodward, with those baby blues, looking as innocent as a Botticelli angel. He never fooled me. It takes an alleycat to know another one. Did I ever tell you what really happened between Newman and me? If that doesn't grab you, what about what went on between James Dean and Newman? Let me tell you about this so-called model husband if you want to look behind those famous peepers.*"

—Marlon Brando

Drawn from firsthand interviews with insiders who knew Paul Newman intimately, and compiled over a period of nearly a half-century, this is the world's most honest and most revelatory biography about Hollywood's pre-eminent male sex symbol.

This is a respectful but candid cornucopia of once-concealed information about the sexual and emotional adventures of an affable, impossibly good-looking workaday actor, a former sailor from Shaker Heights, Ohio, who parlayed his ambisexual charm and extraordinary good looks into one of the most successful careers in Hollywood.

Whereas the situations it exposes were widely known within Hollywood's inner circles, they've never before been revealed to the general public.

But now, the full story has been published—the giddy heights and agonizing crashes of a great American star, with revelations and insights never before published in any other biography.

PAUL NEWMAN'S BABY BLUES
A Gaggle of Lovers, Friends, Enemies, Acquaintances, and Admirers Recall Newman's Tempestuous Early Decades

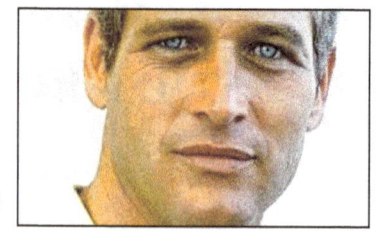

Known to Hollywood insiders, but never before revealed to the general moviegoing public, this carefully researched biography focuses on the adventures of a highly desirable young man on Broadway and in Hollywood.

AT THE PEEK OF NEWMAN'S POPULARITY and male beauty, a survey revealed that 46% of American women would have preferred him as a bed partner to any other male. A former sailor from Shaker Heights, Ohio, he parlayed his ambisexual charm and extraordinary good looks into one of the most successful careers in Hollywood.

Newman once won the tongue-in-cheek "Unzippered Award" for having never been sexually associated with anyone other than his wives. Porter punches holes in that bag of myths to reveal that when Newman was known as the sex symbol of Hollywood, he dated abundantly from the A-list, enjoying off-the-record sexual and emotional trysts with Elizabeth Taylor, Marilyn Monroe, Judy Garland, Audrey Hepburn, and Grace Kelly, plus a coterie of "cougars" that embraced Joan Crawford, Vivien Leigh, Susan Hayward, Ava Gardner, Rita Hayworth, and Lana Turner.

As has been rumored in underground Hollywood for years, Newman also had a closeted life as a bisexual. This biography exposes the megastar's bisexual history and his liaisons with, among others, Marlon Brando, James Dean, Anthony Perkins, and Sal Mineo.

Porter's biography also deals with such touchy subjects as underground speculation about Newman and his relationships with co-stars Tom Cruise and Robert Redford. Falling like a bomb are revelations about the death of his only son, Scott Newman.

According to Porter, "This is a highly personalized biography which I pulled together over many decades, based on insider reports from Newman's friends and enemies. It focuses mainly on Newman's interactions, personal and sexual, with other entertainment industry players during the 1950s and 1960s. It also contains some very revealing upfront material on Newman's early life, particularly his experiences in the U.S. Navy during the 1940s."

Paul Newman, The Man Behind the Baby Blues is one of at least forty celebrity biographies written by Porter, who began gathering insider information about Newman back in 1959, following an introduction by Tennessee Williams. Information came from a sources as diverse as playwright William Inge, author of the play, Picnic, which launched Newman as a Broadway sensation, and actress Geraldine Page, who co-starred with Newman in Sweet Bird of Youth. Porter then continued collecting stories about Hud, Cool Hand Luke, and Butch Cassidy until the day Newman died.

As revealed within the pages of this book, the private Newman was remarkably different from the public face he revealed. He was filled with contradictions: Model husband. Ideal dad. Bad father. Macho heterosexual. Closeted bisexual. Loyal companion, Heartbreaking, two-timing lover. The star summed up his life like this: "Whenever I do something good, right away, I've got to do something bad, so I know that I'm not going to pieces."

Presented are revelations about Newman's heretofore suppressed clandestine relationships with Gore Vidal, Jacqueline Kennedy, Tennessee Williams, Steve McQueen, Montgomery Clift, and Susan Strasberg.

This is a pioneering and posthumous biography of a Hollywood Dream. It's all here—the giddy heights and the agonizing lows of a great American star.

A world class American Icon

Paul Newman
1925-2008

CLIMBING THE LAVENDER LADDER
PAUL NEWMAN'S SECRET LIFE AS A BISEXUAL

by Danforth Prince,
President, Blood Moon Productions

In the opinion of many of his fans, Newman's emotional and sexual involvements with the women in his life (Monroe, Crawford, Taylor, Grace Kelly, Audrey Hepburn, and perhaps most importantly, Joanne Woodward) are more compelling than the equivalent relationships he shared with men.

But according to Darwin Porter, the full story of what Newman did as a means to his end in Golden-Age Hollywood hasn't ever been fully revealed—until now.

During a span of more than 50 years, insiders on Broadway and in Hollywood have spoken of Paul Newman's closeted life. Details about the megastar's bisexual history have been among the entertainment industry's worst-kept secrets.

For decades, the underground press has included Paul Newman on their list of bisexual or gay stars, a list that included Rock Hudson, Roddy McDowall, Richard Chamberlain, Farley Granger, Tab Hunter, Burt Lancaster, Marlon Brando, James Dean, Montgomery Clift, and countless others. "WAS PAUL NEWMAN GAY?" ran one headline. Yet another proclaimed: "DEEP INSIDE THE HOLLYWOOD CLOSET: RUMOR MILL IMPLICATES PAUL NEWMAN."

Even during Newman's lifetime, Larry Quirk, the dean of Hollywood biographers, wrote about Paul Newman's "homosexual panic" and how he maneuvered his way "up the lavender ladder." Quirk was making veiled references to his casting couch interludes with playwrights Tennessee Williams (author of *Cat on a Hot Tin Roof*--its film adaptation propelled Newman to stardom) and William Inge (author of *Picnic*, the play that launched Newman's legend on Broadway).

According to Darwin Porter, the secret life of Paul Newman reached the peak of its exposure and speculation during the 1970s, when Newman acquired the film rights to *The Front Runner*, a best-selling novel about a homosexual coach who falls desperately in love with his star (male) athlete.

In his role as the film's producer, Newman originally offered the role of the athlete to Robert Redford, who refused to play a gay character, fearing that it would harm his image at the box office. Consequently, Newman negotiated with Cal Culver, America's leading gay porn star of the 1970s, to interpret the role. Cal, a friend and confidant of Darwin Porter, later revealed to the gay press that he had had an affair with Newman. Additionally, Darwin's best friend, novelist James Leo Herlihy, had an affair with Newman when he was trying to persuade him to star as Joe Buck in the film version of his novel, *Midnight Cowboy*.

Many of Newman's personal friends, particularly those from the Actors Studio, spoke privately over the years about Newman's sexuality. They included actress Janice Rule (who later became a psychotherapist, with a respected practice in New York City), Rod Steiger, Geraldine Page, Eartha Kitt (who was introduced to Newman via her best friend, James Dean), and "Vampira," (aka Maila Nurmi), TV-land's first Goth, and a famous personality of the 1950s.

Tony Perkins, a friend of Herlihy's, privately admitted that he'd sustained a sexual affair with Newman when they both lived at the Château Marmont in Los Angeles in the 50s. The self-admittedly gay writer Gore Vidal spoke openly about his near-obsessional fixation on Newman during Newman's appearance in Gore's teleplay of *Billy the Kid*. And during one particularly complex point in their relationship, Paul Newman and his then "mistress," Joanne Woodward, shared a Malibu beach house with Vidal and his "husband," Howard Austen. Throughout that chapter of their lives, all four members of the ménage remained "artfully nonspecific" as to the direction of the emotional links going on within that beach house.

Sal Mineo, another friend of Darwin's, confessed to having sustained a sexual affair with Newman that began on the set of *Somebody Up There Likes Me*. Sal confessed his undying love for Paul to yet another author, Larry Quirk, who published this then-first-time news in a book released by Taylor Publishing Company. Later, an unauthorized feature story on Newman revealed that Jackie Witte (Newman's first wife) threatened to leave him when she learned about his affair with James Dean.

Brooks Clift, another of Darwin's friends, revealed the details of an affair that his brother, Montgomery Clift, had had with Newman. And actor Frank McHugh, a close friend of Spencer Tracy and a member of the hard-drinking "Irish Mafia" of Hollywood, claimed that he accidentally walked in on Newman and the recently deceased actor Jack Lord, catching them together "in an embarrassing position." Newman, Lord, and McHugh were each at the time filming a teleplay together.

For more on the startling details associated with the bisexual side of the actor whom no one seemed to be able to get enough of, Blood Moon hereby presents Darwin Porter's newest biography. Best wishes to all of you, and many thanks.

FRENEMIES AND FRIENDS
WHAT THEY SAID ABOUT HIM:

"You can't help feeling sorry for guys like Newman. They have too much to lose if they make one false step. Look what *Confidential* did to Tab Hunter. Whenever Joanne Woodward came up, Newman became all macho. He was sad in many ways. Having to pretend to be what he wasn't. But most of us Hollywood hunks in the 1950s had to do that."

Matinée heartthrob **Jeffrey Hunter**

"Hell, guy, you just can't seem to realize what's happening. You're the new kid on the block. Every gay and every horny broad in Hollywood wants to go to bed with Paul Newman. You're doing pretty well for a married man. I've always had this belief that if a married man played it right, he can have more fun than single blokes."

Rod Steiger

"Paul Newman has the potential of becoming a magnificent actor if he ever gets through this complex he has about playing boy-macho."

Joan Crawford

"Even Newman's baby blues couldn't lure the women away from those TV boxes. We should have stripped him down more and shot the film with him half naked. That day will come for movies, I predict."

Robert Wise, lamenting the failure of the Paul Newman film he directed, *Until They Sail*

"Mr. Newman, Mr. Newman! Would you like to see my body?"

Sandra Dee, at 14

"I never got around to screwing Paul Newman, although I certainly intended to. He had as much sex in the 50s as I did, but whereas he got away with it, I didn't"

Rock Hudson

"Newman is just as much of a narcissist as Gore Vidal, but he disguises it completely, and, like the most skilled of actors, puts up a mask to confuse the world. I suspect he will go far in an industry that is all about illusion. There is no self-awareness in this handsome young man at all. He is an obvious homosexual, but does not dare admit that to himself. He's a selfish rogue while pretending to be benevolent, supporting all the right causes. He has a facile charm but no depth. In spite of the hot sun out here, he already knows that California is a cold, harsh land. He does not want it to hurt him. So what will he do? What must he do? He will inflict emotional pain on others, therefore avoiding the pain of having the blows strike him first. I predict Newman will turn into a cardboard figure. There will be no reality to him. He can't be real. A tragedy, really. But, this is, after all, Lotusland."

Anaïs Nin

PAUL NEWMAN'S DIVERSIONS, TEMPORARY PASSIONS, TROPHIES, AND/OR EMBARRASSING INDISCRETIONS

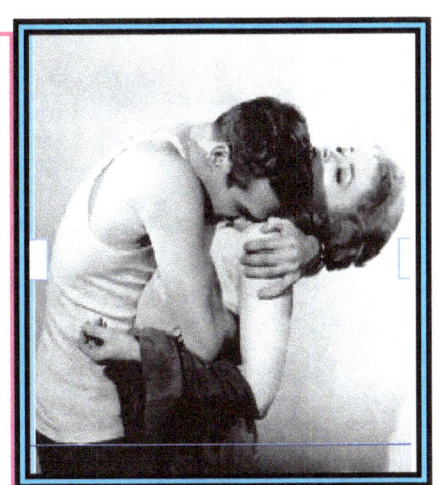

Marlon Brando

Jackie-O

Montgomery Clift

Marilyn Monroe

Steve McQueen

Grace Kelly

Robert Redford

Elizabeth Taylor

Joan Crawford

Tom Cruise

Audrey Hepburn

James Dean

BLOOD MOON'S RESPECTFUL FAREWELL TO A GREAT AMERICAN MOVIE STAR

KIRK DOUGLAS
MORE IS NEVER ENOUGH

DARWIN PORTER & DANFORTH PRINCE

DRIPPING WITH TESTOSTERONE, A YOUNG HORNDOG SETS OUT TO CONQUER HOLLYWOOD

Of the many male stars of Golden Age Hollywood, Kirk Douglas became the final survivor, the last icon of a fabled, optimistic era that the world will never see again. When he celebrated his birthday in 2016, a headline read: LEGENDARY HOLLYWOOD HORNDOG TURNS 100.

He was both a charismatic actor and a man of uncommon force and vigor. His restless and volcanic spirit is reflected both in his films and through his many sexual conquests.

Douglas was the son of Russian-Jewish immigrants, his father a collector and seller of rags. After service in the Navy during World War II, he hit Hollywood, oozing masculinity and charm. Conquering Tinseltown and bedding its leading ladies, he became the personification of the American dream, moving from obscurity and (literally) rags to riches and major-league fame.

The *Who's Who* cast of characters roaring through his life included not only a daunting list of Hollywood goddesses, but the town's most colossal male talents and egos, too. They included his kindred hellraiser and best buddy Burt Lancaster, John Wayne, Henry Fonda, Billy Wilder, Laurence Olivier, Rock Hudson, and a future U.S. President, Ronald Reagan, when winning the highest office in the land was virtually unthinkable.

Over the decades, he immortalized himself in film after film, delivering, like a Trojan, one memorable performance after another. He was at home in *film noir*, as a western gunslinger, as an adventurer (in both ancient and modern sagas), as a juggler, as Tennessee Williams' "gentleman caller," as a Greek super-hero from Homer's *Odyssey*, and as roguish sailor in the Jules Verne yarn, exploring the mysteries of the ocean's depths.

En route to his status as a myth and legend, his performances reflected both his personal pain and the brutalization of the characters he played, too. In *Champion* (1949), he was beaten to a fatal bloody pulp. As the sleazy, heartless reporter in *Ace in the Hole* (1951), he was stabbed with a knife in his gut. As Van Gogh in *Lust for Life* (1956), he writhed in emotional agony and unrequited love before slicing off his ear with a razor. His World War I movie, *Paths of Glory* (1957) grows more profound over the years. He lost an eye in *The Vikings* (1958), and, as the Thracian slave leading a revolt against Roman legions in *Spartacus* (1960), he was crucified.

All of this is brought out, with photos, in this remarkable testimonial to the last hero of Hollywood's cinematic and swashbuckling Golden Age, an inspiring testimonial to the values and core beliefs of an America that's Gone With the Wind, yet lovingly remembered as a time when it, in many ways, was truly great.

The longest surviving male star from Golden Age Hollywood, Kirk Douglas, once said:

"If you are born a complete nobody, and have dreams of becoming a somebody, know that it's going to be a rough, lonely, and rocky road, filled with potholes, before you get where you're going."

"Be aware you might not get there, especially if you head to Hollywood by train, plane, car, or your trusty thumb stuck out on the highway."

"I was warned that Hollywood has the world's largest boulevard of broken dreams. I arrived in town planning to avoid that boulevard, regardless of how many detours I had to take."

"What happens to you on the way to the top is called life, with all its ups and downs, its pain and sorrow, but also its joy and happiness."

"I experienced it all, the deepest regrets, the greatest thrills, and, yes, stardom beyond my wildest dreams."

"Sometimes forbidden love knocked on my door, Lots and lots of beautiful women who wanted what I had to give them. In most cases, what appeared to be love in the forgiving moonlight never lasted when that sun in the morning brought a golden dawn to the Pacific Coast. I woke up, faced reality, hastily put on my clothes, and headed out the door back to home and hearth until my next adventure."

"My circumcised Jewish cock brought thrills to dozens of women. Mae West might have turned me down, but who needed that old drag queen when you had Lana Turner, Marlene Dietrich, Rita Hayworth, Linda Darnell, Ingrid Bergman—and the beat goes on."

KIRK DOUGLAS WAS A *CHAMPION* IN THE RING, *SPARTACUS* ON THE BATTLEFIELD, AND A MAN WITH A *LUST FOR LIFE.*

HERE, COMPILED AFTER YEARS OF RESEARCH, IS THE MOST COMPREHENSIVE OVERVIEW OF HIS LIFE AND TIMES EVER PUBLISHED.

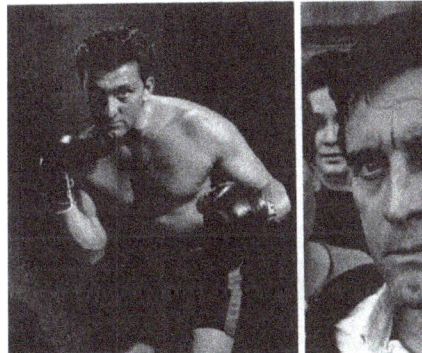

The son of an illiterate Russian "Ragman," **ISSUR DANIELOVITCH** survived poverty and anti-Semitism to pursue the American Dream.

Part Romantic Hero, part Dostoevskiian Anti-Hero, Issur assumed a WASP name and a new Identity as **KIRK DOUGLAS.** Blood Moon's comprehensive biography describes what happened after that.

PETER O'TOOLE: Hellraiser, Sexual Outlaw, Irish Rebel

Darwin Porter & Danforth Prince

When it was published, early in 2015, this book was widely publicized in the *Daily Mail*, the *New York Daily News*, the *New York Post*, the *Midwest Book Review*, *The Express (London)*, *The Globe*, the *National Enquirer*, and in equivalent publications worldwide

One of the world's most admired (and brilliant) actors, Peter O'Toole wined and wenched his way through a labyrinth of sexual and interpersonal betrayals, sometimes with disastrous results. Away from the stage and screen, where such films as *Becket* and *Lawrence of Arabia*, made film history, his life was filled with drunken, debauched nights and edgy sexual experimentations, most of which were never openly examined in the press. A hellraiser, he shared wild times with his "best blokes" Richard Burton and Richard Harris. Peter Finch, also his close friend, once invited him to join him in sharing the pleasures of his mistress, Vivien Leigh.

"My father, a bookie, moved us to the Mick community of Leeds," O'Toole once told a reporter. "We were very poor, but I was born an Irishman, which accounts for my gift of gab, my unruly behavior, my passionate devotion to women and the bottle, and my loathing of any authority figure."

Author Robert Sellers described O'Toole's boyhood neighborhood. "Three of his playmates went on to be hanged for murder; one strangled a girl in a lovers' quarrel; one killed a man during a robbery; another cut up a warden in South Africa with a pair of shears. It was a heavy bunch."

Peter O'Toole's hell-raising life story has never been told, until now. Hot and uncensored, from a writing team which, even prior to O'Toole's death in 2013, had been collecting under-the-radar info about him for years, this book has everything you ever wanted to know about how THE LION navigated his way through the boudoirs of the Entertainment Industry IN WINTER, Spring, Summer, and a dissipated Autumn as well.

Blood Moon has ripped away the imperial robe, scepter, and crown usually associated with this quixotic problem child of the British Midlands. Provocatively uncensored, this illusion-shattering overview of Peter O'Toole's hellraising (or at least very naughty) and demented life is unique in the history of publishing.

Left, **Peter O'Toole** plotting vengeance as **Henry II** in *Becket;* and *right* shooting up an oasis as **T.E. Lawrence** in *Lawrence of Arabia*.

THE PASSION OF THE WORLD'S GREATEST ACTOR

"God put me on this earth to raise hell! And I did."
—*Peter O'Toole*

"If Peter had been any prettier, he would have been billed as Florence of Arabia."
—*Noël Coward*

"Princess Margaret was insatiable. Calling every day, couldn't get enough of me."
—*Peter O'Toole*

"My greatest sexual thrill involved going to bed with Peter and some girl at the same time."
—*Richard Burton*

"If there's not a dame on this set I can't screw, my name's not Peter O'Toole."
—*Peter O'Toole*

"Peter was the only man I preferred in bed to Dick [Richard Burton]."
—*Elizabeth Taylor*

"Katharine Hepburn called me a pig and a drunk. She even bashed my head a few times with an empty liquor bottle. But I adored her. I told her that one night with me would cure her of her lesbianism."
—*Peter O'Toole*

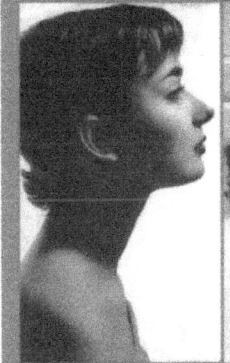

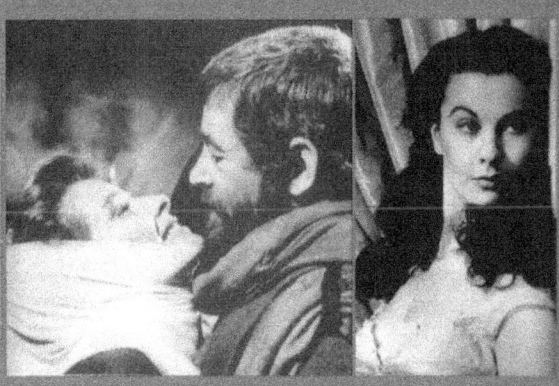

PETER O'TOOLE

Hellraiser, Sexual Outlaw, & Irish Rebel
An Unprecedented New Look at the 20th Century's Most Outrageous Actor

Born to a vagabond bookie working the U.K's racetracks, Peter O'Toole became "the most notorious sailor in Her Majesty's Royal Navy" and then worked as a street vendor, a paparazzo, a newsman, and a steeplejack before drifting into the London theatre.

After his spectacular success in David Lean's four-hour epic, *Lawrence of Arabia*, he announced, "I've arrived! Ignore me at your peril!" He then went on to be nominated for seven Oscars before emerging as the Crown Prince of the British Theatre.

An orgiastic hellraiser, he starred in week-long binges and sex orgies of near Biblical proportions, bedding everyone from Elizabeth Taylor to Princess Margaret, who relentlessly pursued him. Mercurial acting talent on the screen was combined with a lethal off-screen life that "would have landed most blokes in jail" (his words).

In 2015, Blood Moon released the world's most comprehensive *exposé* of the eccentric, hell-raising actor.

Here's **Peter O'Toole** in *Caligula* (1972) as the syphilis-ridden and very dangerous psychotic, **Tiberius**, Emperor of Rome. Still viewed as an authentic (and pornographic) overview of ancient Rome, it was described at the time as "the most debauched movie ever made."

Blood Moon's exposé of PETER O'TOOLE--one of the Baddest of the Bad Boys of the London stage and later, of Hollywood, received a *tsunami* of favorable reviews and news coverage after its release in 2015.

The pages that follow replicate just a few of them.

Here's how it was reviewed by Vinton McCabe in the NEW YORK JOURNAL OF BOOKS.

Something decidedly odd is going on at Blood Moon Productions, whose Babylon Series has recently released its latest Hollywood biography: *Peter O'Toole: Hellraiser, Sexual Outlaw, Irish Rebel*.

Where, in the past, the subjects of these "tabloid biographies" (written in chapters that resemble nothing so much as photocopies of *The Enquirer* and *The Weekly World News*) have been written about in a manner that some readers might consider salacious (Nancy Reagan, in her youth, is alleged to have been particularly skilled at treating her gentlemen callers to oral sex, Zsa Zsa Gabor is said to have had sexual congress with both John F. Kennedy *and* Richard Nixon) the latest celebrity to be put under the microscope—the aforementioned Peter O'Toole—is treated with something alarmingly akin to respect.

Which might, under other circumstances, be considered a good thing. But consider the subtitle: *Hellraiser, Sexual Outlaw, Irish Rebel*.

Understandably, the suggestion that Peter O'Toole had a fling with England's Princess Margaret Rose on the island of Mustique might, in some (royal) households, be enough to grant him the title of "sexual outlaw," but after all the allegations of sexual misconduct and/or experimentation ascribed to various Reagans, Kennedys, and Gabors, to say nothing of writers along the line of Gore Vidal, Tennessee Williams, and Truman Capote, and a string of Hollywood all-stars from Barbara Stanwyck to Marlene Dietrich to that ultimate hellraiser (and a sexual outlaw who knew what being a sexual outlaw was all about), Errol Flynn, the stuff that O'Toole is said to have attempted leaves him several notches down on the outlaw scale from his dear friend Richard Burton, and many, many slots below the ultimate outlaw, Mr. Flynn.

What Peter O'Toole mostly appears to be is very consistent actually, especially where his goals, self- congratulatory comments, and rude behavior are concerned.

In all these, he started out pretty early in life.

For instance, on his 18th birthday, he called his best friend to tell him that he had decided to give up his job at a local newspaper and run away to London:

"I decided that I don't want to be a journalist," he said, "I don't want to write about the affairs of other people. I want journalists writing about my affairs. I think I want to be a famous actor . . . I've decided to storm the formidable walls of London Town . . . I'm heading south to conquer. Get out of my way [Sir Laurence] Olivier, or else I'll knock you down and walk over your tired old body to claim my right in the spotlight."

In this brief quote, O'Toole reveals two of the major themes of his life: ambition and the need for attention/fame.

What he proposed next to his friend on the day of his 18th birthday, August 2, 1950, illustrates another lingering theme:

"In the meantime, let's get pissed. Booze is the most outrageous of drugs. That's why it's my preferred choice."

Getting pissed and staying pissed seem to have been intertwined goals for O'Toole that placed second only to heterosexual intercourse on his ongoing bucket list. Acting, it seems, came in third.

When it came to sexuality, O'Toole insisted that he was decidedly straight and reportedly turned down Laurence Olivier, John Geilgud, Noel Coward, and Alan Bates, among many other interested suitors. This is despite the fact that many found his enraptured dance when first fitted with Arab robes in *Lawrence of Arabia* as a sign of fey tendencies. And the fact that his role as a "babe magnet" in *Casino Royale*—a role that had been cast with Warren Beatty, who quit the film, allowing O'Toole to take it over—was met with reviews that sighed with their regret that Beatty had been replaced. O'Toole, the reviewers insisted, made for a poor on-screen lothario. And the fact as well that the nuns in the Catholic school he attended as a child gave him the nickname "Bubbles."

And then there's this: while discussing the experience in Catholic school, O'Toole reportedly commented, "Nuns aren't that smart. Imagine denying yourself cock all your life. If I were a heterosexual woman, I would take on at least six men a night from early morning to midnight."

Hmmm.

Still, Peter O'Toole got around. He made a wager with a friend that he could bed British actress Diana Dors, as well as Anita Ekberg and Jayne Mansfield and won the bet. And reportedly had an affair with the then-Mrs. Richard Burton, Elizabeth Taylor, while the three of them, the Burtons and O'Toole, were filming an adaptation of Dylan Thomas's *Under Milk Wood*.

Princess Margaret Rose, Countess of Snowden. Well intentioned, but often blocked from expressing her true feelings, this tragic "younger sister of the Queen:" was looking for love and perhaps a handsome prince.

Here's **Peter O'Toole**, cast as the Prince of Denmark in the National Theatre's 1963 production of *Hamlet*. Was he, for a time, the best Shakespearan actor in the English-speaking world? Regardless of who did it best, Margaret Rose, for a while, at least, selected him as her friend and playmate.

Here's **Peter O'Toole** in *Caligula* (1972) as the syphilus-ridden and very dangerous psychotic, Tiberius, Emperor of Rome. Still viewed as an authentic (and pornographic) overview of ancient Rome, it was described at the time as "the most debauched movie ever made."

[*While cheating on his wife Sian Phillips often enough to ultimately send her into the arms of another man, O'Toole did at least once rather famously state, in a spirit of fairness, that, "She's a free woman. Just because she's married doesn't mean she has to be a servant to her man. There's a wedding ring on her finger, not in her nose."*]

Here's **Peter O'Toole**, in bed with **Elizabeth Taylor** in a money-losing production of Dylan Thomas' **Under Milkwood** (1972). They're each portraying a resident of the fictional Welsh village of Llareggub.

Did they do it alone, or was Richard Burton also involved in the scene?.

The Peter O'Toole who emerges from these pages is less a hellraiser than a braggart, less a sexual outlaw than a womanizer who proved to be a poor husband and a worse father, and less an Irish rebel than a pugnacious drunkard. He is, as presented in these pages, something of a bore.

But there is also Peter O'Toole the artist. Peter O'Toole the actor, who attained an iconic status early on with *Lawrence of Arabia*, who more than held his own on-screen against Katharine Hepburn in *A Lion in Winter*, and who returned after a period of flops and attempts to put his drinking behind him with *The Stuntman* and *My Favorite Year* and who acknowledged both his old age and his personal failures with a late-life minor masterpiece with *Venus*.

Where the gossip in this biography is played down compared to others written by the same authors, it is in the study of the man and the specifics of his movies that it succeeds.

And the biography produced seems less entertainingly outrageous than the others produced by the House of the Blood Moon, more centered as a traditional Hollywood bio, giving the reader some rather good anecdotes about the making of this full film catalogue. And, indeed, the chapters dedicated to the making of *Lawrence of Arabia*, from the details of the nose job that O'Toole was required to endure in order to secure the role to a lively recreation of O'Toole's bromance with Omar Shariff, form the beating heart of the book and are very satisfying indeed.

Here's **Peter O'Toole** with **Audrey Hepburn** in that stylish romp about art forgeries and *haute couture*, **How to Steal a Million** (1966).

Even better—and equal to any salacious details that the authors have given us in any of their other, more outrageous, biographies—is any section of the book in which the Burtons appear. Tales of drunken binges, threesomes, banquets with food flown in from around the world, and battles, bruises, and screeched oaths bring the book to vibrant life and raise the question as to why the authors have not until now turned their attention to the most famous, oversized couple in world history: Liz and Dick?

If ever there were to be a perfect blending of authors and subjects, it would be Richard Burton and Elizabeth Taylor and Darwin Porter and Danforth Prince.

That would surely be the stuff of which bestsellers and Lifetime mini-series are made.

No one could portray an eccentric, arrogant, outraged, and aristocratic Brit like **Peter O'Toole**.

He's seen above satirizing the "mad as a hatter" British aristocracy in **The Ruling Class** (1972). A commercial failure at the time, it was described by O'Toole as "a comedy with tragic relief." It's now a cult classic.

Vinton McCabe is a critic-at-large, whose running commentary of pop culture began more than 20 years ago in the pages of the Advocate Newspapers of CT and MA, continued on the pages of New England Monthly, and blared out of radios tuned to WGCH in Greenwich, and other Connecticut stations. He is the author of the novel **Death in Venice, California.**

PETER O'TOOLE

"I'VE DONE EVERYTHING POSSIBLE"

by Darwin Porter

Insouciant, offensive, brilliant, and brash, actor Peter O'Toole once said, "God put me on this earth to raise hell—and I did just that."

His week-long drug and drinking binges, coupled with sex orgies, reached near Biblical proportions. It was said that he matched Don Juan's legendary total of 1,033 seductions.

Hailed by some critics as the greatest actor of the 20th century—move over Olivier and Gielgud—he was nominated for eight Oscars as Best Actor of the Year, but lost every time, although he did win an Oscar for Lifetime Achievement in 2003.

This charismatic man lives again in the pages of my latest biography, *Peter O'Toole—Hellraiser, Sexual Outlaw, & Irish Rebel,* written with co-author Danforth Prince.

Growing up in industrial Leeds in England, the son of a crooked Irish bookmaker, O'Toole claimed, "I was part of the criminal class, not the working class." Discovering sex as a very young teenager, he later proclaimed, "There is nothing on earth as good as a man and a woman."

He mesmerized the world by appearing in white flowing robes in *Lawrence of Arabia* (1962), hailed as one of the greatest films of all time. Marlon Brando had turned down the role of T. E. Lawrence, the Imperialistic Brit who helped to unify the Arabs of the Saudi Peninsula in a successful campaign to overthrow the Turkish Ottoman Empire.

Flirtatiously, playwright Noël Coward told O'Toole, "If you were any prettier, you'd be called "Florence of Arabia."

O'Toole went on from there to make some 90 other films—some of them memorable, others so horrible that studios didn't want to release them. As one reviewer said, "O'Toole would overact; he would be ridiculous, but he was never dull and was often riveting. He battled alcoholism and came to look and behave like his own ghost near the end of his life. We are unlikely to see the likes of him again."

In 1958, he married the brilliant Welsh actress Siân Phillips, a turbulent liaison that would last until 1979, when she divorced him to marry a younger actor. He proclaimed, "The happiest married men I know have a wife to come home to—not to come home *with.*"

His bosom buddy, a rival on the screen and in the boudoir, was Richard Burton. O'Toole had seduced Elizabeth Taylor before Burton met her. Originally, she had wanted O'Toole to co-star with her as Marc Antony in *Cleopatra* (1963).

In addition to Taylor, O'Toole's affairs included some of the world's most beautiful women, ranging from Vivien Leigh to Ava Gardner to Audrey Hepburn. He even went aristocratic at times, conquering the Duchess of Alba and Sarah Churchill (Sir Winston's daughter). But often, his conquest was some "wench" he met in a pub during one of his legendary drinking forays.

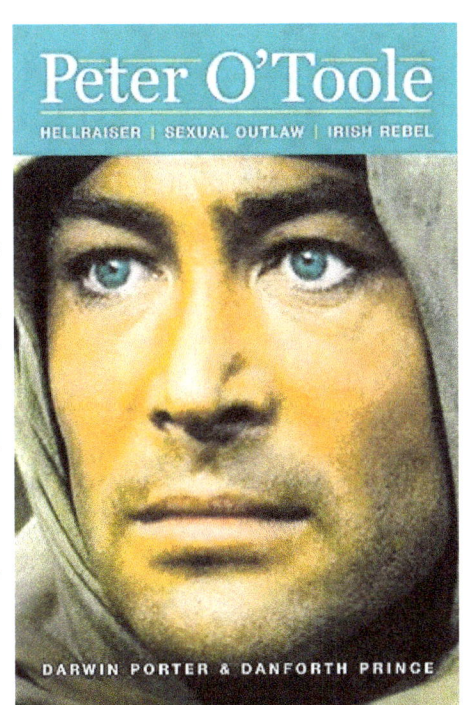

"I was a disreputable rake," he confessed. No affair was more notable than Her Royal Highness, Princess Margaret, the "Black Sheep" of the House of Windsor. He later told Burton, "I found her insatiable."

In spite of a cycle of dissipation he pursued on a virtually epic scale, he outlived most of his friends, dying in 2013 at the age of 81.

In his final years, he said, "the only exercise I get these days is walking behind the coffins of my friends, those who actually exercised."

He was a headline maker. When he starred as *Hamlet* (1963), in London, he called it "the worst play ever written." His controversial performance as *Macbeth* (1980) was hailed as the world's most atrocious. "The Bard is turning over in his tomb," wrote one reviewer, who likened his performance to that of "monstrous Bette Davis in *What Ever Happened to Baby Jane?*"

His own comment: "I was as popular as a pork sausage in a synagogue."

Reporters always found him good copy. One from London's *Daily Mail* asked him how he wanted to be remembered.

"For making the world's best French toast."

He also was asked what was his greatest thrill.

He answered, "To go out pubbing one night in London and to wake up in Mexico."

Darwin Porter's biography reveals the drama-within-the-dramas associated with the celebrated Anglo-French genius **Jeanne Moreau**. **O'Toole** is pictured in the *left photo* as a hapless (and English) foreign diplomat trying to avoid being enrolled as the sex slave of the sex-crazed Russian Empress in *Great Catherine* (1968)..

The middle photo shows the world's then-most famous transsexual, **April Ashley,** as she appeared during the peak of their affair; and

The right-hand photo shows **O'Toole** as Henry II, emoting with his drinking buddy and frenemy, **Richard Burton** as **Thomas Becket** during their filming of the Oscar-winning historical drama, *Becket* (1964). Becket, a principled Saxon commoner who was later designated as the **Archbishop of Canterbury**, arranges debaucheries for the king when he isn't busy running Henry's court.

  w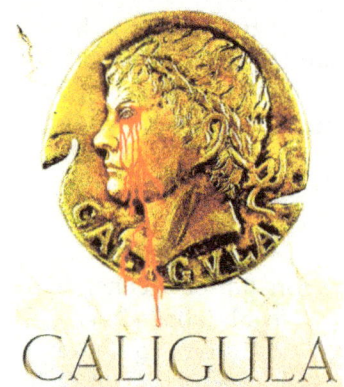

 ***

Peter O'Toole's life and times intersected, sometimes intimately, with some of the most watched celebrities of his era: *Left Photos:* His co-star, **Katharine Hepburn,** as Eleanor of Aquitaine, "the most famous woman of the Middle Ages," as she appeared in Peter O'Toole's homage to a dysfunctional Imperial family, *A Lion in Winter* (1968).

Middle photos: Lifestyle guru and founder/President of **Penthouse**, **Bob Guccione,** from around the time he financed a film whose costs almost instantly spun out of control, *Caligula* (1979). It showcased **O'Toole** in his portayal of Tiberius, an insane, syphilitic tyrant.

Right photos: The distinguished British actress, **Helen Mirren,** shown here as Caesonia, "the most promiscuous woman in Rome." Mirren, of course, went on to portray other, more restrained figures, including Queen Elizabeth II.

Book Review News from Blood Moon Productions and from

FILMS *in Review*

PETER O'TOOLE: Audiences loved him in *Lawrence of Arabia*. Later, he reigned as both a film star and "babe magnet" hounded, worldwide, by the tabloids, adulated in both London and Hollywood.

And now, the film historians at FILMS IN REVIEW have weighed in with their opinion of his recent biography from Blood Moon Productions. Here's the review, lifted verbatim from the much-anticipated CHRISTMAS COLUMN, 2015, as authored by film producer and cinema historian Roy Frumkes, whose biography appears below:

PETER O'TOOLE – HELLRAISER, SEXUAL OUTLAW, IRISH REBEL

BloodMoonProductions.com. Writers: Darwin Porter & Danforth Prince. 620+ pages. Book Smell: subtle.

It has to be a reflection of modern technological advances, it can't be anything else: all the Blood Moon books, most of them several hundred pages in length, are written by the same two people – Porter & Prince. I mean, how is that possible? Each book should have taken two years. Well, it must be something to do with the ease of writing with WORD, combined with the extraordinarily easy access to information on the internet. I've never seen a more thorough use of these modern breakthroughs than here.

And while the book has the feeling, at times, of collage, it's never any less than fun, and it's infinitely more substantial than a mere gossip tome. I mean, I loved Kenneth Anger's Hollywood Babylon books (I had the pleasure of putting him up at my apt for a few days once, and that was fun, too), but they (and this, at first glance) are nothing more than gossip. However in their cumulative, lurid glow, like Weejee's LA photos, the O'Toole bio becomes something more than what is on the surface – much, more, certainly than what Anger gave us. O'TOOLE takes itself a level more seriously than gossip, and its text is informative, both about the British stage and the American screen.

In terms of glorious gossip, however, wait till you get (just as an example) to page 126. O'Toole is invited by Jules Buck, his friend and business partner, to join him for drinks with two other friends, who turn out to be Ava Gardner (they meet in her suite at the Savoy Hotel in London) and Burt Lancaster, neither of whom O'Toole had previously met, and both of whom had acted together in Robert Siodmak's THE KILLERS. Their unexpurgated stories that evening are absolute jaw-droppers. Lancaster's bi-sexuality and Gardner's sexual appetites are tossed away like everyday, casual knowledge. Their fast-flowing repartee and awareness of each other's sexual adventures pile on, paragraph after paragraph, story after story, and it's heady stuff. Add in some bizarre here-say out of nowhere about Evita Peron, and it's a kinetic, wonderfully written chapter. And there are plenty more to follow.

I mentioned this book to FIR's quirky film critic, Victoria Alexander, and after reading it she ordered the one on Elizabeth Taylor and said it was just as good. Blood Moon has found a winning formula.

For access to the orginal text of this review, click on: http://69.195.124.61/~filmsinr/2015/12/20/christmas-column-2015/

Roy Frumkes, the author of this review, followed his childhood dreams of filmmaking, and has been producing, writing and/or directing motion pictures for thirty years. Roy was a member until 2013 of the National Board of Review of Motion Pictures since he got out of college in 1966. He wrote for FIR for thirty years before purchasing the magazine from the NBR in '96 with co-owner Joe Anderson. Prior to that Roy was Managing Editor of the home theater magazine *The Perfect Vision*. From 1985 to 1994 Roy co-produced and co-directed the annual D.W.Griffith Awards Ceremony, working with the likes of Paul Newman, Bette Davis, William Hurt, Steven Spielberg, Kirk And Michael Douglas, Sidney Poitier, Jodie Foster and Sean Connery.

Currently, Roy teaches film history and screenwriting at The School of Visual Arts, which he considers the finest film school on the East Coast

For More about this book, click on KNEWS, Southern California's News and Talk Radio, which discusses the role of Peter O'Toole as the stage and screen's most enigmatic Hellraiser. Bill Feingold interviews Danforth Prince about an actor whose first and last names EACH had phallic implications https://youtu.be/t3oU356dhPI

In June of 2015, Blood Moon's biography of *Peter O'Toole* was designated by **The New York Book Festival** as Runner Up to Best Biography of The Year. *Blood Moon: Entertainment About How America Interprets Its Celebrities*   www.BloodMoonProductions.com

Peter O'Toole Affair: Did 'Lawrence Of Arabia' Get It On With Queen Elizabeth's Sister Princess Margaret?

By Victoria Guerra in *FOOD WORLD* Magazine
May 26, 2015 11:13 AM EDT

Known as one of the best film actors of all time after breathtaking performances like the title role in "Lawrence of Arabia" and even voicing critic Ego in the Pixar favorite "Ratatouille," the famous "bad boy" genius actor has a new biography under way - and it talks about a supposed Peter O'Toole affair with **Princess Margaret.**

Classic Hollywood glamour won't ever die even if most of its biggest stars have already passed away, and rumors about some of the time's biggest performers still continue well into the 21st century, decades after their prime - including Peter O'Toole's affair with a royal.

Besides the new revelation of Peter O'Toole's affair, other "gossip" that has continued to live long after stars' primes include new information about the death of "West Side Story" legendary actress **Natalie Wood** in the 80s, **Sophia Loren** discussing her infamous picture with J**ayne Mansfield, Rock Hudson**'s ex boyfriend speaking out publicly for the first time after and even the recent discovery that there was a tunnel connecting **Kirk Douglas'** home to **the Playboy Mansion.**

According to *Financial Express*, a new biography about the "*Becket*" actor has revealed Peter O'-Toole's affair with **Princess Margaret**, the younger sister of **Queen Elizabeth of England** - when he was married to Welsh actress **Siân Phillips** and the royal was ending her marriage to **Lord Snowdon**.

The *New York Daily News* reports that the Peter O'Toole affair claims first came out in a new biography of the actor called "*Peter O'Toole: Hellraiser, Sexual Outlaw, Irish Rebel*," written by authors **Darwin Porter** and **Danforth Prince.**

The Mirror reports that the book claims that the iconic actor and the royal allegedly enjoyed a secret holiday in the Caribbean and a similar one in a private villa in Morocco in the 1970s after having met years previously at a screening of O'Toole's film "*Lord Jim*."

The biography claiming Peter O'Toole affair with the princess will come out next month.

—**FOOD WORLD NEWS**

In Reference to Blood Moon's biography of Peter O'Toole, the largest-circulation Broadsheet in the World, THE DAILY MAIL, published THIS (the text on the pages that follow) in their edition of May 22, 2015

***

Peter O'Toole was the Hellraiser who told Burton:
'I've slept with Liz and she says I'm better in bed than you."

Peter O'Toole was famed for wild boozing.
But a new book claims his biggest thirst was for women
Biography reveals infamous womanizing of Peter O'Toole,
ONE OF LAST GREAT HELLRAISERS OF THE BRITISH STAGE

Book claims he had affairs with Elizabeth Taylor, Audrey Hepburn, Vivien Leigh,
Diana Dors - even Princess Margaret. One night he tested his friendship with Richard Burton
by claiming Taylor - his wife - thought he was better in bed

By Tom Leonard in New York for the DAILY MAIL
PUBLISHED: 19:32 EDT, 22 May 2015 | UPDATED: 00:44 EDT, 23 May 2015

A frail, sad, and in-decline **Peter O'Toole** in his last movie,, *The Decline of an Empire*. He died before its release in 2014

April Ashley was one of the world's most beautiful models and had already had **Elvis Presley** propose marriage to her when she met the actor Peter O' Toole. He and **Omar Sharif** were filming the 1962 epic *Lawrence Of Arabia* and the young O'Toole swept Ashley away when they met at a party thrown by Spanish leader General Franco's daughter near Seville in southern Spain.

As she later lay in bed with O'Toole, she whispered in his ear: 'I was born a boy.' As Miss Ashley, a former merchant seaman and the first British person to undergo sex-change surgery, later recalled: "Peter was too far gone at that point to worry about what sex I had been born."

According to a new book, legendary actor Peter O'Toole had affairs with numerous stars including **Elizabeth Taylor**, pictured with O'Toole and her husband **Richard Burton**

It's an astonishing tale but, as the last of the great hellraisers of British stage and screen, it's easy to accept such outrageous stories about Peter O'Toole. He was a star who revelled in his notoriety and debauched reputation.

The white-suited dandy with the cigarette holder and the piercing blue eyes once threw a New Year's Eve party at his Hampstead home, saying the house rule was: "Fornication, madness, murder, drunkenness, shouting, shrieking, leaping, polite conversation and the breaking of bones; such jollities constitute acceptable behaviour."

A more complicated personality than his fellow thespian dissolutes, **Richard Burton, Richard Harris and Oliver Reed,** the unrepentant, hard-drinking troublemaker was also a self-described romantic who claimed to know all 154 of Shakespeare's sonnets.

"All the larks I got up to as a young actor were never reported, thank God," he said a few years before his death aged 81 in 2013. 'If anyone had dared to talk about my sex life in my prime, I'd have said very simply: "Remove your eye from the keyhole."

The last of the great hellraisers of British stage and screen, Peter O'Toole was a star who revelled in his notoriety and debauched reputation

Now a rip-roaring new biography has put its eye to that keyhole and spied a star whose sexual high-jinks were almost as dissipated as his alcoholic ones.

According to **Peter O'Toole: Hellraiser, Sexual Outlaw, Irish Rebel**, outside his stormy 20-year marriage to Welsh actress **Sian Phillips,** he had affairs with **Elizabeth Taylor, Audrey Hepburn, Vivien Leigh, Diana Dors** — even **Princess Margaret.** The book's American authors, **Darwin Porter** and **Danforth Prince,** have a track record of dredging up old stories and gossip about stars who were spared such public scrutiny when they were alive.

Born and raised in poverty in rural Ireland and later in a rough suburb of Leeds, O'Toole was obsessed with his own sexual gratification and lost his virginity to a prostitute when he was 13. He always liked to insist he was not working class but 'criminal class'.

His drinking was legendary. Once, playing Shylock in his mid-20s in an early RSC production of *The Merchant of Venice*, O'Toole came on stage to deliver a crucial speech and was so intoxicated he started spouting lines from *King Lear*.

Fellow RSC members at Stratford-on-Avon once watched him down a bottle of whisky in one go and at an aftershow party he sat on stage with a pedal bin on either side — one filled with beer and the other with brandy, alternately scooping a two-pint mug into each.

Even if his drunken rowdiness frequently landed him in a police cell, his fine looks and tall, lean frame meant he was always a hit with the ladies. They also gave him a good start in acting.

As a student at RADA, he said he was so outnumbered by women that he didn't do any work the first year and "just fucked myself stupid."

He could be charming when he wanted but in private it was often a different story. He married the elegant **Sian Phillips** in 1959 after they fell in love while playing a brother and sister in an RSC play.

Life with him could be exhilarating — he once came to pick her up in a yellow sports car, told her to get her passport and headed off for Rome. O'Toole, the world's most terrifying driver, then took a wrong turn and they ended up in Yugoslavia.

"After one year of marriage," he said, "For me life is either a wedding or a wake."

His impulsiveness could also be maddening. Disapproving of his wife's clothes one day, O'Toole hurled her entire wardrobe out of a window and she spent the next few days having to wear his clothes.

On another occasion, he bought her a Morris Minor but borrowed it for a trip to Bristol. That night, police rang her to say a sozzled O'Toole was in the cells after wrecking her vehicle by driving it into a squad car.

Phillips managed to stick out the marriage for two tempestuous decades, giving him two daughters before having an affair. O'Toole, discovering she had finally rebelled from her life of drudgery, kicked her out of their Hampstead house.

In her biography, she described how, when she wasn't raising her family on her own while her husband was filming, she had to endure this "abominable' binge-drinking, crockery-hurling tyrant" whom she never dared challenge.

According to the new book, O'Toole had quite a nerve in throwing her out for having an affair because he had enjoyed a string of them. Predictably, they were invariably with women who shared his penchant for hard living and drinking. "I'm good at picking fast women and slow horses," he once said.

When O'Toole co-starred with **Ursula Andress** in *What's New, Pussycat* in 1965, news of a rumored affair made the tabloids.

April Ashley was one of the world's most beautiful models and had already had **Elvis Presley** propose marriage to her when she met the actor **Peter O' Toole**. As she later lay in bed with O'Toole, she whispered in his ear: "I was born a boy."

Richard Burton was for many years O'Toole's favourite drinking buddy until, said O'Toole, their carousing came to an abrupt end when his friend married Elizabeth Taylor. The book claims that O'Toole and Taylor *(pictured in bed on set of the film Under Milk Wood)* started an affair when she was married to the American singer **Eddie Fisher**

Could there have been another reason? The book's authors think so, claiming O'Toole and Taylor started an affair when she was married to the American singer Eddie Fisher and staying in a suite at the Dorchester in London.

The actress, it is claimed, had been impressed with O'Toole's Shakespeare stage performances and wanted him to play Marc Antony alongside her *Cleopatra* in the 1963 epic of the same name. Of course, the part eventually went to Richard Burton and his affair with Taylor started there on the set.

It is alleged that O'Toole continued to see Taylor romantically for years. Then, he "severely tested" the friendship with Burton one night when both were very drunk and O'Toole reportedly confided to Burton: "She tells me I'm much better in the sack, at least more reliable, than you are." **Vivien Leigh** and **Laurence Olivier,** another famous acting couple, were also friends of O'Toole. It's claimed O'Toole long envied actor **Peter Finch**'s affair with the beautiful Leigh after she split up from Olivier.

He got his own chance near the end of her short life when he watched her perform in a Noël Coward play and took her to dinner. After agreeing that actors should never marry, Leigh invited him back to share her "lonely bed."

O'Toole later confided to a friend he had to make love in a room festooned with nine photographs of Olivier, but "still managed to rise to the occasion."

The list of sexual conquests didn't stop there. As well as his liaison with transsexual **April Ashley**, it is claimed that O'Toole ended up, after another Andalusian society party, naked in bed with **Sarah Churchill,** the hard-drinking actress daughter of **Sir Winston Churchill**. The actor reportedly told friends he couldn't remember if anything had happened between them.

O'Toole and **Princess Margaret** were good friends, the Princess once surprising his colleagues when she dropped in on a rehearsal of O'Toole's notoriously awful 1980 production of *Macbeth.*

O'Toole spent more than two years making *Lawrence Of Arabia*, the film that turned him into an international star. As his wife stayed at home bringing up their first child on her own, he recalled carousing in the "fleshpots" of Beirut during filming, enjoying bathtubs filled with champagne, and once gambling away nine months' wages in one night. Again, his drinking was out of control.

According to **Alec Guinness,** a local dignitary invited the film's stars to a party only for O'Toole to get in a row with their host and hurl a glass of champagne in his face. "O'Toole could have been killed — shot or strangled," Guinness told a friend. "And I'm beginning to think it's a pity he wasn't."

On another occasion, O'Toole was out boozing with his friend **Peter Finch** one night when a pub refused to serve them as it was after closing time. O'Toole's solution was to buy the pub, writing out a cheque on the spot.

Next morning, having sobered up, he rushed back to the pub. Fortunately, the landlord hadn't yet cashed it. The actors became friends with the landlord and even went to his funeral. But they got drunk first and, having become noisily emotional at the graveside, realised to their horror they were attending the wrong service.

Alcohol permeates nearly every story of O'Toole's exploits. He was sipping champagne when, in 1964, **Diana Dors**, Britain's answer to Marilyn Monroe, allegedly seduced him as she sat wearing a diaphanous black *négligée* in the sitting room of her London flat.

Two weeks later, she invited him to one of her infamous orgies and he apparently went, though primarily to speak to her guest of honour, an American movie star named **Bruce Cabot**, about Hollywood.

Jayne Mansfield, equally blonde and busty but American, was also in O'Toole's sights in his glory years of the Sixties, it is claimed. Their night of passion came after three bottles of pink champagne in her suite at The Dorchester. He is said to have visited her home in Los Angeles where they swam in her heart-shaped pool.

The new book claims he had a fling with **Audrey Hepburn** before they started filming in Paris, with O'-

Toole visiting her suite at the Ritz three nights in a row and telling a friend: "She seems too good to be true." Drama ensued when, during filming, she confided she was pregnant. Either he or her husband, actor **Mel Ferrer**, could be the father. She subsequently miscarried, it is claimed. Whether the affair ever happened, O'Toole later described Hepburn publicly as "delightful but troubled."

And what of **Princess Margaret**?

A tryst with O'Toole sounds far-fetched but the actor **David Niven** is widely believed to have had an affair with her and perhaps also **Peter Sellers**, so it is not impossible.

Certainly they were good friends. The Princess once surprised his colleagues when she dropped in on a rehearsal of O'Toole's notoriously awful 1980 production of *Macbeth*. (O'Toole was at the time in a relationship with the play's First Witch, alias **Trudie Styler**, the future wife of rock star **Sting**.) It is claimed the actor's friendship with Margaret started after they met at the 1965 Royal Command performance of the film *Lord Jim.*

O'Toole was invited to a string of parties at Kensington Palace where she would reportedly complain to him about her worsening relationship with husband **Lord Snowdon**. On one occasion, in the Seventies, O'Toole flew to Morocco to join her at the famous **Villa Taylor in Marrakesh,** where **Churchill** and **Roosevelt** had stayed during the 1943 Casablanca Conference.

The villa's owner said she gave **Princess Margaret** Churchill's old suite complete with a vast bath. O'Toole occupied an adjoining suite with connecting doors. The new book also claims O'Toole later joined Princess Margaret on her Caribbean island getaway, Mustique, but their relationship petered out in 1975.

Did any woman ever turn him down? **Katharine Hepburn,** who is widely believed to have been a lesbian, proved impervious, but that's not to say he didn't try to get close to her.

He starred with her in *The Lion In Winter*. Shooting a scene on a lake, Hepburn was out in a boat so O'Toole paddled out to talk to her, only to trap his finger between their vessels.

The tip of his finger was severed and with no doctors around, O'Toole carried it back to shore, dipped it into a glass of brandy to preserve it and later put it back on, wrapped in a poultice. Only when he took the bandages off did he discover he'd drunkenly put it back the wrong way round.

O'Toole said he was often asked if Lawrence of Arabia was homosexual. Indeed, the same question was frequently asked about him. His response? "I think I've established my straight certificate by seducing a scad of *(female)* movie stars and a bevy of barmaids."

O'Toole claims he never indulged in homosexuality but had plenty of offers. One such, says the book, came early in his acting career from **Cary Grant**. Visiting his hometown of Bristol while O'Toole was working there, the Hollywood star reportedly made a "subtle" pass after inviting O'Toole for dinner at his hotel.

Perhaps O'Toole never became notorious for his womanizing because the world was so distracted by his Olympian drinking, which he largely gave up in 1975 after stomach cancer almost killed him. Some insist he was always simply too inebriated to be much success as a Don Juan, but that may be a little naïve.

As a teenager, O'Toole scribbled in his notebook: "I will not be a common man. I will stir the smooth sands of monotony." Even if we may never know the full sordid details, nobody can deny he didn't succeed.

Peter O'Toole: Hellraiser, Sexual Outlaw, Irish Rebel by **Darwin Porter** and **Danforth Prince** is available everywhere now.

REPLICATING THE DYSFUNCTION OF MEDIEVAL EUROPE'S MOST FAMOUS FAMILY

It's Christmas of 1183. Two memorable actors (**Katharine Hapburn** and **Peter O'Toole**) brilliantly portray **Eleanor of Aquitaine** and **Henry II** in *The Lion in Winter* (1968).

BOOK REVIEW NEWS

Peter O'Toole:

**They loved him in London,
They adored him in Hollywood,**

**and now, they've reviewed him critically in
THE MIDWEST BOOK REVIEW:**

FOR IMMEDIATE RELEASE: Blood Moon's seminal biography of Peter O'Toole, the Anglo-Irish superstar described by some critics as the best actor of the 20th Century, has been critically reviewed by Diane Donovan, Senior Reviewer at the highly prestigious *Midwest Book Review*. Her text is replicated below:

Peter O'Toole: Hellraiser, Sexual Outlaw, Irish Rebel
Darwin Porter & Danforth Prince
Blood Moon Productions
ISBN 9781936003457 Softcover, 6"x9", 632 pps with photos $26.95 www.bloodmoonproductions.com

"One might expect that *Peter O'Toole: Hellraiser, Sexual Outlaw, Irish Rebel* would hold the usual biographical survey of the actor's life and times; but in fact it's a story that offers something far greater: an analysis of O'Toole's life and career that features a new look at the actor's passion, controversies, and determination to 'raise hell'.

"Lest readers think this will be a rehash of prior biographies, it should be mentioned that *Peter O'Toole: Hellraiser, Sexual Outlaw, Irish Rebel* represents decades of research by writers who define their efforts as being steeped in media and celebrity stories - and therefore replete with the high tension, drama, and eye-popping gossip and grit of Hollywood's most outrageous moments and characters.

"So don't anticipate a casual coverage: it's an account of a hellraising, outrageous personality and is itself steeped in the culture it investigates, cultivating lively language, newly-revealed shocking truths, and passionate descriptions to capture the life and times of a film star who, according to Peter O'Toole, "...became the toast of international society. The decadent part, those who live just to fornicate on the Costa del Sol. It's the new gathering place for panty sniffers, child molesters, drunkards, prostitutes, pimps, gigolos, pillheads, and poon stalkers. I adore it. It seems that all the big names want to go to bed with me. A lucky few actually manage to accomplish that splendid feat."

"Outrageous? You bet. It's not for the morally faint - and that promises that *Peter O'Toole: Hellraiser, Sexual Outlaw, Irish Rebel* will be a frequent flyer out of library collections and film reference holdings alike."

MORE ABOUT THIS BOOK, AS FORMATTED ON YOUTUBE:
KNEWS, Southern California's News and Talk Radio, discusses the role of Peter O'Toole as the stage and screen's most enigmatic Hellraiser. Bill Feingold interviews Danforth Prince about an actor whose first and last names EACH had phallic implications https://youtu.be/t3oU356dhPI

Peter O'Toole, Hellraiser, Sexual Outlaw, Irish Rebel, a **Videotaped Description**: https://www.youtube.com/watch?v=k5f4dIbXTLk

In June of 2015, Blood Moon's biography of *Peter O'Toole* was designated by **The New York Book Festival** as Runner Up to Best Biography of The Year.

Depicted above is Blood Moon's President, **Danforth Prince**, with **Rebecca Li-Huang**, whose poignant memoir of her emigration to the U.S. from China (*Green Apple, Red Book*) was also designated as winner of a prestigious literary award.

GLOBE
CELEBRITY NEWS

REVEALED! BOOZER O'TOOLE'S HOLLYWOOD HAREM

MOVIE icon Peter O'Toole flew under the radar as a ladies man, but the Lawrence of Arabia hunk bedded a slew of screen beauties including Audrey Hepburn and Elizabeth Taylor.

His steamy romp with Liz got him in trouble with his longtime drinking buddy, Richard Burton, his co-star in 1964's Becket.

During a night of guzzling, O'Toole told Burton he'd also been with Liz, adding, "She tells me I'm much better in the sack, at least more reliable than you are."

His boast "shattered" the friendship of the two stars, according to a new tell-all due out June 15, Peter O'Toole: Hellraiser, Sexual Outlaw, Irish Rebel.

Authors Darwin Porter and Danforth Prince write that Liz met and had a fling with O'Toole after seeing him on stage. She wanted him to play Mark Anthony in her 1963 Cleopatra flick.

The part eventually went to Richard Burton and his affair with Taylor started there on the set.

But the authors reveal that "O'Toole continued to see Taylor romantically for years." The hellraiser's conquests also included Britain's Princess Margaret, Vivien Leigh, actress Diana Dors and Jayne Mansfield.

But the notorious boozer kept a special place in his heart for Audrey Hepburn, his leading lady in the 1966 flick How to Steal a Million.

They had a fling before filming started in Paris. Weeks later, Hepburn told him she was pregnant and didn't know if he or her hubby, Mel Ferrer, was the father, say the authors, adding she later miscarried the baby.

The book says O'Toole described the beauty as "delightful, but troubled" and "too good to be true."

PETER LOST PAL BURTON AFTER BEDDING LIZ

New book dishes on O'Toole

Peter bedded Burton's babe Liz. Below, he also romped with Audrey Hepburn

OMAR SHARIF RAVAGED BY DEMENTIA

SCREEN hunk Omar Sharif starred in some of Hollywood's biggest flicks, but now the Alzheimer's-stricken actor can't remember them – or what happened yesterday!

The Egyptian-born star of Funny Girl, Doctor Zhivago and Lawrence of Arabia still knows he's a famous actor, but he recently stared at a photo of him with then-wife Hamama and infant son Tarek and asked: "Who's this?"

Sharif, 83, also confuses fans with people he once knew. "Often, he thinks it's someone he knew from before and whose name he has forgotten," says Tarek, 58. "Most of the time it's a fan."

Tarek says the illness makes Sharif, who mainly lives in hotels, "insecure." Because of his poor memory, he often refuses to leave his room. Ironically, he was once one of the Top 10 bridge players in the world, relying on his memory to win tournaments.

Omar (left) and Peter O'Toole in Lawrence of Arabia

BLOOD MOON

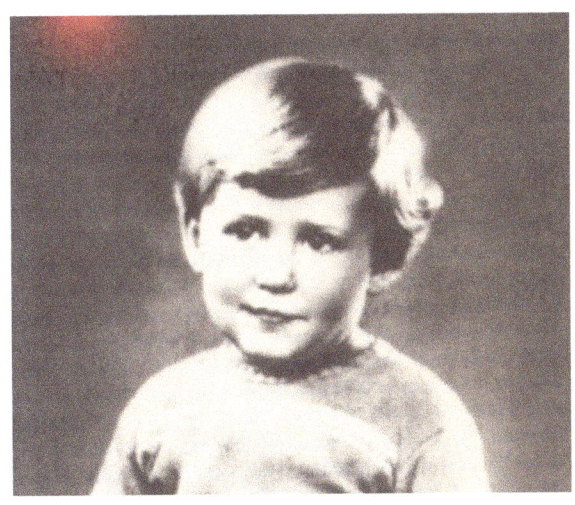

Peter O'Toole as a five-year-old.

Offensive, brilliant, promiscuous, brash, and born to raise hell, he was beaten by nuns, molested by priests, and—in his own assessment—"became a Lager Lout at thirteen, a member, like Dad, of the criminal class."

As he phrased it, "At five years old, I was an Irish laddie. I looked like a cherubic saint, and I was named after a saint. But trust me, I was no bloody saint."

OUTRAGEOUS COMMENTS FROM THE MAD IRISHMAN, PETER O'TOOLE

"I grew up in Leeds, but I was born an Irishman, which accounts for my gift of gab, my unruly behavior, my passionate devotion to women, and the bottle, and my loathing of any authority figure."

"I believe in reincarnation. I can solve for you one of the great murder mysteries in English history. I was Jack the Ripper. There was nothing more exciting to me than taking a butcher knife and slitting open a whore's belly, watching her entrails spew forth."

"I hid my true personality from my fans—my hair-trigger temper and my violent tendencies. I inherited those from my drunken Irish bookmaker dad. I once hit a cop, a restaurateur, a film critic—and I was notorious for smashing television sets like Elvis Presley."

"I'm not from the working class. I'm from the criminal class."

"The greatest problem facing any young actor on the English stage, especially one as gorgeous as I was, is avoiding the clutches of some of England's most stately homos, Laurence Olivier, John Gielgud, Noël Coward, *et al.*"

"I'm not an actor. I'm a movie star."

"Why did millions of gay men assume I was one of them after seeing *Lawrence of Arabia?*"

"I've never looked for women. When I was a teenager, perhaps. Then I met this stripper from Barcelona, name of Bubbles LaRue, who taught me everything I needed to know about sex—and a lot I didn't need to know. I'd still be with her had she not tried to hire me out as a boy whore."

"I will not be a common man. I will stir the smooth sands of monotony."

"I woke up one morning to find I was famous. I bought a white Rolls-Royce and drove down Sunset Boulevard, wearing dark specs and a white suit, waving like the Queen Mum."

"My favorite food from my homeland is Guinness. My second choice is Guinness. My third choice would have to be Guinness."

"Always a bridesmaid, never a bride my foot! Did you hear that, you bloody Oscar pickers?"

"Pope Paul III (1534-1549) was the greatest thief in the history of the Church."

"Public crucifixion is no fun."

"There are only three indispensible things: the audience, the actor, and the author. The rest is dross."

"There's always a hunger, when you're young, to go from peak to peak and avoid the valleys."

"As a star, I had a reputation to live up to every night of my life. At a Hollywood party, I spotted little Peter Lorre, that heavy-lidded, campy, thrilling eccentric and world-weary sardonic. I walked over to him, grabbed him, and kissed him madly, ramming my serpent-like tongue down his throat from which emerged the famously sinister voice on screen. After withdrawing my tongue, I bit his tongue like a vampire, tasting his blood. What else was there for me to do?"

"At one point I was far too gone to worry that April Ashley had been born a boy. She was a world-class beauty."

"I have a darling idea, Dickie (Burton). In the opening scene of *Becket,* we're screwing the same wench. Let me go with you to your suite at the Dorchester and join you and Elizabeth in bed for the night. It can be a rehearsal for our upcoming scene Monday morning."

"Ursula Andress is a bloody sex symbol and all that, but a really nice woman. She told me that all she had to do was run through a film with nothing on."

"The night after Princess Margaret seduced me, I was seen driving around London in her Rolls-Royce Phantom, which she had discarded for a new one."

"When we made *Lion in Winter,* I called Katharine Hepburn a female impersonator. But I just adored the dykey bitch. Even when she hauled off and slapped my face. We had a violent relationship, which was fine with me. I've always had this masochistic streak in me."

"How can I compete with the bosom of Sophia Loren in *Man of La Mancha?* To do so, the director will have to photograph me in a jockstrap."

"You know my favorite review for *The Ruling Class?* Vincent Canby of *The New York Times* claimed that with my blonde wig, I looked like Barbara Stanwyck in *Double Indemnity.* High praise indeed, to be compared to this stately dyke, (who's) second only to Katharine Hepburn in the lez department."

"The director of *Caligula*, Tinto Brass—I called him Tinto Zinc—gave me this Sumerian girl to follow me around. I nicknamed her Betty, the Collapsible Crutch. I was also followed by thirteen naked men as my guards. They were selected for their very large penises and given only Robin Hood hats to wear, nothing else. "I was willing to appear nude and with an erection in *Caligula* if called for. But Tinto Zinc told me that at this stage of his life, Tiberius could only be sexually aroused by being penetrated. When I saw those four-foot phalluses being brought onto the set, I opted out."

"I want my *Macbeth* to be the bloodiest in history, darlings. Do you know that if you stab a living man with a sword, blood spurts out seventeen feet. After opening night, critics claimed that my *Macbeth* was the worst in history. I was compared to Bette Davis in *What Ever Happened to Baby Jane?* I was as popular as a pork sausage in a synagogue."

"Elizabeth Ashley told me she smoked a lot of dope. She also made it with a lot of guys. She was almost as pretty as Audrey Hepburn. Neither of them had any tits."

"It's a razor's edge, a romance with an old man and a young woman."

"The only exercise I take is walking behind the coffins of friends who took exercise."

"As for my final curtain, I chased my own rainbow to the end. No, I didn't find a pot of gold... Only an empty crock. It didn't smell like Chanel No. 5."

"Over time, I went on to become the greatest stage and screen actor of the 20th Century, as immodest as that sounds. So, I'm a braggart. Well, I've got bloody something to brag about!"

"I've done everything that's possible to be done."

O'Toole's portrayal of the sociopathic, syphilitic Roman emperor, Tiberius, is alive and thriving within the minds of anyone who ever screened what probably morphed into the most notorious film of 1979, *Caligula.*

In the photo above, Tiberius (O'Toole) embraces his horrified (but equally bloodthirsty) successor, Caligula, as portrayed by **Malcolm McDowall.**

THOSE GLAMOROUS GABORS

Bombshells from Budapest, Great Courtesans of the 20th Century

Darwin Porter & Danforth Prince

Zsa Zsa, Eva, and Magda Gabor transferred their glittery dreams and gold-digging ambitions from the twilight of the Austro-Hungarian Empire to Hollywood. There, more effectively than any army, these Bombshells from Budapest broke hearts, amassed fortunes, lovers, and A-list husbands, and amused millions of voyeurs through the medium of television, movies, and the social registers. In this astonishing "triple-play" biography, designated "Best Biography of the Year" by the Hollywood Book Festival, Blood Moon lifts the "mink-and-diamond" curtain on this amazing trio of blood-related sisters, whose complicated intrigues have never been fully explored before.

***

"You will never be Ga-bored…this book gives new meaning to the term compelling. Be warned, *Those Glamorous Gabors* is both an epic and a pip. Not since *Gone With the Wind* have so many characters on the printed page been forced to run for their lives for one reason or another. And Scarlett making a dress out of the curtains is nothing compared to what a Gabor will do when she needs to scrap together an outfit for a movie premiere or late-night outing.

"For those not up to speed, Jolie Tilleman came from a family of jewelers and therefore came by her love for the shiny stones honestly, perhaps genetically. She married Vilmos Gabor somewhere around World War 1 (exact dates, especially birth dates, are always somewhat vague in order to establish plausible deniability later on) and they were soon blessed with three daughters: Magda, the oldest, whose hair, sadly, was naturally brown, although it would turn quite red in America; Zsa Zsa (born 'Sari') a natural blonde who at a very young age exhibited the desire for fame with none of the talents usually associated with achievement, excepting beauty and a natural wit; and Eva, the youngest and blondest of the girls, who after seeing Grace Moore perform at the National Theater, decided that she wanted to be an actress and that she would one day move to Hollywood to become a star.

"Given that the Gabor family at that time lived in Budapest, Hungary, at the period of time between the World Wars, that Hollywood dream seemed a distant one indeed. The story—the riches to rags to riches to rags to riches again myth of survival against all odds as the four women, because of their Jewish heritage, flee Europe with only the minks on their backs and what jewels they could smuggle along with them in their decolletage, only to have to battle afresh for their places in the vicious Hollywood pecking order—gives new meaning to the term 'compelling.' The reader, as if he were witnessing a particularly gore-drenched traffic accident, is incapable of looking away."

—*New York Review of Books*

Born in Central Europe during th twilight of the Austro-Hungarian Empire, three "vonderful wimmen"—Zsa Zsa, Eva, and Magda Gabor—transferred their glittery dreams and gold-digging ambitions to Hollywood. They supplemented America's most Imperial Age with "guts, glamour, and goulasch," and reigned there as the Hungarian equivalents of Helen of Troy, Madame du Barry, and Madame de Pompadour.

More lethal than any army, these Bombshells from Budapest conquered kings, dukes, and princes, always with a special passion for millionaires, as they amassed fortunes, broke hearts, and amused sophisticated voyeurs on two continents. With their wit, charm, and beauty, thanks to training inspired by the glittering traditions of the Imperial Habsburgs, they became famous for being famous.

In time, these Magyar temptresses would collectively entrap some 20 husbands and seduce perhaps 500 other men as well, many plucked directly from the pages of Who's Who in the World.

At long last, Blood Moon lifts the "mink and diamond" curtain on this amazing trio of blood-related sisters, whose complicated intrigues have never before been fully explored.

Researched over decades, this sweeping historical epic is by Darwin Porter, an ardent chronicler of America's entertainment industry. One of the world's leading celebrity biographers, he has already profiled the lives of dozens of other icons and movie stars. He now invades the boudoirs of the three Gabor sisters, revealing the secrets of the most notorious mantraps since Eve.

"Dahlinks, this Magyar mother raised a trio of the world's most beautiful daughters. I want each of them to marry a king...perhaps a prince, at least."

                                                                                --Jolie Gabor

Views of the Gabor family before the upheavals of World War II.

Left photo, left to right: Eva, Zsa Zsa, and Magda, pose on the beach at Lake Balaton, in central Hungary, in a cheesecake photo with the family's formidable matriarch, Jolie.

Right photo:, left to right: Magda (later the Countess of Warsaw), Zsa Zsa (later acknowledged as the most famous Hungarian in the world); and Eva (the sister most devoted to the pursuit of a career in America's entertainment industry), appear poised, at their mother's direction, as a romantic reincarnation of "The Three Graces"

Prologue

Jolie Gabor

It was four o'clock on a dull gray February afternoon in the Hungarian capital of Budapest. The year was 1924. Behind the wheel of her Mercedes, painted a battleship gray, Jolie Gabor was rolling down Andrassy út, known as "The Fifth Avenue of Budapest."

In those days, only six ladies of Budapest owned and drove their own cars.

In the seat beside her sat her beloved daughters—nicknamed "Magdika," age 9; "Zsazsilka," 7; and "Evika," 5.

Suddenly the sun broke through for the first time that day, adding at extra sparkle to Jolie's diamonds. While getting dressed, she'd told her beautiful daughters, "These are my daytime diamonds. For the evening, I really dazzle. That's when a woman should bring out the king's ransom stones."

She wanted to make a spectacular appearance that afternoon at tea. Both Jolie and her daughters wore scarlet-colored dresses that matched the upholstery of the Mercedes. The clothing had been designed by Jeanne Lanvin, who also designed matching gray coats for each of the Gabors, which duplicated the exact color of the vehicle itself.

The fashion-conscious Jolie preferred the French designer because she was celebrated for her mother-and-daughter outfits and exquisite *robes de style,* as well as for her modern and global approach to fashion. Before heading out, Jolie had also doused her daughters in *Après l'Ondée* by Guerlain (1906). "It's a piece of art created from hellotrope, violette, and iris that gently touches our skin like a scent from heaven."

Arriving at the Café Gerbeaud, the Gabors were greeted by a doorman in a puce-colored uniform. Starched, gloved, and beribboned, the daughters emerged first onto the sidewalk.

Franz Lutsky was the manager of the Café Gerbeaud, on Vörösmarty tér, which had been founded in 1858 by Swiss confectioner Emile Gerbeaud. It was Jolie's favorite rendezvous. He always reserved the best table for her. Privately he referred to her as "This Magyar mother hen with her three beautiful spring chickens."

Although the café was bustling at that time of day, nearly all of the patrons stopped to take note of the new customers making such a glamorous entrance.

Later, Magda would recall, "Everything that mother did in those days was to teach us a lesson. That day at the café, the lesson involved how to make an entrance. Her forever advice was, 'When you arrive in town, don't keep it a secret.'"

The Gabors were about to embark on a life so glamorous Jolie often said in later years, "No one would believe it!"

As designer Donald F. Reuter put it: "The early lives of the Gabors is a fascinating tale that reads like a cross between *Doctor Zhivago* and *Gypsy,* with a generous sprinkling of *Fiddler on the Roof* and *Auntie Mame* thrown in for good measure."

With a grand flourish, the *maître d'hotel* guided Jolie, followed by her "three *vonderful wimmen*" down the long railroad-style layout of the café until they arrived at one of the sitting areas, decorated in a tone of scarlet that matched their dresses. The aging waiter, who had been born in 1854, knew what to bring to table. The aromatic coffee had been dispensed from a *cafetière* whose perimeter was sheathed in hand-painted panels of Herend porcelain—one of only three on Earth, and the confection he brought was the celebrated chocolate-and-marzipan royal torte. "It's positively sinful," Jolie told her daughters. "But a woman born into a man's world must be sinful to advance herself."

Away from her domineering husband, Vilmos Gabor, Jolie always seized the opportunity to lecture her daughters about the future roles they'd play.

"*Dahlinks,* each of you will grow up to become a fabled Hungarian beauty. But you must never become a delicate porcelain figure. The blood of Attila the Hun flows through your veins, the blood of Genghis Khan. You were meant to conquer as the daughters of a once-great empire. Your homeland is a nation of powerful warriors and passionate lovers. Each of you will grow up to marry a king…or at least a prince."

"A few months ago, in the lobby of the Ritz Hotel here in Budapest, I was stunned to encounter the handsome, charming, and very rich Prince of Wales—with his entourage—parading through. Last week, I sent him a letter acknowledging our meeting, along with that gorgeous photograph of you, Zsa Zsa. I told him that you were growing more beautiful every day, and that in just a few years, you'd be one of the most dazzling beauties of Europe, fit to sit on his throne as Queen of England when he becomes King."

Zsa Zsa wasn't embarrassed or intimated by Jolie's behavior and point of view. In fact, she amplified her mother's idea with: "I'd be a queen and rule over all the British colonies—and I'd also become the Empress of India."

A COMPREHENSIVE BIOGRAPHY OF THE ONCE-MOST-FAMOUS ENTERTAINER IN THE WORLD

JACKO

The Social and Sexual History of Michael Jackson

This is the world's most unbiased report on the trials and tribulations of a performer whose fame surpassed, in some places, that of either the U.S. President or Jesus Christ. From investigative reporter Darwin Porter—the biographer who Unzipped Marlon Brando and brought Babylon back to Hollywood.

It illuminates the life of The Gloved One from cradle to grave, including his meteoric rise to fame, insights into his fall from grace, and the desperate but ongoing attempts to revive his career. Published post-mortem to MJ's tragic death in June of 2009, it provides shocking insights into his triumphs and disasters, and an estate that will be disputed for decades.

An award-winning finalist in Foreword Magazine's BOOK OF THE YEAR contest, this is unlike any other biography of the superstar ever written.

"I'd have thought that there wasn't one single gossippy rock yet to be overturned in the microscopically scrutinized life of Michael Jackson, but Darwin Porter has proven me wrong. Definitely a page-turner. But don't turn the pages too quickly. Almost every one holds a fascinating revelation."
—**Richard LaBonte.** *Books to Watch Out For*

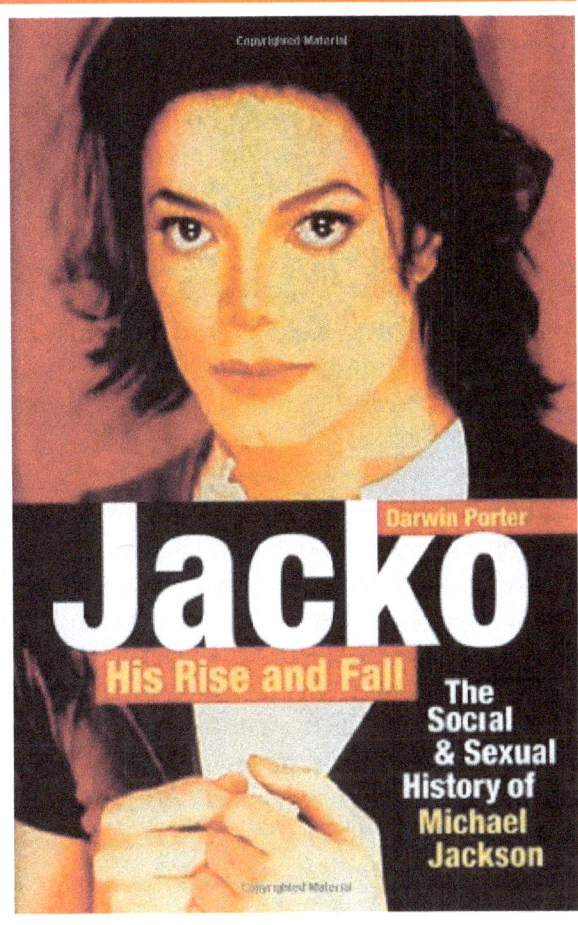

"Don't stop till you get enough. Darwin Porter's biography of Michael Jackson is dangerously addictive."
—*The London Observer*

This biography was authored by Darwin Porter and originally released in 2007, during the lifetime of MJ, who presumably was aware of its existence and opted to allow its sale and distribution to proceed without any legal protests or publicly expressed objections.

At the time of its release, it was the only significant biography of Michael Jackson published during the previous fifteen years, a remarkable circumstance, considering the superstar's widespread fame and controversies.

Post-millennium, Michael became an object of ridicule and scorn, hounded by the press and bleeding from a river of lawsuits. This book examines the mechanics of his decline, as it describes an American icon who wandered into a treacherous Garden of Eden and tasted its forbidden fruit.

In this book, Michael interacts with an all-star cast whose members included Elizabeth Taylor, Katharine Hepburn, Jane Fonda, Madonna, Princess Di, Mick Jagger, Paul McCartney, Diana Ross, Brooke Shields, Sammy Davis Jr., Johnnie Cochran, Sophia Loren, Frank Sinatra, Fred Astaire, Cary Grant, Mae West, Liberace, Lisa Marie Presley, and that dad of hers.

JACKO, HIS RISE AND FALL

Despite Michael Jackson's spectacular fame, no one has ever published a comprehensive biography with inside information about his highly dramatic life. All of that changed with the release of this book.

Meticulously researched over several tumultuous decades, it explores and explains many of the secrets that Michael Jackson wanted to keep hidden from the world. It examines the man behind the myth, a public figure whose eyes are often hidden behind dark glasses, his face obscured by an even darker mask.

It's peppered with quotes from the subject himself. But for deeper insights, author Darwin Porter turned to the hundreds of Jackson associates who were linked to the growth, maintenance, and decline of his spectacular career and severely bruised public image.

Ironically, long after the headlines died, thousands of celebrity watchers and pop music fans continued their obsession with this charismatic star, wildly celebrating his acquittal from child molestation charges in California. But after restless wanderings in Bahrain, Ireland, England, and France, where Michael will go next is a question the author tries to answer.

Ironically everyone knows Michael's music, but despite its commercial and artistic success, the world is more concerned with what he does whenever he's not onstage. His saga is unique in the American entertainment industry, moving from the poverty of America's Rust Belt (Gary, Indiana) to the oil-enriched desert sands of Bahrain, with detours to Neverland, Michael's private Land of Oz.

The most talked-about and written-about megastar in history, Michael Jackson is stranger than we ever knew, as will be revealed within the pages of this biography.

Three views of the most famous (and most maligned) entertainer of his era: **MICHAEL JACKSON.**

This is the story of a brown-skinned boy with a big nose who moonwalked his way into "the world of white," with a re-sculpted face and financial assets that the rest of the world felt free to pillage. Michael's talent was and is the stuff of legends. He didn't exactly pounce out of the womb singing and dancing…but he came close.

Michael is Peter Pan, the child-man who invited to his bed boys who were too young, yet too far advanced in their savvy, not to react sometimes with venom. Jordie Chandler walked away with $25 million after "sleeping over." Cancer-stricken Gavin Arvizo, who sued Michael and lost, got nothing.

During the 1980s, at the peak of his career, Michael was the most famous man on the planet, a sex symbol known for wearing fetish gear and grabbing his crotch onstage. Post-millennium, he became the object of ridicule and scorn, hounded by the press and by the courts, the object of as many as 50 new lawsuits a year. This book examines the route of his decline. It's a story of a pop-culture icon who wandered into a treacherous Garden of Eden and tasted its forbidden fruit.

This biography will lead you to a rare, behind-the-scenes look at Michael Jackson, with insights into a glittering cast of characters that only a lifetime like his could have linked together. They include Jackie Onassis, The Reagans, the Clintons, Elizabeth Taylor, Katharine Hepburn, Jane Fonda, Madonna, Princess Di, Prince (the singer), Mick Jagger, Paul McCartney, Diana Ross, Tatum O'Neal, Brooke Shields, Sammy Davis Jr., Coretta Scott King, Quincy Jones, Berry Gordy Jr., Johnnie Cochran, Sophia Loren, Frank Sinatra, Louis Farrakhan, and even Lisa Marie Presley and Elvis.

Enquiring minds might ask: "Is Michael a pedophile or an innocent victim of his own fame? You decide. Within this book, like the evidence in a jury trial, it's all spread out before you.

It's been said that what Michael wants engraved on his tombstone is "Don't Judge Me." Hopefully, after reading this book, observers of the Jackson saga might form some unexpected conclusions of their own.

Getting to Know Blood Moon's
MAGNOLIA HOUSE SERIES

DID YOU KNOW?

That the origins of our Magnolia House Series were inspired by Donald Trump?

We spent the early months of 2016 laboring over a guidebook to the Fame and Fury of Donald Trump. We envisioned it as a "compendium of cringe." Source material derived from recaps of TV news and from reporting by *The New York Times, The NY Daily News*, and the *New York Post,* but with the "seasonings" for which Blood Moon is famous.

NBN's "rank and file" was prepped and primed, optimistic about high-volume sales, and flush with impressive advance orders. **WHAT COULD POSSIBLY HAVE GONE WRONG?**

Without warning, days before its widely publicized release, the NBN flipped, refusing to get involved. Their awkwardly orchestrated betrayal sabotaged months of advance planning.

We regrouped. Ours was not the first ambitious publishing vision sabotaged by issues and players associated with THE DONALD. In the days that followed, we arranged for alternative distribution.

Interestingly, **Donald Trump, The Man Who Would Be King** went on to win multiple literary awards and many stunning reviews. Seven years later, we repackaged and re-released it on the 4th of July, 2024, in advance of Trump's "comeback" second term.

We present this information as an illustration of the trauma and betrayals associated with the creation of Blood Moon's Magnolia House Series. With the understanding that none of the books within that series has ever been associated with, or distributed by, the NBN, the series incorporate many of our best, most seasoned, and most mature titles. Most have been extensively reviewed, and some have won impressive literary awards. It is with that understanding that we present, on the pages that immediately follow, descriptions of each of the titles within the series.

What Is Magnolia House?

Built in stages between 1830 and 1866, and closely associated with the ambitions and traumas of the Civil War, it's our resident headquarters, a landmarked "*grande dame*"with memories to sustain and stories to tell.

In the months that followed, we crafted and produced a double-volumed overview of the building's history. They relay its celebrity associations from before our tenure there, and also during the decades we occupied the premises.

INTRODUCING BLOOD MOON'S
MAGNOLIA HOUSE
AND THE SERIES THAT BEARS ITS NAME

HOW DO YOU DESCRIBE A BOOKISH, MAGNOLIA-SCENTED LANDMARK?

As depicted below, **Volumes One and Two** of Blood Moon's **Magnolia House Series** were conceived as affectionate testimonials to a great American monument, **MAGNOLIA HOUSE,** our company's nurturing and very tolerant historic home in Staten Island (NYC) It has a raft of stories to tell—some of them about how it adapted to the publishing industry's radically changing tastes, times, circumstances, and values.

VOLUME ONE (ISBN 978-1-936003-65-5) focuses on its construction by a prominent lawyer during the booming (Northern) economy before the Civil War; its Gilded-Age purchase by the widow of the Surgeon General of the Confederate States of America; and later, its role as a branch office of THE FROMMER GUIDES during the heyday of the American travel industry. It was an era rich with insights into the celebrity secrets their reporters on the job in "London, Paris, and "Hollywood on the Tiber" (privately, until now) unveiled, years later, through Blood Moon Productions.

VOLUME TWO (ISBN 978-1-936003-73-0) is an *haute* celebrity romp through the half-century of Broadway, Hollywood, and publishing scandals swirling around Magnolia House's visitors and their frenemies…a "Reporters' Notebook" with everything that arts industry publicists didn't want fans and critics to know about at the time.

Each of these books is a celebration of the fast-disappearing
PRE-COVID AMERICAN CENTURY,
And both are available now through internet purveyors worldwide.

from BLOOD MOON PRODUCTIONS at MAGNOLIA HOUSE
Award-Winning Entertainment about
America's Legends, Icons, & Celebrities

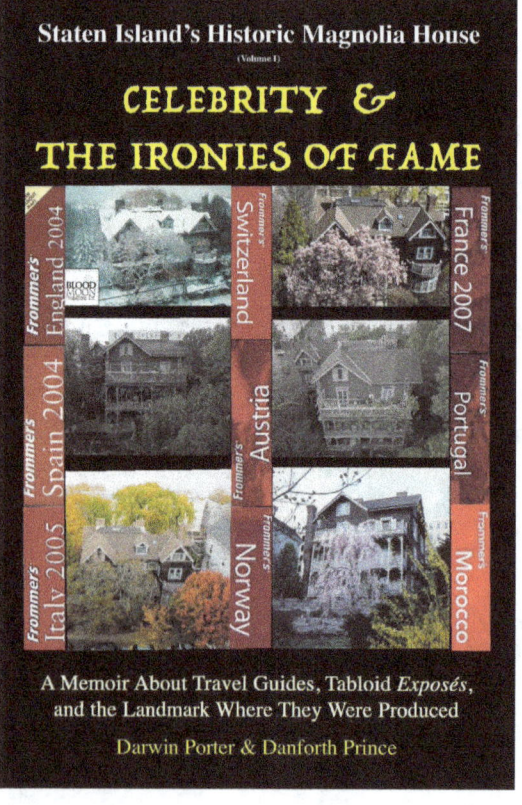

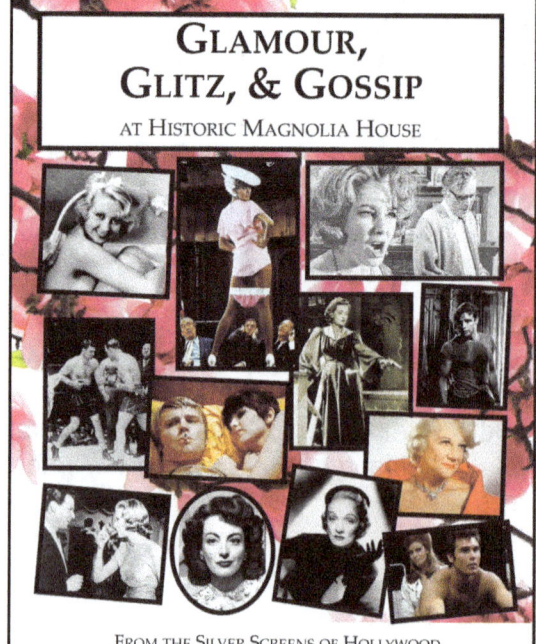

WHAT DOES NEW YORK CITY SHARE IN COMMON WITH L.A. AND SAN FRANCISCO? THEIR RESPECTIVE BOOK AWARD FESTIVALS EACH APPLAUDED HOW BLOOD MOON DEFINED THE FONDAS: HENRY, JANE, AND PETER

BOOK AWARD NEWS:

THE FONDAS: TRIPLE EXPOSURE
A ROLLICKING, DOUBLE-BARRELLED OVERVIEW OF A VERY FAMOUS AMERICAN FAMILY

On July 25, 2023, the Awards Committee at the prestigious **NEW YORK BOOK FESTIVAL** defined Darwin Porter and Danforth Prince's double-volume overview of **THE FONDAS** as **WINNER of their BEST BIOGRAPHY OF THE YEAR** Award.

Their decision arrived in the immediate aftermath of the hotly contested **San Francisco Book Festival**, where the same double-volumed set was defined as RUNNER UP to Best Biography of the year, too.

The most comprehensive (and to some, shocking) overview of their lives ever published—it brings new life and an upgraded cultural importance to this talented and influential trio of biologically related stars.

WHO WERE THE FONDAS?: During the climactic peak of Classic Hollywood, **Henry Fonda** was the reassuring archetype of the American male—at least on film. In private, he married five times (two of his wives committed suicide), soldiered on through active military service in the Pacific during World War II, and seduced legendary ladies (*or dragons, depending on your point of view*) who included Bette Davis, Jean Harlow, Greta Garbo, Joan Crawford, Lucille Ball, and Marlene Dietrich.

His very outspoken daughter, Jane, led a tumultuous, scandal-soaked life of her own, one indelibly linked to the "New Wave" and "New Hollywood" of the 60s, 70s, and 80s. Spectacularly famous in Europe and the U.S., she morphed from a bilingual onscreen sex kitten into the notorious "Hanoi Jane," later making a film comeback as an Oscar winner. Her love affairs embraced everyone from Warren Beatty to the Black Panthers.

The least-known, perhaps least "likable" member of this tumultuous trio, **Peter Fonda** led a privileged life laced with drugs, high adventure, and seductions—a thrill-seeking "Easy Rider" racing across the landscapes of the 1960s, 70s, and 80s as the "Bad Boy Gone Wild"—often bringing with it a "wafty and pointless psychedelia."

THE FONDAS—It's all here in two delicious volumes. If you want to know what went on in Hollywood after the klieg lights went off, consider reading them. The private "ecstatic and agonized" lives of a celebrity-soaked entertainment industry pro, his daughter, and his son are documented as never before, lives set on fire by triumph, tragedy, passion, heartbreak, wide acclaim, scalding denunciations, and suicides.

IN 2022, IN HONOR OF THE 40TH ANNIVERSARY OF HENRY FONDA'S DEATH, BLOOD MOON PRODUCTIONS RELEASED VOLUME ONE OF A TWO-PART BIOGRAPHY CELEBRATING THE LIFE AND CAREER OF ONE OF THE AMERICAN CENTURY'S MOST CELEBRATED ACTORS

HENRY FONDA

DARWIN PORTER AND DANFORTH PRINCE

TWO MONTHS LATER, IT WON THE COVETED BEST BIOGRAPHY AWARD FROM THE HOLLYWOOD BOOK FESTIVAL

Throughout his forty-five year career, **Henry Fonda**—a stable, reassuring archetype of the American male—never gave a bad performance. immortalizing himself in such films as *Young Mr. Lincoln, The Grapes of Wrath,* and *Mister Roberts*. The torments of his introverted private life vied with his on-screen dilemmas. Personal dramas included five wives (two of whom committed suicide) and involvements in many of the seminal events (including active service in the Navy during World War II) of the 20th Century. His affairs starred such mega-divas as Lucille Ball, Joan Crawford, and Bette Davis, and with his second wife, Frances Seymour, he founded a Hollywood dynasty with movie star children, Jane and Peter.

This, **Volume One (1905-1960)** covers Henry's origins in Depression-era Nebraska, his rise to fame, his complicated dynamics with other celebrities, and his middle-aged years navigating his passion for acting with the business realities of Hollywood.

Volume Two (1961-1982), also available now, covers his complicated relationships with his famous and newsworthy daughter, Jane, and his (deceased) son, Peter.

Together, these books give the clearest, most detailed overview of this great American actor ever published.

All this and more from Blood Moon Productions, an award-winning publishing enterprise that specializes in exposing long-suppressed secrets hidden during Hollywood's Golden Age.

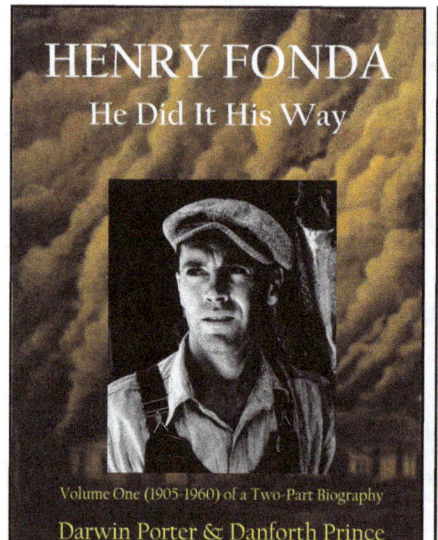
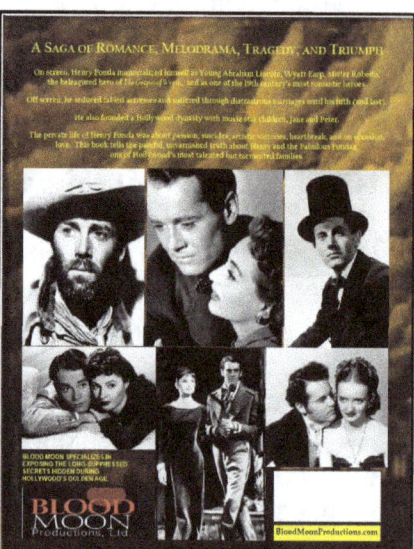

HENRY FONDA: HE DID IT HIS WAY
Volume One (1905-1960) of a Two-Part Biography

Darwin Porter & Danforth Prince   345 pages, with hundreds of photos
ISBN 978-1-936003-84-6

A YEAR LATER, ON FLAG DAY, 2023, IN TIME FOR A GREAT AMERICAN HOLIDAY, BLOOD MOON RELEASED VOLUME TWO OF ITS TWO-PART BIOGRAPHY OF THE AMERICAN CENTURY'S MOST CELEBRATED CINEMATIC DYNASTIES

THE FONDAS—HENRY, JANE, & PETER

TRIPLE EXPOSURE   INTERTWINED SAGAS OF DYSFUNCTION, TRAGEDY, AND TRIUMPH

Darwin Porter & Danforth Prince

Throughout his forty-five year career, Henry Fonda,—a stable, reasuring archetype of the American male—never gave a bad performance. Personal tragedies included five wives (two of whom committed suicide) and affairs which starred such mega-divas as Lucille Ball, Joan Crawford, and Bette Davis.

This, **Volume Two (1961-1982)**, of Blood Moon's FONDA project, turns klieg lights on three emotionally intertwined mega-celebrities, two of them Oscar winners: The lanky and boyish American hero, **Henry**; his beautiful daughter, "the eternal rebel," **Jane**; and his son, **Peter,** a preppy-looking thrill-seeker indelibly linked to the "bad boy on a bike" narratives of the 60s.

It's the second, and final, installment of Blood Moon's coverage of the FABULOUS FONDAS, one of Hollywood's most talented but tormented families. It reflects the private agonies of a father, daughter, and son engulfed by the divisions of their respective generations and the ironies of the American Experience.

THE FONDAS: HENRY, JANE, & PETER
TRIPLE EXPOSURE
Volume Two (1961-1982) of a Two-Part Biography
360 pages, with hundreds of photos

It joins Volume One, HENRY FONDA: HE DID IT HIS WAY (1905-1960). the already-available winner of a Best Biography of the Year award from the Hollywood Book Festival. Together, as a pair, this two-volume set gives the clearest, most detailed, and clearly unvarnished overview of the Fondas ever published.

JUDY GARLAND & LIZA MINNELLI
TOO MANY DAMN RAINBOWS

DARWIN PORTER & DANFORTH PRINCE

Judy and Liza were the greatest, most colorful, and most tragic mother-daughter saga in show biz history. They live, laugh, and weep again in the tear-soaked pages of this remarkable biography. Darwin Porter and Danforth Prince have compiled a compelling "post-modern" spin.

According to Liza, "My mother—hailed as the world's greatest entertainer—lived eighty lives during her short time with us."

Their memorable stories unfold through eyewitness accounts of the typhoons that engulfed them. They swing across glittery landscapes of euphoria and glory, detailing the betrayals and treachery which the duo encountered almost daily. There were depressions "as deep as the Mariana Trench," suicide attempts, and obsessive identifications on deep psychological levels with roles that include Judy's Vicky Lester in *A Star is Born* (1954) and Liza's Sally Bowles in *Cabaret* (1972).

Lesser known are the jealous actress-to-actress rivalries. Fueled by klieg lights and rivers of negative publicity, they sprouted like malevolent mushrooms on steroids.

As Judy faded into the 1960s, Liza roaringly emerged as a star in her own right. "I did it my way," Liza said. She survived the whirlwinds of her mother's drug addiction with a yen for choosing all the wrong men in patterns that weirdly evoked those of Judy herself.

For millions of fans, Judy will forever remain the cheerful adolescent (Dorothy) skipping along a yellow brick road toward the other side of the rainbow. Liza followed her down that hallucinogenic path, searching for the childhood, the security, and the love that eluded her.

Judy Garland, an icon whose memory is permanently etched into the American psyche, continues to thrive as a cult goddess. Revered by thousands of die-hard fans, she's the most poignant example of both the manic and depressive (some say "schizophrenic") sides of the Hollywood myth.

Deep in her 70s, Liza is still with us, too, nursing memories of her former acclaim and her first visit as a little girl to her parents at MGM, the "Dream Factory," during the Golden Age of Hollywood.

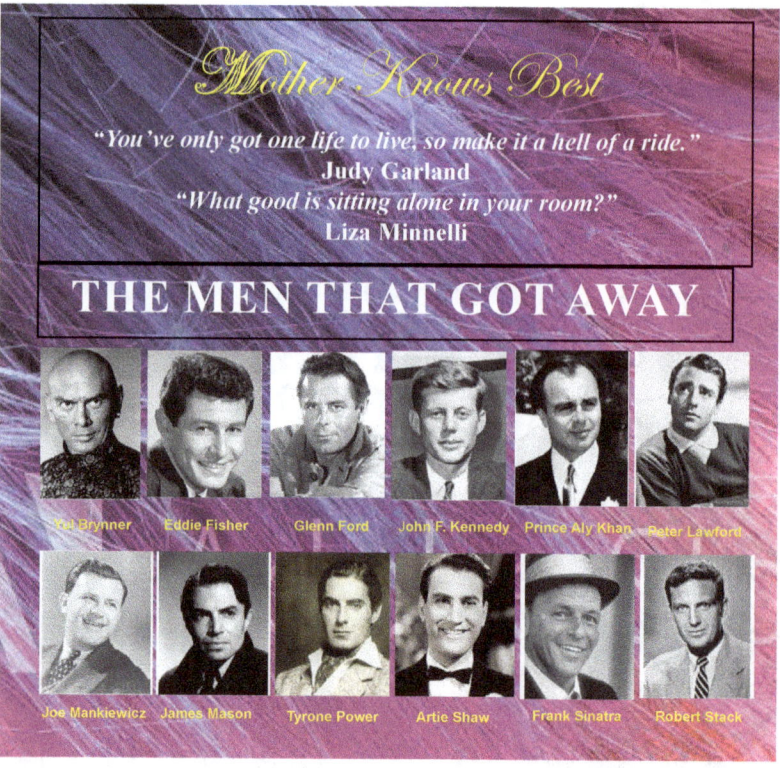

The Seductive Sapphic Exploits of
MERCEDES DE ACOSTA
Hollywood's Greatest Lover

Darwin Porter & Danforth Prince

IF YOU ASSUMED THAT THE GREATEST LOVERS ARE MEN, some of the most famous "cult goddesses" of the early- and mid-20th-Century might emphatically disagree.

At Magnolia House, in the final years of her life, the celebrated, notorious, and once-fabled Spanish beauty, **MERCEDES DE ACOSTA** (1892-1968) was a frequent visitor. To Darwin Porter, she confessed and recited fabulously indiscreet stories about her romantic same-sex exploits among the theatrical and cinematic elite of New York, London, Paris, and Hollywood.

It reveals "Sapphic Standards" from the heyday of Silent Film and the early Talkies that no other book—even her own (*Here Lies the Heart*, published in 1960)— ever dared to make public.

If you assumed that the greatest lovers are men, some of the most famous actresses of the early- and mid-20th-Century might emphatically disagree.

To film historian Darwin Porter, in the final years of her life, the notorious Spanish beauty MERCEDES DE ACOSTA (1892-1968) confessed indiscreet truths about her romantic exploits in New York, London, Paris, and Hollywood. Her targets were women, each of them celebrated in the theater, filmmaking, and literary scenes.

This book focuses on the "stories behind the story" of some of the women who evolved into America's most admired stage and early screen goddesses. Here, culled from firsthand accounts, is an unvarnished, unapologetic glimpse at what happened AFTER the vamps and sirens of the first half of the 20th Century walked down the red carpet of show-biz fame and in rare cases, fortune.

Mercedes de Acosta's love affairs were with women, each a figurehead in art, the theater, and the filmmaking and literary scenes. They included **Greta Garbo, Marlene Dietrich, Nazimova, Gertrude Stein, Alice B. Toklas, Eva Le Gallienne, Tallulah Bankhead, Jeanne Eagels, Katharine Cornell, Eleanora Duse, Isadora Duncan**, and **both of Valentino's wives**. This is probably the best portrait of *avant-garde* Broadway and early 20th-century filmmaking ever published. A pithy, photo-packed softcover with 474 pages and many dozens of photos

Here are Some of the Legendary Celebrities Who Were Exposed (or "Compromised') in the Confessions of Mercedes de Acosta

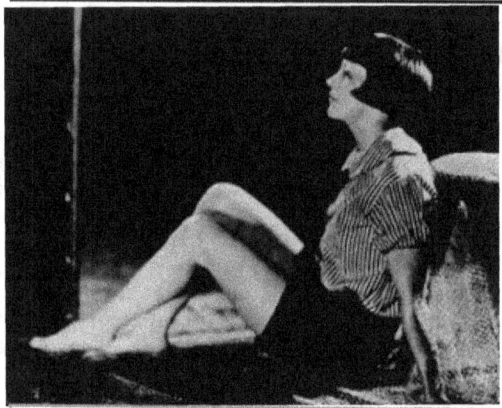

Silent Screen Vamp **Jean Acker**

Philanthropist and arts patron **Rita Stokes Lydig**

Stage star and the former Toast of London, **Tallulah Bankhead**

Stage diva **Ethel Barrymore**

"The aristocracy of Broadway," **Katharine Cornell**

"The Mother of Modern Dance," **Isadora Duncan**

"The world's most fabulous woman," **Marlene Dietrich**

Italy's most celebrated actress, **Eleanore Duse**

Socialite, trendsetter, and interior decorator, **Elsie de Wolfe (Lady Mendl)**

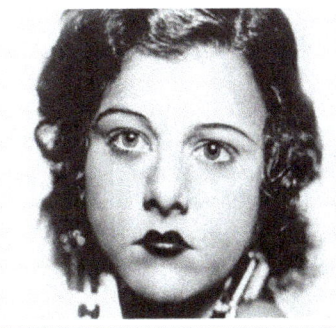

Torch singer, heiress, and murderess **Libby Holman**

Young **Greta** "The Divine" **Garbo**

Violet Ward "and her lover" circa 1900 at the Alice Austen House ("Clear Comfort" now a museum on Staten island), as photographed by Queer Icon & long-time Staten Island resident **Alice Austen**

Silent screen *tragedienne* & megastar **Jeanne Eagels**

John ("The Great Profile) **Barrymore**

Russian prima ballerina **Tamara Karsavina**

The Wizard of Oz's Good Witch of the North, **Billie Burke**

French cabaret entertainer and model for Toulouse-Lautrec: **Yvette Guilbert**

Photographer pioneer **Gertrude Kasebier**

Evelyn Nesbit, as photographed by **Gertrude Kasebier**

Anonymous but expressive subjects of the then new-fangled art of photography, circa 1899

Broadway Uber-Diva
Eva Le Gallienne

Comedienne and Stage Star
Beatrice Lillie

Broadway investor and theatrical agent
Bessie Marbury (left), with **Elsie de Wolfe**

Philanthropist & Activist
Anne Morgan,
daughter of J.P. Morgan

Suicidal Hollywood star
Ona ("Belle Watling") **Munson**

Silent Screen Diva & "Force of Nature"
Nazimova

Rudolph Valentino's imperious second wife
Natacha Rambova

Art Connoisseur and *Zeitgeist* star
Gertrude Stein (*standing*) with her long-time companion, **Alice B. Toklas**

Novelist, philanthropist, and Francophile, **Edith Wharton**

MERCEDES DE ACOSTA

Inspiration, Enabler, Muse, Mentor, &

SEDUCTRESS OF THE WORLD'S GREATEST ACTRESSES

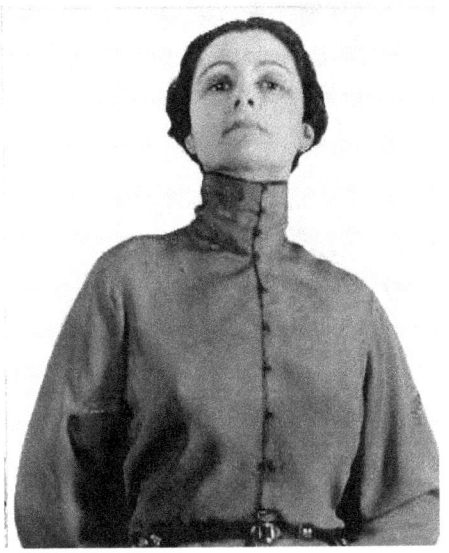

Until she was seven years old, the legendary Spanish beauty, **Mercedes de Acosta**, was convinced she was a boy. She tried to convince others of that, too. However, her world came tumbling down on her when a ten-year-old boy challenged her to show him her penis. He took her behind a bathhouse, unbuttoned his pants, and pulled out his penis, playing with himself until it was erect.

At this point, he was joined by five other boys, all of whom produced erections for her. When challenged to show her own privates, she ran screaming back to her bedroom, where she cried for two days and nights.

She later wrote, "On this hot afternoon, everything in my young soul turned monstrous and terrible and dark."

The inset photo shows Mercedes after she'd lost an eye after surgery for removal of a tumor. Stylish to the last, she wore that patch with a sort of panache.

In her final years, desperately in need of money, she had to sell her jewelry and private papers, including personal letters from Greta Garbo and Marlene Dietrich, to pay medical bills.

She spent the end of her life, as she told Darwin Porter, "learning just simply and quietly to be."

She was seventy years old in 1966, when she died, the long-time survivor of one of the 20th Century's most fascinating lives.

DAISY CHAIN
A Witty, Sometime Cruel, Late-Night Parlor Game Invented by Truman Capote

Whenever he was feeling provocative and bitchy (which was most of the time), a puckish **Truman Capote** would, if the company were amenable, play one of his favorite parlor games. He called it "Daisy Chain."

If the players had a large enough inventory of salacious gossip, and no compunction about revealing other people's indiscretions, "Daisy Chain" could link ANYONE to almost ANYONE ELSE through their previous sexual or romantic indiscretions.

According to Capote, **Mercedes de Acosta**—a socially well-connected eccentric whose lesbian adventures usually defied conventional social circuits—provided some of the most consistently reliable links in his parlor game.

Capote paid a price for his wit: Tennessee Williams described him as "a sodomite's delight, a monster unleashed from virginal portals," and when he got too caustically witty, in print, most of his friends and parlor game playmates brusquely abandoned him forever.

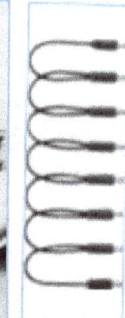

Wallis Warfield Simpson
(aka The Duchess of Windsor)

King Edward VIII abandoned the British throne to marry her. After that, she was both reviled and sought-after as a source of delicious gossip.

Francis Spellman was a predatory homosexual and the Cardinal Archbishop of New York.

At the Vatican, it was no secret that he had "this thing" for acolytes and choir boys.

Blood Moon Productions proudly announces A NEW EDITION of its 2014 compilation of lurid, vintage scandals from the Golden Age of Camelot. It focusses on the most watched, most enigmatic, and most controversial woman of the 20th Century, and it's called

JACQUELINE KENNEDY ONASSIS
HER TUMULTOUS LIFE & HER LOVE AFFAIRS

Darwin Porter & Danforth Prince

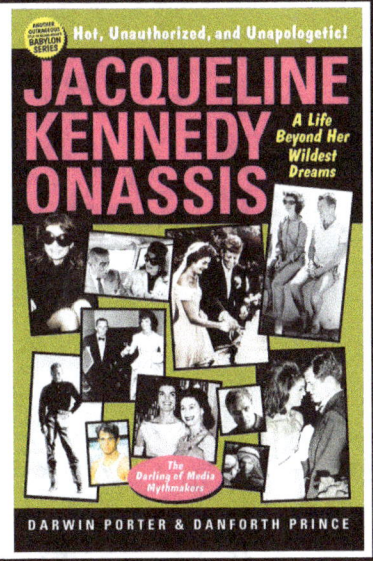

JACKIE INVADES "WASHINGTON BABYLON," EUROPE, & BEYOND

This is a new edition of the most compelling compilation of cash-soaked ambition, sexual indiscretion, and social embarrassment about a former first lady ever published,

Available now from **Ingram** and from **Amazon.com** worldwide, in honor of one of America's favorite Valentines.

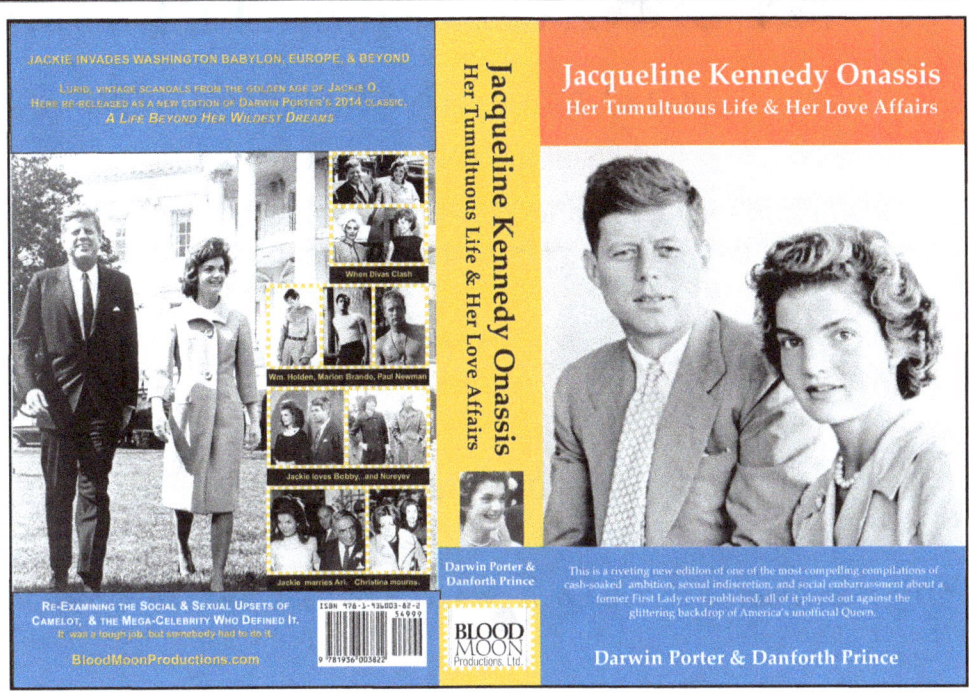

JACQUELINE KENNEDY ONASSIS
HER TUMULTUOUS LIFE & HER LOVE AFFAIRS

Conceived in direct and sometimes defiant contrast to the avalanche of more breathlessly respectful testimonials to the life and legacy of "America's Queen," this book is the latest installment in Blood Moon's endlessly irreverent MAGNOLIA HOUSE series.

RE-EXAMINING THE SOCIAL AND SEXUAL UPSETS OF CAMELOT AND THE MEGA-CELEBRITY WHO DEFINED IT.

IT WAS A TOUGH JOB, BUT SOMEBODY HAD TO DO IT.

"Jack treated me like a Victorian wife, and I suffered the pain of his infidelities."
--Jackie to her friend, Carly Simon

"Jack's presidency was sandwiched between that of a general whose mistress claimed he was impotent and a Texas clodhopper who should have been castrated like a bull."
Jackie on Presidents Eisenhower and Johnson

"Lady Bird was such a pigeon she'd run down the street naked if Lyndon commanded it."
--Jackie on Mrs. Lyndon B. Johnson

"Because of you, my son is growing up to be a fruit."
--Jackie to Peter Lawford

"The President is divorcing Jackie to marry me and make me First Lady."
--Marilyn Monroe to Frank Sinatra

"Don't ever bring that tramp into my home ever again."
--Jackie lecturing John-John on Madonna

"I fell in love with Jackie the first day Jack brought her home—how envious I was. I could stare for hours drinking in her beauty. I decided to wait my chance."
--Teddy Kennedy to (Florida) Senator George Smathers.

In the pages that follow, we've listed some of the
CHAPTER HEADINGS

that divide the various sections of our ode to America's
MOST FASCINATING, EVER, First Lady and Celebutante
JACQUELINE BOUVIER KENNEDY ONASSIS

"A LIFE BEYOND HER WILDEST DREAMS"

Baby Jackie and Black Jack Bouvier

Jackie Grows Up with "The Black Prince"
Her Gambling, Womanizing, Bisexual Father

Jackie in Europe (and Engaged)

"An American Geisha" Auditions Ivy League Beaux

How Jackie Surrendered Her Virginity in a Paris Elevator

The Newport Debutante
& the Senate's Most Eligible Bachelor

Jack & Jackie Get Married!
Their Mexican Honeymoon: A Recipe for Marital Disaster

Jackie's Married Life:
No Magic, and No Fireworks, but
Lots of Adultery and Life-Threatening Surgeries

Suicidal, Jackie Submits to Electro-Shock Therapy

Gore Vidal and the JFKs
Confronting the World's Most Famous Couple

Jack and Jackie Reveal Their Secrets to America's Most Cynical Social Historian

First Lady of Camelot
"I Hate that Name, It Sounds Like a Race Horse"
—Jacqueline Kennedy

Flying on Dr. Feelgood's Speed, Mythmaking Jack & Jackie Are Idolized by Millions

Assassination
JFK and Jackie Fly to Texas for a Date With Destiny
Gunshots from Dallas are Heard Around the World

The Thousand Day Reign of Camelot

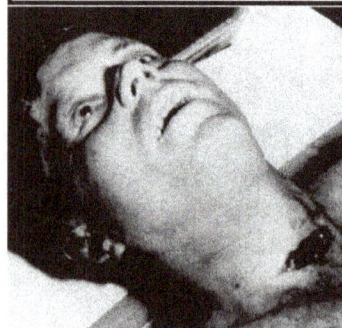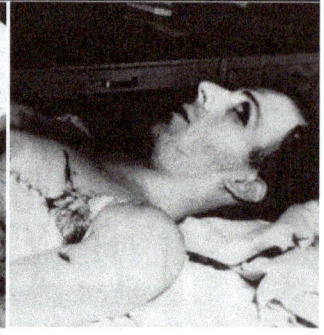

Jackie's Road
to the White House

At the Los Angeles Democratic Convention, Marilyn Defines JFK as "Very Penetrating"

Jackie and MM
—The World Knew Them by their Nicknames
"Jackie, I want you to meet Miss Marilyn Monroe"
—Truman Capote

Sharing Poisonous Secrets
Jackie in a Face to Face with JFK's Mistress

Bobby Kennedy
The Lancelot in Jackie's Camelot

A Shared Tragedy Evolves Into an Abiding Love

America's Queen Vs. The Literati

Competitive Bitchfests: Jackie is Repeatedly Embarrassed by Norman Mailer, Gore Vidal, & Truman Capote

Jackie's Taste for A-List Movie Stars

After Dates with Sinatra and Brando, She Awards Top Honors to William Holden

Jackie's Lovers, Listed in Alphabetical Order

Friends and Flings—What's Love Got to Do With It?

JFK Orders Paternity Test on Caroline and John Jr.

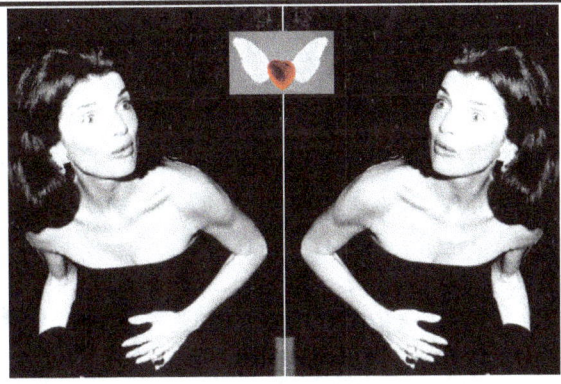

Rudolf Nureyev— From Russia With Love
"Tales of Tatar Tail"

The Kennedys Confront "Rudi in the Nudi"
Jackie and Lee Vie for the Reincarnation of Nijinski

Capote Vs. "Jackie & La Principessa"

The Tormented Saga of Capote's Lost Friendship With America's Most Famous Sisters

Jackie, Grace, & The Bullfighter

Jackie Tangles With Her Serene Highness, The Princess of Monaco

Jackie vs. Elizabeth Taylor
Rival American Divas Battle for Love, Glory, and Men

The Queen of Ancient Egypt Slugs It Out
With the Queen of the Potomac

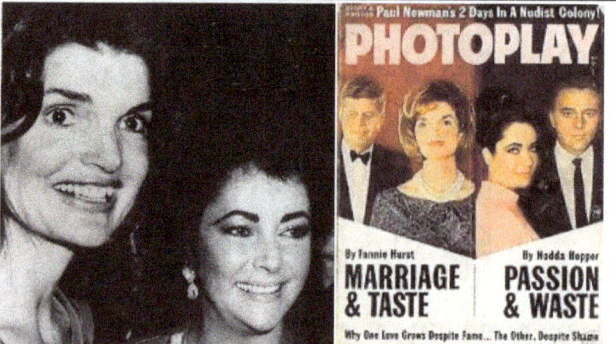

Jackie Marries Onassis
("A Grizzled Satrap")
And Enrages Half of America

Jackie O. and Daddy O. Mesmerize the World
A Bizarre Marriage Pact / Jackie's Bottomless Closets

Alexander and Christina
Onassis' Children Vs. "Our Evil, Gold-Digging Stepmother"

Greek Drama: Ari's Doomed Children
Rape, Early Deaths, and a Hired Assassin

Teddy Kennedy, Lion of the Senate
Coveting His Brother's Wife

Discovered: Teddy's Declarations of his Enduring Love for Jackie

Jackie's Nude Photos
"The Billion Dollar Bush"

Playboy and Penthouse Reject the Jackie Nudes,
But Hustler and Screw Each Score Publishing Bonanzas

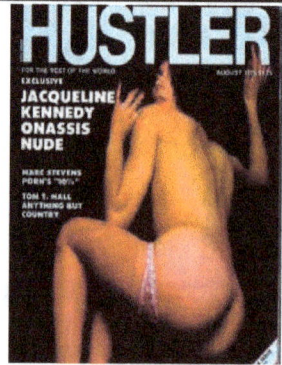 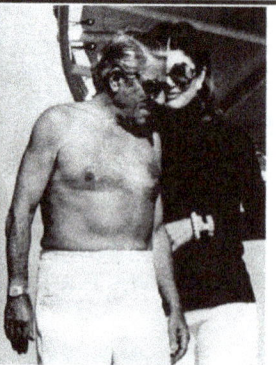

LUCILLE BALL & DESI ARNAZ

BECAME THE MOST CELEBRATED DUO IN THE HISTORY OF TELEVISION
IN TWO VOLUMES, BLOOD MOON HAS RELEASED THE MOST STARTLING, CANDID, AND UNVARNISHED OVERVIEW OF THEIR LIVES EVER PUBLISHED.

Half of America gathered every Monday night around the little black box in their living rooms to watch the antics of Lucy and Ricky Ricardo, a Cuban bandleader with his wacky, high-spirited wife.

The early struggles of Lucy and Desi were epic. As a girl, she at times was literally chained in her backyard in Jamestown, New York. As a teenager, she broke away and earned a reputation as "The Jamestown hussy," riding around with Johnny DeVita, a local hoodlum.

Born to wealth and privilege in Cuba, Desi, at the age of twelve, was escorted to the local bordello by his father to lose his virginity.

His family lost everything in the Cuban Revolution and fled to America. In Miami, Desi got a job cleaning out canary cages. He was eventually hired by bandleader Xavier Cugat because, "I beat hell out of those Afro-Cuban drums."

Meanwhile, in Manhattan, Lucy was struggling to break into show business, hustling "sugar daddies" and stage-door Johnnies who gave her money and gifts. Once, when desperate, she became a nude model. "A gal's gotta eat."

In the 1930s, she made it to Hollywood and worked making films for RKO. The executives used her as a gussied-up hooker to "entertain" out-of-town film exhibitors.

[Ultimately, she got her revenge. In one of the most ironic "fiscal revolutions" in show-biz history, she bought the studio.]

Drifting to Hollywood, Desi spotted Lucy on a sound stage "dressed like a two-dollar whore who had been badly beaten by her pimp." Their tempestuous marriage, characterized by long separations, staggered along for two decades.

By the early 1950s, the careers of both Desi and Lucy had headed south. There was a lot of resistance among TV executives who objected to his Cuban accent. But *I Love Lucy* was launched nevertheless and shot up in the ratings like a rocket, morphing into the most successful sitcom in TV history.

"With gold arriving in wheelbarrows" (Desi's words), they bought the four-block RKO Studios. Desilu Productions was launched, becoming the largest motion picture and television studio in the world.

In 1960, after their divorce, Lucy appraised her husband: "He is a Jekyll and Hyde type. He drinks, gambles, and chases the broads from thirteen to thirty, even Carrie Fisher. He's awash in broads, lots of booze, and that gay actor, Cesar Romero, is his devoted slave. Desi is destructive, but always building something. If it's big, he has to break it down."

"Love?" she asked. "I was always falling in love with the wrong man. Even Desi."

Desi, too, summed up his many years of marriage: "We were anything but Lucy and Ricky Ricardo on the tube. Those guys had nothing to do with us. Lucy and I dreamed of success, fame, and fortune. Guess what? **It all led to hell."**

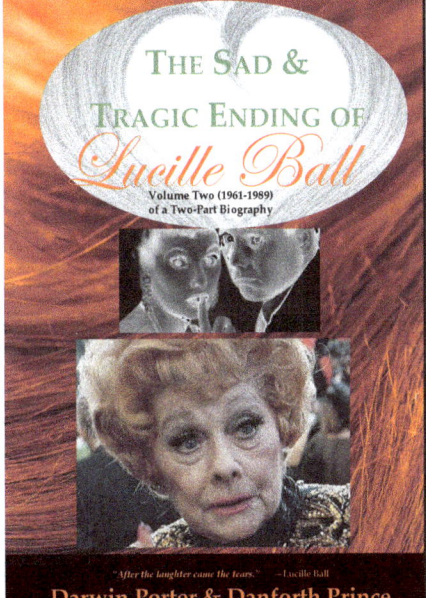

LUCILLE BALL & DESI ARNAZ

THEY WEREN'T
LUCY AND RICKY RICARDO
VOLUME ONE (1911-1960)
OF A TWO-PART BIOGRAPHY

Darwin Porter and Danforth Prince
ISBN 978-1-936003-71-6
Softcover, 530 pages, with photos, available everywhere now

THE SAD & TRAGIC ENDING OF

LUCILLE BALL

VOLUME TWO (1961-1989)
OF A TWO-PART BIOGRAPHY

Darwin Porter and Danforth Prince
ISBN 978-1-936003-80-8
Softcover, 550 pages, with photos, available everywhere now

THIS BOOK ILLUSTRATES WHY *GENTLEMEN PREFER BLONDES*, AND WHY MARILYN MONROE WAS TOO DANGEROUS TO BE ALLOWED TO GO ON LIVING.

Less than an hour after the discovery of Marilyn Monroe's corpse in Brentwood, a flood of theories, tainted evidence, and conflicting testimonies began pouring out into the public landscape.

Filled with rage, hysteria, and depression, "and fed up with Jack's lies, Bobby's lies," Marilyn sought revenge and mass vindication. Her revelations at an imminent press conference could have toppled political dynasties and destroyed criminal empires. Marilyn had to be stopped…

Into this steamy cauldron of deceit, Marilyn herself emerges as a most unreliable witness during the weeks leading up to her murder. Her own deceptions, vanities, and self-delusion poured toxic accelerants on an already raging fire.

"This is the best book about Marilyn Monroe ever published."

—**David Hartnell,** Recipient, in 2011, of New Zealand's Order of Merit (MNZM) for services to the entertainment industry, as defined by Her Majesty, Queen Elizabeth II.

Winner of literary awards from the New York, Hollywood, and San Francisco Book Festivals

DARWIN PORTER MEETS THE ULTIMATE BLONDE

"**With scrupulous research, Darwin Porter pretty much sums up the underside** of American entertainment, political and criminal activities during the mid-Twentieth Century. He does not paint a pretty sight, but Porter does present, with scathing honesty, the Monroe death lies and cover-ups, stopping just short of JFK and RFK. And for those who still believe that lone gunmen were responsible for the deaths of the Kennedy Brothers, is that the sound of sleigh bells on the roof? "It's been said that he deals in muck because he can't libel the dead. Well, it's about time someone started telling the truth about the dead and being honest about just what happened to get us in the mess in which we're in. If libel is lying, then Porter is so completely innocent as to deserve an award. In all of his works he speaks only to the truth, and although he is a hard teacher and task master, he's one we ignore at our peril. To quote Gore Vidal, power is not a toy we give to someone for being good. If we all don't begin to investigate where power and money really are in the here and now, we deserve what we get. Yes, Porter names names. The reader will come way from the book knowing just who killed Monroe. Porter rather brilliantly points to a number of motives, but leaves it to the reader to surmise exactly what happened at the rainbow's end, just why Marilyn was killed. And, of course, why we should be careful of getting exactly what we want. It's a very long tumble from the top."

--**ALAN PETRUCELLI**
Examiner.com

Who Killed Marilyn Monroe?

DR. ENGELBERG: "I'm calling from the home of Marilyn Monroe. She's dead."

LOS ANGELES POLICE SERGEANT JACK CLEMMONS WAS THE FIRST ON THE SCENE: "I had this eerie feeling that I'd come upon a murder. The cover-up had begun four hours before."

Like the sirens of Greek mythology, Marilyn was an irresistible temptress who captivated powerful men. On her road to ruin, the once-vulnerable waif had mutated into a temperamental vixen, seducing and provoking dangerous men presiding over the military mechanisms of the Free World and the innermost sanctums of organized crime. She knew too much. A walking time bomb, she could topple political dynasties and jail Mafia dons. Her naked body held the clues. But less than an hour after the discovery of Marilyn Monroe's corpse in Brentwood, a flood of theories, tainted evidence, and conflicting testimonies began pouring out into the public landscape.

This book examines the relentless sense of peril surrounding Marilyn during the year before her death, and the mass hysteria that followed in its wake. No death in the 20th century, other than that of JFK himself, ever sparked more cover-ups, lies, criminal thefts of vital data (including body parts), bribes, perjury, myths, incompetent investigating, distorted medical records, unauthorized leaks, outrageous rumors, and a *blitzkrieg* of bizarre books that obscured more than they revealed.

This investigative report lays out evidence, stripping it of its links to the self-interest of whoever gave it, and separates what really happened from thousands of distorted and misleading testimonies.

Into this steamy cauldron of deceit, Marilyn herself emerges as a self-enchanted and unreliable witness during the weeks leading up to her murder. Her misunderstandings, vanities, and delusions poured toxic accelerants on an already raging fire. After the shattering events of August 5, 1962, when Marilyn's nude body—an object of desire for thousands of fans—was wheeled in for voyeuristic doctors to examine and dissect, a legend was already being born.

BLOOD MOON: STRIPPING AWAY THE CENSORSHIP AND SECRECY FROM THE SCANDALS OF HOLLYWOOD'S "GOLDEN AGE." IT'S A TOUGH JOB, BUT SOMEBODY HAS TO DO IT!
BLOODMOONPRODUCTIONS.COM

ISBN 978-1-936003-79-2

"Here we are, Pussy, at this God-forsaken place, a land of shadoes, a burial bground for prehistoric monsters. And your soon-to-be ex-husband, Arthur Miller, calls this drama "The Misfits". Is that what we are, Pussy? Hollywood will use us, rip the flesh from our bones, and then bury us with those extinct reptiles."

—Montgomery Clift to Marilyn Monroe

"I got a call from Life magazine's bureau chief, Richard Stolley, at six that Sunday morning. 'Marilyn Monroe's dead. Go to the morgue and shoot what you can.'

"I rounded up three bottles of the most expensive whisky I could find. It was a bribe to the guy in the morgue. 'Ever seen a dead body before?' he asked before he led me to a steel-lined refrigerated corridor.

"He opened a door to wheel out a corpse. A white sheet covered her body. He tied a tag to her left big toe. Its inscription read CRYPT 33—MARILYN MONROE."

—Photographer Leigh Weiner

"I'd like to think that if Sinatra were still alive, he'd be taking a swing at both Darwin and Danforth for spilling so many juicy, juicy secrets! I love the Porter/Prince books. They are the biographies I dreamed about as a child."

—Paul Bellini, in FAB Magazine, Toronto

"Porter's book concludes with an account of Marilyhn's death that would certainly have gotten the author a pair of cement over-shoes or a bullet in the head, had he published it 30 years ago. Marilyn played with some very very dangerous people and in the end, she paid a high price for it—but what a ride she had!"

—Tobias Grace

"With this sizzling book, Blood Moon scores again."

—Richard LaBonte, Books to Watch Out For

MARILYN'S DEATH ELICITED OUTRAGE FROM ALMOST EVERYBODY
Here's How It was Reviewed by Some of Her Contemporaries:

"A simple, decent-hearted kid whom Hollywood brought down, legs parted."

—Director **Elia Kazan**

"More and more, Marilyn was involving herself with some of the most dangerous men on the planet, power figures who played rough and would stop at nothing. What did a blonde sex goddess mean to them? Some of them regarded her as no more than a whore, an easy lay for them to pick up and discard."

—**Shelley Winters**

"Marilyn's death is of historical interest. There is no statute of limitations on murder."

—L.A. District Attorney **Ira Reiner** in 1985

"They murdered Marilyn. The amazing thing is why after all these years they didn't find a reason to murder me, too."

—**Frank Sinatra**

"The title of the movie we were going to make said it all: Something's Got to Give."

—**George Cukor**

"It is doubtful that either Kennedy saw past the beauty and the intelligence to the truly shattered nature of her personality—one which, as her psychiatrist later admitted, would have made her a candidate for an institution had her name not been Marilyn Monroe."

—**Anthony Summers**

"Clues that pointed to foul play vanished. Once cleaned up, the death scene indicated suicide. All of Monroe's bed linen and personal laundry had already been washed and put carefully back in cupboards. By sealing the crime scene, Fox was merely adhering to the tradition of studio policy, sanitizing real-life Hollywood murder scenes."

—**Patte B. Barham,** veteran Hollywood reporter

"Marilyn was slapped around. On the tapes, you could actually hear her being slapped, even hear her body fall to the floor. One of the men said, 'What do we do with her body now?'"

—**"Tom,"** a "Deep Throat" wiretapper inside Bernard Spindel's operation

"Marilyn's death was to apear to be an accidental suicide, exploiting her false reputation for reckless overdosing. Marilyn Monroe would commit suicide according to their schedule. Maf, her small poodle, was her only bodyguard that night, and he was barking ferociously."

—Detective **Milos Speriglio**

"There are those who see Marilyn Monroe's death as the seed of assassinations to follow—those of her boyfriends Jack and Bobby Kennedy."

—**Norman Mailer**, to poet Norman Rosten

"My feeling was that she (Eunice Murray) had been told what to say. It had all been rehearsed beforehand. And why was she washing Marilyn's sheets at that ungodly hour of the morning?"

—**Sergeant Robert Byron** of the LAPD

"I'm often asked to comment on Marilyn Monroe, and the autopsy I performed on her. Words fail me, so I quote from the Latin poet, Petrarch: 'It's folly to shrink in fear, if this is dying. For death looked lovely in her lovely face.'"

—**Dr. Thomas T. Noguchi**, Marilyn's coroner

"You might call it a convenient death. She died just before the shit was about to hit the fan."

—**J. Edgar Hoover** to Guy Hotell

The Mistress of Camelot

O, Time,
Be kind.
Help this weary being
To forget what is sad to remember.
Lose my loneliness,
Ease my mind
While you eat my flesh.

—**Marilyn Monroe**

AUTHOR'S MEMO

Consistent with the trend in modern biography, this book deals with reconstructed quotes, which are presented as told to me by various sources at the time. Word-for-word conversations were reported "as remembered," which means that the exact wording of dialogues may not be correct, but the points being made, as well as the action taking place, have been honored and replicated.

Any memoir or biography of Marilyn Monroe always invites a host of attacks, many of them so violent in expression that the attacker in some cases has ended up paying damages to the author either in court or as part of out-of-court settlements. Many of these attacks are senseless and without reason. Others, of course, are valid, but too often intemperate.

Let's look at it this way: It is truly amazing that a luminous movie star of the 1950s can still shine her light into the 21st Century and beyond. The world has moved on, and Hollywood is no longer that place she set out to conquer at the end of World War II. Yet her memory lingers to enchant each new generation.

It seems that everyone who ever met Marilyn left with a very different opinion of her, and many of those who met her are staunchly committed to defending that opinion, even if misguided. This book brings together not one, but a wide sampling of points of view about Marilyn. If those being quoted did not "know" Marilyn as well as they thought they did, they should be forgiven, as Marilyn probably did not know herself.

I'm grateful to those who shared their experiences of Marilyn with me, for, in spite of the differences in their respective points of view, a portrait of this fabled star nonetheless emerges.

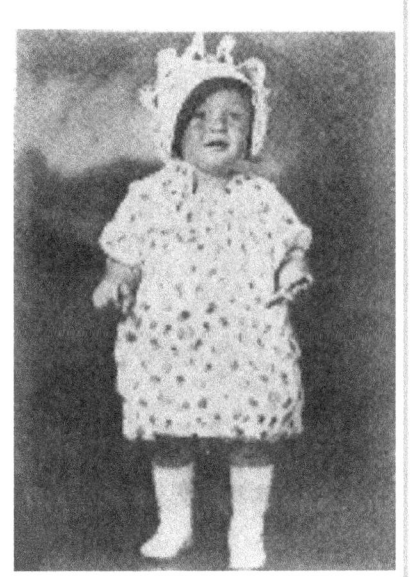

Imagine it is the year 2012: Marilyn is eighty-four years old, with remaining traces of her former beauty. Beside her sits her twenty-four-year-old boyfriend, her latest conquest. With champagne, still her favorite drink, they're watching the latest Monroe-inspired movie, TV series, or documentary.

After the telecast, the young man asks, "Marilyn, is that what really happened? I mean, did you really go to bed with President Kennedy?"

She giggles as she reaches over to kiss him. "Something like that, sweetie, something like that. Memory fades as time goes by. But what a hell of a story from an orphan who nobody wanted."

Blood Moon's
Hollywood Remembered

Glitz, Glamour, Triumph, & Tragedy

How Blood Moon Productions captured the attention of
The American Tabloids during the decline of
The Entertainment Industry's Golden Age

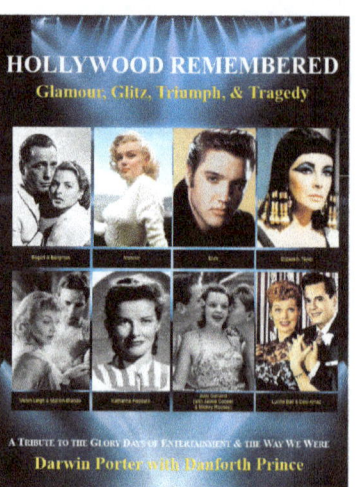

July 4, 2025: Blood Moon Productions (www.BloodMoonProductions.com) proudly announces the release of *Hollywood Remembered*, a 450-page compendium of "short stories" inspired by **Darwin Porter's** long exposure to the backlot intrigues of the entertainment industry's "Hollywood Heyday."

It's envisioned as an oversized coffee table book of enduring interest to anyone who ever loved classic films and the scandalous intrigues associated with its players. It's not for the timid. Pages are splashed with incisive commentary and photographs of a fabulous era swept away by changing times.

Its inspiration derived from twenty years of Darwin Porter's monthly contributions to *Boomer Times*, a glossy magazine and "Sunday supplement" of *The Miami Herald's* subscribers in Dade and Broward Counties, Florida. It was spearheaded by **Anita Finley**, a South Florida gerontologist who doubled as a spokesperson for her state's "politically connected" population of Baby Boomers.

According to Blood Moon's president, Danforth Prince, "The core values of **Anita Finley** and **Darwin Porter**—who define Baby Boomers as "Old-Time Hollywood's Greatest Fans"—always dovetailed neatly. This book is envisioned as a joint celebration of the staggering literary output of both *Boomer Times* and **Blood Moon Productions**. As such, we've dedicated it to **Ms. Finley**. The *Grande Dame* of Florida's Boomers.

"We also envision this as an **autobiography of Blood Moon Productions** and an end-of-life tribute to its creative director, **Darwin Porter**. If not for his archival skills, many once-underground truths about The American Century would have died with their last first-hand witnesses. But thanks in part to Porter's staggering descriptive output, thousands of once-repressed facts have been recorded and digitalized for future historians and fans. In fact, for the Library Trades, we've categorized this one-of-a-kind new book as a resource for MEDIA STUDIES.

"With a release expected on that Greatest of American Holidays, The 4th of July, Blood Moon's HOLLYWOOD REMEMBERED will challenge traditional beliefs about celebrities and the sociologies that nurtured them. "

With a special tribute to the celebrities whose luminous images still enthrall us on movie screens today, thanks for taking a look at this portrait of the ferociously unfettered "indie" that briefly reigned as a magnet for tabloid publicists, and as one of the hottest independent publishing ventures in the world.

Blood Moon's HOLLYWOOD REMEMBERED:
Glitz, Glamour, Triumph, & Tragedy

By Darwin Porter with Danforth Prince
ISBN 978-1-936003-92-1

This book is a testimonial to the scrappy independent press that repeatedly captured more media flash than any equivalent publisher in the English language—all based on exposing "imbalances" in the public's perception of the most influential dream factories in the history of humankind.

| WINNER: NY BOOK FESTIVAL 2024 |
| BEST ANTHOLOGY OF THE YEAR |
| *Hollywood Remembered—* |
| *Glamour, Glitz Triumph, & Tragedy* |

FROM NEW YORK TO HOLLYWOOD, NEW ZEALAND, AND BEYOND, BOOK REVIEWERS AND COLUMNISTS ARE GOING GAGA FOR:
HOLLYWOOD REMEMBERED
BLOOD MOON'S TESTIMONIAL TO "THE WAY WE WERE."

BOOK AWARD NEWS: For Immediate Release, August 2, 2024

Yesterday, judges at the prestigious **NEW YORK BOOK FESTIVAL** designated ***HOLLYWOOD REMEMBERED*** —Blood Moon's Ode to Golden Age Hollywood—as the WINNER of one of its **BEST BOOKS OF THE YEAR** Awards.

Their decision was announced by the Festival's president, Bruce Haring: "We celebrate the authors of these award-winning books, wishing them recognition for their archivizations of facts and ways of life that, without their efforts, might be lost forever. We applaud them for their hard work, and we wish them luck in their future endeavors."

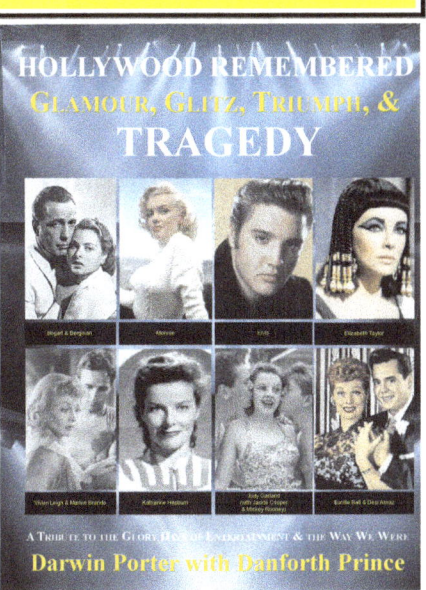

ENQUIRING MINDS ARE ASKING:
WHO ELSE MADE A FUSS OVER THIS BOOK LAST WEEK?

ANSWER: **DAVID HARTNELL**, New Zealand's answer to Hedda Hopper, Cindy Adams, and Emily Post. Praised as the CLASSIEST Hollywood Obsessive in the History of Journalism, with a Social Media Following of Millions of "Down Unders," he's the only Entertainment Columnist to be applauded and recognized by Her Majesty, the (late) Queen Elizabeth II. His Hollywood gossip columns appear in **NZ Woman's Weekly, Woman's Day** and the **Sunday News.** His catchphrases ***"I'm not one to gossip but..."*** and ***"my lips are sealed"*** have become part of New Zealand's popular culture.

In the 2011 Queen's Birthday Honours, he was appointed a Member of the New Zealand Order of Merit, for services to entertainment. His review of Hollywood Remembered is replicated on the next page.

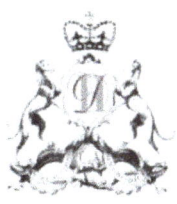

David H.W. Hartnell MNZM
Patron "The Variety Artists Club of New Zealand"
Patron "The Brotherhood of Auckland Magicians"
Ambassador St James Saviour
Ambassador Prostate Cancer Foundation of New Zealand
david@davidhartnell.com
PO Box 78042, Grey Lynn, Auckland 1245, New Zealand

According to David Hartnell, "I'm not one to gossip but ………

"This week an amazing oversized coffee table book *Hollywood Remembered—Glamour, Glitz, Triumph, & Tragedy* by Darwin Porter and Danforth Prince arrived from Blood Moon Productions in New York. It is the best tribute of the Golden Glory Days of Entertainment in Hollywood ever written.

"This is the BEST book of its kind ever published, a staggering compendium of short stories inspired by Darwin Porter's long exposure to the backlot intrigues of the entertainment industry's Hollywood Heyday. It's for anyone who's ever loved classic films and the scandalous intrigues associated with its players. It's not for the timid. Pages are splashed with incisive commentary and photographs of a fabulous era swept away by changing times.

"Critics around the world have hailed Porter and Prince's celebrity biographies as the best of their kind. Even after 50 odd years writing and talking about Hollywood and its stars, I learned quite a few things from within its pages that I didn't know.

"I award this stunning publication five out of five very large gold stars! If you love movie stars, Hollywood celebrity history and gossip from the heydays of Hollywood, this is the book for you!

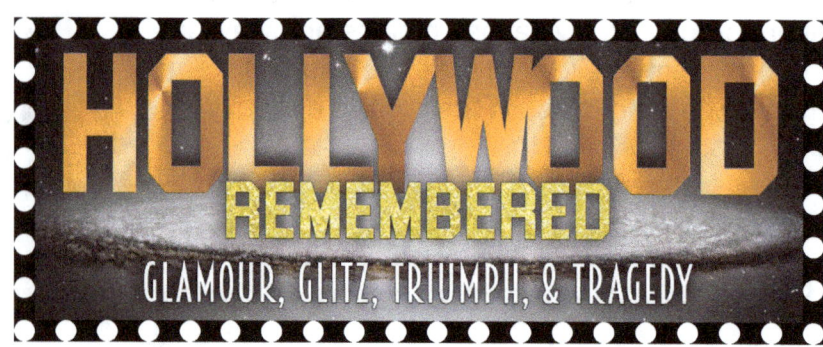

"According to Blood Moon's president, **Danforth Prince**: 'For the Library Trades, we've categorized it as a resource for Media Studies. We envision it as **an autobiography of Blood Moon Productions** and an end-of-life tribute to its creative director, **Darwin Porter.** If not for his archival skills, many once-underground truths about The American Century would have died with their last first-hand witnesses."

"But thanks to Porter's staggering descriptive output, thousands of once-repressed facts have been recorded and digitalized for future historians and fans. *Hollywood Remembered* will challenge traditional beliefs about celebrities and the sociologies that nurtured them. With special tributes to the celebrities whose luminous images still enthrall us on movie screens today, thanks for taking a look at this portrait of the ferociously unfettered indie that briefly reigned as one of the hottest independent publishing ventures in the world."

This is the story behind the story of the small, scrappy independent press,
Blood Moon Productions,
whose celebrity *exposés* (more than 50 of them) generated *tsunamis* of tabloid flash
during the decline of the entertainment industry's golden age.

It's a story about Media, the Hollywood Dream Factory, and the clumsy, treacherous
juggernaut known as FAME. It's about the fantasies that the entertainment industry
crafted, and the secrets it conspired to conceal.

It offers an "on the down low" view of entertainers who delighted us, who captured our
imaginations, and who paid heavy prices for the pedestals on which we placed them.

It's also a memorial to belief systems and values that in many cases have
Gone With the Wind.

From "Deep in December" of our lives *(or, if we're lucky, from Deep in September)*,
we offer it as a tribute to the way we were.

Here it is…*Hollywood Remembered*…an idiosyncratic, scrappy anthology
like nothing that's ever been seen before. It says a lot about the American version
of Fame and/or Infamy that you might not have expected.

Happy reading…and may your memories burn bright.

www.BloodMoonProductions.com

CHALLENGING THE STATUS QUO'S
BELIEFS ABOUT CELEBRITY
AND THE IRONIES OF FAME

IT'S A TOUGH JOB,
BUT SOMEBODY'S GOT TO DO IT.

BOOK RELEASE & CELEBRITY NEWS

FOR IMMEDIATE RELEASE   Blood Moon proudly announces the release of what its president, **Danforth Prince**, describes as "a 250-page 'wild card,' that combines aspects of a bookseller's catalogue with a memoir, an autobiography, and a manual for media studies.

"It was inspired by new (and in many cases, horrifying) realities in North America's book distribution patterns after the "going out of business" announcement of one of our distributors, the **National Book Network**. It's also a late-in-life effort to document our research methods and to explain how two eccentric but agile writers managed to accumulate so many gossipy, historically compelling *exposés* of American and international celebrities."

"THIS IS IT." he said, "Our best shot at compiling, for estate purposes and as an effort to revise our distribution networks, an annotated CATALOGUE—with commentary, sidebars, and source material—of our *oeuvre*."

"How things got DOWN and LOW at Blood Moon will never happen again," Prince continued. "Our saga, as an independent publishing venture, is unique. This book spins insights into the quirky small press that brazenly compiled and published, within a span of fewer than fifteen years, almost 50 tell-all biographies, film, and gossip guides that many editorial venues would have refused to touch."

"We present it as **a bookseller's catalogue on steroids**. To this book's 'from the cradle' overview of our publishing history, we've added narratives that illustrate our investigative techniques, and eagles'-eye views of the *milieux* in which—for a few decades, at least—we thrived. A historic archive, it's soaked with nostalgia for priorities and belief patterns about the American Century that have Gone With the Wind."

"This is also a testimonial to old-fashioned "up-close-and-personal" (i.e., "non-internet") conversations. In our case, many were with living witnesses to dramas-within-dramas that were crucial to that compelling all-American phenomenon known as SHOW BIZ."

THE YEAR OF ITS PUBLICATION, THIS BOOK WON A RESPECTED LITERARY AWARD FROM THE LOS ANGELES BOOK FESTIVAL.

BLOOD MOON PRODUCTIONS
Its Origins, Its *Oeuvre*, Its Sources, & Its Legacy
Darwin Porter & Danforth Prince
Softcover, 242 pages, 8 ½" x 11"
with hundreds of color photos & illustrations
ISBN 978-1-936003-94-5

Available everywhere now

Entertainment About Celebrity
and the Ironies of Fame

A Review of Blood Moon Productions

Darwin Porter & Danforth Prince's overview of Blood Moon Productions

9781936003945 $49.99   www.BloodMoonProductions.com

Anyone interested in Hollywood history, gossip, drama, and major players will likely well know of the prolific publisher Blood Moon Productions, whose works have profiled celebrities, ribald atmospheres, and legendary encounters on and off the silver screen.

This review was written by Diane Donovan (photo above), senior reviewer for Bookwatch, California Bookwatch, The Midwest Book Review, and Donovan's Literary Services.

What they won't know is how Blood Moon began, evolved, and became a powerful entity fueled by the "Neitzsches of Naughtiness," Darwin Porter and Danforth Prince. This is why Blood Moon Productions: Its Origins, Its Oeuvre, Its Sources, and Its Legacy is simply outstanding—a "must have" acquisition for any library collection seeing popularity with any of their publications.

It's already a fact that Porter and Prince have profiled and preserved the legends of modern times, from Marilyn Monroe and Elvis Presley to Humphrey Bogart and Carrie Fisher. A dip into Blood Moon Productions examines the wellsprings of not only the dynamic duo's Hollywood interests and connections, but exactly how they can churn out so much weighty and compelling writing in a short span of years.

How weighty and prolific? Think two or three yearly, at about five to seven hundred pages long, packed with rich stories and photos about major public personalities.

Their revised focus here is not to say that gossip has been set aside for practical review of personal lives and a publishing house's development. Indeed, as with all their books, gossip, juicy stories, and high drama permeates this synthesis of the many Hollywood lives and encounters Danforth and Darwin have experienced over decades of work.

The writing is as impeccable as its headliners (think 'chapter titles' on steroids), as in the book's second part about Darwin Porter: "The most famous person you've never heard of, he's what would have happened if Walter Winchell had fathered a child with Hedda Hopper."

Who would not be inspired to read all about him, fueled by the heady analysis of Darwin Porter, who reviews Danforth's vivid life and choices.

And, the color. Most photo-filled Hollywood books rely relatively little on color imagery; but no expense has been spared here ... and it shows.

Quite simply, any Hollywood-centric library collection would be hard pressed to find anything even remotely like Blood Moon Productions in Hollywood literature.

Steeped in the culture from whence it was born, Blood Moon Productions is risqué, ribald, rollicking, and powerfully personal, and is highly recommended for a broad audience of fans of gossip, Hollywood personalities, and the individual ambition and connections which have driven and motivated Porter and Prince to stand out from the crowd of Hollywood wanna-be writers.

Bravo! More, please.

"Blood Moon, in case you don't know, is a small publishing house on Staten Island that cranks out Hollywood gossip books, about two or three a year, usually of five-, six-, or 700-page length, chocked with stories and pictures about people who used to consume the imaginations of the American public, back when we actually had a public imagination. That is, when people were really interested in each other, rather than in Apple 'devices.' In other words, back when we had vices, not devices."

—The Huffington Post

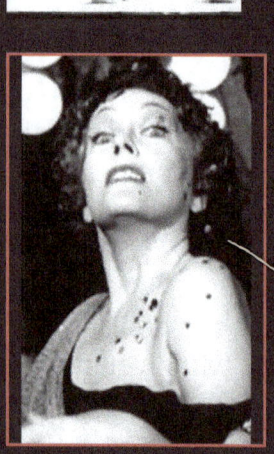

Blood Moon Productions, Ltd.

"ENTERTAINMENT ABOUT HOW AMERICA INTERPRETS ITS LEGENDS, ICONS, AND CELEBRITIES"

BloodMoonProductions.com

ISBN 978-1-936003-94-5

November & December 2016

PHYLLIS CREORE, "THE CANTEEN GIRL"

The Voice that Brought Hope to Millions of G.I.s During World War II Becomes a Centenarian

By the time you read this, Americans will have gone to the polls, ending one of the most contentious presidential election campaigns in U.S. history. Not liking either Donald J. Trump or Hillary Clinton, many voters chose not to vote at all. Others who did cast ballots won't know for several months (or years) whether they made a wise or a regrettable choice.

In all the hullabaloo of the closing weeks of the presidential campaign, the death of "The Canteen Girl" (Phyllis Creore) went almost unnoticed. When she died at the age of 100 in Manhattan, it signaled the end of an era, and the death of the last female icon of World War II.

Beginning shortly after the U.S. entry into World War II, following the Japanese attack on Pearl Harbor, the soothing alto voice of this beautiful blonde brought music and a message of hope to homesick soldiers fighting on remote Japanese-held islands in the South Pacific.

Lyrics of her theme song included: "I wish you luck in everything you do/That all your cares will disappear from view."

At one time, I got to talk to her at the Broome Street Art Gallery in Manhattan. She told me, "I wanted to present the voice and conjure up the image of the girl these boys left behind to go off to war. I wanted them to know how grateful we were that they were fighting for our freedom, and that we on the home front loved them and awaited their victorious return."

"I got hundreds of marriage proposals, often from seventeen-year-olds recently enlisted," she said. "Many of these boys, away from home for the first time, and many afraid for their lives, were desperately lonely. I reached out to

Two views of the woman whose voice was projected across the atolls of the Pacific as a morale-builder during the darkest years of World War II: Introducing **Phyllis Jeanne Creore.** aka "The Canteen Girl."

Her personal and musical styles were unique and will never come again. Her radio audiences, from positions scattered across the atolls and coral reefs of the Pacific, were young, lonely, confused, testosterone-driven males hankering for home and the sounds of the girls they left behind. **Phyllis Creore** was reliably and steadily on hand, ready to rescue them, at least from afar.

them."

"The world no longer remembers me, I'm sure, but my boys did. Many wrote to me for years, telling me about their post-war lives, sending me photographs of their wives and children. It saddens my heart to think that many of these fine, brave men are no longer with us. Just thinking about them always brings tears to me."

"It was the greatest thrill of my life, to sing and to talk to these young men, sending out a message of hope transmitted on shortwave radio to the troops abroad. Of course, I had to compete with the notorious Tokyo Rose."

Phyllis was referring to several actresses, each known as "Tokyo Rose" who broadcast pro-Japanese propaganda during the war. GIs endured the outlandish propaganda for access to the program's then-cutting edge American music. But in vivid contrast to Phyllis, the actresses collectively known as Tokyo Rose wanted to lower American morale, urging soldiers to put down their arms and surrender. Tokyo Rose often mocked the U.S. soldiers, teasing them cruelly by planting suspicions that men who had remained in the U.S., sometimes classified as 4-F, were stealing their wives and girlfriends.

At the end of the war, only Iva Toguri, a Los Angeles-born former U.S. citizen was arrested for her portrayal and persona of Tokyo Rose. Convicted of treason and imprisoned after the war, she was released from prison in 1956.

Phyllis Creore married Ted Westermann, a film-industry executive, in 1946. She later developed a second life as an artist, exhibiting in New York City. Most of her final years were spent in seclusion in her Fifth Avenue apartment, surrounded with scrapbooks bulging with letters "from my G.I.'s."

She was grateful for the letters she received from Franklin and Eleanor Roosevelt, each of whom thanked her for her wartime broadcasts. When not broadcasting during the war, Phyllis was a regular at the Stage Door Canteen near Times Square. *[A hit song of that era was entitled, "I Left My Heart at the Stage Door Canteen."]* Having opened in March of 1942, the Canteen catered to soldiers scheduled for more or less immediate transport to the battlefront. Phyllis, along with actresses who included, among others, Lauren Bacall, could be seen dancing the jitterbug with soldiers. Tallulah Bankhead might be giving away kisses, and Helen Hayes smiling sweetly and spreading mustard on their hot dogs.

My great friend and frequent house guest was the actress and cabaret entertainer, Greta Keller. Back in Berlin during the late 1930s, she'd been the favorite singer of Adolf Hitler until Goebbels discovered that she was Jewish. Reacting to a telephonic warning from her friend, Conrad Veit (who, ironically, portrayed a Nazi in Casablanca in 1942), she fled from Berlin a few hours before the SS descended on her apartment with the intention of shipping her off to a concentration camp.

During Greta's subsequent residency in New York City, the U.S. government asked her to sing and deliver German-language American propaganda for broadcast to German soldiers battling against the Allies. In addition to performances of "Lili Marleen" aimed directly at their weary heartstrings, she worked to persuade them that they were losing, and that their continued resistance would contribute to the deaths of millions of their fellow citizens and the destruction of much of their Fatherland.

The voices of these female propagandists and singers from World War II have been silenced with the passage of the decades, but they live on in recordings, many of them nostalgic reminders of that dreadful time in the early 1940s when Western Civilization itself was in danger of obliteration.

Decades after her wartime memories were built, **Phyllis Creore** retained stacks of neatly organized file folders filled with sweat-stained, handwritten letters from G.I.s who worshipped her—perhaps as an archetype, but nonetheless sincerely—from afar.

Each of the handwritten letters, by anyone's standards, is a tear-jerking testimonial to Phyllis' musical expressions of love across the abyss of time and space.

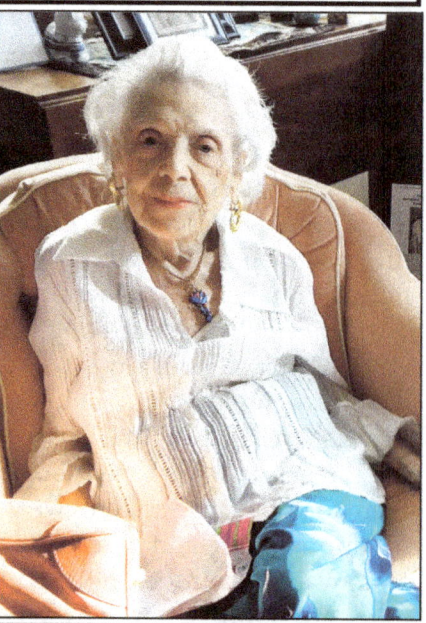

Phyllis Creore Westermann in her NYC apartment in March of 2016, on the occasion of her 100th birthday.

When a podcaster at the party gushed, *"You're part of history!"* she responded, with a laugh, *"Well, it took 70 years of waiting!"*

May 2015

"FLY ME TO THE MOON"

The Durability of Bart Howard's Blockbusting Classic Proves that an Underlying Fascination with THE MOON is part of the American Psyche

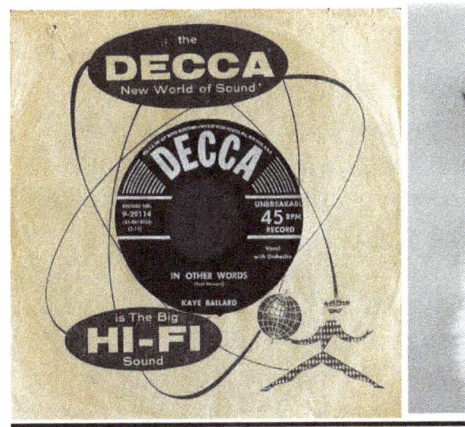

Left photo: The first pressing, released in April of 1954, of the first-ever recording of *"Fly Me to the Moon"* by Bart Howard, as sung by **Kaye Ballard**, as she appeared in the late 1950s.

One lovely summer night in 1954, a wonderful friend of mine, composer Bart Howard, went for a walk along a lake. There was a full moon glowing that night. He returned to his cottage and sat down in front of his piano. In twenty minutes, he wrote, a song he formally named "In Other Words," but which most consumers remember as "Fly Me to the Moon."

He'd go on to write 50 other songs, but nothing to equal "Fly Me to the Moon." As he told me, "I've lived off that song ever since, and I have to go to the bank every day." The song's durability was enhanced by later renderings by Frank Sinatra, Tony Bennett, Ella Fitzgerald, Peggy Lee, Nat King Cole, Connie Francis, and Sarah Vaughan.

Released by NASA as a simulation of its **Apollo 11 Moonwalk**, this photo shows what Armstrong and Aldrin looked like during their moonwalks of 1969.

Bart was delighted when his song became the first ever played on the moon. In July of 1969, the commander of Apollo 11, Neil Armstrong, one of the people who heard it, on site, was the first person to walk on the moon. As he famously broadcast to millions of listeners back home, "That's one small step for man, one giant leap for mankind."

His Moonwalk was replicated a few moments later by Buzz Aldrin, who carried with him a portable cassette which played "Fly Me to the Moon" to some 450 million listeners.

Today, space tourism has already been launched. I turned down an opportunity to be a small part of it when I met with an editor for the Frommer guidebook series, of which I was the chief writer.

She pitched an idea to me: "Would you like to write a book called *Frommer's The Moon: A Guide for First-Time Visitors?"*

Thinking she was joking, I said, "I don't like to write books on planets I've never visited."

But she was serious. In time, Frommer would actually publish such a book written by a German, Werner ("Tiki") Küstenmacher, who had fallen in love with space travel as a child. I agreed to help with the research and to help publicize it, the first ever such book.

He even owns a plot of land on the moon. Yes, real estate is being sold for some

First (and only) edition of *Frommer's Guide to the Moon,* as marketed by The Frommer Guides, **Darwin Porter's** "alma mater."

future home on the moon.

Transits are also being sold for future visits there, and they're not cheap.

The Frommer Guide featured all the lunar attractions such as the "Sea of Tranquility," or excursions to "the Dark Side of the Moon." Previewed were such attractions as the Colossal Crater Copernicus, 58 miles in diameter, or Epsilon Park in the Liebnitz Range near the Moon's South Pole. Visits were described to the "Sea of Death," a gigantic crater 93 miles across. Also recommended was a visit to the Gruithuisen Gamma, a 12-mile-wide circular mountain mass whose peak looks like a collapsed pudding.

Practical details were also provided, including tips about eating, drinking, sleeping, and radiation dangers. On the practical side, visitors were told about how to urinate in space, and how to keep yourself fastened to your toilet seat so you won't float away during an awkward moment. Showers were out but sponge baths were in.

Even the subject of sex was reviewed. Ulrich Walter, a German physicist and astronaut, reported that in space, one's libido tended to be at a low ebb. To date, only one married couple has been sent into space. In 1992, Mark C. Lee and Jan Davis were aboard Space Shuttle Mission 47, but they provided no XXX-rated details.

Presumably, future moon travelers will want to bring home souvenirs for family and friends. There are probably no gold or precious metals there, but plenty of moon rocks to pick up as souvenirs.

For getting around, a "Moon Buggy" is recommended. Some were left behind during the Apollo Mission. New batteries will be needed.

Bart Howard only wanted to fly to the moon. Once you get there, you won't be able to fly around, as there is no atmosphere.

Companies such as Virgin Galactic and XCCR are working to make space tourism a future possibility. Russia has already pioneered flying passengers aboard a Soyuz Spacecraft to its international Space Station, charging $20 to $40 million per seat. Halted in 2010, flights are to resume in the autumn of 2015.

In Tokyo, Obayashi Enterprises is the world leader in blueprints for colonizing the moon. Scientists are at work exploring how bacteria can be used to make clean air and how plant cultures can provide sufficient nutrition. Its inventors are designing "Japanese Moon Cities."

Despite its renown among Boomers, **"2001: A Space Odyssey"** is underestimated by Gen X-ers as bizarre and painfully slow with a soundtrack that's completely (and for a movie about outer space, realistically) silent.

Some 60s-era viewers compared it to looking through a kaleidoscope while on acid, with an unexpected ending that features monkeys squabbling over a water-hole.

Although considered one of the best science fiction films of all time, when it was first released, hundreds walked out of theaters. Nonetheless, it retains an eerie fascination for anyone interested in Outer Space and its frontiers.

Movie buffs have been visiting the moon since the days of silent films. Director Stanley Kubrick's *2001: A Space Odyssey* remains the genre's masterpiece, coming out around the same time as the Apollo 11 landing. Most of the films are cheesy fare, including Zsa Zsa Gabor's *Queen of Outer Space*, a 1958 tale about a revolt against cruel Venusian queen. (Zsa Zsa, looking fabulous, played a scientist.)

Currently on DVD is a stark drama entitled *Moon*. The director was David Jones, son of rock royalty David Bowie. If you prefer to stay on Planet Earth, and if you want to continue to think of the moon as a romantic image in the sky, you can always catch Betty Grable in *Moon Over Miami* (1941) on Turner Classics.

And if you prefer your lunar musings to remain frothy, light-hearted, and fun, Hollywood has already done most of the "heavy lifting" for you. Photos above present the Moon, and everything else in Outer Space, as high camp—and no one did it better than **Zsa Zsa** *(see photo, right)*

September 2012

JOAN RIVERS
Ready, Aim, FIRE!

The unsinkable Joan Rivers has just turned 79. She's the first to admit that after a series of botched cosmetic surgeries, she looks like a surprised catfish.

Known for her loud, raspy voice and heavy Brooklyn accent, she has made a career of poking malicious fun at herself and roasting celebrities on the bonfire of their own vanities.

Currently, she's touring America, promoting her most outrageous book yet, *I Hate Everyone…Starting With Me*.

She made her debut in 1959 in a play called *Driftwood*, playing a lesbian who's hot for the then-unknown actress, Barbra Streisand. Since then, she's never gone away, though many a movie star such as Julia Roberts wishes she had.

Today, she'll take "any gig anywhere so long as there's a stage and a paycheck." For two decades, the duenna has hawked her jewelry collection on QVC. No actress escapes her attacks when she's the host of E! Network's *Fashion Police*. She's known as the "smother-mother" on WEtv's *Joan & Melissa: Joan Knows Best?* For years, Joan's 44-year-old daughter, Melissa, has pursued a career in Rivers' shadows, but she lacks her barb-slinging mother's ability for dead-on zingers.

Rivers has bitter memories of when she played fashion cop and stood on the red carpet at the annual Academy Awards presentations. She never awarded any "Oscars" for the dress of Hollywood stars—and was often told to restrain her cattily devastating remarks. "My God, I even had to be nice to Nicole Kidman, who married Tom Cruise. I can assure you that marriage wasn't for sex."

In this century, Rivers will take almost any movie role she's offered. Perhaps her lowest point was in 2006 when she appeared as Princess Clara's "*vajoana*" in an adult animated show. She told entertainment reporters, "Honey, if you'll appear as a vagina, a victim of too many plastic surgeries, you'll do anything."

Through the vagaries of her career, Prince Charles has always been her most loyal fan. In contrast, her list of enemies would stretch from New York to Buckingham Palace.

She offended Elizabeth Taylor so severely that the screen icon once threat-

In the years before her death in 2014, **Rivers** was the trenchant host for the cable TV show **Fashion Police**," presiding over a panel that eviscerated the famous and pseudofamous for their appearances on red carpets, worldwide. Some of the butts of her jokes never fully recovered.

But despite their cruelty, viewers organized **"When it comes to fashion, Joan is never wrong"** fan clubs. Others insisted that tuning in to an episode was akin to attending their version of church.

One of her biographers (Leslie Bennetts) called her **Joan the Impaler,** "one of the world's most uninhibited mean girls," who "focused her rage on ridiculing other women."

Her fans loved her anyway (or perhaps because of it), insisting that although Rivers was exhausting at and times infuriating, she was a reminder that feminists are as complex and contradictory as everyone else.

America's then-premier late-night TV host, **Johnny Carson,** looks at **Joan Rivers** with something approaching adoration during one of her frequent appearances on this show. After she became a favorite of his, he made her the show's first permanent guest host in 1983

Later, when she announced she was leaving to be the centerpiece of a competing late-night talk show, he bitterly denounced her and never spoke to her again.

ened to sue. Most of Taylor's weight was put on when she was married to the Republican senator from Virginia, John Warner, who nicknamed her "Chicken Fat." Rivers quipped, "When we were young, all of us wanted to look like Elizabeth Taylor. Now we do."

Rivers had two marriages—the first to James Sanger in 1955, a union that lasted six months; and again to Edgar Rosenberg in 1965. (He committed suicide in 1987.) In her 1997 book, *Bouncing Back*, she asserted that she, too, almost committed suicide.

In her latest book, she seemingly offends everyone—even the beloved Betty White. "I'm sick and tired of losing all the sassy grandma roles to her when I thought I had a closed market. I think it's high time someone pushed that b---h in front of a train."

She also said, "I hate famous stroke victims who don't realize it's time to get out of the public eye. Case in point—Kirk Douglas and Dick Clark." Clark, of course, died after she wrote that.

Rivers freely admits that "my own day will come when I can only smile, wave, and not speak."

She was always great with an exit line, as when she asked Camilla Parker Bowles, Prince Charles' wife, "Do you know a rich Russian who'd like to buy my palatial East Side apartment in Manhattan? Marie Antoinette would have lived in it if she had money."

Rivers once quipped, "I've had so much plastic surgery, when I die, they'll donate my body to Tupperware."

On August 28, 2014, she entered as an outpatient at a clinic in Yorkville in Manhattan. It was for a minor throat procedure. However, during the operation, she stopped breathing. She was resuscitated and transferred to the Mount Sinai hospital in East Harlem, where she was put on life support. She never woke up from a medically induced coma and died on September 4, 2014 from brain damage cased by a lack of oxygen, according to New York's Medical Examiner's Office.

At her funeral, Howard Stern (of all people) delivered the eulogy. He claimed, "She was brassy in public, classy in private, a troublemaker, trail blazer, and pioneer to comics everywhere."

Her daughter, Melissa Rivers, on January 26, 2015, filed a malpractice lawsuit against the clinic and the doctors who performed the surgery on her mother. In May of that year, the lawsuit was settled out of court for an undisclosed amount.

Joan Rivers....and **Melissa**....became regular *schtick* in the *haute* world of red carpet galas.

What are two of **Joan Rivers'** stage (and sometimes late-night TV) lines that diehard fans still remember years after her death?

"My face has been tucked in more times than a bed sheet at the Holiday Inn," and *"My vagina is like Newark; men know it's there, but they don't want to visit."*

Joan Rivers spent more than a half century as an insult comic, saying, in her distinctive Brooklyn accent, shameless, outrageous, and spectacularly tasteless things, clawing her way, rung by rung, up the comedic ladder. She was also brave, self-satirizing, and at her best, hysterically funny.

In 2025, eleven years after her death, NBC rescuscitated her image with a television tribute. In it, an armada of New Age comedians paid tribute.

May 2010

Much Ado About Nothing

Kitty Kelley's Bestselling *Exposé* of
OPRAH WINFREY
Lacks New Dirt

From the poison pen of celebrity slasher, Kitty Kelley, comes her latest nationwide best seller, simply entitled *Oprah*. According to reports, the talk show diva is "spitting mad" about Kelley's latest tome.

Oprah has made millions by prying deep secrets from her guests, or getting Tom Cruise to jump up and down on her sofa like a madman. But when the spotlight is turned on her, Oprah apparently feels too much of the glare.

Kelley has written bios on Jacqueline Kennedy Onassis, Frank Sinatra, Nancy Reagan, Elizabeth Taylor and the Bush family. The biographer revealed some of the most sordid aspects of those celebrated lives, including lurid details of Nancy as a Hollywood starlet "whose phone number was passed around."

But in *Oprah*, Kelley did not find such a rich biographical field to plow. The reason is twofold. First, Oprah's relatives had already sold many of the indiscreet stories to the tabloids. Also, Oprah herself has revealed many of her secrets to millions of her fans.

Scandal-mongering **Kitty Kelley,** whose sweet smile belies the daggers she's thrown at the reputations of some of her subjects, shows off her newest exposé. The subjects of some of her other tell-alls are depicted on the next page.

Even so, the tabloids went headline mad, heralding old secrets that had already been aired, notably the diva's alleged lesbianism (a crush on Diane Sawyer, for example), time lodged as a teenage hooker, her wild cocaine binges, and the mystery surrounding the identity of her father. Oprah told disgraced author James Frey, "I too smoked crack in Baltimore and did cocaine in Chicago." The charge that Oprah traded sexual favors for money so she could buy drugs to support her habit has also been aired before.

At the age of 14, Oprah gave birth to a baby boy, naming him Vincent. He lived for only five weeks and she never saw her kid.

The most damaging revelation about Oprah is that she invented a sob story about her childhood to gain sympathy from her audience. These tales from the bowels of Mississippi include alleged sexual abuse as a child. "I don't believe a word of this," said Katherine Carr Esters, Oprah's cousin. "She was spoiled, petted, and indulged better than any little girl in these parts. I confronted her as to

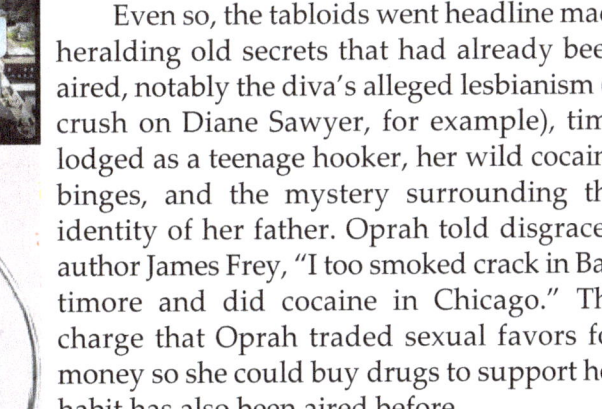

From her earliest moments, **Oprah Winfrey** (depicted as a child in the photo above) realized that she wasn't made for life in a menial job in her home town of Kosciusko, Mississippi.

A byline of modern celebrity states that "Offense is, indeed, sometimes the best defense,"

To that effect, **Oprah's** fan magazine, "O," celebrated her ambiguous links to her best friend and "gal pal," **Gayle King**, in a front-page cover story.

why she told all those lies. She said it's what people want to hear. She told me, 'the truth is boring.'"

It appears that Oprah would do anything for a rating, claiming she was so poor that she had to adopt two cockroaches—"Melina and Sandy"—as her only pets.

Naturally, Kelley dishes Oprah's love life, including her affair with John Tesh of *Entertainment Tonight*. He reportedly said, "I woke up one night and saw my white body next to her black body and couldn't take it anymore." He fled in the middle of the night.

Oprah's steady beau, if he could be called that, is Stedman Graham, 59. But the suggestion is clearly made that he is a mere smokescreen to disguise the real love of Oprah's life, Gayle King, Oprah's longtime "gal pal". Oprah's alleged lesbianism has long been fodder for the tabloids.

Unless someone has a video camera concealed in Oprah's bedroom, audiences may never know the exact details of the Winfrey/King association.

Let's admit, however, that Oprah has been extremely generous to King, giving her a $3.6 million home in Connecticut and a $7 million apartment in New York. One Christmas, Oprah wrote out a check to King for $1.25 million "so both of us can be millionaires."

That's a lot better than what Diane Sawyer got—dozens of gigantic sprays of orchids and a one-karat diamond toe ring.

Vernon Winfrey, a Tennessee barber, helped raise Oprah when he was the boyfriend of her mother, Vernita Lee. Oprah took his name, of course. He too has claimed that the media mogul was "fast and loose" in recalling her childhood. He also accused King of being "a dirt hog" and a "street heifer," blaming her for his present alienation from Oprah.

Kelley does not identify the man suspected of being Oprah's real father. Let's do it for her. He is Norh Robinson, an 84-year old Navy vet from Kosciusko, Mississippi, a town she abandoned at the age of six.

When pressed, Oprah snapped at reporters, "I will not be taking a paternity test, ever!" My new daddies keep popping up, some of them calling me to tell me they need a new roof."

Now living as a dirt poor farmer in a rural VA hospital, Robinson has publicly asked Oprah to "please admit I'm your father!"

You probably won't hear Kitty Kelley making references to her new book on the talk show circuit. The biographer has claimed that Oprah has used her influence to "blackball" her from appearances on such shows as *Larry King* on CNN.

Nearly 17 years ago, Oprah abandoned plans to write her own story. According to Gayle King, she stopped work on her memoirs "because Oprah felt she still had a lot of living to do. I think it will be a hell of a book when she writes it – and a hell of a movie."

Diane Sawyer, one of the most influential journalists of her era, seen here in 1972 with then-President **Richard Nixon**

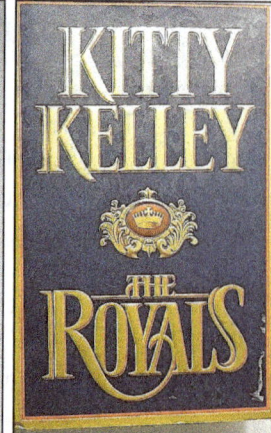

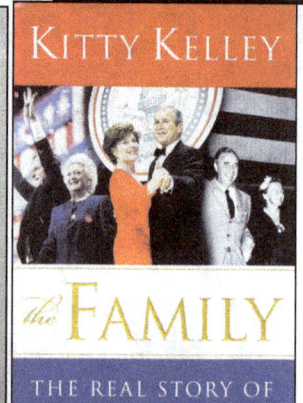

Kitty Kelley was one of America's most controversial biographers, revealing secrets about such famous personalities as Jacqueline Kennedy Onassis. She was also the first to expose starlet **Nancy Davis'** private life as an MGM starlet before she married **Ronald Reagan**. It seems that Miss Nancy "was known as "The Fellatio Queen of Hollywood."

August 2018

CELEBRITY
INTERNET & SOCIAL MEDIA
FRAUDS

"Is that really you, Beyonce?"

From athletes to movie stars, celebrities in all fields are plagued with thousands of fans or charlatans who are impersonating them on social media. Sometimes these phony celebrity social media accounts are just for fun, but often, they are frauds to cheat fans out of money. Bogus profiles litter the landscape, a major headache to Facebook Twitter, and Instagram, among others. Facebook alone reported that it has removed 583 million accounts: Even its executive, Mark Zuckerberg, has had fake accounts established in his name.

Fans might ask the question, "Is that really you, Oprah, Justin, or Beyonce, or are you an impersonator? It's roughly estimated that a fake account posts something online every four seconds.

Some fraudulent accounts are so crudely conceived that only the most gullible are sucked in; others are incredibly professional and authentic-looking. Such was the case with Empire actor Derek Luke. Every photo on his fake account was captioned and personalized with heartfelt messages from the star.

Dr. Elle Boag, a lecturer in social psychology, claims, "People often imitate a celebrity if they feel alone or bored. They may not have friends, and they like to attract people pretending to be someone they are not. It's a form of escapism, an extension of fan fiction."

"Some people like to lie and manipuli;te others," Boag said. "It entertains them and makes them feel powerful. You can be anybody you want to be. Why not a celebrity? Perhaps you're a 45-year-old bored housewife who gets a kick out of impersonating Justin Bieber in your spare time?"

Sometimes, crimes are committed. While on vacation, Bieber was snapped in the nude on a beach. One middle-aged man posted the nude photo of the star on a fake account and solicited some of his young fans, girls ages 13 to 14, to send him nudes of themselves. He received hundreds of responses before he was arrested.

When there was speculation that Oprah Winfrey might run for president, fake accounts were set up in her name, urging supporters to send campaign contributions to clearly designated post office boxes, each of them false. Thousands upon thousands of dollars were fraudulently collected in her name. An account was fraudulently established under the name of Chris Pratt, whose authentic social media sites correctly define him as one of the stars of the mega-hit *Jurassic World*. It had him soliciting sex from some of his young fans. As a countermove, he had to issue warnings on his own (authentic) Facebook account that the the sexual solicitations were bogus and unauthorized.

Another fake account offered to sell a sex tape of Beyonce and her

Whether their warnings are conveyed **through words or through illustrations** *(see above)* consumer watchdogs and security experts are saying, frequently and loudly, that "there is a strong possibility of on-line fraud associated with virtually anything you do on social media."

rapper husband, Jay-Z, for fifty dollars. Hundreds e-transmitted payment, but no such tape existed.

Based on fake social media postings, country singer Kip Moore has had some awkward moments, too. Women have materialized from the audience at his concerts, informing him that they've left their husbands because Moore had posted that he loved them. But despite Moore's innocence, many women turned on him, calling him a "scumbag."

A watchdog company that protects celebrities from exploitation took a survey, finding that the greatest number of fake accounts (almost 2,000), had been inspired by the Brazilian heartthrob known simply as Neymar, a player for that nation's soccer team. SportsPro named him "the most marketable athlete in the world."

Second runner-up for the number of fake social media accounts established with various derivations of his or her name was a Texan, Selena Gomez, who shot to fame through the Disney Channel's hit TV series, Wizards of Waverly Place.

Mega-star Jennifer Lawrence is very outspoken about not having (or wanting) an Instagram account, yet at least twenty fake Instagram accounts exist with confusing derivations of her name.

Some "real" negative postings from "real" celebrities can be lethal to a social media venues resale value. When Kylie Jenner, a player in the Kardashian-Jenner empire, announced that she was angry with and would no longer post on Snapchat after a re-design of its platform, the value of its stock dropped by one billion dollars.

It's easy to believe that because of all this upset and confusion, there might be a "rethinking" of social media and its usefulness. Perhaps the headaches, damage, and danger involved aren't worth maintaining such accounts.

The Association of Certified Fraud Examiners discovers Internet-related fraud conspiracies all the time. To an increasing degree, they're associated with either Cryptocurrencies or with fraudulent celebrity endorsements. **Buyers, BEWARE!!**

August 2022

Polls Illuminate the "Everyday Dumbness" of Many Americans

"Who Ever Heard of Eleanor Roosevelt?"

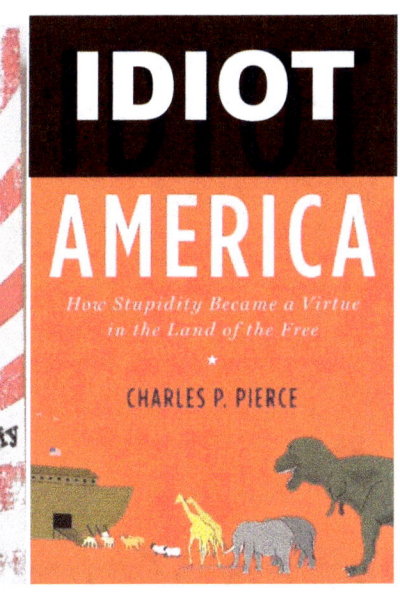

Somewhere in America, every day, various groups, including the widely respected Gallup Polls and World Public Opinion polls, are conducting rigorous surveys of public opinions. The results usually agree on one important premise: Whereas Baby Boomers were and are the best-informed sociological subdivision in human history, many polls reveal that Millennials and members of Generation Z are often weirdly (some say "astonishingly") misinformed in events associated with key events of 20th Century history.

High percentages of the U.S. population, they reveal, believe that the Holocaust was caused by Jews. Among recent arrivals to the U.S., many young immigrants from non-European countries have never heard of either World War I or World War II.

Seven percent thought the U.S. Civil War was fought by Americans trying to free themselves from the restrictions of being an English colony.

Adding to the confusion, towering figures of the 20th Century had little name recognition within the general U.S. population: Eleanor Roosevelt, Ernest Hemingway, and Thomas Edison have been all but forgotten. Only eight percent had heard of Clark Gable, Bette Davis, and Humphrey Bogart. Dwight Eisenhower and General Douglas MacArthur fell into the category of "Who?". And among the U.S. Presidents of the previous half-century, Jimmy Carter and Gerald Ford were the least known (i.e. almost completely unknown).

Through pollings, the National Science Foundation ascertained that 27% of Americans believe that the sun revolves around the earth. The same 27% also believe that God determines the winner of football games. About 45% of the U.S. population believe that ghosts and demons are real, personal, and sometimes "in your face." And a Gallup Poll concluded that 84% of women and 72% of men believe in angels.

In forty-nine states, a majority of Americans would not be able to pass the standard American Citizenship Test. In noted contrast, Vermonters scored high on questions associated with citizenship issues and in most other "all around fact-checking" tests too.

Yet even in the best-informed markets, ironies abound: Although 71% of Americans want to reduce government spending, most of them don't want to eliminate either Social Security or Medicare.

A survey from the World Public Opinion group found that the majority of Americans believe that excessively generous foreign aid is the cause of our deficit. Yet before the war in Ukraine, foreign aid was only one percent of the U.S. budget.

Getting almost no name recognition in various polls was John Adams, the second U.S. President (1797-1801) and George Washington's two-term (1789-1797) Vice President. Cantankerous and brilliant, he loudly asserted, during his tenure in power, that Thomas Jefferson (later, his vice president) was a spy for the French. Jefferson defined Adams as a "pigheaded and intemperate prima donna," and Benjamin Franklin thought Adams was "absolutely mad."

[What did make the president mad was his free-spirited wife and advisor, Abigail, who insisted on doing her own laundering of her undergarments, hanging them out to dry in the East Room of the White House.]

Adams, who would surely have been horrified by results of recent polling and the "dumbing down" of the U.S. population, had advice for future generations: "Democracy doesn't work if people aren't paying attention." He also said, "An informed America makes a strong America."

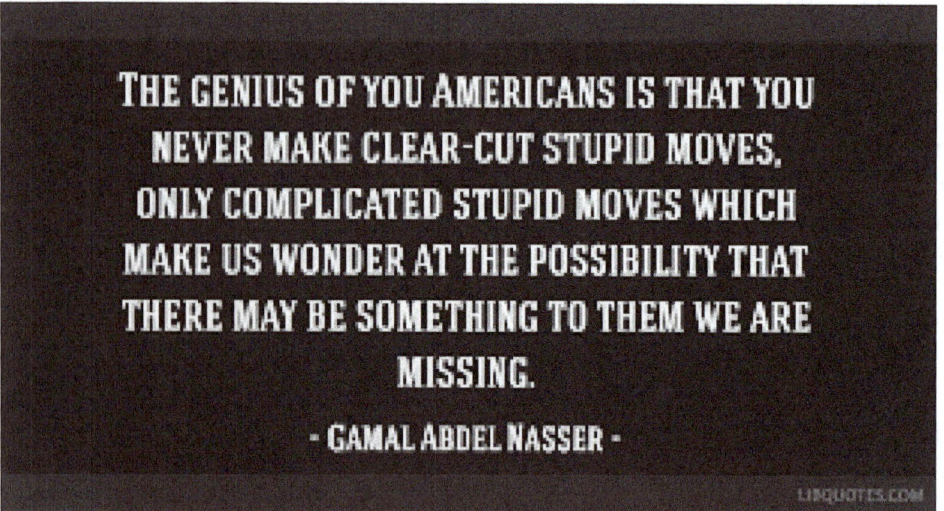

October 2022
The State of the Sunshine State

HURRICANES

Repeatedly, Florida's Coasts Have Slowly Recovered from Disastrous Storms

Can It Continue?

Emerging from the poverty-stricken Blue Ridge Mountains, my widowed mother and I arrived on Miami Beach in 1950, the beginning of that resort's Golden Age.

She was, to use an outdated term, the "Girl Friday" to Sophie Tucker, "The Last of the Red Hot Mammas" and the reigning Queen of Miami Beach.

I rushed home every day after school to meet whatever visiting movie star was calling on her. They included everyone from Judy Garland to Frank Sinatra.

Outside, pink Cadillacs glided along the boulevards at night; nightclubs booked legendary entertainers; restaurants tantalized palates, and plush beachfront suites lured the rich and famous.

Of course, I had heard dark stories about hurricanes, none more horrendous than the 1928 hurricane that killed a record 2,500 people. But those storms seemed distant.

All of that changed for me in 1960 when I became a very young bureau chief of *The Miami Herald* in Key West. From the sky, **Hurricane Donna**, one of the most destructive in Florida history, descended. Most of the Florida Keys were wiped out, but except for wind and water damage, Key West was more or less spared.

Gregory Hemingway, son of Ernest, and I, in a small plane, flew over the Keys to survey the damage. Spotting a building—any building—with an intact roof seemed impossible.

In the days and weeks ahead—with varying degrees of optimism—I wrote bulletins about how the Keys were "coming back." Some predicted it would take a decade. Locals were both resourceful and industrious, first restoring power and water, then clearing the debris of cars that had landed on top of houses or boats that were stacked in piles at marinas.

That same drive and energy are being shown today in the wake of **Hurricane Ian's** landfall that began on Caya Cota Key, launching its devastating assault up the coast.

Florida's Gulf Coast has become a subdivision of the massive worldwide destruction of homes that include those lost to forest fires in California, buildings bombed in Ukraine, and floods that put one-third of Pakistan under water.

The death toll and injuries to residents of Florida seem to get worse every year. In 1960, President Eisenhower, in the closing months of his term in office, provided generous government relief. We expect President Biden, who called Ian "one of the worst hurricanes in Florida history," to do the same.

After power and water were restored along the Gulf, the massive task of debris removal began at once in towns that were ravaged from Naples to Fort Meyers. Reconstruction will be massive, especially difficult for sen-

> **Hurricanes** from the Caribbean often make landfall in Florida, bringing lashing waves, 185 mile-per-hour winds, and life-threatening flooding. Roofs are often blown away and entire buildings destroyed. What is not mentioned is the loss of family albums and heirlooms accumulated over generations.
>
> As Hazel Dawson once told a reporter from *The Miami Herald*, "My past was just wiped out, all those pictures in family albums...You might say they were Gone With the Wind."

ior citizens who lost everything.

But hopefully, the courage and will to start over again will be there, and it won't be easy. But since the dawn of time, the loss of dwellings and homes is woven into history. Comebacks usually occur, although at speeds which vary.   Of one thing, we can be certain: The sons of mothers-to-be who survived the ravages of Florida's most recent hurricane will probably not be named Ian.

Michael

Helene

Unnamed Category 4 Storm

Sandy

December 2022

IS IT INCEST?

When a Mother Is Artifically Inseminated & Gives Birth to Her Son's Baby?

Today, you can't watch any TV news channel without some host mentioning the word incest. Before the late 1940s and the birth of television, the word was almost never used.

It's now frequently used in the ongoing debate over abortion. Millions favor outlawing abortion except in the case of incest or rape. Other, more militant, groups don't want abortion performed even when a pregnancy derives from rape or incest. The debate will likely linger for years.

Of course, incest has existed since the dawn of time. Most cases focus on fathers with daughters, or perhaps a brother or uncle with a sister or niece.

Yet still, for the most part, mother-son incest is still a love that dare not speak its name. Most victims prefer never to discuss it, although that is changing. When ABC-TV aired a broadcast on the subject, the studio was bombarded with confessions from men who had been seduced by their mothers. Various psychiatric associations are studying some of these victims to determine what damage may have been done to their mental health.

[As a side note, and most amazingly, mother-son porn flicks—a favorite of voyeurs—are generating millions of dollars.]

One of highest-profile cases of a mother giving birth to her son's child is unfolding now in Utah. Its details have become fodder for the tabloids.

Jeff Hauck, 32, is married to Cambria, 30. They are the parents of two sets of twins. After her last pregnancy, Cambria experienced great difficulties and later had a hysterectomy.

In the weeks that followed, Jeff made seven deposits in a sperm bank, since they wanted even more kids.

Galvanizing the situation, Jeff's mother, Nancy Hauck, who is 56 and approaching menopause, volunteered to become the surrogate mother—and none too soon.

Her son was delighted.

Over a period of twelve weeks, Nancy received daily fertility-enhancing hormone treatments administered by her husband, an optometrist. Then an embryo, fertilized in a lab with her son's sperm, was implanted in her uterus. Within a few months, the Haucks announced that Nancy was pregnant and scheduled to give birth to a girl.

Hollywood has not ignored the burgeoning interest in the Hauck's situation. Right now, two screenwriters, including Fred Baring, are at work on a film scenario that showcases mothers pregnant with their sons' children.

The Utah case is unusual but not unheard of. Nancy Hauck's pregnancy is not morally or medically interpreted as incest by anyone involved in the case, although some outsiders disagree.

Even so, a question remains: Will the little girl, as she matures, refer to Nancy as her mother or as her granny?

MOTHER KNOWS BEST

Two sub-components of the Hauck family. *Upper photo:* **Jeff Hauck** with his mother, **Nancy**, and *lower photo*, **Cambria** with her mother-in-law, **Nancy**.

Nancy volunteered, and successfully carried, as a surrogate mother, the child whose egg and sperm were donated by her biological son **(Jeff)** and her daughter-in-law **(Cambria)**.

June 2014

Celebrating 24 Years of PRINT, RADIO & WEB

Boomer Times
& Senior Life

Listen to Boomer Times Radio Shows! Saturdays 5-8am, WSBR 740am

babyboomers-seniors.com
boomerexpofl.com   cure-symposium.com

 Like us on    Click BoomerTimes

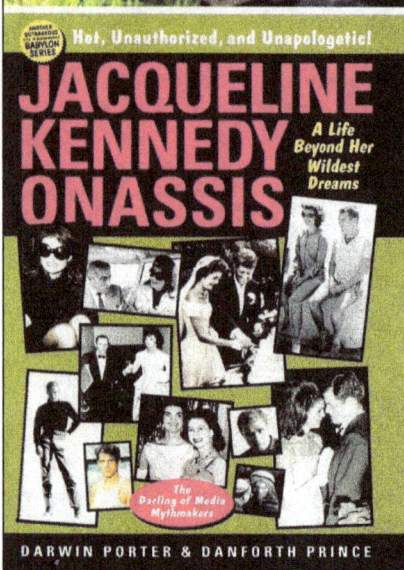

November 2021

THE RETURN OF THE WOOLLY MAMMOTH

The sci-fi film, *Jurassic Park,* created a sensation across America when it opened in movie theaters in the summer of 1993. Its theme centered on a disastrous attempt to create a theme park of cloned dinosaurs. A series of lucrative spin-off films followed, the latest, *Jurassic World: Dominion,* set for release in the summer of 2022.

Science fiction may one day become a reality. Some world scientists, working for a privately funded investment group called Colossal, are spending millions of dollars hoping to bring back the magnificent but extinct woolly mammoth to the Tundra of Siberia.

The huge animal roamed the earth 55 million years ago, and some mammoths last inhabited Wrangel Island in the Arctic Ocean as late as 4,000 years ago.

For a genetic "renaissance," the mammoth was chosen over other species because of the discovery of frozen carcasses in Siberia and Alaska, from which DNA samples were extracted.

In 1929, news electrified the world that 34 mammoths were discovered frozen in Siberia with soft tissues such as skin, flesh, and organs intact.

In the last few weeks, Colossal announced it is now moving ahead in its laboratories to bring back the mammoth, perhaps using the bodies of present-day elephants, its nearest relatives. Every scientist involved admits that the outcome, although gargantuan, will be possible, although ethically complicated. "Who," scientists have wondered, "will decide whether they can be set loose, perhaps to alter world ecosystems in unforeseen ways?"

The U.S. government has announced that with present climate change conditions, some one million plant and animal species many disappear from the planet within a century. Only this past summer, the ivory-billed woodpecker, which once graced the bayous of the American South, has not been spotted in years. The song of the Hawaiian Kauai O'o bird exists only in recordings. Hundreds of other plant and animal life in the last century have been moved from the Endangered Species list to the roll call of the Extinct.

Other "ethically complicated" breakthroughs are predicted by scientists in decades and centuries to come. Dr. Peter Bracket even suggested, jokingly, or otherwise, that "one day we might have George Washington, even Elizabeth Taylor or Marilyn Monroe, make their comebacks."

"And if we can get Moscow to turn over the charred remains of Hitler, removed from the Berlin bunker during the closing hours of World War II," he continued, "we might put *Der Führer* on trial for crimes against humanity."

Artist's conception of an alive and thriving Woolly Mammoth.

January 2019

A (Horrifying) Tour of Yesterday's Medical Oddities

Readers of *Boomer Times* are kept abreast of all the latest developments in medicine and "wellness" innovations that can lead to a longer, healthier life.

That was hardly true for our distant ancestors, who often found going to a "doctor" would lead to their death. To call some of those practitioners of medicine "quacks" would be too polite a term.

The Cinemax show, *The Knick*, portrayed a horrifying world before modern medicine.

So does a new book, *The Mystery of the Exploding Teeth and Other Curiosities from the History of Medicine* by Thomas Morris, a London-based medical historian.

It's like a *Ripley's Believe It or Not* stroll down memory lane to a centuries-old world of horrific operations, quack cures, superstitions, and even "deadly dentures."

The title derives from a cases of acute, probably abscessed, toothaches followed, mysteriously, by the tooth breaking apart with great force.

Antique medical beliefs went far beyond "the leeches-and-mercury" cure. Is there a problem with your head? A red-hot frying pan pressed into your face was the cure.

A virtual "cure for everything" involved taking several pipefuls of tobacco and blowing smoke into a patient's bowel through a tube inserted into the patient's anus. Samuel Taylor, a doctor in London in the 1870s, recommended that for most of his patients.

Bleeding, through the opening of veins or the applications of leeches, was the cure for almost everything. If not that, gruesome anal insertions were all the rage, as doctors seemed to have an obsession with the rectums of their patients.

Operations often morphed into executions, leading to a patient's death. In rural settlements without even a so-called "doctor," the local hog butcher was summoned wielding a knife and a bottle of gin to help the patient endure the pain.

Sal ammoniac, a salty, smelly substance derived from camel urine in Egypt, was frequently recommended as a medica-

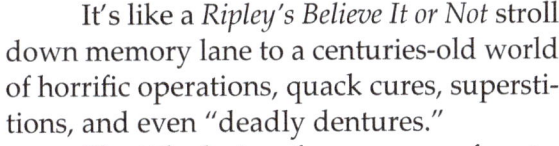

Without antibiotics and in an age when venereal viruses, including syphilis, were rampant, many people suffered from the agonies of **blocked bladders**. Medieval catheters consisted of a metal tube, which was painfully inserted via the urethra, into the bladder. Sometimes the bladder got drained, sometimes it didn't.

Treatment of kidney or bladder stones consisted of a physician's assistant sitting on top of the victim, with his or her legs strapped behind his or her neck. The physician would then insert two fingers up the victim's rectum, searching for hard pellets, simultaneously pressing a fist against the victim's pubic region, just above the pelvis, until he detected what might or might not be a stone. It was then extracted with an unsterilized knife (without anesthetic or antibiotics) from the victim's bladder. One can only imagine the horror.

Cataracts were corrected by cutting the lens then pushing it deeper into the eye, in a (horrifying) technique called "needling" or "couching." Although it allowed the entrance of light back into the eye, the resulting vision was permanently out of focus. Yet many patients believed that since they had been almost blinded by cataracts, then any sight—even blurred—was better than full blindness.

The surgery wasn't usually considered as non-life-threatening (whatever that meant). Since the patient was already mostly blind, if the surgery went poorly and they lost the eye, other than the physical agony involved as part of the procedure, their life wouldn't be much different. If it went well, they might have their vision partially restored. Such was the medical beliefs at the time.

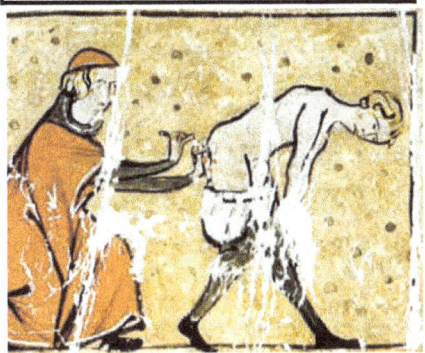

Hemmorhoid treatments: European monks (or medicine men) would insert a red-hot iron tube up a person's rectum. Then fantasize and/or pray.

tion. Hot glasses placed upside-down on a patient's back were said to draw out "evil humors." Laxatives, many of them derived from hideous ingredients, were often employed, leading to awesome, sometimes blood-soaked, explosions into chamber pots. Mustard plasters were heated to temperatures so hot that, when applied, they peeled off the skin.

The book relates how a patient with a 56-pound tumor had to be cut open. The surgeon made a number of mistakes, including haphazardly removing his genitals as part of the process.

If something were wrong with a patient's intestines, doctors instructed him or her to swallow a parasitic tapeworm in the belief that it would devour other parasites or pests. Then—in theory, at least—the tapeworm, with the pest inside, could be forced to leave its host through induced vomiting.

Some "healers" advocated that opium mixed with the vomit of a crow would work as an analgesic.

In Edinburgh in 1862, a Dr. Hastings widely advocated swallowing the excrement of boa constrictors as a cure for tuberculosis.

If a pregnant woman experienced difficulty with her unborn fetus, her belly was slathered with honey and then a colony of bees was let loose to sting her.

During long sea voyages, a stricken sailor often had to turn to a shipmate handy with a knife, a needle, and thread.

One had to watch one's diet, as cucumbers were "evil" and tomatoes "poisonous."

During the Crusades, warriors departing from England put chastity belts on their wives. In a bizarre twist, a jealous fishwife from Faro, Portugal, pierced her lover's penis with a tiny golden padlock for which only she held the key.

In Paris in 1824, a cart ran over a man's stomach, pushing a section of his intestines down into his scrotum. The cure? First, leeches, then a recommendation to walk around with a harness that supported the world's largest known pair of testicles.

The trick for patients of olden days was to survive "the cure."

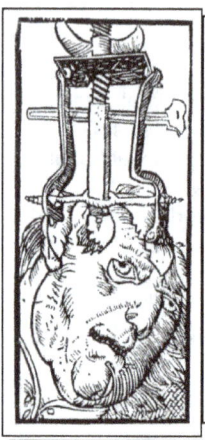
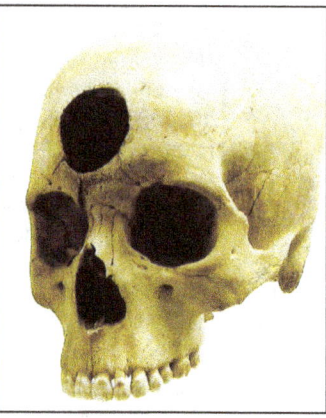

Trephination, or **trepanning**, has been practiced since Neolithic times. It involves drilling a hole in the skull, perhaps for the release of evil spirits, or for the treatment of migraines, epilepsy, or mental disorders, or to relieve intracranial pressure caused by bleeding or swelling in the brain caused by head injuries.

The practice was widespread across medieval Europe and, unless infections set in, survivable, as evidenced by post-surgery skulls with evidence of bone regrowth.

A systematic focus on the control (or lessening) of **infection on the battlefield** didn't really begin until World War II. Amputation of wounded limbs as a means of treating gangrene was common during the American Civil War, as part of standard practice that began in the 16th Century.

Standardized ambulance and transportation services from battlefields wasn't invented until the Crimean War (1853-1856), when the British lost more soldiers to disease than to combat. Then, thanks in part to Florence Nightingale, specialized units were formed to handle the movement of wounded soldiers and medical equipment to and from battlefields.

Pior to that, and almost never with anesthesia, surgeons provided (horrifyingly primitive) care to injured soldiers, extracting arrows, spears, bullets, and shrapnel; crafting splints for fractured bones; sewing up wounds; cauterizing heavy bleeding; dressing burns; amputating limbs; performing scalp surgeries for mental illness; draining abscesses; and trimming overgrown gum tissue for the survivors of scurvy.

Whatever Became of Napoléon's Penis?

The speculation, even the mystery, still lingers. Exiled in October of 1815 after losing the Battle of Waterloo, the former French emperor was sent into exile on the Isle of St. Helena in the South Atlantic Ocean. He died on that island on May 5, 1821.

Here, the history of "privates" gets murky. Dr. François Carlo Antommarchi conducted an autopsy in which he is said to have surgically removed the penis of the former emperor.

The doctor may have been bribed at the request of Napoléon's chaplain, who preserved it in alcohol, smuggled it out of St. Helena, and sailed with it to his home in Corsica.

There, it remained until 1916, when a bookseller from Maggs Brothers in London acquired it for an unknown price.

In 1924, another bookseller, A.W.W. Rosenbach, bought it and sailed with it across the ocean to the Port of New York and from there to his home in Philadelphia. Interpreting it as an object of "morbid curiosity," he rented it to the Museum of French Art in Manhattan, where it was viewed by hundreds of curiosity seekers.

The reviewer for *Time* magazine described it to his readers, comparing it to "a maltreated strip of buckskin showlace." Another writer described it as "a small, shriveled eel," and yet another thought it evoked "a small piece of leather."

Rosenbach later sold it to a collector, Donald Hyde, who kept it until his death. His wife then sold it to a friend of her husband, John F. Fleming, another bookseller. How much she got for it is not known. One report has her giving it away, as she found it "disgusting."

It was later sold to yet another collector (name unknown), who tried to make a deal with Christie's in Manhattan to sell it to the highest bidder. No buyer seemed to want the little thing.

After its failure at auction, it became the property of one James Conmyn, who wanted to get rid of it for a price. With that in mind, he contacted Eric LeVine, who collected artifacts from the Napoleonic era.

From LeVine, this "treasure" eventually went to yet another artifact collector named John K. Lattimer, who bought it for only $3,000 in 1977. It is believed to be currently owned by his daughter, who at one point was offered $100,000.

Who will ultimately end up with this Napoleonic "keepsake" remains a mystery.

Judith Pascoe, writing in *The New York Times,* found the penis "barely recognizable as a human body part." A TV documentary on Channel 4, *Dead Famous DNA,* said that the penis measures one inch. It is not known how long it was, alive and erect, although speculation at the time was that it was little more than three inches long. So far, it is believed that either during the life of its owner or after its preservation in formaldehyde, it was never photographed.

Three views of "the scourge of Europe," **Napoleon Bonaparte,** (aka **Napoleon I**) in stances that range from the artfully glorified to the physically exhausted. Few other men of his era invited such admiration and loathing.

Because many servants or fellow soldiers had probably viewed Napoleon's penis during his lifetime, many bawdy jokes ensued.

The first wife of Napoleon had been Joséphine de Beauharnais (1763-1814), the Empress of France from 1804 until their marriage was annulled in 1810.

Her marriage to the emperor was her second. Her first husband, rumored to have been "heavily endowed," was Alexandre de Beauharnais. He was guillotined during the Reign of Terror, and she was imprisoned for five days after his execution.

Before her marriage to Napoléon, Joséphine was rumored to have had many affairs, often with officers in the French Army. Napoléon married her in 1804. In addition to her role as Empress of France, as Napoléon's consort, she later became Queen of Italy.

Two days after her wedding, her husband left Paris to head the French Army in its invasion of Italy. He wrote love letters to her during his campaign: "I awake full of you. Your image and the memory of your intoxicating pleasures have left no rest to my senses."

Joséphine was rumored to have been highly sexed. She could not wait for Napoléon's return, so she launched an affair with a handsome, dashing Hussar lieutenant named Hippolyte Charles. When word of their affair reached Napoléon, he was furious.

It 1798, Napoléon led his army into an invasion of Egypt. He was known to have had an affair with Pauline Fourès, the wife of a junior officer. His fighting men called her "Napoléon's Cleopatra."

Other than his love for Joséphine, one of the reasons he'd married her was his strong desire to produce a male heir who would one day preside over France as Emperor Napoléon II.

Joséphine never managed to produce one. When the potentiality of that ever happening grew dim, he had his marriage to Joséphine annulled on January 10, 1810.

Wife #1:
Joséphine de Beauharnais
Queen of the French (1804-1810) and

Wife #2:
Marie Louise of Austria, Duchess of Parma, as she appeared in a Daguerrotype of 1847.

Death came to Joséphine on May 29, 1814. The cause was pneumonia. She had begged to join Napoléon in exile in St. Helena, but he had rejected her offer.

Still hoping for an heir, after the annulment of his marriage to Joséphine, Napoléon married Marie Louise (1791-1847), the Duchess of Parma in 1810, making her Empress of France and Queen of Italy. She would hold that lofty position until his abdication on April 2, 1814, despite the fact that the dictator had sarcastically announced that he was "marrying a womb."

Marie Louise gave birth to a son, Napoléon II, in March of 1811. At birth, he was assigned the title "King of Rome," although he was later "demoted" to "the Duke of Reichstadt." Alas, in 1832, in Vienna at the age of 21, he died from tuberculosis. Suffering from pleurisy, his mother died in December of 1847.

Left photo: Portrait of **Napoleon II,** painted in 1832 and *(right)* his tomb, within **Les Invalides** in Paris, with iconography and rococo surpassed only by the effigies there associated with this famous father.

The penis of Napoleon I is not the only body part that generated a lot of brouhaha around the time of its owner's death. Whereas Napoleon II was originally buried in the Imperial Crypt in Vienna, in 1940, Adolf Hitler ordered that some of his body parts be transferred to a position near those of his his father, in Paris, as a gesture of respect to the French. Perhaps ghoulishly, his heart and intestines, however, remained in urns within the imperial Crypt in Vienna, in honor of his Habsburgundian mother, **Marie Louise.**

March 2021
Nobody Lives Forever

SISTER ANDRÉ
The Oldest Woman in the World

Sister André *(aka **Lucile Randon**)*

In the city of Toulon in southeastern France, there resides a woman who is verified as the oldest in the world. Since she joined a Catholic order in 1944, she's been called Soeur (Sister) André, born Lucile Randon on February 11, 1904, during the era when Theodore Roosevelt was in the White House.

She is blind and in a wheelchair at the Ste. Catherine Labouré nursing home. In the same establishment, were 88 other residents, 81 of whom contracted the Covid virus, which killed ten of them.

As a teenage girl, she opposed the invention of the airplane and motor vehicles. "I knew they would be turned into weapons of war to kill millions, and I've survived two World Wars to see my fear come true."

"I survived the first pandemic in 1918, and I knew I could pull through yet another one," she told the French press. "Once a year on my birthday, I indulge in my favorite dessert, a peach-flavored Baked Alaska with a glass of champagne. I'm looking forward to having that treat again on my 118th birthday in 2022."

Incidentally, she is not the oldest verified person on earth. That honor goes to Kane Tanaka of Japan who is 118. Most people who are more than a century old live in the U.S. or Japan.

The oldest verified person who ever lived was 122 years old. Jeanne Calment (1875-1997), also a French citizen. All these survivors of "a century of living" are called "supercentenarians."

"My advice to the world," says Soeur André, "is never give up hope and trust in God. Stay strong even in your darkest hours, and, if you live long enough, you'll have plenty of those."

Kane Tanaka, photographed as she appeared at 117.

***

This column appeared in the March 2021 issue of Boomer Times. On January 12, 2023, Sister André, that French supercentenarian, was the last living person on earth born in 1904, so far as it is known.

In February of 2022, the French president, Emmanuel Macron, sent the nun birthday greetings from Paris.

"I feel I would be better off in heaven," she said, "but the good Lord doesn't want me yet."

With her passing, Maria Branyas became the oldest validated living person. She was born in 1907.

Jeanne Calment, the now-deceased oldest verified person who ever lived, 122 years old at the time of her death, as she appeared at the age of 40.

Born in San Francisco in 1907, American-Catalan **Maria Branyas** died in Olot, Spain, on August 19, 2024. The photo depicts her as she appeared in her 20s.

Gertrude Mokotoff
A Mayor at 71, a Bride at 98

Gertrude Mokotoff made headlines when she became mayor of Middletown, New York, at the age of 71. Before that, she'd been President of the City Council.

The daughter of a tailor, she had been born in Brooklyn on August 20, 1918. She attended Brooklyn College before earning her master's degree at Columbia University.

At the age of 23, she married Dr. Reuben Mokotoff, a cardiologist in Manhattan. Even though he had a thriving medical practice, they tired of big city life and relocated in Middletown, New York. There, he became an immediate success, and she started the first training program for electron microscopy technicians, while raising a brood of four very bright kids.

Their successful, productive marriage lasted 61 years, and she mourned the death of her husband when he died in 2002. She might have considered retirement at her age, but impulsively, she decided "to give politics a try."

That led in time to her becoming the president of the Middletown City Council. Although Middletown had, for many years, consistently voted Republican, she ran as a Democrat and won. After that, she ran for a second term and won again.

To keep fit, she always worked out at the local gym. There, she met Alvin Hann, a widower from a previous marriage. They began to date, discovering that both of them had a great love of opera.

One night, he drove her into Manhattan to attend a performance of Mozart's *The Marriage of Figaro*. During the drive back to Middletown, she decided that he was never going to propose marriage to her, so she asked him--a retired businessman and a fellow nonagenarian-- to marry her.

The wedding took place just days before her 99th birthday. "So what?" she said. "I'll soon be 99. That is just a number. Today, the day I'm marrying, I'm only 98. So, boys, let's not rush this, okay?"

The wedding, presided over by Mayor Joseph Destefano, took place at the Middletown City Hall. Her 71-year-old daughter was maid of honor, and his son, Mark, age 71, was best man.

When the press surrounded her, she told the newsmen, "It's never too late to fall in love."

Regrettably, she died at the age of 100 on October 28, 2018.

Gertrude Mokotoff and **Alvin Mann** at their wedding on August 5, 2017, in Middletown, New York.

February 2022

Pentagon Launches Probe of UFOs

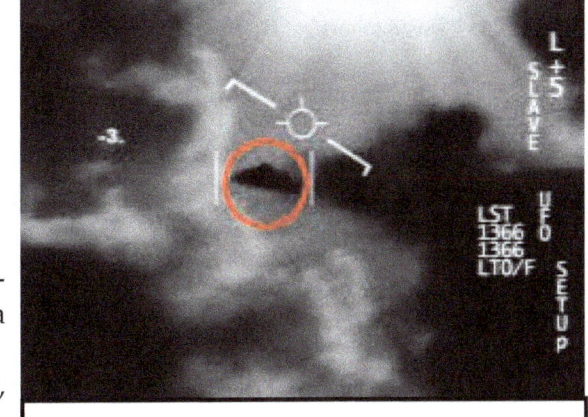

An unidentified aerial phenomenon (UAP) as captured by the sensors of a U.S. Navy Jet.

It was reported that the first bit of business addressed by then-President Bill Clinton after he took office in 1993 was a call for a summation of secret government files about UFOs.

The late Senate Majority Leader, Harry Reid of Nevada, said, "The American people deserve to know more—and hopefully, they will soon. The U.S. Senate needs to take a serious, scientific look at UFOs and any potential security implications."

Another former President, Barack Obama, suggested, "We need to spend a lot more money on a weapons system to defend ourselves against potential alien invaders."

Early last year, the U.S. government issued an official report that was immediately denounced. It discounted some 120 "eyeball-to-eyeball" confrontations military pilots had with UFOs, despite the fact that the alien craft could perform aerial feats impossible to execute with present Earthling technology.

Pilots who encounter such phenomena are now being taken seriously. On November 23, 2021, it was announced that millions of dollars would be spent by a newly formed organization, The Office of Airborne Object Identification and Management Synchronization Group (AOIMSG). Today, that organization is at work assessing UFO sightings and any associated threats to safety of flight and national security.

Caught on camera, a sighting of a **UFO** over Minnesota.

Avril Haines, the Director of National Intelligence for the Biden Administration, said "There is always the question of alien space craft. Is there something else that we simply do not understand that might come extra-terrestrially?"

Luis Elizondo, a former U.S. Army Counterintelligence Special Agent, has gone much farther. "Unidentified craft in space have already interfered with and actually brought offline our nuclear capabilities." His allegations have been telecast on The History Channel.

Although officially debunked (yet believed by millions), the alleged crash of a flying saucer on July 8, 1947, in Roswell, New Mexico has been a hot issue since the first news broke two years after the end of World War II. A sci-fi TV series, Roswell, New Mexico, since its debut in mid-2018, has become a big hit.

The world's greatest astronomers make the claim that there are as many as 40 billion earth-sized planets in our "known" universe, each positioned from twelve to fifty light years from Earth. Each of them orbits around a sun-like star in the vast galaxy (the Milky Way) that contains our planet.

It is extremely unlikely that spacecraft from earth will set out anytime soon to explore locations more than 24 trillion miles away. It's also likely, because of the vast distances involved, that any spacecraft visiting earth will be "staffed" with drones instead of biologically viable "living" creatures.

According to the Pentagon, as applauded by many who labor in the sciences, today's research involves bringing accidental and anecdotal observations about UFOs into the mainstream of transparent, validated, and systematic scientific research. Where will it lead? Almost certainly to a better, less "scatter-shot" approach to understanding the universe that surrounds us.

Long-time "skywatchers" of *Boomer Times* define this, its December 2022 cover, as the "**unexpected UFO**" of the magazine's history.

In its preface, **Anita Finley,** its publisher, made a surprise announcement to readers throughout South Florida: A notification of her recent WEDDING to **Commander John Derr** of the U.S. Navy.

In addition to adding a wedding photo to the artwork's lower left cover *(see the lower left corner of the illustration below)***,** she included a news announcement on that edition's PAGE 4:

"For those who know me personally, I want to share my special news: I married John Derr on November 21st in a simple private ceremony at the courthouse in Port Charlotte, Florida. My family and friends are very happy for us.

MY ADVICE? If you find a new love, be ready to meet the challenges of a special relationship and **GO FOR IT.**

December Delicious Dreams to all of you from Anita Finley
Gerontologist & Publisher, **Boomer Times & Senior Life Magazine**

June 2022

The Return of the Victory Garden

Mayor Eric Adams of New York City, as well as mayors and governors of some other cities, urged Americans in the summer of 2022 to plant a Victory Garden.

Baby Boomers grew up in an era where markets overflowed with reasonably priced fruit and vegetables. But during World War II, and even during World War I, so-called "Victory Gardens" were planted from coast to coast.

Along with rationing stamps, they reduced pressure on the food supply and allowed shipments of food to be diverted to our men and women engaged in wars in and around the Pacific and Atlantic Oceans.

First Lady Eleanor Roosevelt ordered that a Victory Garden be planted in the rear of the White House grounds. Later, First Lady Michelle Obama ordered the planting of a "Kitchen Garden," there, too.

By the spring of 1943, there were eighteen million Victory Gardens in the United States. Twelve million tons of fruit and vegetables were harvested by "soldiers of the soil."

Today, lower income families are hard hit, especially since February 2021 when food prices have risen by eight percent, even fifteen percent on some items. In a lot of metropolitan areas, rents have gone up a staggering 33%, cutting into food budgets.

City dwellers can plant gardens on rooftops, vacant lots, in their backyards (if they have one), even on window sills.

In the late 1960s, when I bought my home in St. George, on the North Shore of Staten Island, fifteen Lithuanians lived here. They had turned the back lot into the most varied small garden I'd ever seen, with the widest possible range of fruit and vegetables, from rhubarb to strawberries. They grew heads of cabbage, which they turned into sauerkraut which they stored, fermenting in salt, in two huge wooden barrels for the winter.

In New York, Columbia University's Urban Design Lab is overseeing a network of community gardens to help food-deprived families. Members function, to some degree, as role models to equivalent groups in other towns and cities.

Columnist Jullian Abbott wrote, "The future is uncertain. There's no way to be sure that food shortages and skyrocketing prices will continue. But we can't wait until it's too late. We can increase our chances to eat healthy fruits and vegetables by starting our Victory Gardens today."

During World War II, First Lady **Eleanor Roosevelt's White House victory garden** was one of some 18 million roughly equivalent food patches. Collectively, they provided 40% of the country's vegetable crop and "liberated" millions of dollars for the war effort.

In 1945, during the final days of the war **President Harry Truman** urged Americans to "Grow more victory gardens. Grow them at home, at workplaces, in community plots, and on farms; grow them bigger and better, and maintain them for the harvest."

By then, thanks to rationing and expanded agrarian output, America was not only feeding itself but exporting huge amounts of food to other (sometimes starving) nations.

Happy Valentine's Day 2014, from Boomer Times:

HINT: Both it's color scheme and the triangle it promoted were PINK

THE CRUDE, FLORIDA-BASED OBSESSION WITH BASHING HILLARY

Hillary & Her Boy Lover from Outer Space?

In researching my latest celebrity biography, *Bill & Hillary, So This Is That Thing Called Love,* I discovered that as First Lady, Hillary Clinton made more frontpage exposé headlines in *Weekly World News* than any other American.

Originating in Lantana, Florida, the mass circulation tabloid moved its headquarters to Boca Raton in the late 1990s. The paper was published between 1979 and 2007, reaching its peak in the '80s with a circulation of 1.2 million. Founded by Generoso Pope, Jr., the paper was a sister publication of *The National Enquirer*.

The tabloid was largely fictional, known for its outrageous cover stories, often based on supernatural or paranormal themes. Most often, its "news" verged on the satirical, with black-and-white covers heralding its revelations in "Second Coming" headlines. One edition claimed GARDEN OF EDEN FOUND! Hundreds of believers, mostly evangelicals, flocked to their travel agents to book passage to Colorado, the alleged site of this biblical paradise.

As amazing (and horrible) as it seems, a survey showed that some 150,000 of its faithful readers believed every word the sensationalist rag sheet printed.

Hillary was accused of having an affair, in the White House, with P'lod, a creature from Outer Space. The alien was alleged to have impregnated her. The paper went on to say that she gave birth to P'lod's son.

According to *Weekly World News,* her romance with the alien ended after a jealous Bill got into a fistfight with P'lod, and the president had him locked away in the slammer. In the meantime, Clinton was busy with a three-breasted intern, who was presented on the cover in all her mammary glory.

Revelations about other presidents were also featured. It was revealed that all our founding fathers were gay, and that George Washington and Abraham Lincoln were actually women. Lincoln was also thought to be insane.

The paper presented George W. Bush as lacking in intelligence. *World News* chronicled his plans to run for pope after his term in the White House ended; his love affair with Attorney General Janet Reno, and his intention to nominate Yoda as Secretary of Defense. Vice President Cheney was said to be a robot, who had to make frequent trips to the hospital to get rewired.

DUMB & DUMBER

Three of the four replicas of front pages of *Weekly World News* bash **Hillary**—the fourth delves into some of the overblown subtleties of **Kim Kardashian's butt**.

Although some of that publication's themes elicit guffaws (***"how could people read things this stooopid?!"***), overall, we are "not amused' (as Queen Victoria might have said, if she'd seen (and believed) any of them.

As a means of displaying how DUMB many of the rag machine's themes were, we've replicated some of them on this page and the one that follows.

Our final words of advice? **CAVEAT EMPTOR!** (Buyer Beware) and **DON'T BE STOOOPID!!!**

Actually, however, we think that this one might be true.

235

Word was leaked that Saddam Hussein and Osama bin Laden were secretly married, and that Saddam was going to undergo a sex-change operation.

A recurring theme claimed that prominent figures thought to be dead were actually alive, including Marilyn Monroe, John F. Kennedy, and country singer Hank Williams. A very old Adolf Hitler was discovered living in Brazil and determined to become the oldest man in recorded history.

But nothing captured the imagination of its readers more than those **ELVIS ALIVE!** headlines, based on alleged frequent sightings of Elvis. Photos—as a policy, doctored and Photoshopped—depicted a gray-haired, balding Elvis coming out of a Burger King.

Feature articles included accounts of prehistoric creatures discovered in a block of Arctic ice, and relics from the past also showed up, including the sandals of Jesus. After 9/11, terrorism was a feature, including an exposé that Kim-Jong-un of North Korea planned to invade and conquer the United States.

"Bat Boy," a scary humanoid discovered in the Lost World Caverns of West Virginia, became the most popular feature. It was said that he planned to run for president in 2028. Bat Boy even became the star of a Broadway musical and the subject of a best-selling book, Going Mutant: Bat Boy Exposed!

Other stories featured pictures of the Loch Ness Monster, Bigfoot, time travel, and alien abductions. The world's biggest baby, fattest woman, and fattest cat (Tonya) were regularly depicted, including the world's fattest married couple.

With circulation dwindling—perhaps because consumers eventually got tired of the publication's bizarre blend of satire, humor, science fiction, and news, *Weekly World News* ceased to be printed in 2007. It was later reconfigured into an online periodical.

Today, in its online version, it no longer focusses as obsessively on Hillary. Instead, it frequently features presidential candidate Donald Trump. *World News* reported that he recently purchased Scranton, Pennsylvania, a cash-strapped, depressed town in Pennsylvania's Rust Belt, and that he's planning to turn it into a film-making capital to rival Hollywood.

"It's a dumpy town," Trump is quoted as saying, "but I'll pave its streets with gold. I'll get the biggest movie stars to move there and erect palatial mansions."

BILL & HILLARY
So This Is That Thing Called Love

The first book of 2016 about the world's most famous couple, *Bill & Hillary—So This Is That Thing Called Love*, is now at Amazon.com and at book stores throughout America and abroad. It's co-authored by myself and Danforth Prince.

It generated international headlines even before its release.

The first question everyone asks is, "Is it pro- or anti- Clinton?" an issue that's central within nearly every biography ever published about this fascinating marital team. Having ruled over the Free World in the 1990s, they're now plotting a return.

The answer to that key question is "neither." Whereas the book explores the seedy past of the Clintons in excruciating detail, it contrasts the boorish behavior of their worst enemies—many of whom ended up in jail. Scandal piles upon scandal, as it's associated with a presidency that set new rules for round-the-clock media coverage of a sitting president.

With no intention of being flippant, in a style you've seen in early Blood Moon productions, we conceived and wrote this book as entertainment. The book is not a political tome so much as it is the story of a love affair, a collaboration between partners, a troubled, scandal-soaked marriage.

Love, Bill & Hillary Style: Was their marriage a cynical, conjoined-at-the-hip alliance of political convenience? Or was it love? That's the question around which this new release from Blood Moon Productions was built.

The saga began when a pair of brilliant, edgy, and intensely ambitious political activists met at Yale in 1970 and plotted their collective futures. Their agenda involved first grasping the presidency for himself, and later, for her. Obviously, at least the first half of that long-standing and obsessive ambition has already been achieved.

The big question explored within the book is this: Was it a cynical, conjoined-at-the-hip alliance of political convenience? Or was it love?

Amazingly, this seemingly iron-studded marriage has survived pandemics, marital infidelities, political vendettas, betrayals, fistfights, backroom stabbings, raw ambition, endless Congressional investigations, and impeachment proceedings.

Thebook follows the Clintons' setbacks and "Teflon comebacks," their tragedies and triumphs, their good years and bad years, their "Bimbo Eruptions," their serial infidelities, their tabloid embarrassments, and their maddening failures.

In spite of all this, there were some stunning achievements during the moments when they were actually allowed to govern (i.e., when they weren't being summoned for depositions).

Hillary once publicly ridiculed Tammy Wynette for the lyrics of her hit song, "Stand by Your Man," but over the course of many years, disappointments, and betrayals, standing by her man is exactly what the First Lady did.

The Clinton saga—sometimes defined as "One Nation Under Sex"—is an uncensored tale about an unconventional marriage that changed the course of our lives and the world.

Everyone interviewed—over the years they have numbered in the hundreds—had strong opinions about the Clintons, and no one ever

Country boy, big city girl: An unlikely pairing. But together, **Bill & Hillary** ended up ruling the Free World—for a while, at least.

Years after their exit, their associated scandals—enormous at the time—seem benign in comparison to the more sinister, more blatant ones of MAGA and the Tangerine Menace.

seemed neutral about Hillary. On the eve of the upcoming presidential elections, many voters anticipate a historic event: the first female president ruling over the dawning of a new Age of Aquarius. In volatile contrast, her most venomous "snakebite enemies" (her words) interpret her as a "Femi-Nazi who will usher in a Reign of Terror."

Bill also elicits mixed reactions, his admirers hailing him as the world's greatest elder statesman, a global humanitarian, and one of the five greatest presidents of the 20th Century.

In vivid contrast, George H.W. Bush (i.e., "Daddy Bush") had a different view: "He is a womanizing, Elvis-loving, non-inhaling, truth-shading, war promoting, gun-hating Baby Boomer from hell itself."

In this latest Blood Moon biography, it's all here—Clinton rumors realities are laid bare: Who is Chelsea's biological father? Who is Bill Clinton's biological father? Why was he labeled a homosexual during his first run as Congressman from Arkansas? Why is Hillary still defined in some quarters as a lesbian? Is Bill a cross-dresser? Did Hillary murder her lover, Vince Foster? Did Monica Lewinsky really believe she would become the next First Lady? Did investigator Kenneth Starr consider forcing the President to disrobe so that his penis could be photographed and compared to its description by Paula Jones, who was suing him at the time for sexual harassment? What quotes were expurgated from the Gennifer Flowers tapes as unfit for public consumption? Did Bill attempt to seduce Jackie Kennedy Onassis? Did he lie on the "casting couch" of Pamela Churchill Harriman, doyenne of the Democratic Party? What happened the night Barbra Streisand stayed for a "sleep-over in the Lincoln Bedroom? Was Sharon Stone really Bill's West Coast mistress? What did Hillary say in private about her mother-in-law, Virginia Kelley? *(ANSWER: "An over-painted, broken-down redneck whore who belongs in a white trash trailer park.")*

On the morning Hillary left the White House after her husband's second term, she stood under its portico and, aping Arnold Schwarzenegger, proclaimed, "I'LL BE BACK!" The potholed highway to the White House is only halfway complete.

Bill & Hillary—So This Is That Thing Called Love

From Blood Moon Productions, Biographers of the Rich & Famous. 6x9 Softcover, with lots of photos. 532 pages ISBN 978-1-936003-47-1. Available everywhere now.

Likable, engaging, and charismatic—everyone called him **"The Comeback Kid."**

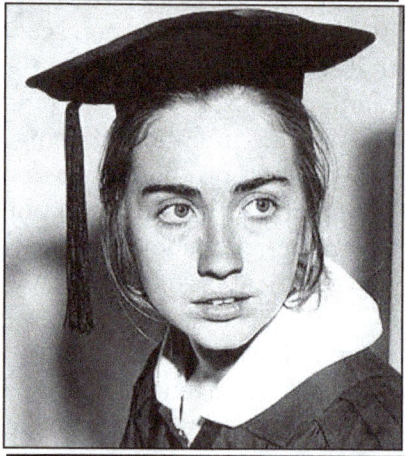

Rabble-rousing at Wellesley—where **Hillary** developed a personal style that some say prevailed throughout the remainder of her career

**VIEWS OF A PRESIDENTIAL ADMINISTRATION
and the (in retrospect, benign) scandals that shook it to its core**

Left to right: Photo #1: "**Billary,**" celebrating one of many political victories *Photo #2* First Daughter **Chelsea Clinton** on the cover of *Elle* *Photo #3.* **Deep Doo-Doo, Deep Whitewater.** *Photo #4* Fabled and notorious, **Pamela Harriman**, billionairess daughter-in-law of Winston Churchill, became a vocal supporter and fundraiser *Photo #5.* National scandals of his own from the most pompous and punitive moralist in Washington, Clinton tormentor and disgraced college administrator, **Kenneth Starr.**

DOUG EMHOFF
Exactly WHAT Is a "Wife Guy?"

An all-new phrase, "Wife Guy," has entered The Dictionary of American Slang, and Merriam-Webster' Collegiate Dictionary's next edition will list "Second Gentleman," as an official term of formal address.

Both were created for Doug Emhoff, the husband of the multiracial Kamala Harris, the first black U.S. Vice President and the first of South Asian origin.

Emhoff has broken yet another "glass ceiling" in the history books: He is the first Jewish spouse of a U.S. President or Vice President.

Harris has said, "Call Doug whatever you wish, but I'm sticking to what I've always called him: 'Honey.'"

Both Harris and Emhoff are 56, each having entered the world in 1964. [He's older than she is by seven days.]

Just who is Doug Emhoff?

On a blind date set up by a friend, Emhoff and Harris bonded immediately and began to see each other exclusively. They were married in Santa Barbara on August 22, 2014. At the time, their combined net worth was $5.8 million.

> **Doug Emhoff** never shrank in the shadow of a superstar spouse. Throughout most of the 2024 presidential campaign, his cellphone sported a sticker that read: "A Woman's Place is in the White House."
>
> **Kamala Harris** made history as the first woman of color nominated for vice president by a major political party. After her acceptance speech, Emhoff, beaming, made his entrance, walking alongside another prominent plus-one — Jill Biden — onto a convention hall stage in Wilmington, Delaware, to join their headline-generating partners.
>
> When Joe Biden, the Democrats' presidential nominee, introduced Kamala as his running mate, he told Emhoff: "Doug, you're going to have to learn what it means to be a barrier-breaker yourself." If Biden and Harris had won the presidential election of 2024, Emhoff would become the nation's first second gentleman.
>
> His romance with Harris feels scripted by Hollywood. His first meeting with her was part of a blind date set up by a (well-connected) mutual friend. From L.A. and San Francisco, respectively, they eventually connected by phone and scheduled a date for that weekend, when plans called for her to be in L.A. Their relationship blossomed quickly. "He seemed so genuinely comfortable with himself," Harris wrote. "That's part of why I liked him immediately."
>
> Nomenclature for the "recomposed" new family? Cole and Ella Emhoff, his children from a previous marriage, call Harris "Momala."

He'd been married before, to the movie producer Kerstin Emhoff, with whom he produced two children. Cole, Emhoff's son, is a graduate of Colorado College, and his daughter, Ella, is studying at the Parsons School of Design in New York.

Born in Brooklyn, Emhoff gravitated West, where he became a graduate of the University of California's Law School. A litigator, he became a partner in the DLA Piper Law Firm, representing clients in copyright and trademark disputes at its branches in California and Washington, D.C.

He has since abandoned those duties and is now on the faculty of Georgetown University Law Center. There, he teaches a course in intellectual property and entertainment law.

From the beginning, he showed a fervent and dedicated support of his wife. When a protester moved toward her on the campaign trail, trying to grab her microphone, he jumped up from his front row seat and rushed to her rescue.

On his Twitter account, he wrote, "I am a proud husband and an advocate of social justice and equality. I may be the first Second Gentleman, but I will not be the last."

Karl Marton, author of Hidden Power, claimed, "Emhoff's main role will be what so many wives have been over the millennia: a really great support to their spouse."

A new survey of what is called "gender-inverted roles," revealed that 41 percent of American moms are the sole or primary support of their families.

On the 2020 campaign trail, Emhoff met Chasten Glezman Buttigieg, the husband of Pete Buttigieg, who is now the Secretary of Transportation. Chasten told Emhoff, "One day, I, too, will be the Second Gentleman when Pete is elected President."

PETE BUTTIGIEG
The First Openly Gay Cabinet Member

Pete Buttigieg ran unsuccessfully against Joe Biden for President. Once in office, Biden named him U.S. Secretary of Transportation. Before that, he was nicknamed "Mayor Pete," a reference to his being the 32nd mayor of South Bend, Indiana, from 2012 to 2020.

A graduate of Harvard College and the University of Oxford, he was later an intelligence officer in the U.S. Navy Reserve. He was deployed to Afghanistan for seven months in 2014.

While serving as mayor, Buttigieg came out as gay in 2015. He later married Chasten Glezman, a schoolteacher and writer, in June of 2018. Chasten now goes by the name of "Chasten Buttigieg."

The secretary and his husband became parents in August of 2021 by adopting two newborn fraternal twins.

In his race for the Presidency, and by winning the primary in conservative Iowa, Buttigieg became the first openly gay candidate to win a presidential primary or caucus.

He then dropped out and endorsed Biden, who nominated him Secretary of Transportation in December of 2020. He was confirmed by a vote of 86 to 13, making him the first openly gay cabinet secretary in U.S. history. He was opposed by noted homophobes.

Some people have suggested that the cabinet minister has a super intellect, as he has some knowledge of such languages as Norwegian, Spanish, Italian, Maltese, Arabic, Dari Persian, and French. In addition, he is a talented musician, playing guitar and piano.

Here's **Pete Buttigieg** (right) then the U.S. Transportation Secretary, in 2021, seated on a hospital bed with his husband, **Chasten**, and their two adopted children. As such he's the first Cabinet secretary to become a parent while in office.

"We're delighted to welcome **Penelope Rose** and **Joseph August Buttigieg** to our family," Mr. Buttigieg, 39, said on social media, sharing this photo of his daughter and son for the first time since they announced that they were finalizing the process of becoming parents.

Mr. Buttigieg surfaced in national politics when he entered the presidential race in 2019 as mayor of South Bend, Indiana. Mr. Buttigieg and Chasten, a former middle school teacher, were married in 2018. Since Mr. Buttigieg entered the national spotlight, they have successfully overturned many prevailing perceptions of gay relationships.

Pete Buttigieg (right figure in each of the photos above) lives in Washington, D.C., with his husband, **Chasten Glezman Buttigieg.** Buttigieg met Glezman on the dating app *Hinge* in summer 2015.

Many writers have suggested that if Buttigieg ever won the presidency (most unlikely), he would be the first gay U.S. President. Actually, James Buchanan (1857-1861) was. His lover was William Rufus King, who had served as Vice President under Franklin Pierce. In Washington, Buchanan and King were derisively called Miss Nancy & Aunt Fanny.

This episode is devoted to the difficult, much-overrated, long-suffering creatures defined by a sometimes ungrateful nation as

FIRST LADIES

They've included presidential spouses defined as "Raving Lunatics," a "Fellatio Queen," & "An Overdressed Belle Showcasing her Big Tits."

#1. Martha Washington

Martha Washington, called "The Mother of Our Country," was First Lady from 1789 to 1797, a period of service she likened to being "a state prisoner." She'd married poor boy George Washington in 1759.

Before that, she was wed to Daniel Parke Custis, who was actually her godfather and twenty-one years her senior. He died in 1757, leaving her with two children, 17,000 acres of land, and 300 slaves. She became one of the richest women in the colonies.

It was said that George married her for her money, because he was really in love with his married neighbor, Sally Fairfax.

In many ways, it was an absentee marriage. During the eight years of the Revolutionary War, George made only two trips to Mount Vernon and on each of them, stayed for only two days.

Some historians have defined Washington as "a ladies' man," but there may have been another, secret, side to him.

Author Michael Bronski wrote: "It was in 1778 that Washington began a romantic, if not sexual, affair with Jean de Lafayette. In his letters he referred to the French general as "the man I love," and in his letters to Washington, Lafayette called him "my sweetheart."

Another historian wrote, "When Washington met Lafayette on the battlefield at Yorktown, the younger Frenchman kissed him from ear to ear with as much ardor as ever an absent lover kisses his mistress on his return."

When they had to part, Lafayette asked for a locket of Washington's hair "to carry with me always."

#2. Dolley Madison

Dolley Madison was married to President James Madison and served as First Lady from 1809 to 1817. She may have been as close as America came during the 19th Century of having an empress. And long before the emergence of Jacqueline Kennedy and Melania Trump, she was the first fashion icon in the White House.

The term "First Lady" was introduced by her, and she's been hailed as the suma inter pares (first among equals) of presidential spouses.

One of her admirers was Aaron Burr, who may have taken her virginity. It was he who introduced her to Madison, who married her in

Martha Washington
Did she have to share George with the Marquis de Lafayette?

Dolley Madison had to flee from the White House to escape British Redcoats who wanted to kidnap her for public trials and humiliations in London.

1794.

"Little Jemmy," as she called her husband, became Secretary of State in 1801. Because President Thomas Jefferson and Vice-President Burr were widowers, Dolley became the de facto hostess of the White House.

In all of American history, she was the most prepared to be First Lady.

After the British chased her from the White House, she returned and moved into a private home with Jemmy. Overnight, she became the toast of Washington, giving parties even though the capital had been ravaged.

She was the best-dressed woman outside London and Paris, wearing elegant gowns of silk and satin. She had an ample bosom and shocked Washington society by her plunging décolletage. She also introduced the wearing of turbans from which two-foot feathers spouted. She was also addicted to snuff.

At the end of her life, she was a pauper, begging for money and trying to hawk her tell-all memoirs. Her drunken, gambling son, John Payne Todd, squandered her money. Like Martha Washington, Dolley had been married before, having wed John Todd, Jr., in 1790.

Since her death in 1849, her fame and legacy have grown, and she is now ranked as one of the most celebrated First Ladies in American history.

#3. Mary Todd Lincoln

Mary Todd Lincoln was First Lady from 1861 to 1865 and married to Abraham Lincoln. Her most famous sound bite was, "What world of anguish this is—and how I have been made to suffer."

By 1839, she moved to Springfield, Illinois, where she met a lanky lawyer, Abe Lincoln, a young man who had no money and lacked social graces.

Unknown to her at the time, he was living with Joshua Fry Speed for four years, sleeping with him in a small bed and becoming his lover.

Lincoln's biographer, Carl Sandberg, phrased it poetically and delicately: "Providence had given these two men streaks of lavender, spots soft as May violets."

Mary Todd Lincoln learned that her husband preferred young soldiers to her.

Mary's relationship with Abe was turbulent, filled with arguments and jealous rages, but she prevailed and married him in 1842. Even as a girl growing up, she told her parents, "One day, I want to be wed to the President of the United States."

She urged Abe to go into politics, and he was elected to the U.S. Congress in 1846. She became one of his most ardent supporters, almost nightly urging him on.

In 1860, the newly formed Republican Party nominated him as their presidential candidate, and her dream was coming true. Of course, as the world knows, his election blew up into a Civil War and, ultimately, his assassination.

When her favorite son, Willie, died in 1862, she tried to communicate with her dead son by holding séances at the White House. Then, months before her husband's death, she warned Lincoln that she'd had a premonition of his assassination.

Her final years were tragic as she sold Lincoln's possessions to raise money for herself and her two remaining sons. One disaster followed another, as her youngest son, Tad, died in 1871.

Four years later, an Illinois court judge pronounced her insane. Her oldest son, Robert, testified that she was crazy.

After Lincoln's death, his biographers began to reveal aspects of his secret life.

In 1831, Abe, then 22, became involved with 19-year-old Billy Greene. The younger man later claimed, "The moment I laid eyes on Abe, I noted that his thighs were as perfect as a human being could be. We shared a bed so small that if one of us turned over, the other would have to do likewise." He would recall his time with Abe as "the most glorious period of my life."

When Abe was 28, he moved to Springfield, Illinois, where on his first day in town, he med Joshua Fry Speed, 23. The young man invited him to share his bed, and Lincoln did just that for four ears.

As reported, Joshua became the love of Lincoln's life. And he was heartbroken, almost suicidal, when Joshua moved back to Kentucky where he was a slave owner.

Lincoln's law partner, William Herndon, wrote that "Speed, more than onyone dead or living, was devoted to Abe. No two men have ever been more intimate. They shared everything together—and not just a small bed."

As President of the United States, Abe Lincoln became involved with Captain David Derickson of the 150th Pennsylvania Volunteers, knicknamed "The Bucktail Brigade." Lincoln was 53 at the time, and the captain 44.

The President was outside Washington reviewing troops when he first met the captain. He asked him to ride back to Washington with him, and, according to reports, the captain never left his side for the next four months. They became so close that the President even let him sit in on Cabinet meetings, discussing how the Civil War was going. The two men often inspected troops together.

When Derickson was called back to his post, the President countermanded the order, telling General Grant, "The Captain and I are getting quite thick."

Later, Virginia Woodbury, wife of the Assistant Secretary of the Navy, interpreted the relationship as "scandalous. The Bucktail soldier is devoted to the President and even sleeps with him."

Thomas Chamberlin, Derickson's commanding officer, wrote: "The Captain has advanced so far in the President's confidence that he spends every night in bed with him at Lincoln's summer retreat from Washington. He even makes use of Lincoln's nightshirt."

It was in their bedroom at his summer retreat that Lincoln began to write the Emancipation Proclamation.

Ida Saxton McKinley was one of the richest First Ladies to ever occupy the White House.

#4. Ida Saxton McKinley

Ida Saxton McKinley was the wife of President William McKinley and First Lady from 1897 to 1901, the year her husband was assassinated. Most of the time during her tenure at the White House, she remained in bed because of various ailments. She used the time effectively, crocheting 3,500 pairs of slippers.

#5. Grace Coolidge

Grace Coolidge, wife of Calvin Coolidge, lived in the White House from 1923 to 1929. She first spotted her future husband aboard a steamship when she peered into his bathroom through a porthole. He was naked, standing in front of a mirror. "Then and there, I decided he would be my husband," she later claimed.

Grace Coolidge decided to marry the future president after seeing him naked through a bathroom window.

#6. Bess Truman

Were it not for Bess Truman, the White House as it appears today would not be standing. After Roosevelt's death in 1945, Harry Truman and his wife, Bess, moved into the White House. On their first night, their bed almost fell through the rotting floor. She learned that there were plans to raze the entire building and to construct an all-new copy. She objected, asserting that the White House was a historic monument and its original walls and shape and structure should be preserved to the degree that it was structurally possible. She and Harry moved out as work began.

Harry Truman with **Bess.** She saved the White House—as it existed at the debut of their administration—from being demolished into rubble as part of its reconstruction.

#7. Jacqueline Bouvier Kennedy

Jackie Kennedy served as First Lady from 1961 until her husband's assassination in Dallas in November of 1963. During her tenure at the White House, she became the most famous woman in the world. Known for her beauty, charm, and grace, she "reigned" in stark contrast to the style of Mamie Eisenhower, married to the two-term President and former General Dwight Eisenhower.

During Jacqueline's time there, she had to rear two children and deal with her philandering husband. In his day, JFK would seduce such stellar women—as well as dozens of lesser-known ones—as Joan Crawford, Hedy Lamarr, Lana Turner, Marlene Dietrich, Judy Garland, and Marilyn Monroe.

One night, Jacqueline told the gossipy author Truman Capote, "The man I really wanted to marry was William Holden."

The JFKs: "I had to share Jack with numerous women during his tenure as president."

#8. Nancy Davis Reagan

The former MGM starlette, Nancy Davis, was married to President Ronald Reagan , and they ruled over the White House from 1981 to 1989. Ironically, as Reagan became one of the most popular Presidents, she became one of the most unpopular First Ladies.

During her days as a starlet at MGM, Davis became known as "The Fellatio Queen of Hollywood." She sustained several high profile affairs, including romances with, among others, Yul Brynner, Broadway star Alfred Drake, Peter Lawford, Robert Walker, Frank Sinatra, and Spencer Tracy.

Her first choice of a husband was Clark Gable, but he spurned her offer.

SHOW-BIZ PROS **Nancy Davis Reagan** as she appeared in 1957 in *Hell Cats of the Navy*, a movie she made with her husband, the future U.S. President, Ronald Reagan. They married in 1952, after his divorce from superstar Jane Wyman, in 1948.

FIRST LADYSHIPS
A vehicle for Public Service?
Or a Laboratory Experiment for the creation of Monster Egomaniacs?

Left to right in photo, left, **Nancy Reagan, Lady Bird Johnson, Hillary Clinton, Rosalyn Carter, Betty Ford,** and **Barbara Bush,** as they appeared together in 1994 at a fundraiser for the U.S. Botanic Gardens in D.C.

Historians who included Michael Beschloss have commented on their table positions and body language.

FIRST LADIES
The Hardest Unpaid Job in the World

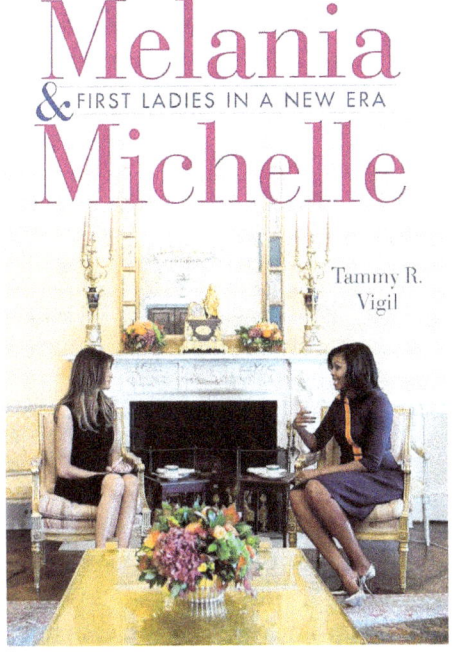

Few American First Ladies endured the pain and humiliation that Patricia Nixon, the wife of Richard Nixon, faced in the White House where she lived from 1969 to 1974.

Her husband was forced to resign over the Watergate scandal, and the camera recorded her holding back her tears.

The remarkable differences among First Ladies have been revealed once again in the new book, *Melania and Michelle: First Ladies in a New Era*, by Tammy Vigil. This is a nonpartisan book that pinpoints the wide differences between these two highly placed figures. Vigil claims that the only thing the two have in common is that whatever they do will find some group hating and denouncing them.

Michelle had to face false rumors spread to millions of people on the web that, because of her well-muscled arms, she is a man in drag. Another "fake news" item appeared under the head—MICHELLE OBAMA IS TRANSGENDERED.

Take popularity, for example. Michelle is one of the most popular women in America, rating at least a 53% approval, although some polling has put her at 65%. In contrast, Melania lags way behind: Only one in four Americans approve of her.

First Lady Do's and Don't's seem to be on everybody's mind with the changeover of Presidential administrations that followed Trump's return to power in 2025.

A new book documents and describes the differences First Ladies have demonstrated—especially **Melania Trump** and her predecessor, **Michelle Obama.**

During her tenure in the White House, Michelle called herself "Mom-in-Chief," referring to how she reared her two daughters under the glare of a spotlight. In contrast, Melania does everything she can to conceal her son, Barron, from the press.

As a skilled lawyer and litigator, Michelle was prepared for the job, battling hostile lawyers in front of judges. In the White House, she was not exactly a co-president, but a skilled negotiator and adviser behind the scenes.

Melania, to much of the world, appears like a "trophy wife," standing by her husband silently and always looking beautiful, exquisitely dressed, and made up, sometimes referred to as the "Mannequin First Lady."

She actually is an intelligent woman who speaks more languages than any other First Lady. She rarely comments on political issues, though she has denounced "bullying." She made one widely printed comment: "I wish he wouldn't tweet so much."

First Lady **Pat Nixon** with her politically traumatized husband, **Richard Nixon**, in what appears to be an uncharacteristically (and rare) happy moment.

Sporting a broad-brimmed hat that almost concealed her emotions, **Melania Trump** receives a kiss from **The Donald** under the Rotunda of the Capitol during his second inauguration, in January of 2025. It more or less coincided with their 20th wedding anniversary.

She also had to endure the humiliation of having nude pictures released that she'd posed for in the 1990s, some where she shared a lesbian embrace with another model.

[Long before Melania, Jacqueline Kennedy Onassis had to endure even more revealing nudes taken of her secretly on the Greek Island (Skorpios) owned by Aristotle Onassis.]

Of course, both Michelle and Melania have made missteps. When Barack Obama won the Democratic primary, his wife said, "For the first time in my life, I am really proud of my country." She was instantly denounced as unpatriotic.

At the GOP convention in 2016, that nominated her husband, Melania gave the shortest speech in First Lady history. Regrettably, one hawk-eyed reporter revealed that part of it was plagiarized from Michelle's 2008 convention speech.

Every American First Lady has faced trials and tribulation, some, of course, far more than others.

Take Dolley Madison, First Lady from 1809 to 1817. During the War of 1812, British troops planned to raid the White House, kidnap her, ship her to London, and parade her naked through the streets as a war trophy.

Alerted that the British were coming, she fled from the White House, taking only Gilbert Stuart's portrait of George Washington and some beautiful red draperies.

After eating the dinner she had planned that night, the British general burned down the White House.

The United States won the battle, and at the victory celebration, Dolley showed up in a stunning scarlet gown made of drapery material. The scene was repeated years later by Scarlett O'Hara (the draperies she converted into a dress were, in her case, green) in *Gone With the Wind*.

No First Lady was ever as commanding as Eleanor Roosevelt, wife of FDR, who was First Lady from 1933 to 1945, some of the darkest years in American history. The Roosevelts had to be a beacon of hope during the Great Depression and during World War II, the greatest conflict in world history.

She made her mark, becoming "the ears and eyes" of her crippled husband, as she toured relentlessly, trying to right a wrong wherever she found it. She stood for women's liberation, civil rights, and a host of other liberal causes.

In 1942, the worst year for the Allies, she took a dangerous flight to war-torn London, where she walked the bombed-out streets. She brought tears of joy to Londoners who lined the streets. "She gave us hope when it appeared that all was lost," said a widow who had lost both her husband and her three children in "The Blitz."

Mrs. Roosevelt capped a remarkable career in 1948, three years after leaving the White House. At the United Nations, she ruled Soviet delegates out of order and passed the first-ever Declaration of Human Rights, immortalizing herself and making her the greatest woman of the 20th Century.

Chances are that no one now alive will ever see the likes of Eleanor Roosevelt anytime soon. What they are likely to witness is the first female President of the United States introducing the "First Man."

DANCING BUSHES: George (Bubba) with his wife **Laura** dancing on a carpeted replica of the Presidential Seal.

With almost universal acclaim, the greatest-ever First Lady was **Eleanor Roosevelt,** a forcefully hard-working champion of humanitarian causes in many different arenas.

She appears *on the left* as a fashionable but socially repressed bride in 1905. On the *upper right*, she poses with Franklin Delano Roosevelt, her four-time-elected husband, in 1932.

Lower right photo: A lioness of progressive causes, Eleanor appears at the United Nations in 1948, forcing through passage of the Universal Declaration of Human Rights. She succeeded despite powerful denunciations from the Soviet delegates who opposed her.

Eleanor Roosevelt befriended a young **Darwin Porter,** co-author of this anthology, during his time as a bureau chief for the *Miami Herald.* From his first interview emerged a profile that *the Herald* entitled "Portrait of a Great Lady." In the years that followed, Darwin escorted Mrs. Roosevelt, at her request, to political rallies and fundraisers of merit in New York City. Their relationship remained strong, supportive, and vital from the late 1950s until the death of Mrs. Roosevelt in 1962.

Lacerating First Ladies Is an American Tradition

"Attacking spouses is off-limits—it has no place in American politics," said Ted Cruz, the failed Republican presidential candidate and senator from Texas. "It's frankly disgusting."

It all began in Utah in the spring of 2016, when an anti-Trump PAC published a photo of Melania Trump lying naked on a bearskin rug for the January, 2000 cover of the British *GQ* magazine.

To retaliate, Donald Trump retweeted a glamorous shot of his wife next to an unflattering photo of Heidi, Cruz's wife.

Actually, Cruz was wrong. Dating from the early days of the Republic, attacking Presidential wives has long been part of dirty protocols in Washington.

The tradition dates back to the days of Dolley Madison (1768-1849). With her magnificent turbans and gowns with plunging *décolletage*, she was the first fashion diva to inhabit the White House. She was also a devout user of "snuff tobacco."

In 1808, Charles C. Pinckney, the Federalist candidate for President, spread the rumor that James Madison "pimped" his wife to the widowed incumbent, Thomas Jefferson, in exchange for his endorsement. In the aftermath, Dolley was widely denounced as a "political whore."

No presidential wife had been attacked as much as Rachel Jackson (1767-1828), the wife of Andrew Jackson. In the last year of her life, her name was dragged through the mud by her husband's enemies. She was mocked for being "grossly obese—to fat to fit into a girdle"—as well as an ignorant fool. She was called "The Beast."

She had been previously married to the insanely jealous Lewis Robards when she was seventeen. He almost fought a duel with Jackson over her. She married the future President in 1791, but later found out her divorce was not official. In the campaign, she was accused of being "a bigamist and an adulterer." She died right before Christmas of 1828, and was therefore spared the fate of being First Lady, a role she dreaded.

Long before such polarizing figures as Eleanor Roosevelt and Hillary Clinton, Mary Todd Lincoln (1818-1882) suffered an onslaught of criticism. Born in slave-holding Kentucky, she perhaps would be diagnosed as bipolar today. The White House staff privately referred to her as "The Hellcat." When her son, Willie, died in 1862, she conducted daily séances. She went on shopping sprees, charging gowns and outfits her husband could not afford. On one jaunt, she purchased 400 pairs of gloves.

When her half-sister's husband died fighting for the Confederate Army, she draped the White House in black bunting, a defiant act that almost led to angry Yankees storming the grounds.

Frances Cleveland (1864-1947), nicknamed "Frank," caught the eye of Grover Cleveland when she was in diapers. When her father died in a buggy accident in 1875, "Uncle Cleve" became her guardian. There were rumors of child molestation.

Twenty-seven years her senior, he became the first sitting president to have his wedding at the White House. He admitted to having fathered an illegitimate child in Buffalo. Eventually, the Clevelands had a child of their own, Ruth. A candy bar, called "Baby Ruth," was named after her and became the most popular treat in America.

Frank was accused of cheating on her husband, as she was seen on the arm of a handsome young male escort.

Cleveland lost his bid for re-election to Benjamin Harrison, but the couple won the next election and returned to the White House in 1893. When the press

No, It's not one of Melania's unregulated bitcoins, although if it had been, no one would have been surprised. It's a replica of her custom-designed FLOTUS Seal, accessorized with all the symbolic trappings of the Oval Office.

It's been flagrantly thrust in the faces of friends and frenemies alike, another flashy and expensive grab for power associated with the *fashionista*, First Lady, and nude model.

Ted and Heidi Cruz, reacting to Trump's unflattering comparison of Heidi to the allure of Melania—naked or not.

Andrew Jackson's long-suffering wife Rachel. The attacks upon her were so vitriolic that her premature death, just before her husband's inauguration, were blamed on them, directly

could find no scandal about Frank, they made up unflattering stories about her and published them.

The parade of first ladies came and went, with scandalous stories about most of them. Ida McKinley (1847-1907) was said to be insane and locked away at the White House. She actually suffered from epilepsy. In 1901, after his re-election to office, McKinley was shot by an anarchist and died eight days later.

As the 20th Century moved on, Eleanor Roosevelt (1884-1962) was the most reviled—also the most beloved, of First Ladies. Secretly, she was accused of being a lesbian. Years later, her love letters to Lorena Hickok, a reporter for the Associated Press, were published.

Jackie Kennedy (1929-1994), married a notorious philanderer, John F. Kennedy. Perhaps to get back at him, she vacationed, in Italy in 1962, where she had a torrid affair with Fiat czar Gianni Agnelli, the uncrowned King of Italy.

After JFK's assassination, she became the most popular woman on earth. She lost that position when she married Aristotle Onassis, the Greek shipping magnate. She was widely denounced as an "international gold-digger and prostitute."

Nancy Reagan (1921-2016) was one of America's most unpopular First Ladies. She was ridiculed for her interest in astrology, and was disgraced when Kitty Kelley, in an unauthorized biography, revealed that during her days in Hollywood as an MGM starlet, she was labeled "The Queen of Fellatio."

Michael Reagan, Ronald's adopted son with his first wife, Jane Wyman, said, "If Nancy knew that one day she would become First Lady, she would have cleaned up her act when she was a starlet."

Ida McKinley, who was widely rumored to have been insane, looking dour with her equally dour-looking husband, **President William McKinley**, at a banquet before his assassination in 1901.

Frances Cleveland, the ward and later child bride of the two-term President **Grover Cleveland,** as she appeared in a portrait by the Gilded Age's "society portraitist," Anders Zorn in 1899.

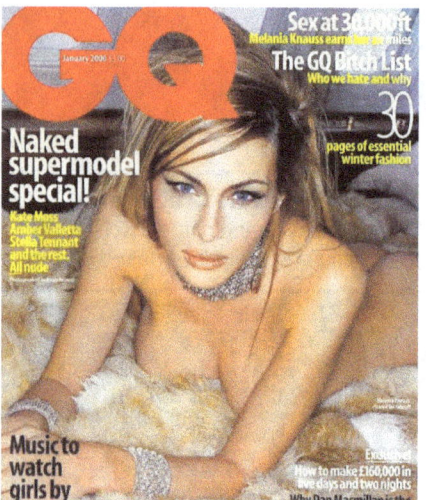 

THERE BUT FOR THE GRACE OF DONALD

It was a postmodern, Trump-era First, wherein a First Lady's naked charms are laid out, bold and broad, for friends and foes, Republicans and Democrats, communists and capitalists, to ogle.

Late-night comedians had a field day...and inspired other aspirant New Americans to try to emulate the success of the former **Melania Knauss**, a once-impoverished model and immigrant from Slovenia.

Since those early (now embarassing) indiscretions, she's the most gossiped about and most widely emulated *fashionista* on the planet.

February 2021

ONE OF AMERICA'S FAVORITE BLOOD
SPORTS: LACERATING FIRST LADIES

REMEMBERING DOLLEY MADISON

Upper photo: **Dolley Madison** and *lower photo:* her husband, **President James Madison.** in office 1809-1817.

Five days after January's mob assault on the U.S. Capitol, the ex-First Lady, "Cover Girl" Melania Trump, issued a widely ridiculed statement: "I find it shameful that surrounding these tragic events, there has been salacious gossip, unwarranted personal attacks, and false misleading accusations about me—from people who are looking to be relevant and (who) have an agenda."

That statement was instantly attacked for its implied self-centeredness. Anita McBride, chief of staff for an earlier First Lady, Laura Bush, was among the first to weigh in: "At a time when the nation is hurting so badly, and we are craving moral authority from our leaders, this should not be about how Melania may feel maligned."

Since the dawn of the United States, every First Lady has come under attack, some in ways almost excruciatingly painful. "Being pilloried in the press is part of the job description," said Eleanor Roosevelt who endured a relentless barrage of devastating attacks during her precedent-breaking reign (1933-1945). Today, she's acclaimed by most historians as our greatest First Lady.

Eleanor wasn't alone in having to cope with attacks: The notorious Hollywood history of starlet Nancy Davis was dug up, and as First Lady ("Mrs. Hail to the Chief" Ronald Reagan), attacks on her reached a fever pitch, especially after it was revealed that she was relying on astrology to help direct the political maneuverings of her husband.

Few First Ladies have endured the ongoing venom aimed at First Lady Hillary Clinton during her extension of health insurance to more Americans, especially children. During her 2016 campaign for president, deeply disturbing verbal assaults ("LOCK HER UP") were levied based on (in hindsight) relatively innocuous accusations involving some missing e-mails.

But in retrospect, perhaps the most vilified presidential wife in U.S. history was Dolley Madison, First Lady (and wife of our fourth president, James Madison) from 1809 to 1817. At the time, his detractors called him "the pygmy president" because of his height (5'4"). Today, he's revered as "The Father of the U.S. Constitution."

Dolley had lost her first husband when she was 26: Attorney John Todd, Jr., and her young son were felled by the yellow fever epidemic then sweeping through Philadelphia.

Perhaps in an attempt to emotionally recuperate, she moved to Washington, where her mother ran a boarding house. One of the boarders, a rising young politician named Aaron Burr *[later Vice President during the administration of the third American President, Thomas Jefferson]* fell in love with her and wanted to marry her as soon as his wife, then suffering from cancer, died in New York.

Burr made the mistake of introducing the arousing, vivacious young widow to another rising politician, James Madison. Perhaps based on political ambitions of her own, she agreed to an alliance (in this case, marriage) with him, coquettishly defining him as "a darling man who looks like he's on his way to a funeral."

[Throughout Madison's life, he'd suffered from various illnesses: dysentery, rheumatism, hemorrhoids, and more. It therefore came as no surprise when she discovered, on their wedding night, that he was impotent, too.]

To compensate, she found herself another influential lover, the politically and socially prominent George Washington, who had long ago tired of his portly wife, Martha. *[Martha, owner of 300 slaves at the time he married her, had been the richest woman in the North American colonies. Tall and broad-shouldered, Washington had an obvious physical fault: His wooden teeth had a tendency to rot.]* As Dolley and he played cards, or whatever, they'd often share, together, the arrival of dawn. He referred to her as "the sprightliest partner I ever had." *[Was he talking about cards?]*

Wanna discuss palace intrigue? Thomas Jefferson, President from 1801-1809, designated Dolley's husband, James Madison, as his Secretary of State and moved him and his buxom wife into the White House. Madison was accused at the time of "shamelessly pimping his wife to his boss."

Jefferson's wife, Martha, had died in 1782. Now a widower, Jefferson vowed never to marry again, preferring involvement with a number of mistresses, including Dolley, instead. During Jefferson's presidential tenure, she was often at his side, presiding like a First Lady at parties, dinners, and political events.

She also continued her affair with Burr, Jefferson's Vice President. She was greatly distressed in 1804 when Burr killed Alexander Hamilton in a duel.

At last, one of Dolley's carefully nurtured dreams came true when her husband, James Madison *[Jefferson's Secretary of State, remember?]* became the fourth President (1809-1817) of the United States.

Charges of "Petticoat Politicking," and accusations that he was using his wife's sexual favors to charm and seduce his political enemies were levied against Madison before, during, and after his campaign. Yet despite the vitriol, some historians cite "James & Dolley" as the inventors of bipartisanship in Congress, even though that term didn't exist at the time.

Dolley became the victim of almost endless vituperation: One of Madison's Federalist enemies denounced her from the floor of Congress, citing evidence of her "promiscuity that will make the hairs of my fellow congressmen stand erect as porcupine quills. She is oversexed, adulterous, an insatiable thing, a complete floozie. She has seduced three presidents, one vice president, countless politicians, and even foreign diplomats."

Throughout her reign, first as a political superstar and then as First Lady, Dolley became known for her lavish parties at which she appeared in towering turbans with plunging *décolletage* that revealed magnificently ample breasts.

During her tenure as First Lady, 209 years before before 2021's mob assault on the Capitol, the District of Columbia faced an even more destructive attack by the British in 1814.

In residence at the White House, after surveying the "victuals" laid out for a state dinner she'd organized, Dolley learned that the British troops of Rear Admiral Sir George Cockburn were massed together on the outskirts of town, heading toward the Presidential Palace, presumably to burn it. Cockburn had already announced his intention of raping her, kidnapping her, and hauling her back to England to parade, in chains, through the streets of London as a spoil of war.

Hastily, Dolley ordered her slaves to remove Gilbert Stuart's famous portrait of George Washington from its frame, and to rescue the expensive red velvet curtains that she'd recently hung in the drawing room.

Then she fled into the night with her slaves. Cockburn laid siege to the city and burned many public buildings after consuming, with his officers, the dinner that Dolley had arranged for that night's State Dinner.

Months later, she returned to the burned-out capital. Although her husband wanted to abandon it and move the seat of government to Philadelphia. Dolley stood firm, promoting the rebuilding of Washington, and demanding that her slaves assist in the erection of a new Presidential mansion. After she ordered that it be painted white, the term "The White House" came into vogue.

James Madison died in 1836, almost twenty years after the end of his presidency. Dolley, wiser and now removed from public scrutiny, would have serious money problems in the years ahead. Yet while she remained alive, every incoming president visited her at her home, a ritual that to some resembled a pilgrimage and rite of passage, always seeking her blessing.

Zachory Taylor became President in 1849, the year of Dolley's death. He later told the press and the nation, "Dolley Madison has been our First Lady for half a century." She had only months to live, dying at the age of 81. Taylor himself soon died from the cholera epidemic then sweeping across Washington.

Cited in the decades that followed as one of the key figures in the establishment of American Democracy, her legend had just begun.

An artist's rendition of **Dolley Madison** *(right)* directing the White House staff before the invasion of Washington (and the burning of the White House) by the British during the War of 1812.

FRANKLIN & ELEANOR
Adultery in the White House

Franklin & Eleanor, keeping up appearances in 1941

Franklin and Eleanor, the most towering male and female figures of the 20th century, are making a comeback, but not in ways they'd appreciate.

Acclaimed historian Joseph E. Persico, who collaborated with Colin Powell on his autobiography, has written an explosive new book: *Franklin and Lucy: President Roosevelt, Mrs. Rutherfurd, and the Other Remarkable Women in His Life.* The book deals in part with FDR's decades-long affair with Lucy Mercer Rutherfurd. It also explores Eleanor's sexual liaisons with both men and women during her husband's years in power.

Filmmakers in Hollywood are preparing a documentary on the private lives of Eleanor and Franklin. Ever since Watergate, Hollywood has discovered that films about the private lives of presidents make for fascinating cinema, as in the case of Richard Nixon and John F. Kennedy. Currently playing in theaters across the nation is Oliver Stone's take on George W. Bush as depicted in the controversial movie simply entitled *W*.

Lucy Mercer Rutherfurd

For long-time Roosevelt watchers and devotees such as myself, Persico's book does not reveal a lot of new information. But for a new generation less familiar with the FDR saga, the biography explodes like TNT.

In 1905, FDR married his fifth cousin, "the ugly duckling," Eleanor, whose uncle was Theodore Roosevelt. "It's a good thing to keep the name in the family," Theodore said. From the beginning the marriage was anything but idyllic, although it produced four sons and one daughter. Even from the marriage's debut, the handsome and dashing young FDR was a notorious flirt.

In 1918, Eleanor discovered a pack of love letters exchanged between her husband and her social secretary, Lucy Mercer. She threatened her young husband with divorce unless he ended his relationship with Lucy. To save both the marriage and his political career, he promised that he would. But he lied.

Marguerite (Missy) LeHand

From that day forth, Eleanor cut off all intimate contact with her husband, who turned elsewhere for his sexual pleasures.

In 1921, Franklin was stricken with polio, which led to the loss of his use of his legs and his confinement for the rest of his life to a wheelchair. Amazingly, that fact remained unknown to most of the American public at the time. Nevertheless, as *The New York Times* put it, "In plain English, he could still sustain an erection."

With his libido intact, FDR took a second mistress, Marguerite (Missy) LeHand, the daughter of an alcoholic Irish Catholic gardener. She was described as having "lips parted in that strange secret smile composed of cunning influence, forever baffling."

When Missy came to work for FDR as a secretary, he was smitten. He began an affair with her that would last until her death in 1944 of a cerebral embolism.

For reasons of her own, Eleanor wasn't as upset over her husband's affair with Missy as she had been with Lucy. "After all, the pot can't call the kettle black," said Sir Winston Churchill, the seventh-cousin-once-removed of FDR.

Eleanor, meanwhile, had been having affairs of her own. In 1928, this prim and proper Victorian woman threw off the shackles of her own strict upbringing and launched two simultaneous affairs—one with a woman, another with a man.

In his official role as governor of New York, FDR assigned a handsome, virile, New York State trooper, Earl Miller, as his wife's bodyguard. A bodybuilder and notorious womanizer, Earl launched an affair with Eleanor.

She was 45, Earl was 32. Her many lesbian friends were disturbed by this new liaison, and utterly horrified by the way Miller "manhandled" her in public.

Eleanor and Earl even made what was jokingly referred to years later as a "soft core porn film" entitled *The Kidnapping of the First Lady*. For years, the film was believed to have been destroyed, but Persico found clips from it, publishing them in his new book. In the home movie, Earl, in a tight-fitting bathing suit, plays a bearded pirate with a bandanna. He abducts Eleanor, and hauls her away with him "for immoral purposes." Based on appraisals of the still shots from that film, Eleanor appears to be enjoying her kidnapping.

An equal opportunity seducer, Eleanor also took up with Lorena Hickok, a notorious, cigar-smoking lesbian, who stood five feet eight inches tall, and weighed more than 200 pounds. A journalist who was assigned to cover the Roosevelts for The Associated Press, Lorena drank a quart of bourbon a day and referred to herself as "one of the boys." "I dress like a man, talk like a man, and curse better than any sailor," she said.

Earl Wilson with **Eleanor**

Eleanor fell under her spell, launching an affair that would last from 1928 to 1940, when Lorena dumped the First Lady for a female tax-court judge.

Eleanor's steamy love letters to Lorena were published in the 1998 book *Empty Without You*. In one of the letters, Eleanor wrote: "I wish I could lie down beside you tonight and take you in my arms. I ache to hold you close. Most clearly, I remember your eyes, with a kind of teasing smile in them, and the feeling of that soft spot just northeast of the corner of your mouth against my lips."

In the meantime, FDR was keeping busy with other affairs of his own, not only with Missy, but with women who included Margaret (Daily) Suckley, a distant cousin; Dorothy Schiff, publisher of *The New York Post*, and Princess Martha of Norway.

Lorena Hickok

By this time, Lucy Mercer had married Winthrop Rutherfurd, a wealthy sportsman and dog breeder, who was old enough to be her father. When he died, and with Missy dead, FDR resumed his affair with Lucy in 1944. In fact, Lucy was sitting with FDR when he died in 1945, as he was having his portrait painted in Warm Springs, Georgia. Immediately after his death, before Eleanor arrived in Georgia to accompany her husband's body back to Washington, all evidence of Lucy's presence was removed from the President's retreat.

After Lorena abandoned her, Eleanor took up with young Joseph Lash, who would later become her most famous biographer. She was horrified to learn that army intelligence had taped "the sounds of sexual intercourse" during an illicit weekend the First Lady spent with Lash at the Blackstone Hotel in Chicago. The tapes were later played for FDR in the Oval Office.

FDR was hardly buried in the ground at Hyde Park before Eleanor's longtime admirer, Bernard Baruch, proposed marriage to her. Previously, the financial wizard had worked closely with her, thanks to his directorship of the War Industries Board. Politely, she rejected his offer of marriage, and also refused to accept offers to run as the first female candidate for President of the United States.

Thanks to these high-drama interchanges among Franklin, Eleanor, Lucy, Missy, Earl, Joseph, Princess Martha, and the entrances and exits of various other women, FDR's White House was the focal point of more adultery than a 1970s-era key-swapping party.

Joseph Lash

In retrospect, Bill Clinton's White House appears tame.

April, 2012

SANDRA LEE

Navigating, with difficulties, through the Labyrinth of Romance & NY Politics

Eleanor Roosevelt, long married to New York Governor Franklin D. Roosevelt, was once the First Lady of New York State. Today, the Empire State doesn't have a First Lady, but a "First Girlfriend."

She's the chic, beautiful, and sophisticated Sandra Lee, the celebrated star of Semi-Homemade on the Food Network. She's also the main squeeze of Andrew Cuomo, the popular New York governor who is increasingly viewed as a leading candidate for the Democratic nomination for president in 2016 if Hillary Clinton doesn't run.

The son of another New York governor, Mario Cuomo, Andrew married Kerry Kennedy, Robert F. Kennedy Jr.'s little sister, in 1990, and they have three children, including Michaela, plus twins Cara and Mariah. But when Andrew caught Kerry cheating on him in 2003, he divorced her. Of course, she's not the first Kennedy to have indulged in adulterous relationships.

A bachelor again, Andrew met the blonde-haired, chicly dressed Sandra at a *soirée* in the Hamptons in 2003. She found him a "huge muscle-bound man," and it was love at first sight. An advocate of physical fitness, Sandra refuses to be drawn into political debates with Governor Chris Christie in neighboring New Jersey, though she was rumored to have called him "the whale blubber candidate."

Today, Sandra and Andrew divide their time between the governor's mansion in Albany and an elegant residence in Westchester County.

Sandra didn't always have it so good. Her drug-addicted mother left home when Sandra was only fifteen, leaving her to raise four siblings on food stamps and welfare.

By her sheer will power, drive, talent, and ambition, she educated herself and step by step evolved into a media star on TV. But she pooh-poohs the notion that she's the next Martha Stewart. "Martha is Martha, and I am me," she says. However, K-mart and Sears have dropped Martha's line in favor of Sandra by Sandra Lee's home line, and her cookbooks have sold four million copies.

In the kitchen, she is no Julia Child, or devotee of those beef stocks that take five hours to cook. Sandra is well acquainted with the can opener and such packaged ingredients as Cool Whip and Velveeta. Her appeal is to mainstream housewives with little time to spare.

She is most notorious for her Kwanzaa cake, which one food writer referred to as "a crime against humanity." Start with a (store-bought) glazed angel food cake and dump a can of apple pie filling into its ring. Then garnish it with corn nuts and pumpkin seeds. Presto! A "celebration dessert" in five minutes.

Sandra denounces her critics as food snobs. However, she is upgrading her image, and is developing a new *Food Network* TV show under the Sandra Lee brand.

She is also upgrading her wardrobe, having once adopted Cher as her fashion role model. Once she came out on her TV show dressed as Marilyn Monroe appeared in *Gentlemen Prefer Blondes*. Today, she's more influenced by the fashion dictates of *Vogue*'s Anna Wintour or *Glamour*'s Cindi Leive. There is speculation that if she makes it to the White House, she'll be a Jackie Kennedy-like fashion role model for the 21st Century.

A wonderful but contentious and complicated state: Here's **New York's coat of arms.**

Andrew Cuomo stopping for a photo op with **Sandra Lee.**

On the home front, Sandra enjoys being a mother to Andrew's three daughters and admits that each of them keeps urging her to marry their dad. But so far, the couple seems content to live as they are. Although Andrew is known for his "fiery, bulldog temper," she claims he's a pussycat around the house.

At the age of forty-five, she looks like the golden queen of the senior prom at college. When a reporter asked her how she keeps her spectacular looks, she said, "You're so full of it. Don't work me. But I look great, don't I? God, tell me I do."

Sandra Lee with Ben Youcef.

EDITOR'S NOTE:
This column, published in the tradition of Marcel Proust's Remembrance of Things Past, *is an example of how what seems an idyllic life, with hopes and reams for the future, can change within weeks or at least within a few years. The same fate that awaited Sandra Lee and Andrew Cuomo happens to hundreds of other couples in different ways, although not with such high profiles as the once "Dynamic Duo."*

Andrew Cuomo served as the 56th governor of New York from 2011 to 2021. Before that, his father, Mario Cuomo, was elected Governor three times.

In 2021, Andrew was forced to resign his office amid numerous allegations of sexual misconduct. At the time of his resignation, he was the longest-serving governor in the United States still in position.

Left photo: **Chris Christie** of New Jersey Right photo: **Martha Stewart.**

Many women came forth alleging sexual harassment. The governor's attorneys denounced the allegations as false, but the charges persisted until Cuomo was forced from office. In a statement, the governor said, "I now understand that my interactions may have been insensitive or too personal."

In the wake of her separation from Cuomo, Sandra Lee underwent a complete hysterectomy seven years after her double masectomy. She told the press, "I am happy not to have any more halo of worry hanging over my head."

As of this writing, Miss Lee, since 2021, has been involved with a boyfriend, an Algerian, Ben Youcef, who is thirteen years her junior. She called him "her sweet boyfriend;" and openly thanked him for his support during her medical horrors. Friends of the couple affectionately refer to them as "Bendra."

In November of 2025, Cuomo launched a widely publicized bid for a political comeback, running for mayor of New York City in that year's election. In the primary, despite leading in most Democratic polls, he lost to the otherwise relatively unknown Zohran Mamdani in what was widely evaluated as a major upset. After switching his political affiliation from Democratic to Independent, he continued his run, then lost again to Mamdani in the general election.

Cheerfully roaring through an abbreviated "make it easy on yourself" **Kwanzaa cake** recipe, **Sandra Lee** breaks time constraints in most of the recipes she crafts.

Andrew Cuomo announced his bid for NYC mayor in March 2025. He initially ran in the Democratic primary but lost to **Zohran Mamdani,** later launching an independent bid for mayor in July of the same year.

June 2017

Springtime in Paris Meets the Fires of Early Autumn

EMMANUEL MACRON

Mating Games for the *Président de la République*

The election of the youngest president in the history of France has focused world attention on May-December romances. A former civil servant and investment banker, Emmanuel Macron, 39, is married to Brigitte, the First Lady of France, who is 65. Ironically, Macron is now the stepfather of Laurence Auzière, who was born in 1977, the same year as himself.

Actually, a May-December marriage is the wrong term. More appropriate to the Macrons' situation is "May-September." Attractive, charming, hardworking, and supple, Brigitte might be experiencing the first few falling leaves of autumn, certainly not the cold winds of December.

While attending high school in his home town of Amiens, France, 15-year-old Macron asked to confer with his teacher, Brigitte Auzière, one day after school. Alone in the empty classroom, she asked him how she could help him. "You can begin by giving me a long, lingering kiss," he told her. When she objected, he said, "It's all right. I'm going to make you my wife." He ignored the fact that at the time, she was a married woman with three children.

When his parents learned of his obsession with his teacher, Macron was shipped off to Paris to complete high school. He promised Brigitte, "I'll be back."

He lived up to his promise, and, so it was rumored, their intimate relationship continued for decades. In 2006, she finally divorced her first husband, banker André-Louis Auzière, and, at last, married Macron in 2007.

He'd gone from teacher's pet to teacher's husband. In the 2016 election, Macron defeated his Alt-Right competitor, the National Front's candidate, Marine Le Pen. Her supporters launched more attacks on Macron's private life than they did on his policies. He was accused of having gay affairs and mocked as "Brigitte's toy boy." His enemies spread false rumors that she had to wipe the jam off his mouth after breakfast and give him a smack on the butt when he misbehaved. She was also denounced as a "menopausal Barbie."

He dismissed such charges as sexist. "There are many younger men out there who would like to date older women, but hold back because of an appalling double standard in society. It's always been all right for

It was an (unconventional) love story that evoked a HUGE reaction from a nation that's fascinated with the nuances of love. Here are the *Président de la République*, **Emmanuel Macron**, with the schoolteacher who made him her pet, the former **Brigitte Auzière**

Affable and urbane, with movie-star good looks, **Macron** is the most charming and charismatic French President to be elected in LOOONG time. Here, standing, he celebrates France's victory over Croatia at the 2018 World Cup in Moscow.

older men to marry younger women. Take my counterpart in America, *(a reference to Donald and Melania Trump)*, the President and his First Lady."

During the French presidential election, a Parisian psychiatrist, Dr. Françoise Gerber, issued an opinion that we consider apropos, smart, kind-hearted, and pertinent:

"Expect a lot of scrutiny if you're a woman marrying or dating a young man. Don't necessarily go for a societally approved marriage, but go with the man who has captured your heart, who has an energy level to match your own, and who appreciates the beauty that time has etched into your face, and your experience which has mellowed you into the remarkably fine woman you are today."

***

In Hollywood, May-September romances have long been commonplace. Clark Gable got the ball rolling when, as a 17-year-old, he came under the influence of his acting teacher, Josephine Dillon, born in 1884. He later married her, but she received abusive and insulting mail from his fans until her death in 1971. The King of Hollywood had died in 1960.

In the Oscar-winning patriotic tearjerker, *Mrs. Miniver* (1942), Richard Ney played Greer Garson's son. The following year, he married her.

In more recent history, Demi Moore, after divorcing Bruce Willis, wed Ashton Kutcher, despite a 16-year age difference.

The beat goes on. In 2009, Samantha ("Sam") Taylor-Wood directed Aaron Johnson as John Lennon in the biopic, *Nowhere Boy*. He was only 18; she was 42. In England in 2012, the director and her leading man were married, each taking the surnames, "Taylor-Johnson."

They have two daughters. Aaron's most recent picture is Tom Ford's thriller, *Nocturnal Animals* (2016). Sam recently directed *Fifty Shades of Grey*.

Vive la difference! was the response of some hipster entertainment-industry couples when it came to explaining the chronological gaps between couples in love.

Examples of older women falling for younger men include *(left photo)* **Josephine Dillon**, **Clark Gable**'s acting coach and wife;

Greer Garson, shown on the *upper right* with **Richard Ney**, her co-star (he portrayed her son) in *Mrs. Miniver* (1942);

and **Ashton Kutcher**, sixteen years younger than his wife and *inamorata*, **Demi Moore.** Their love affair ultimately ended in the divorce courts.

A Veteran Travel Writer Mourns
THE WILLFUL DESTRUCTION OF
UKRAINE
& Other Sites of Historic Interest

In the late 1950s, Arthur Frommer published a best-selling guidebook to the capitals of Europe and named it *Europe on $5 a Day*. It opened up postwar travel to many low-budget visitors left in droves to explore then-inexpensive Rome, Paris, London, Florence, and Venice. As a then-young and idealistic reporter, I was hired to write about, in depth, the travel scenes of Western Europe: England, France, Spain, Switzerland, Italy, and many other (at the time) less-visited countries such as Portugal and Denmark.

American travel to Western Europe flourished, and there emerged a demand from readers who wanted travel guides to destinations behind what Winston Churchill had chillingly defined as "The Iron Curtain."

Off I went on an amazing voyage of discovery, promoting then-exotic "new frontiers" in travel.

Since Frommer had already published the travel guide I'd researched and written to West Germany, it seemed logical to begin with an "expansion" into East Germany, known at the time as the *Deutsch Demokratische Republik*, then under Soviet control.

It was nearing midnight as my car pulled into "Checkpoint Charlie." I drove into Eastern Europe for the first time as a border guard shined a flashlight directly into my face. "You have blue eyes, so you are welcome," he said to me, without much, it seemed "political finesse."

Wherever I went in East Germany, I knew I was being spied upon and followed. Perhaps it was Vladimir Putin himself—stationed at the time in East Berlin as a professional bureaucrat of the Soviet Union's KGB—who ordered that I be followed in case I was a spy.

As years went by, some of the tourist authorities for the various Eastern European government got to know me and the travel guides I was producing. Things became easier as the perception spread that I was bringing in tourists with hard currencies to spend.

More of my Frommer guides followed, including a prominent one to Hungary that featured the ancient and fascinating capital of Budapest, which many westerners combined with visits to neighboring Austria.

At the time, the most poignantly glorious touristic destination of Eastern Europe was Prague, the monument-studded capital of Bohemia. Many of its touristic attractions survived World War II. Today, the city's entire historic core is a UNESCO World Heritage Site.

Two views of **Darwin** exploring, as an early writer & researcher at **The Frommer guides**, the touristic marvels of Europe.

This iconic title was associated with a travel guide series for which **Darwin Porter** developed and expanded over the course of five eventful decades..

It highlighted the postwar Go-Go years of European (and world) tourism, when dozens of countries "opened up" either for the first time, or after long closures forced upon them by the rigors of World War II.

Now, to Darwin's horror, Vladimir Putin is willfully destroying many of the touristic glories that once were the pride of the nations that contained them. Ukraine, for now, is a premier example. Others are in danger of following.

Could it be that Boomers, during their postwar heyday, enjoyed touristic options that will never reach the lofty heights of their Arthur Frommer-era diversity—ever again?

In the U.S.S.R.'s territory of Georgia, it was a shock to see many commemorative statues honoring Josef Stalin, a "hometown hero" despite his mass murder of millions of other Soviets.

I visited (and wrote about) landlocked Armenia, in the highlands of Western Asia, home to a rich cultural heritage dating back to 860 B.C. During World War I, 1.5 million Armenians were slaughtered by Turks in one of recent history's most prolonged acts of genocide.

In Bulgaria, it was wise for motorists to carry some local currency. The underpaid police often stopped motorists for alleged traffic violations. For payment of the equivalent of $5 in local currency, ("For your children!" I always said with a smile while passing off the bribes) foreign motorists could almost always continue on their merry way.

Americans used to flock to Romania for visits to Transylvania in search of the Castle of Dracula, made famous in Bram Stoker's 1897 Gothic novel. Partly in jest, innkeepers warned that vampires don't usually emerge until after midnight.

There are (or were, in an era when politics with Russia were less fraught than they are today) so many other countries to explore: Azerbaijan, for example. Positioned as a buffer zone between Eastern Europe and Western Asia, it boasts the Caspian Sea as its eastern frontier.

How many people do you know who have explored landlocked Uzbekistan, where the Uzrel is the dominant language? Uzbekistan, you'll quickly learn, was a flourishing independent kingdom in the 8th-6th Centuries, B.C.

Armenia

Sofia, Bulgaria

The best for last was the once-glorious nation of Ukraine, populated with handsome and industrious people with a richly folkloric and fertile culture. It used to be the friendliest destination in Eastern Europe, with staggering numbers of sophisticated hipsters fluent in English.

In its historically important city of Lviv, forty miles from the border of Poland, some 2.5 million visitors used to flock to its annual jazz festival. Those days are gone.

Those early dreams of mine—now dying or altogether dead—involved the transformation of Eastern Europe into thriving touristic destinations. Hopefully, they'll emerge from the present Russian massacres into a happier future. It's my fervent hope that the people of Ukraine will arise from their ashes. No nation deserves to suffer as much as it has. Now, its citizens are facing destructive onslaughts equivalent to what their grandparents faced from the Nazis during World War II.

I fervently hope that the carnage of Russia's cruel aggression toward its Western neighbors will not drag on endlessly.

After all, Putin can't live forever.

Lviv, Ukraine.

Kiev, Ukraine.

The Curious Ironies of
TRICIA NIXON

(Remember Her?)

First Daughter, First Lady, or Future Queen?

When he was President of the United States, Richard M. Nixon had a dream: He had two beautiful daughters, and he wanted to arrange marriages for each of them with the sons of powerful families.

Conspiring with Mamie Eisenhower, he had already engineered the wedding, in 1968, of his younger daughter, Julie, to David Eisenhower, the grandson of former U.S. President, Dwight D. Eisenhower. Still going strong today, the marriage produced two daughters and a son. In 2010, Julie and David co-authored a book on Ike, detailing his role in winning World War II.

After Julie married, Nixon focused on nuptials for his older daughter, Patricia ("Tricia"), born in 1946. He referred to the blonde beauty as "a budding Grace Kelly," but he feared that at the age of 24, she was "getting a little long in the tooth."

He envisioned her marrying into a political family, and perhaps starting a new dynasty, based on the genetic union of the Nixon with the Bush families.

He knew that George H.W. Bush had a 22-year-old son, George W. Bush, who had reached a marriageable age. He invited the young man to a dinner in Washington to honor the astronauts of the Apollo 8 mission, which had orbited the moon. It was agreed that at the party, Tricia would be the date of "Baby Bush," as Nixon called him.

Bush was already intoxicated when he arrived at the White House to pick up Tricia to escort her to a lavish dinner. He arrived with the intention of taking her out on the party circuit after dinner before returning her to the White House. At first, the White House security detail was not going to let him inside the gates. In his recent memoir, Bush himself admitted what a disaster their date had been.

"At dinner, I reached for some butter, knocked over a glass, and watched in horror as a stain of red wine crept across the table toward Tricia. Then I fired up a cigarette, prompting a polite suggestion from Tricia that I not smoke. The date came to an end immediately after dinner, when she asked me to take her back to the White House."

His aides later informed Nixon that "young 'W' is a drunkard, a womanizer, and has the personality of a frat house animal."

Moving on from the Bush fiasco, Nixon had an even bigger dream, and that involved the uniting of the House of Nixon with the House of Windsor, then residing in Buckingham Palace.

For years, Nixon had told confidants, "Liz and I are kissin' cousins," referring, of course, to Queen Elizabeth II.

Burke's Peerage, the official record-keeper of Britain's nobility, has long stated that Richard Nixon, the son of a Whittier, California, grocer, was actually a direct descendant of King Edward III (d. 1377). That made Nixon very distantly related to both QEII and Sir Winston Churchill.

"I felt that the president secretly wanted to be an English lord,"

Three views of then-First-Daughter TRICIA NIXON

Upper photo: Pretty and single, an unwilling role model for **conservative Miss Americas.**

Middle photo: At the White House, under the glare of matchmakers yearning for a marital alliance with **Charles, the Prince of Wales,** and

Lower photo: Artfully poised with a look resembling a princess, and clad in embroidered silk organdy, **Tricia Nixon** appears in the White House's Rose Garden on June 12, 1971 with her groom, **Edward Finch Cox**. Other than the royal trappings, the ceremony was as American as apple pie. A critic snidely fumed, "The dozens of florists who provided the ceremony's thousands of flowers were almost as carefully culled as the guest list itself."

Herb Klein, former Nixon aide, revealed. "He longed for social distinction."

Anholt Smith, who had known Nixon since childhood, claimed, "He behaved like a Napoléon, very imperious. He gave you the feeling you were traveling with God."

One afternoon, Nixon startled his aides by announcing, "You're looking at the father of the future Queen of England."

In his search for a son-in-law, he focused on Princes Charles, who at 21 was young, free, single, and the world's most eligible bachelor. In 1970, Nixon invited him to the White House for an official visit. Charles seemed fit and virile, capable of producing an heir to the British throne. He had a lean, athletic form and was known for peeling off his shirts to reveal a hairy chest and toned pecs. He enjoyed playing polo and galloping with the fox hunters.

Nixon had Tricia immaculately groomed and dressed to meet her Prince Charming.

Anthony Holden, royal biographer, said, "Seating plans constantly had Charles and Tricia side by side, while the program had them spending all of each day together—even to being left alone with each other in various parts of the White House. "

Unlike the David/Julie mating, Charles and Tricia turned out to be an incompatible couple. Charles later claimed that he was "distinctly annoyed" at having Tricia pushed onto him. He also told aides that he found Nixon's daughter "plastic and artificial."

Eventually, and with a mind of her own, Tricia chose her own husband, wedding Edward Finch Cox, a Harvard Law student, on June 12, 1971 in the Rose Garden of the White House. Today, he is a corporate attorney in Manhattan, and the parent of a son, Christopher Nixon Cox, with Tricia.

Charles returned to England and, in time, proposed marriage to Amanda Knatchbull, Lord Mountbattan's granddaughter. She rejected his proposal. He later became besotted with Anna ("Whiplash") Wallace, a socially prominent beauty, but she dumped him, too, claiming, "He ignored me at the Palace Ball."

Finally, he married Lady Diana Spencer, and, as the saying goes, "The rest is history, chronicled in embarrassing detail in bio films, TV documentaries, and in countless books, newspapers, and magazine articles.

On March 19, 2015, during the administration of Barack Obama, Prince Charles returned to the White House for another State visit. At the time, although President Obama had two very young daughters, matchmaking this time was out of the question.

Charles was escorted by Camilla, his former mistress and now his second wife, the Duchess of Cornwall.

SCENES THAT PREFACE A WEDDING

The December 1968 wedding of Tricia's younger sister, Julie Nixon (born 1948) to the grandson (David Eisenhower) of former president Dwight D. Eisenhower, was markedly less ostentatious that that of her sister, Tricia. three years later. It was viewed at the time as the marital union of two of the country's most powerful political families.

The couple, celebrity sweethearts of the year, were determined to keep the ceremony private. "Whether my father won or lost, we had no desire to be married in the White House," Julie told a reporter years later from their home in Berwyn, PA. "We were not interested in being minor celebrities or in the hoopla."

In the photo above, Julie's mother (First Lady **Patricia Nixon**) shares a laugh with former First Lady **Mamie Eisenhower** during their planning of the nuptials. They had met for the first time during the 1952 Republican convention, where it had been announced that Richard Nixon would be Dwight Eisenhower's running mate.

YOUNG, FOOLISH, TIPSY, and SOAKED IN REPUBLICAN PARTY POLITICS

Future president **George W. Bush** from around the time he behaved "drunkenly and loutishly" during an "arranged by someone else" date with **Tricia Nixon**. News of its disastrous outcome was widely publicized as far away as the U.K.

The Saturday Evening Post
(Spring 1972)

Julie & David Eisenhower

"They certainly had a lot in common, these children of very famous families, accustomed all their lives to being on stage. Both were good-looking, intelligent, clean-cut, intense, conservative—none of the sixties rebelliousness for these two. They were the kind of kids every Republican would like to have for children."

Stephen E. Ambrose, *historian and author of* **Nixon: The Triumph of a Politician 1962-1972** *(1989)*

August 2015

Obama to Africa:
"I'll Be Back!"

In July of 2015, at least a dozen documentary filmmakers, including two from Hollywood, flew to Kenya and Ethiopia to accompany President Obama on his return to Africa. Highlights of his trip included a stopover in Kenya, the birthplace of his father, Barack Sr., who eventually abandoned his wife and son. In his native Kenya, he became a major economist.

Obama's trip to Kenya was the first to his father's homeland since winning the White House, as well as the first visit of a sitting American president. But he promised it would not be his last. Upon leaving, he told Kenyans, "I'll be back," mirroring the famous movie line uttered by Arnold Schwarzenegger.

During his state visit, Obama was clearly "a rock star" to that nation's youth. When his helicopter touched down at Kenyatta University, hundreds of students mobbed him, lining the streets as they waved and cheered, took photographs, and wore T-shirts with welcoming messages—HOPE, COURAGE, CHANGE.

In urban Nairobi, there was more of a security bubble around him, and he wasn't allowed to mingle with the crowds as he wanted to. At the city's Safaricom Indoor Arena, as the public address system played, "I'm coming home," he was greeted by some 4,500 cheering people.

He addressed the throng in Swahili, calling out, "Habari Zenu," meaning "How are you?" He also told them he was anxious to dig into some "ugali and sukumawiki" (bread made with maize flour and greens.).

"He's not just our familia," said Auma Obama, one of his many aunties. "He gets us! He gets us!"

He had an extended family reunion, which included members he met for the first time. "There are cousins and uncles and aunties who show up that you didn't know existed."

Obama's personal and presidential politics in Africa, during the final year of his presidency. In the middle and lower photo, Michelle and/or Malia and Sasha, are with him.

Many historians interpreted it as one of the most important diplomatic outreaches of his administration.

The president's welcome by Kenya's brutal dictator, Uhuru Kenyatta, was polite but restrained. He wasn't too happy hearing Obama's message of "tough love." Obama lectured him on corruption in government, gay rights, counter-terrorism, and women's rights.

On counter-terrorism practices, a Human Rights Watch accused the government of "extrajudicial killings, arbitrary detention, and torture." Gay sex is punished by 14 years in a dank prison with subhuman conditions.

Obama called Kenya's treatment of women "stupid," comparing it to a society that as a team "doesn't use half of its players."

This most recent visit was in sharp contrast to his first trip to Kenya as an impoverished student, when he lived among the people, visiting his ancestral home, and eating, drinking, and sleeping among the locals.

Before leaving, Obama promised Kenyans he would come back as part of his post-White House life. That message brought hope to the young people of Africa, as the filmmakers discovered during their interviews with students.

Currently, Africa has more than a billion people, 200 million of whom are between the ages of 15 and 24. "If change comes, it will not be from our ossified leaders holding onto power," said student Omar Allimadi. "It will come from frustrated young people who will rise up to take over a newly emerging Africa."

Many young people expressed the hope that Obama would return and run for president of Kenya, claiming that as the son of a Kenyan father, he would have that right.

Many students read into Obama's parting statement a future intention. "Your country is better off if you have new blood and new ideas. I'm still a pretty young man."

"Although the current leadership would oppose him, Obama would be sure to win," claimed student Simon Oudo, 25, who also washes cars for ten dollars a week. "As our native son, he owes half of his identity to our troubled country and, by greater measure, to Africa itself. He's in a unique position to bring change and hope to us. He could become another Nelson Mandela. Will he meet that challenge? History is calling to him. But will he hear its siren?"

School teacher Rashid Nakhungo, 42, said, "Obama could return and lead us into a brighter future, or else he can choose to stay in America, growing rich off book deals, $350,000 speeches, and living in luxury and comfort. The choice is up to him. I hope he will choose to truly win that Nobel Peace Prize that was prematurely awarded to him."

During Obama's two-day visit, he also flew to Addis Ababa, Ethiopia, another troubled country, a U.S. ally with serious human rights violations.

He brought a message of democracy and proclaimed, "I stand before you today, announcing to all within the sound of my voice that the future of Africa is up to Africans. I'm not just a lecturer from the west, but a native son come back home to tell you that I have a personal stake in the success of the continent of my roots."

Two views of **Barack Obama** with his paternal grandmother **Sarah Onyango Obama** (aka "Mama Sarah").

Upper photo: As a student during his first trip to Africa to visit the family of his father, Barack Obama, Sr., and

Lower photo: As the American President, in 2015, during his state visit to Kenya.

Portrait of the 44th First Family

Left to right: **Michelle, Malia, Barack,** and **Sasha Obama,** posed for a family portrait in the Oval Office in 2011. Barack's ground breaking administration ran from 2009 to 2017

POLITICS

Boomer Octogenarians and Their "Silver Tsumani"

The Federal Department of Health and Human Services, in a recent report, asserted that the 85-and-older population is projected to double from its present 6.6 million to 14.4 million by 2040. Readers of this magazine are likely to be among the most deeply affected. The first of the Baby Boomers, born in 1946 in the aftermath of history's greatest war, will become octogenarian in three short years. And three former presidents, Bill Clinton, George W. Bush, and Donald Trump, will become octogenarian before the end of this decade.

Celebrities who have recently joined (or are on the verge of joining) the "Octogenarian Club" include Paul McCartney, Harrison Ford, Michael Bloomberg (former mayor of New York City), and Joy Behar.

Joe Biden is not a Baby Boomer. On November 20, 2022, he became the first octogenarian to sit in the Oval Office. When he entered the world, America was a very different place, and the most disastrous war in world history was raging.

The Allies were 18 months from launching the D-Day landings on the beaches of Normandy. *Casablanca,* starring Humphrey Bogart and Ingrid Bergman, would be released in two months. Bing Crosby was No. 1 on the music charts, and the average annual income was $1,885. (That is not a misprint.) Life expectancy for men was 65. Ironically, that was the age of retirement, too.

It is said that the presidency irretrievably ages, fast, whomever fills that office. Exceptions include George H.W. Bush, who died at 94, and Jimmy Carter, who will turn 99 in October of 2023.

When Trump was inaugurated in 2017, he became the oldest man ever to become president. Biden, however, beat his record. As one columnist noted, "Neither man is a spring chicken." If Biden seeks and is elected to a second term in 2024, he'll be 86 when he departs from office.

As Peter Baker wrote, "The aging of the American political establishment is a testament to medical advances that have not only extended life expectancy but made it possible for many to play productive roles in society long past what their parents or grandparents were able to do. Eighty is the new 70, as it were."

After considerable research, Sheryl Gay Stolberg wrote: "Scientists who study aging stress that chronological age is not the same as biological age—and that the two often diverge as people grow older. It is true that older people tend to decline physically, and the brain undergoes changes. But in people who are active, experts say that the brain continues to evolve, and some brain functions even improve—a phenomenon that experts call 'the neuroplasticity of aging.'"

Dr. Dilip Jeste, a psychiatrist who studies aging at the University of California, sounds a hopeful note. "This idea that old age is associated only with decline is not true. There are studies done all over the world which show that in people who keep active physically, socially, mentally, and cognitively, there is increased connectivity among specific networks, and even new neurons and synapses can form in selected brain regions with older age."

To illustrate some of the ironies associated with how we view our cult heroes, heroines, and icons, we've

---

Baby Boomers have morphed, gracefully or not, into Senior Citizens, with all the perks associated with their status as a (sometimes) united voting block.

With this power comes the added muscle of—in many cases—the security of owning real estate at percentages that surpass that of the general (younger) population. And if events worked out for them and (presumably) if their children have left the nest, many control impressive savings and disposable incomes.

designated Barbra Streisand as "Octogenarian of the Month. The little girl with the great voice from Brooklyn turned 80 in 2022.

Thankfully, she'll be able to live comfortably in her senior years, thanks to her net worth of $400 million.

BLOOD MOON'S OCTOGENARIAN OF THE MONTH

Barbra Streisand in 1966 and (lower photo) with **Robert Redford** in *The Way We Were* (1973).

RUNNERS-UP FOR BLOOD MOON'S OCTOGENARIAN OF THE MONTH

(upper photo): **Harrison Ford**, and (lower photo): **Paul McCartney**

THE DEATH OF AMERICA'S OLDEST LIVING PRESIDENT

On December 29, 2024, **Jimmy Carter**, the 39th President of the United States, passed into history at the age of 100 years and 89 days. He was the longest-lived U.S. President in history and the first centenarian President.

After two years in hospice care, he died at his home in Plains, Georgia, the state of which he had been the 76th governor. A period of national mourning was announced by **President Biden**. The former First Lady, **Rosalynn Carter**, had died on November 19, 2023 at the age of 96.

Carter surpassed the lifespan of George H.W. Bush, who was 94 years old when he died on November 1, 2010. Both men were born in 1924. Biden declared a day of national mourning and a Federal holiday for January 9.

As a Democrat, Carter had sought a second term as President, losing to the former movie star Ronald Reagan in 1980.

In 2002, Carter won the Nobel Peace Prize for his post-presidential work trying to improve the lives of hundreds of Americans.

In a 2019 interview with *People*, Carter claimed that he never expected to live as long as he had, claiming that the secret to a long life was a good marriage.

Women We Love

JACKIE SPEIER

Congresswoman from California

Another Jackie in the White House?

Years Before Her Election to Congress, on a Fact-Finding Mission to Guyana, She Survived Five "Point-Blank" Gunshot Wounds from the Kool-Aid Killers

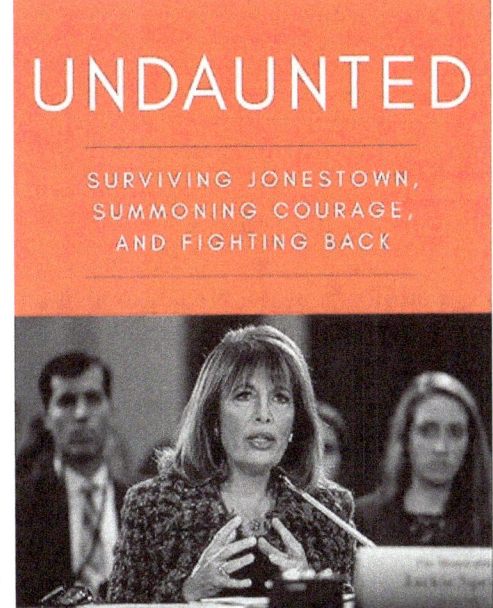

The choices she made at Jonestown, to survive against unfathomable odds, empowered **Jackie Speier** with a resolve to become a vocal proponent of human rights.

Since then, she's been on the right side of history, particularly since the Donald Trump takeover, many dozens of times.

As one year passes and another is rung in, 2018 will go down in history as "The Year of the Woman."

As never before, more women have run for political office—and many have won—not only 120 seats in Congress, but as an occasional U.S. Senator or holder of a state office. Winners include a Native American lesbian from the grain belt state of Kansas.

Each of them has a story to tell, often one of courage, and how they had to overcome roadblocks.

The #MeToo Movement has also shaken up the nation.

To single out only one woman, Jackie Speier has won re-election to California's 14th District (San Mateo County and the southwest quarter of San Francisco). She has a unique story to tell, and does so valiantly in her newly released memoir, *Undaunted: Surviving Jonestown, Summoning Courage, and Fighting Back*, published by Little A.

In 1978, when she was 28, she was working as a staffer in the office of Congressman Leo Ryan. She agreed to fly with him on a fact-finding, rather dangerous trip to Jonestown, Guyana.

Dozens of reports had come in about alleged human rights abuses at the Peoples Temple in Jonestown.

Jim Jones was the charismatic leader of a fanatical cult that consisted mainly of American citizens.

According to reports, many people were being held there against their will.

Jackie had a number of letters to deliver to the followers of Jones from family members back in the States. Once in Jonestown, she was shocked that most of the relatives wouldn't even read the letters from members of their families. "They had a glazed look in their eyes, like they'd been brainwashed."

Ryan and Jackie were introduced to the "Second Messiah," who was sitting on a makeshift throne, like a king. He ordered them to leave Jonestown, citing religious freedom.

That night, many members of his disenchanted flock secretly slipped Jackie notes or spoke to her in private, claiming that they were virtual prisoners, held against their will.

Jackie Speier appears here with California Congressman **Leo Ryan** shortly before their eventful investigation of Jim Jones's Peoples' Temple in Jonestown, Guyana in 1978. Unlike Jackie, who survived five bullet wounds, Ryan was killed in the same attack.

Here's the charismatic Congressman **Leo Ryan** during his voluntary incarceration at Folsom State Penitentiary in 1970. His intention at the time involved an up-close-and-personal exposure to prison life as a means of legislatively correcting its premises.

When news of these "traitors," as he called them, reached Jones, he went berserk, making dangerous threats of retaliation.

The next morning, Jackie commandeered a dump truck, onto which she hustled twenty deserters from the cult. Ryan appeared with his white shirt bloodied. A crazed member of the cult had stabbed him.

She helped one of the evacuees aboard before the truck headed down a rocky road to a small airstrip in the middle of the jungle. She was helping people board a small plane when a red tractor-trailer ominously screeched to a halt only feet from the getaway plane.

A dozen men jumped from the rear of the truck and opened fire with automatic weapons.

Jackie hit the ground near the wheel of the plane, pretending to be dead. In spite of that, a deranged follower of Jones opened fire, shooting five bullets into her back, leg, and right arm before fleeing with the other guerillas on that truck.

To her horror, she noticed that Ryan was dead, his body near that of another corpse, NBC's Don Harris.

For an astonishing 22 hours, which she called "the most agonizing of my life," she lay near death.

At last, a Guyanese cargo plane with soldiers came to the aid of the wounded. Jackie, along with the other survivors, was flown to the United States, where she got emergency medical care that saved her, as she had lost a lot of blood. She later learned that Jones and 900 of his followers had consumed Kool-Aid laced with poison. Almost every member of the cult was dead.

When Jackie regained consciousness in a hospital, she thought of her brave mother, an immigrant, who had survived the "Armenian Genocide."

"While in Jonestown, I vowed that if I ever escaped alive from that hellhole, I would make every day of my life count, each day would be precious to me, and I vowed to live my life as fully as possible. I would devote the rest of my life to public service."

And so she did.

***

Throughout her career, Jackie Speier has taken strong stands on the issues of the day, including "the health of the planet." *Newsweek* included her among its "150 Fearless Women" of the world, and *Politico 50* listed her as one of the top influencers in American politics today.

In some circles, there is talk of running her for President of the United States.

"One day," she says, "not today, nor even tomorrow, but one day, a woman will occupy the Oval Office."

Jim Jones. wearing glasses, was the cult leader whose egomania and Satanic visions led to the death, by cyanide, of more than 900 members of his flock. Many were children

He appears here with some of them, shortly before their collective deaths.

Speier has insisted that Jones and his cohorts orchestrated a mass murder, not a voluntary mass suicide, at Jonestown. "Many of the deceased were children and infants. How could their deaths be defined as voluntary suicides?"

Having retired from the U.S. Congress in 2023, **Jackie Speier** announced that she would run for the San Mateo (California) County Board of Supervisors in 2024, more than 40 years after she was first elected to that same board.

About a year later, she announced on her Facebook page that she had been successfully treated for breast cancer, urging women to NOT skip their annual mammograms. She continues today as a ferocious advocate of human rights from her home district near San Francisco.

JOHN HINCKLEY

The Man Who Tried to Kill Ronald Reagan

His Legal Defense Team Blamed the Insanity that Acquitted Him on His Sexual Obsession with a then-underaged Jodie Foster

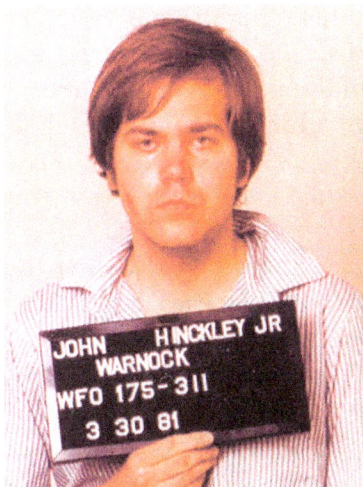

Will Ronald Reagan's crazed would-be assassin, John Hickley, Jr., finally go on trial for homicide? That's a thorny legal issue now facing Federal prosecutors.

On August 4, 2014, James Brady, formerly then-President Ronald Reagan's Chief Press Officer, died—the tragic after-effect, 33 years later, of having been shot in the brain during Hinckley's attempt on Reagan's life. At last, after the decades since that nightmarish event, Brady's death has been officially defined as a homicide.

There is no statute of limitations on homicide. Based on recent court rulings about Hinckley's mental state, the question is, could the Oklahoma-born would-be assassin, now 59 years old, be sane enough to face homicide charges?

Let's go back in time: It is 2:25pm on March 30, 1981, and President Reagan is leaving Washington, D.C.'s Hilton Hotel after a speech to the AFL-CIO.

Suddenly six shots ring out from a .22 caliber Rohm RG-14 revolver. One of the bullets ricochets off the President's armor-plated Lincoln limousine and penetrates his left side. It hits his rib before lodging in the spongy tissue an inch from his heart. A lung is punctured and collapses. He comes very close to instant death.

Police officer Thomas Delahanty and Secret Serviceman Timothy McCarthy were hit, but survived. Jim Brady (his experience an inspiration for partially successful attempts at gun control) was also hit, and subsequently paralyzed for life on the left side of his body.

Almost three months after the shooting, at his trial, Hinckley was charged with thirteen offenses, but found not guilty by reason of insanity. He claimed that the shooting "was the greatest love offering in the history of the world."

Upper left, Mug shot, snapped in 1981, of 25-year-old **John Hinkley** after his attempted assassination of *(upper right)* then-president **Ronald Reagan.**

Lower photo: a self-portrait of **John Hinckley.** His body language replicates a scene with Robert De Niro in *Taxi Driver* (1976) in which De Niro's character threatens death to a "lowlife" who menaces an underaged prostitute portrayed by Jodie Foster.

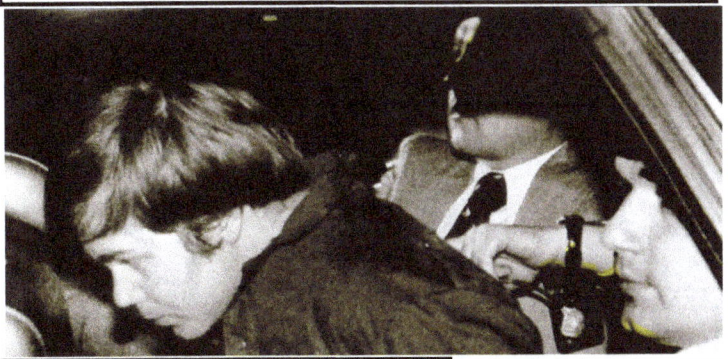

John Hinckley, hauled off for interrogation by the police in the aftermath of his attempted assassination of Ronald Reagan in 1981.

His actions sowed havoc among law enforcement and media observers, and led to the partial paralysis and eventual death of **James Brady** *(photo, right)*, Reagan's press secretary. **The Brady Bill,** aimed at limiting easy access to weapons, was eventually passed after arduous lobbying by his wife and later, widow,

In court, his lawyers cited his romantic and sexual obsession with the then-underaged screen actress Jodie Foster.

Hinckley figured that by killing Reagan, his fame would be the equal of Foster's, allowing him to pursue her while "accessorized" with a name as famous as hers.

As Hinkley's role model, he cited Lee Harvey Oswald, JFK's assassin.

Over the years, Hinckley's lawyers, bankrolled by his wealthy parents, have scored many victories for their bizarre client. His first requests for outside visits came in 1987, but were denied after his room was searched. Police discovered many pictures of Foster, along with letters he had exchanged with serial killer Ted Bundy. Hinckley had also tried to obtain the address of mass murderer Charles Manson.

In 1999, Hinckley was allowed to leave the hospital for supervised visits with his parents. His father had been a financial supporter of George H.W. Bush in 1980. Hinckley's older brother, Scott, had dinner at the home of Vice President Bush's son, Neil Bush, the day after the assassination attempt on Reagan's life.

In 2000, Hinckley was granted unsupervised visits with his family, although that privilege was revoked when it was discovered he'd spent his time gathering up photos of Jodie Foster, and that he had smuggled them back into his hospital.

In 2005, a judge ruled that Hinckley was to be allowed unsupervised visits to his parents' home in Williamsburg, Virginia, up to four annual trips of four nights each. The court determined that his depression and his psychotic disorders were in full remission.

In 2007, he was allowed month-long visits. Two years after that, a Federal judge ordered that he be allowed a dozen annual visits of ten days at a time, and that he be granted a driver's license. Prosecutors objected, claiming that he was still a menace to society and had "inappropriate thoughts about women," particularly Foster.

In November of 2011, his lawyers requested that Hinckley live full time outside the hospital, although the Justice Department opposed that, arguing that he was known to have tricked and manipulated his doctors in the past. But by December of 2013, the court ordered that his outside visits be extended even further.

Since August of this year, however, the possible ruling of homicide in regard to Brady's death has brought a different twist to the Hinckley case. Were his lawyers allowed too much leeway in portraying Hinckley as insane during his trial? Many believe he should have been sentenced to life imprisonment.

In my latest biography, *Love Triangle—Ronald Reagan, Jane Wyman, and Nancy Davis*, I came across two human interest stories not reported

SCREAMING, RESOUNDING CHAOS followed in the immediate wake of Hinckley's shootings.

Hinckley claimed, in court, that his attempted assassination of Reagan was an "unprecedented demonstration of love" to impress actress **Jodie Foster**, who resisted any contact with him either before or during the years that followed the chaos he wreaked.

Depicted above is **Jodie Foster** portraying an teenaged prostitute in the film that Hinckley said, in court, inspired his weaponized attack on Ronald Reagan.

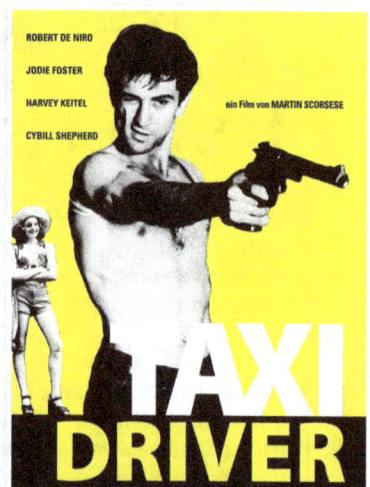

Robert de Niro, another of Hinckley's role models, getting gun-happy, in *Taxi Driver* (1976)

at the time of the assassination attempt on Reagan's life.

Adjacent to Reagan that nightmarish day in 1981 was Jerry Parr, chief of his Secret Service detail. At the sound of pop, pop, pop, Parr grabbed Reagan by the waist, hurled him into the back seat of the limo, and then piled on top of him, presumably shielding his body from further bullets. Not knowing he'd been shot, Reagan cursed him, claiming he'd broken his rib, which may have the object that punctured his lung. "I can't breathe," he cried out in agony.

He later apologized to Parr. "Instead of cursing him, I should have thanked him for saving my life."

Dr. Daniel Ruge, Chief Physician at the White House, was also traveling with Reagan on that fateful March afternoon. Ruge was at his side as they rushed to George Washington University Hospital. When they got there, he ordered that the President be stripped naked so that he could search for the bullet's entry wound. He also ordered immediate blood transfusions. A few minutes later, Reagan was wheeled into the operating room for emergency surgery.

Ruge later claimed he'd made a mistake in not having Vice President George H.W. Bush notified that he should assume the duties of Acting President.

Nancy Reagan and Daniel Ruge had had a long history together. In the mid 1940s, before she left her parents' home in Chicago to try her chances as an actress on Broadway, she'd been involved in a serious relationship with him. Had she not left Chicago to pursue her theatrical ambitions, she might very well have become Mrs. Daniel Ruge instead of Mrs. Ronald Reagan, First Lady of America.

History has some strange twists.

***

In June of 2022, wire services carried the bulletin REAGAN SHOOTER FREED.

A U.S. District Court Judge ruled that Hinckley will have his electronic devices removed and will have unrestricted freedom after spending two decades in a mental hospital.

While confined, he was occasionally allowed to go unguarded in the community in Virginia with certain travel restrictions.

He was also ordered to continue submitting to ongoing therapy following an insanity claim. He stayed with his mother in Williamsburg, Virginia prior to her death in 2021.

At the time of his release, Hinckley was 67 years old. While in recovery, he sharpened his musical skills. In April of 2022, he wrote on Twitter that he would perform on July 8 at a sold-out concert in Brooklyn. However, the concert was canceled after death threats

He has posted music videos on YouTube for songs he recorded, "Places I Have Been," and "You and I Are Free."

In 2022, blogger Joe DeVita published this blurb on the web: **John Hinckley Jr.,** *(photo above)* the man who attempted to assassinate President Ronald Reagan in 1981, is currently seeking musicians for a new band.

"I'm starting a band. I'm looking for a bass player, drummer and lead guitarist. If you would like to be in my band and are serious about this, send bio to P.O. Box 240 Williamsburg, Va. 23187," wrote Hinckley on Twitter.

For his attempt to kill the President in a deranged plot to impress actress Jodie Foster, with whom he was obsessed after seeing her in the 1976 film *Taxi Driver*, Hinckley was ultimately found not guilty on 13 charges by reason of insanity in 1982. Four people were wounded in the shooting, including Reagan, who was shot in the chest via ricochet. One of the victims, **Press Secretary James Brady,** was permanently disabled as a result of his wounds and died 33 years later. The death was ruled a homicide as it was related to the bullet wound he sustained during the initial attack.

Ronald Reagan's
CODE OF THE SECRET SERVICE
Warner Brothers (1939)

Although very few whimsical bits of humor ever emerged from John Hinckley's attempt to assassinate Ronald Reagan, one of the few involved the Chief of Reagan's security team, Secret Service agent **Jerry Paar.**

At the first sounds of gunfire, with enough force to have perhaps broken Reagan's rib, he threw him onto the floor of the Presidential limo, then covered Reagan's body with his own as a defensive shield. After Reagan recovered from his wounds and his indignities, he thanked Parr for having saved his life.

In an ironic twist, Parr, as a young boy, had seen *Code of the Secret Service*, a movie in which Reagan had played Lt. Brass Bancroft of the Secret Service.

The picture was so terrible—at least in Reagan's view—that he pleaded with Warner Brothers not to release it. His request was denied. As an adolescent, Parr saw the movie at a Saturday matinee and decided there and then to become a Secret Service agent like Reagan on the screen.

With that in mind, and in appreciation for the heroism of **Agent Paar,** we here present a photo-montage of one of Ronald Reagan's B movies—one that he later wanted to forget.

Most of the details narrated within this episode were revealed within Darwin Porter's award-winning 2014 overview of the Hollywood adventures of three wannabee actors, two of whom went on to become the most powerful couple in the Free World.

IRONIES ABOUND

Today, thousands of Hollywood players from the Reagan's heyday continue to ask themselves, *"Who at the time, would ever have believed that a B-movie actor, consigned to accepting increasingly dismal roles, would ever wind up as a two-term President of the United States?"*

LOVE TRIANGLE
RONALD REAGAN, JANE WYMAN, & NANCY DAVIS

All the Gossip Unfit to Print
Darwin Porter &
Danforth Prince

Softcover, 636 pages,
with hundreds of photos.
Available everywhere now.

Ronald Reagan with his co-star, **Rosella Towne**

JUSTIN TRUDEAU
"Dreamboat" Sweeps to Power in Canada

North of the border in our good neighbor, Canada, there is a jubilant sense that it's the dawning of the Age of Aquarius. Its secretive, combative, staid, and ultra-conservative prime minister, Stephen Harper, was booted out of Ottawa in November.

Replacing him was the darling of the Liberal Party, Justin Trudeau, a 43-year-old, charismatic, good-looking, and charming new leader. He's been hailed for ushering in the second era of Trudeaumania, bringing back memories of his father, Pierre Trudeau, when he swept to power 47 years ago.

As a liberal, Justin favors such positions as the legalization of marijuana, and he's also pro-Choice. He's for gun control, health care, gay marriage, and immigration, all hot button issues still raging in the United States.

For his cabinet, half of its members are women, some others are from minority groups. "I want my cabinet to look like the face of Canada today."

Except for their political agendas, father and son are not alike. A former Minister of Justice, Pierre was a brilliant lawyer and an intellectual. Before becoming prime minister, Justin was a snowboard instructor, whitewater rafting guide, bungee jumper, camp counselor, high school teacher, nightclub bouncer, and boxer. (He still goes one boxing round every week.) He was also an actor (Hollywood has made offers), having starred in the 2007 CBS miniseries, "The Great War."

Unlike his father, Justin is happily married to Sophie Grégoire, a beauty vaguely reminiscent of Grace Kelly, and they have two boys and a girl. They met when they were children, but reunited in 2003 and were married in 2005. "She is one very, very, very lucky woman," said a former girlfriend. "I should know."

He makes a concession to Sophie: "I'll take you to the ballet if you let me bring a flask of Canadian whiskey."

Like his father, he's pursued beautiful women. When only a boy, he invited Princess Di, during a visit to Canada, to go skinny-dipping with him in a Canadian lake.

Unlike his recent predecessor, Justin has a sense of irreverence. In London, he was photographed mockingly performing a pirouette behind Queen Elizabeth's back. He says the "F" word on inappropriate occasions, and he once performed a male striptease at a charity event. When greeting visitors in his foyer, he often slides down the banister. He's been known to practice yoga in front of the Parliament building, and to smoke pot.

He's also a male pinup. Gay bars from Nova Scotia to Manitoba have plastered their walls with pictures of him in his boxing trunks. Teenaged girls flock to his appearances, yelling and screaming like he was Elvis in 1958.

In a survey of women, the most frequently used word to describe Justin was "dreamboat."

Upper photo: **Then Prime Minister Justin Trudeau** on the cover of the August 10, 2017 edition of *Rolling Stone*

Middle photo: Sporting a tattoo on his left biceps, he's seen sparring in a charity boxing match whose "applause quotient' ricocheted around the world, and

Lower photo: with his wife, **Sophie Grégoire** and their children on Inauguration Day, 2015

As one of three sons, Justin witnessed the disintegration of his parents' marriage. Margaret Sinclair was only half Pierre's age when they wed in 1971. As First Lady of Canada, she became tabloid fodder, having a publicized affair with Senator Teddy Kennedy. "I found Teddy more sympathetic to me than Pierre."

During her husband's stint as prime minister, she ran off and went on tour with the Rolling Stones and reportedly sustained an affair with Mick Jagger.

The Trudeaus separated in 1977, after which Pierre became involved in a high-profile affair with singer Barbra Streisand. As she said at the time, "If I become First Lady of Canada, I'll have to make my movies there and learn French."

Pierre also had a secret affair with Jackie Onassis, when her husband went back to his former mistress, opera diva Maria Callas.

"Now, Jackie wants to be First Lady of Canada," Ethel Kennedy quipped. "I hope he can afford her."

After he broke from Margaret, Pierre dated Canadian actress Margot Kidder, known for playing Lois Lane in those *Superman* movies. He never married again, but had his first daughter with Deborah Coyne. His son Michel had died in an avalanche.

Today, the press is hailing Margaret's comeback in Ottawa. Her erratic behavior in the past is blamed on a bipolar disorder, which landed her in a straitjacket and a padded cell.

"I had to undergo deep, deep treatments to get my brain health back." She also told the press that her greatest joy would involve winning the respect of her children and her grandchildren.

As an asset and a liability, Justin has inherited all of his father's friends, but also his enemies. "I've created a lot of excitement in Canada, a lot of great expectations. Many Americans are comparing Sophie and me to Jackie and Jack Kennedy. That wonderful couple faced great tragedy. My hope is that I'll live to see Canada enter a great new age and to bounce my grandchildren on my knee."

It was the 70s, and EVERYBODY was talking about Margaret Sinclair, Justin Trudeau's beguiling but notorious and very famous mother. Remember her?

Here's Justin Trudeau's mother, the former **Margaret Sinclair,** with 11-month-old **Justin** in 1972.

Margaret's relationship with Justin's since-deceased father, Pierre Trudeau, was complicated. "We had this hugely intergenerational marriage," she said years later in an interview. "I was in my early 20s, and he was a very urbane, sophisticated intellectual in his early 50s. We met in Tahiti when he was Canada's minister of justice and I was 19 and on vacation with my family."

After a two-year courtship, they shocked the rest of Canada by getting married in secret. Only about a dozen people attended the ceremony. It was so private that even Pierre's aides were told he'd gone skiing for the week.

"I was a darling wife when I was good, and when I was bad, I was the worst on the planet. I was fresh out of university. I was a flower child. I was very free-thinking for my time. I called 24 Sussex *(the official residence of the PM of Canada)* the crown jewel of the federal penitentiary system."

In 1979, on the night that her husband's party was overwhelmingly defeated in the Canadian election, Margaret—by then officially separated from him—was photographed dancing at Studio 54. Photos appeared in newspapers across Canada. She and Pierre officially divorced in 1984.

Margaret was diagnosed with bipolar disorder in 2000. In the years that followed, she raised public awareness of mental health issues. "When I was manic, it was grand mania," she says. "Where someone else might have run off with the guy from the 7-Eleven, I ran off with the Rolling Stones. I would spend all my money buying Birkin bags; somebody else would have spent all the grocery money. It's paralyzing either way. You don't have the ability to have a second, sober thought."

Since then, she has remained close to all of her children, including Justin. "I am almost shocked to see that I have grown old. But I am also amused."

Her anti-aging advice: "Get a 25-watt pink bulb and install it in your bathroom."

Without the benefit of decades of hindsight,

WHO WAS THE WORST U.S. PRESIDENT?

In spite of how historically tantalizing that question is, the bad news is that no one will be able to accurately answer it until forty years from now. Public ratings of a President in the months following his exit from office are usually dismissed as unreliable.

For example, Harry S Truman ranked a low 28 percent approval rating when he turned the presidency over to Dwight Eisenhower in 1953. Today, Truman is considered one of the greatest of U.S. presidents.

The former haberdasher from Missouri was having his third glass of bourbon when news reached him during the closing months of World War II that FDR had died. On the day he took office in 1945, he learned for the first time that the U.S. had developed an atomic bomb. He later dropped two of them on Japan, efficiently and quickly ending the greatest conflict in the history of humankind.

What's generally accepted as the most reliable source of presidential approval ratings is the Siena College of Research Institute. In its latest polling, Donald Trump emerged as noteworthy: Although for his overall performance he was rated near the bottom (No. 42 of 44 presidents) he was positioned in 10th place for "luck," and in 25th position as a President who was "willing to take risks."

In a survey of the nation's historians, Trump ranked #45 as the worst president in the history of America.

As a demonstration of the fallacy of early polling, Joe Biden ranked low on the scale of U.S. Presidents even before he took office. Today, he gets high ratings for his handling of the Coronavirus but low scores for the border crisis with Mexico.

So, who is in the "sub-basement" of the White House and usually evaluated as a Presidential disaster?

Until the inauguration of Donald Trump, the worst U.S. president was almost universally believed by historians to have been **James Buchanan** (1857-1861), depicted above with his collaborator, Vice President, and many believe, long-time companion, **William Rufus King**. So prevalent was the gossip about their alleged affair that the pejorative nickname "assigned" to them by their detractors was "Miss Nancy and Aunt Fannie."

The lower illustration, although not specifically associated with them during their administration, demonstrates some of the implications of that insult.

Also high on the list of "most disastrous presidencies" include those of "that racist drunk," **Andrew Johnson** (left photo) and **Donald Trump** (right).

In fairness, most historians believe that true assessments of that require decades of hindsight. But smart money from NYC to Las Vegas are insisting that when the dust settles, **THE DONALD** will emerge as the winner.

Two other "sometimes" contenders in the race for "worst presidencies" include **Richard Nixon** (left) and **George W. (aka "Bubba") Bush**, in part because of his disastrous mendacities about Iraq, its alleged weapons of mass destruction, and the war he sponsored in the Middle East.

Whereas Andrew Johnson was the first President to face impeachment, Trump was impeached twice (a record).

Born into poverty, Johnson labored as a tailor before ascending to the ranks of both governor and later, Senator of Tennessee. Because Lincoln had designated him as his Vice President, Johnson assumed the office of U.S. President a few moments after Lincoln was assassinated in 1865 at the end of the Civil War. In office, Johnson compared himself to Jesus Christ, and feared that Southern states would become "Africanized"—that is, taken over by former slaves. He opposed Emancipation and encouraged efforts to keep blacks as a perpetual underclass.

Traditionally, the official who's usually cited as the worst U.S. President is James Buchanan, a Pennsylvania lawyer who occupied the White House from 1857 to 1861. During his term, he did nothing to stop seven states from seceding from the Union, legislative acts which led to a disastrous Civil War where millions lost their lives. The South was left in ruins.

Buchanan's administration was also, until recently, the most corrupt in U.S. history, as millions of "public dollars" fell into private hands.

He lived in the White House with his intimate friend, William Rufus King, who had served as Vice President during the reign (1853-1857) of Franklin Pierce. Based on homosexual allegations, Congressmen mockingly called the couple, "Miss Nancy and Aunt Fannie," or else "Mr. Buchanan and his wife."

"James and Rufus" threw the most lavish parties in the history of the White House, with the President ordering his staff "to keep the liquor flowing." In 1861, on the dawn of the bloodiest war on U.S. soil in history, he left office.

At least, according to Robert Strauss, author of *Worst President Ever*, "Buchanan had the good taste not to run again and was a nice guy."

No one seriously believes that either **Harry S Truman** (upper tier photos) or **Joe Biden** (lower tier photos) qualify as candidates for "worst president. Yet it was bruited around, loudly, during their administrations that Truman's use of the atomic bomb during the final days of World War II, and Biden's "mishandling" of the Southern Border, qualify them as candidates. We loudly and emphatically disagree,

In the presidency's storied existence — from George Washington to Barack Obama — there has never been a president who, previous to his election, has entirely lacked both political and military service. **Donald Trump** has broken this barrier. Historians assessing his disastrous impact will not be kind.

Finally, since we're talking about misguided, incompetent, and/or corrupt contenders for **WORST PRESIDENT**, let's not overlook **Warren G. Harding** (1921-1923). Most of the irregularities that contribute to this assessment erupted after his early death midterm through his presidency. The biggest of the corruption scandals was Teapot Dome. Among the sexual indiscretions was his alleged fathering of an illegitimate child with his long-term mistress, Nan Britton.

JAMES DEAN

AND THE IRONIES OF HIS FAME

"James Dean was the "Other" (After Marilyn Monroe and JFK) most enduring icon of "The American Century"

—Darwin Porter

"Dream as if you'll live forever; live as if you'll die today."

—James Dean

Two ancient depictions of Cleopatra:

Left: Red-haired 1st Century A.D. fresco excavated from Herculaneum, and

Right: a Ptolmaic bas-relief identified as a portrait, accurate or not, of Cleopatra.

Fame is the most fickle of addictions. She's capricious when, with her magic wand, she bestows her recognition on just a select few.

During their respective eras, many people achieve greatness and a kind of short-term recognition, but in the long course of history; most are forgotten. Only a handful emerge, generations later, to re-capture the imagination of the world.

Cleopatra was not the greatest of the ancient pharaohs—her reign over Egypt was a disaster. But she immortalized herself through (highly politicized) affairs with both Julius Caesar and Marc Antony, then committed suicide with the poisonous bite of an asp as her empire crumbled around her. The drama, purported romance, and epic scope of her story prolonged the life of her legend.

Moving forward to the mid-20th Century:

Despite the huge numbers of household names that emerged, only three of them became enduring pop culture icons: John F. Kennedy, Marilyn Monroe, and James Dean.

As most historians agree, JFK was not the greatest of presidents. Had he lived, he'd have become soiled by the quagmire of Vietnam and his sexual indiscretions, his reputation permanently tarnished.

Marilyn did not have a particularly distinguished career, either. Most of her early films are still unknown to the general public. But as a pop icon, she's remembered and in many cases, celebrated by each new generation. Her affairs with the Kennedy brothers, her controversial death, and perhaps her status as "the ultimate blonde" made her a legend. Each of these three luminaries from "The American Century's" middle years—JFK, Marilyn, and Jimmy Dean—had one element in common: Each of them died young and violently, and each is forever associated with the implicitly tragic motto "Live fast, die young."

Had she lived, Marilyn might have evolved into an aging, blowsy showgirl, desperately clinging to her elusive glory and fast-fading sexual charms. As her last director, George Cukor said,

Left: **Peter Lawford** introducing **Marilyn Monroe** onstage at JFK's birthday celebration at Madison Square Garden, May 19, 1962.

Right photo, **JFK.**

Both of the superstars notoriously linked in the aftermath would be dead within three months and 18 months, respectively, of that widely publicized, dysfunctional, and scandal-soaked celebration.

with pointed irony, "Marilyn was not meant for old age."

In contrast, as the youngest of the three (he died when he was 24), Jimmy might have gone on to make some of the greatest movies in Hollywood. At the time of his death, he could have had virtually any role he wanted in Hollywood. He was big, and growing bigger by the day.

Through Blood Moon Productions, in honor of the 60th anniversary of James Dean's death (September 30, 1955); Darwin Porter released the most complete overview of his unfulfilled life ever told. During the fifty years he spent researching it, hundreds of witnesses, friends, "frenemies," and enemies, emerged with testimonials—many of them soaked with scandal—that have never been published before.

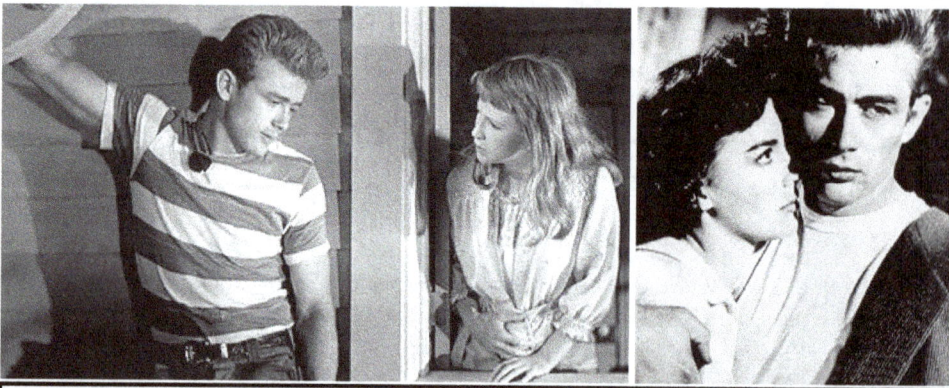

LOVE IS PAIN: Two Views of James Dean from his Most Iconic Films

Left: With **Julie Harris** in *East of Eden* (1955) and *right*, with **Natalie Wood** in *Rebel Without a Cause* (also 1955).

He was fortunate to have known and worked in television with many of the key figures of his life, each with a story to tell. During the course of its compilation (he actually began it back in 1970), he managed to obtain at least three prolonged deathbed" confessions from mentors who loved and/or nurtured him, and who no longer had careers to protect.

Some of the greatest stars, both male and female, seduced him; others detested him. Whereas Marlene Dietrich held him in contempt; Gary Cooper treated him like a son. As actress Geraldine Page told him, "No one ever knew the real James Dean because he only shared one small part of his life with each person, hugging the rest close to his breast.

Intense, handsome, vulnerable, and highly original, he mesmerized moviegoers and still does to this day. Each new generation reads in his legend their spin on what he symbolizes. Marlon Brando, to whom Jimmy was often compared, said, "Nothing fascinates the public as much as an unfinished life. All of us speculate what might have been in our own lives had we taken a different path."

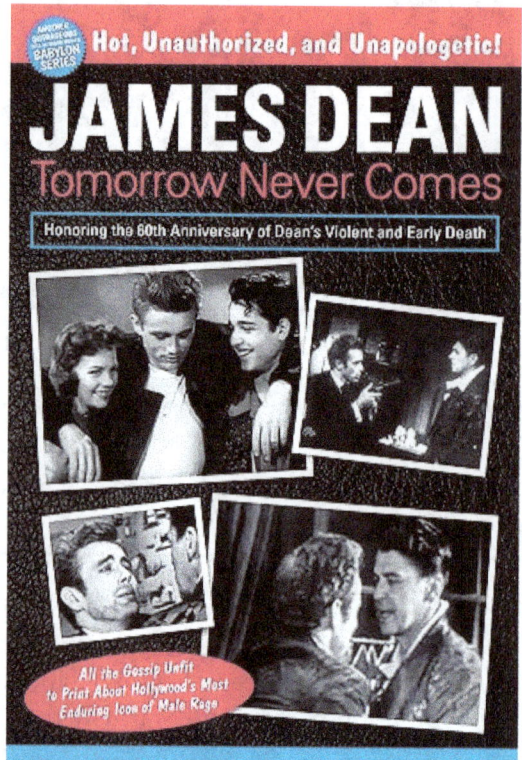

THIS BOOK PROUDLY REVEALS WHAT REALLY HAPPENED TO 1950S MEGASTAR JAMES DEAN

It took until the 21st Century before the last major players told everything they knew

It's about JAMES DEAN: the "punk," "little bastard," and "shameless hustler" who, in his words, "had affairs with some really big names in Hollywood, and a few in Washington, D.C., too."

JAMES DEAN-Tomorrow Never Comes
Biography & Autobiography/Rich &Famous,
by Darwin Porter & Danforth Prince
6x9 Softcover, with photos. 744 pages ISBN 978-1-936003-49-5.

This is a tragic, myth-shattering saga about America's obsession with celebrities.

February, 2019

Death of the Movie Star

Once upon a time, there existed a magic kingdom called "The Dream Factory." It thrived in a place known as "Tinseltown" (aka Hollywood).

In that land before computer-generated effects, talented men and women put everything on the silver screen that the human mind could conjure.

Perhaps a gigantic ape on top of the Empire State Building, holding a helpless Fay Wray in his mammoth hand. Maybe the Land of Oz on the other side of the Rainbow through which Little Dorothy wandered. Perhaps it was Rhett Butler departing forever, informing Scarlett O'Hara, "Frankly, my dear, I don't give a damn." Or perhaps Bogie telling Ingrid Bergman, "We'll always have Paris."

Our parents, and later the postwar Baby Boomers, created what were called "Gods and Goddesses" of the Golden Years of Cinema. An enchanting creature called "The Movie Star" appeared. Some of them could dance (Gene Kelly); others could sing (Frank Sinatra and Judy Garland).

Soldiers in World War II took pinups of Betty Grable and Rita Hayworth with them into battle. A pinup of Rita was pasted onto a plane carrying the first atomic bomb.

At the rate of 90 million a week, Americans flocked to see movie stars emote on the screen. In countless magazines, we lived through their love affairs, ill-fated marriages, scandals, good films, bad films… whatever. We loved and worshipped them.

Fan clubs rose up across America. At personal appearances, these stars were mobbed; the police had to be called in to save them from being stripped of all their clothing. We wanted a piece of them.

Sadly, with the exception of Kirk Douglas and Olivia de Havilland (each 102 years old), these stars have faded into our history. Some disappeared quietly into the Pacific sunset; others waited for the phone call from a producer that never came again.

But while they lasted, their fans could temporarily

The oft-underrated actor **Burt Reynolds** morphed into the greatest film revenue driver of the 1980s.

A star by anyone's standards, he brilliantly satirized the ending of the star system (and the winding down of his own career) in his poignant, "with a smile in my heart" performance as a faded, over-the-hill matinée idol in *The Last Movie Star* (2017).

Even Princess Leia (**Carrie Fisher**) seems bored with her view of "traditionally well-trafficked" stars on the **Hollywood Walk of Fame.**

As landmarks surrounded with urban consumers, **big-city movie palaces** did a lot to prolong the concept of movie stardom.

But with the growth of the suburbs with their then-undeveloped tracks of surrounding acreage came **Drive-Ins.** There, in closed, steamy cars, a lot more than movie kings and queens competed for movie-goers' attention.

abandon their workaday worlds, and with a bag of popcorn, enter a darkened theater and be carried away into fantasy.

The gorgeous women were surrogate mistresses to men in the audience, and those beautiful men like Errol Flynn or Tyrone Power allowed women to dream of what might have been.

Sadly, with the emergence of a new generation and new priorities, the Dream Factory disappeared like a mirage in a mirror. Studio backlots where pirate adventures, wartime battles, Westerns, melodramas, were filmed have been sold to real estate developers who turned the terrain into condos and offices. On the spot where Clark Gable made love to Lana Turner, McDonald's offers empty calories in the form of burgers and fries.

Fortunately, an estimated five to six million Americans, mostly Baby Boomers but an increasing number of young viewers, too, can wander back to Yesterday, thanks to modern, digitalized technology. From the convenience of their den or living room, they savor everything from Edwin S. Porter's *The Great Train Robbery* (1903) to Greta Garbo making love to Robert Taylor in *Camille* (1936). Viewers can hear Marlon Brando screaming "Stella! Stella! Stella!" in *A Streetcar Named Desire* (1951), and Rita Hayworth putting the blame on Mame in *Gilda* (1946 as she reprises what's been called "the sexiest dance ever choreographed."

If you're of a certain age, you've heard of Clark Gable, Gary Cooper, Cary Grant, Barbara Stanwyck, Bette Davis, Joan Crawford, James Cagney, Burt Lancaster, James Stewart, John Wayne, Katharine Hepburn, Spencer Tracy, Claudette Colbert, Lucille Ball, and Hedy Lamarr, who was hailed as "the most beautiful woman in the world."

But times have changed. The 91st Academy Awards presentation is coming up, and after a year of screen rage, silliness, or sublimity, the winners will walk off with gold.

Here is a sample list of actors and actresses who have been cited as worthy of various awards for their performances in the year just passed. The question is, when the winner is announced, will you know who he or she is? They include Steve Buscemi, Daniel Gimenez Casho, Lakeith Stanfield, Yalitz Aparicio, Elsie Fisher, Regina Hall, Simon Russell Beale, Adam Driver, Brian Tyree Henry, Steven Yeun, Sakura Ando, Shayna McHayle, Haley Richardson, Kathryn Hahn, John Cho, and Zain Al Rafeea.

Speaking of stars, the names of some of the biggest weren't widely known even during their heydays. Here's **Florence Lawrence** ("The Girl of a Thousand Faces") during the peak of her fame in 1911.

Widely acknowledged as "the First Movie Star," she starred in more than 300 silent films. Even by 1909, after she had appeared in more than 50 one-reelers, Lawrence was known to her adoring public not by name, but as "**the Biograph Girl.**" Studio owners feared that too high a "recognizability quotient" would encourage their actors demands for higher salaries.

A suffragette who dabbled (unsuccessfully) in film production, she died destitute at the age of 52 in 1938, a victim of suicide by rat poison. The advent of "Talkies' had demoted her to bit parts on "Poverty Row."

REST IN PEACE
FLORENCE LAWRENCE
1886-1938

January 2017

KIRK DOUGLAS

The Very Long Life of a Horndog Megastar after a Century of Conquests

Reliably aggressive and a very good actor: Two views of **Kirk Douglas** in *Champion* (1949).

At last, a decades-long question can be answered. Which big movie star from Hollywood's Golden Age would survive all others? Certainly not Clark Gable, Gary Cooper, Tyrone Power, Errol Flynn, or Robert Taylor. These matinee idols died relatively young.

The answer is Kirk Douglas, the first anti-hero superstar of the post-war era. The owner of the screen's most celebrated cleft chin was born Issur Danielovitch on December 6, 1918, in Amsterdam, New York. Survivor of a serious stroke, he lived to celebrate his 100th birthday in December of 2016, and was met with such headlines as "LEGENDARY HOLLYWOOD HORNDOG TURNS 100."

The longest-lived Golden Age female star was Luise Rainer, who died in London at the age of 104. She was the first actress to win two consecutive Oscars, each of them back to back—*The Great Ziegfeld* (1936) and *The Good Earth* ('37).

Douglas immortalized himself in film after film, but had a rough go of it: He was beaten up in *The Champion* ('49); stabbed in the stomach in *Ace in the Hole* ('51); lost a finger in *The Big Sky* ('52); rolled in barbed wire in *Man Without a Star* ('55); cut off his ear as Vincent van Gogh in *Lust for Life* ('56), had his eye put out in *The Vikings* ('58), was crucified in *Spartacus* ('60), and was whipped by his servant in *The Way West* ('67).

For diehard fans of **Lana Turner** ("The Ultimate Movie Star") *The Bad and the Beautiful* (1952) is an essential "Must-See."

Throughout his career, when he was on talk shows hawking his latest film, interviewers wanted him to reveal the secrets of his love life. Talk show host Dick Cavett didn't want to talk about *A Gunfight* ('71). Instead, he wanted the dish on his leading ladies. "What About Faye Dunaway in *The Arrangement* ('69), or Kim Novak in *Strangers When We Meet* ('60)?" he asked.

Douglas was furious.

But by the time he turned 71, his tongue had loosened during the composition of his autobiography, *The Ragman's Son*. He had been married twice, once to actress Diana Dill, with whom he became the father of the future mega-star, Michael Douglas. After their divorce, he married Anne Buydens, a film publicist.

At fourteen, he lost his virginity to his English teacher. His first movie star seduction was on a rooftop in Greenwich Village with a sultry teenage blonde model, Betty Bacall. Later, she went to Hollywood, changed her name to Lauren, and married Bogie. Although for years, each of them denied her "deflowering," near the end of her life, she said, "Of course he did. Don't be a fool!"

LUST FOR LIFE (1956): **Kirk Douglas'** cinematic interpretation of the tragic, brilliant, and probably insane painter, **Vincent Van Gogh,** was universally praised by art experts and dramatists alike. Ironically, his physicality weirdly resonated that of Van Gogh himself.

In a nutshell, here are some tantalizing insights into how Douglas bedded the screen goddesses of yesterday:

Joan Crawford: "She was the aggressor, ripping off her dress in the foyer, too eager to go upstairs. I was nearly overcome with the fumes of her bad breath."

Rita Hayworth: "I went to bed with my fantasy of *Gilda* (her most famous film '46). I woke up to find a sweet, unsophisticated girl whose likeness had been stamped on the first atomic bomb dropped on Hiroshima."

Evelyn Keyes: "*Scarlett O'Hara's Younger Sister* wrote in a memoir that I was parlor-sized."
Marlene Dietrich: "She preferred fellatio and had sex without preference for gender."
Marilyn Monroe: "She kept me waiting for two hours. I practically had to put things on ice, I was so eager."
Marilyn Maxwell: "She was no lady, telling me she preferred Frank Sinatra."
Ann Sothern: "She played my wife in *A Letter to Three Wives* ('49). We rehearsed our husband-and-wife scenes in my bed."
Ava Gardner: "She turned to me when Sinatra kicked her out of his house."
Patricia Neal: "She cried during the whole thing, claiming she was cheating on the man she loved—the much-married Gary Cooper."
Gene Tierney: "She was a good kisser once you got beyond the overbite."
Lana Turner: "She was my co-star in her most memorable movie: *The Bad and the Beautiful* ('53). She told me I was twice as good as Ronnie Reagan and ten times better than Senator John F. Kennedy."
Pier Angeli: "She wanted to marry me when not in the beds of James Dean, Clark Gable, or the singer, Vic Damone. (He actually married her.)"
Mae West: Early in his career, she auditioned Douglas for her stage show. She insisted he wear skimpy briefs for her inspection. He did not make the grade.

His most bizarre seduction occurred one summer when he worked as a bellboy at a resort in New York State. It was owned by a vicious anti-Semite woman who didn't know he was Jewish. "Before I left that summer, she seduced me. At the point of her glorious climax, I screamed in her ear, 'I'm a Jew!'"

Kirk Douglas, the last surviving Golden Age male star, finally died at the age of 103, living three more years after celebrating his 100th birthday.

His son and fellow actor, Michael Douglas, announced, "to the world, he was a legend, an actor from the Golden Age of Movies who lived well into his golden years, a humanitarian whose commitment to justice and the causes he believed in set a standard for all of us to aspire to."

Portrait of a self-promoting Renaissance Man: Blood Moon's unvarnished posthumous biography of the former Issur Danielovich won some literary awards and some rave critical reviews. Published in 2019, here's the full story of *The Ragman's Son*.
KIRK DOUGLAS, More Is Never Enough ISBN 978-1-936003-61-7. 624 pages with hundreds of photos.

The 1950s Version of

HOLLYWOOD'S CASTING COUCH

As exposed in Darwin Porter's's Newest Biography
Rock Hudson, Erotic Fire

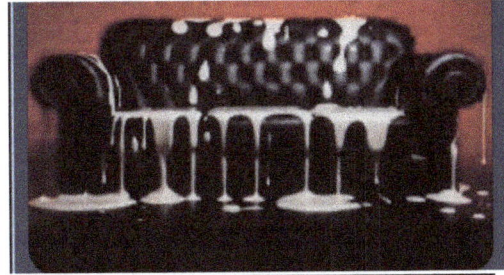

Two photos above: **A Casting Couch,** before and after an audition.

Reviewers are evaluating my latest biography, *Rock Hudson Erotic Fire*, for salacious information about how the casting couch operated during the dying days of Hollywood's "Golden Age." Its release in November of 2017 coincided with an avalanche of charges of sexual harassment currently being splashed across the tabloids, many of them dominating television's 24-hour news cycle. Perhaps beginning with Bill Cosby and in time embroiling producer Harvey Weinstein, accusations against sexually harassing "gropers" have engulfed an astonishingly wide range of men, everyone from Dustin Hoffman to the Rev. Jesse Jackson; Alabama's senatorial candidate Roy Moore; even such unlikely malfeasants as the ex-Prez, George H.W. Bush, 93, who admitted, "I once liked to pat women's rears and was known as David Cop-a-Feel."

During Rock's heyday, the term "sexual harassment" didn't exist, entering the public lexicon as late as 1977. Many young men and women arrived in Hollywood during the post-war years, expecting to extend their sexual favors as the vehicle that would help them break into show business. Rock Hudson, it's revealed, played the game very well, indeed.

After service in the Navy, in the Philippines, during World War II, Rock—handsome, strapping, charming, and hunky—arrived in Hollywood at around the same time as another hopeful, Marilyn Monroe.

They met after she'd been been fired from Columbia, and appeared on the Universal lot (Rock's "home studio") looking for a job. He had ten dollars in his pocket, and she had nothing. Their affair began when he bought her breakfast. It was intense but brief. She advised that if they ever wanted to become movie stars, they each needed to spend lots of time as cooperative hopefuls on as many casting couches as possible.

Her advice played out well—not only for herself, but for him, too. The head of Universal, Ed Muhl, despite his status as a married man and the father of three, fell under Rock's spell. At three o'clock every afternoon, Rock was summoned into Muhl's office, and the door was firmly locked with them alone together in the room. Muhl's rising young star left about an hour later, and within months, he was awarded with a string of starring roles.

Men of various sexual persuasions were not alone in their emphasis on casting couches. Many powerful leading ladies of the day, including **Joan Crawford, Marlene Dietrich,** and **Bette Davis,** maneuvered sexual favors from whomever was awarded laurels as their leading men.

This brings us, of course, back to Rock Hudson: In a series of ro-

Unless you've been cut off from the news cycle for the past decade, you're probably aware of the floods of sexual harrassment charges pouring in, as they relate to "previously unblemished" public figures. Charged with sexually aggressive improprieties have been:

Upper tier, left to right: **Dustin Hoffman, Harvey Weinstein,** and **former President George H.W. Bush,** and

Lower tier, left to right: **The Reverend Jesse Jackson** and Alabama senatorial candidate **Roy Moore,** former Chief Justice of the Supreme Court of Alabama.

mantic encounters that hugely influenced his career, Oscar winner **Jane Wyman** (ex-wife of Ronald Reagan) developed a crush on him and insisted that he be cast as her leading man in the 1954 remake of *Magnificent Obsession*. [*An earlier version of this "four-hanky weeper" had been released in 1935.*] The picture helped morph Hudson into a superstar, leading to his Oscar-winning performance in Edna Ferber's sprawling saga of Texas, *Giant* (1956).

Rock spent many a night at Wyman's home during the making of *Magnificent Obsession*. Her affair with Rock ended abruptly when Rock, Wyman, and her husband, bandleader Fred Karger, flew to Manhattan to attend the premiere of the film.

To her horror, after returning unexpectedly to her suite at the Plaza, she found Karger in bed with Rock. Although she continued her professional relationship with Rock, she divorced her errant young husband shortly thereafter, remarrying him in 1961, and then divorcing him again in 1965. Rock, in contrast, emerged as the world's Number One box office attraction for an undisputed seven years in a row.

Since his widely publicized death from AIDS in 1985, most of the public erroneously assumes that

JILTED JANE: (i.e., megastar diva **Jane Wyman**, ex-wife of the future president, Ronald Reagan), is seen on the left with her husband, bandleader **Fred Karger,** and on the right with her handsome and very promiscuous co-star, **Rock Hudson**, with whom she had fallen madly in love.

Jane was jilted one afternoon at the Plaza Hotel in NYC, when she returned early from a shopping excursion to find her husband and co-star together *in flagrante delicto*. As they'd both discover, **HELL HATH NO FURY LIKE A DIVA SCORNED.**

Rock was gay when, in fact, he was a rampaging bisexual, especially during his younger days. He seduced obsessively, and without gender preference, everyone from Elizabeth Taylor to James Dean, from Lana Turner to the inevitable Miss Crawford, even such bizarre couplings as Tallulah Bankhead and Liberace. He fathered a son, and became sought-after in some of the upper-tier society circuits of Europe, even enjoying sexual intimacies with three royal princesses: Margaret Rose of Kensington Palace; Princess Grace of Monaco; and Princess Soraya, the former queen of Iran.

Researched over a period of decades, *Erotic Fire* reveals details—for the first time—about the often tragic life of this astonishingly successful fallen idol. He was the first mega-celebrity stricken with AIDS, and became, in 1985, the first famous person to succumb to a black death that, in time, killed millions of men, women, and children, especially in the sub-Sahara.

On Rock's deathbed, as cited by Elizabeth Taylor, he said, "If my dying calls world attention to this plague, and people will raise money to try to find a cure, then this will be my shining hour."

Beautiful Elizabeth took up the banner and became the chief fundraiser for AIDS. The rest is history.

Rock Hudson Erotic Fire
Darwin Porter & Danforth Prince
Biography/Rich & Famous.
6x9 Softcover, with photos.
664 pages

ISBN 978-1-936003-55-6.
www.BloodMoonProductions.com

***

In the dying days of Hollywood's Golden Age, Rock Hudson became the most celebrated phallic symbol and lust object in America. Darwin Porter's newest biography tells how he did it. EROTIC FIRE.

Another example of Blood Moon's Award-winning Entertainment About How America Interprets its Celebrities.

The Death of Rock Hudson's Fraudulent Blackmailer
PHYLLIS GATES

James Frey's so-called memoir, *A Million Little Pieces,* about drug addiction and alcoholism, is a national scandal and bestseller in spite of its infamy. Oprah Winfrey first promoted the book to millions of her fans, then turned on Frey, exposing him on TV as a fraud and a liar.

But fake memoirs are old hat to insider Hollywood. Bennett Cerf, publisher at Random House, once told Marlene Dietrich that in her memoirs she must have confused her own infamous life with the saintly days of Mother Teresa. Joan Crawford privately admitted that her self-serving 1962 *Portrait of Joan* "was only fodder for fans."

The world took little note, in January of 2006, of the death of another fake memoirist, Phyllis Gates, who died of cancer at the age of 80 in Marina del Rey. On November 9, 1955, this beautiful "farm girl from Minnesota" married Rock Hudson, the most popular movie star in the world at the time. He died of AIDS at the age of 59 in 1985. Two years later, Gates wrote *My Husband, Rock Hudson*, portraying herself as an innocent victim who didn't know her husband was gay when she married him.

The innocent-faced Gates was a blackmailer and an extortionist, the memoir a lie. Her boss was Henry Willson, a notorious homosexual agent who ruled the male flesh market of 1950s Hollywood, creating "Rock Hudson" (actually Roy Fitzgerald) and numerous other pretty boy stars such as Tab Hunter and Rory Calhoun. Willson paid Gates $50,000 of Hudson's money to enter into this sham of a marriage before scandal-mongering *Confidential* magazine exposed the handsome macho star as a homosexual.

Before working as a secretary for Willson, Gates was known in lesbian circles of the 1950s. She'd been the "girl toy" of the cross-dressing heiress, Jo Carstairs, whose grandfather had left her mega-millions in petroleum dollars he'd earned with John D. Rockefeller.

After her divorce from Hudson in 1958, Gates became infuriated at

Throughout most of his career, **Rock Hudson** was too handsome, too successful, too charming, and too relentlessly unmarried to escape the attention of journalistic yentas. Many of them raised their circulation with speculation about his sexuality.

Here's a front cover of **Movieland Magazine** from the mid-50s gossipping about his links **(will they or won't they?)** to the otherwise unknown parvenue Phyllis Gates.

COMPLICATED, EXPENSIVE, AND ULTIMATELY TRAGIC ATTEMPTS TO AVOID GLBTQ EXPOSURE

Upper photo: Gates' simpering, self-serving, fraud-soaked memoir.

Lower photo: Accessorized with smiles and a wedding cake, **Rock Hudson** and his bisexual bride, **Phyllis Gates,** camouflage their extramarital "gender-nonspecific" promiscuities.

the meager terms she'd agreed to, and wanted more money—millions, in fact. She threatened to blackmail her former mate, demanding 75 percent of his future earnings. She warned him that "25 percent of something is better than nothing." She could have destroyed Hudson's burgeoning career.

Willson to the rescue. He presented Hudson's lawyers with a five-inch file on the nefarious blackmailing schemes Gates had attempted with some of her more famous lesbian friends, an activity that brought her to the attention of the FBI. "It was a Mexican stand-off," one of Hudson's lawyers once told me. "She had us, and we had her." Gates called off her blackmail threats, returning to a quiet life with her lesbian girlfriends—she called them "my sewing circle."

As many a Hollywood star painfully knows, not all blackmailers look like a white-suited Sidney Greenstreet in an old Bogie film. Some of them, as in the case of Phyllis Gates, looked like she could have reigned as queen of a 1950s senior prom.

A Deceitful and Eventually Miserably Unhappy Collaboration

Hudson, Gates, and the orchestrator of the marital ruse, Rock's notorious agent, **Henry Willson.**

NO ORDINARY JOE

One of Phyllis Gates' lesbian flings, it was revealed by Henry Willson, was with **Jo Carstairs,** the ultra-eccentric and very butch heiress to a major block of Standard Oil.

Known as "the Fastest Woman on Water" because of her skill at motorboat racing, she was unapologetically famous for affairs with, among others, Greta Garbo, Marlene Dietrich and—as revealed when things got too hot for Rock Hudson's wife to handle—Phyllis Gates.

Despite Gates's thwarted attempts to blackmail him, **Rock Hudson** emerged in history as a pivotal and influential All-American actor, beloved and admired by his fans, and known for making frothy comedies profitable.

Star of more than 70 films over the course of his 30-year career, he was the first major-league celebrity to contract, and die from, AIDS. His candid "confessions" during the final days of his life increased public awareness of the dangers of sexually transmitted diseases, and made him a new kind of hero after his death.

ROCK HUDSON (1925-1985)
REST IN PEACE, ROCK. WE HARDLY KNEW 'YE

January 2018

HEDY LAMARR

Femme Fatale & **Mother of the Cellphone**

The sultry, enigmatic brunette, Hedy Lamarr, during the dark days of World War II, was hailed as "the world's most beautiful woman."

What is far less known about her fabled life is that she was a world-class inventor, conjuring up an invention that helped revolutionize modern communications, earning her the label of "The Mother of the Cellphone." In 2014, she was posthumously inducted into the National Inventors Hall of Fame.

At last, her remarkable, almost unbelievable story is the subject of a movie, *Bombshell: The Hedy Lamarr Story,* playing in theaters across America this winter.

The review of the movie in *The New York Times* was headlined: "A Hollywood Beauty Who Helped Change the World."

Her story began in Vienna in 1914 when she was born on the eve of World War I, whose aftermath included the collapse of the Austro-Hungarian Empire. She had always wanted to be an actress, and by 1933, she appeared in Gustav Machaty's notorious film, *Ecstasy*, in which she was seen running nude in the woods. In that controversial, *avant-garde* film, she was also depicted in the throes of orgasm. *(Machaty achieved the desired effect by sticking a pin into her).*

She abandoned her career when she married Fritz Mandl, an Austrian arms merchant selling munitions to fuel the Nazi war machine. Ironically, both the sadistic Mandl and Hedy were Jewish.

During that loveless marriage, she entertained, and was entertained by, the elite hierarchies of the Fascist world. She found Hitler "an arrogant, dangerous *poseur,*" and Mussolini "a pompous ass."

In 1937, on a hunt for new talent in Europe, Louis B. Mayer discovered the divorced actress and signed her to an MGM contract, hoping to replace Greta Garbo, who would soon retire.

She became an overnight sensation upon the release of *Algiers* (1938), starring Charles Boyer. Luminous, she was forever after associated with praise for her porcelain skin, her large, marbly eyes, her lilting Viennese accent, her Mona Lisa smile, and her aura of mystery. Throughout the course of the 1940s (the heyday of her film career), she

Chiaroscuro rendering of the mysterious Hedy Kiesler (aka **Hedy Lamarr**).

Hedy Lamarr orchestrated an astonishing collaboration with Louis B. Mayer, head of MGM, during her flight, in 1937, from a repressive marriage to a Nazi munitions mogul.

Mayer accepted her, to some degree, as a "trophy from the other side," sometimes promoting her as an Americanized Teutonic who looked good in frothy tropical skin flicks. The banners on the upper tier show how MGM marketed her in 1942—in this case with obvious dark skin tones as a Polynesian temptress no man could refuse.

The *lower right* photo shows an unhappy **Hedy Kiesler,** the 22-year-old bride of **Fritz Mandl,** a henchman and munitions supplier to Hitler. Some said he married her because of her "celebrity quotient' from her teenaged appearance, nude, in the ultra-avant-garde film, *Ecstase (Ecstasy),* in 1933. The photo was snapped by a reporter in January of 1937 as part of his coverage of that year's **Vienna Opera Ball.**

Decades later, in reference to her flight from her repressive marriage to Fritz Mandl, she said, "It was his game to hold me captive. It was my game to escape. He lost."

Within the bizarre new world she—with huge amounts of luck—created, five other (failed) marriages would follow.

seemed more like a celluloid mannequin than a natural woman.

Some of the era's most famous movie stars seduced her, including Errol Flynn, Charlie Chaplin, James Stewart, Robert Taylor, Stewart Granger, Victor Mature, William Powell, and John Garfield.

Along the way, she picked up five more husbands and had an affair with a young naval hero who had recently returned from the war in the Pacific. "John F. Kennedy was charming, handsome, charismatic, and a real heartbreaker," she said.

As the century progressed, the U.S. government began to pay attention to her ground-breaking invention, which she'd created with the intent of doing something for the war effort. She had her own laboratory for inventions. Her lover, aviator Howard Hughes, lent her some of his top scientists. In return, she counseled him on plane design.

Her greatest achievement, with help from her friend, the avant-garde composer George Antheil, was a radio-controlled torpedo whose navigation systems could not be jammed.

Hedy's invention, which she patented in 1942, foiled attempts to sabotage its trajectory based on rapidly switching frequencies. The system it used for that incorporated "spread spectrums" which, years later, became the foundation for cellular phones and other wireless devices.

Although she feigned indifference, **Lamarr's** youthful involvement, nude, in *Ecstasy* (1933) caused her endless embarrassments from voyeurs at the many chic cocktail parties she attended in NYC, sometimes with **Darwin Porter**, in the "socializing seventies."

In the early 1960s, around the time of the U.S./Cuban missile confrontation, an updated version of Hedy's World War II invention was incorporated into all U.S. naval vessels.

As the years wore on, Hedy tried, unsuccessfully, to rescue her fading beauty with cosmetic surgeries. She and I had signed with the same literary agent, and to some degree, we shared the same circle of friends, and, as such, I visited her often during her retirement in Florida.

Often dazed and confused, she became involved in two shoplifting incidents. The first was in June of 1961 at the May Company Department Store in Los Angeles, where she walked out with gold slippers and various sundries. At the time, her purse contained $14,000 of undeposited checks.

The second shoplifting incident transpired in August of 1991 in Casselberry, Florida. Once again, she walked out with unpaid merchandise—in this case, $21.48 worth of laxative tablets and eyedrops. Eventually, both charges were dropped.

I found her a dear, tormented soul, obsessively sharing memories of a fabled life.

She died on January 19, 2000, age 85, in Altamonte Springs, Florida. Her son, Anthony Loder, flew with her ashes to Austria and tossed them into the winds rustling through the Vienna Woods. She left a $3.5 million estate.

Today, anywhere you go in America, you can see people with cellphones, yet except for Baby Boomers, most of these people have never heard of the mother of that remarkable invention.

As Hedy once told me, "A woman can be beautiful and still have a brain."

Although her talents as an actress were sometimes assessed as "predictable," **Hedy Lamarr** became a foil for many of the most profit-generating male stars of her heyday. *Left to right above*, feature her with **Charles Boyer, Clark Gable, James Stewart,** and **John Garfield.**

March 2018

LATINO, BLACK, & OLDER FEMALE ACTORS
"What About Us?"

Javier Bardem and **Penélope Cruz,** each Latino, brilliant, charismatic, and beautiful, emote together in *Vicky Christina Barcelona* (2008).

In 2015 and 2016, the all-white Oscar nominations provoked an uproar at the Academy of Motion Picture Arts & Sciences, which is 72 percent male and 87 percent white, roughly reflecting the demographics of the movie industry.

These protests led to the creation of the "Oscars So White" movement. By the very next year (2017), the color filters had changed. *Moonlight*, with its African American cast, won as Best Picture of the Year, beating out *La La Land*. And as U.S. society becomes more nominally all-inclusive, additional changes seem inevitable.

Oscar host Chris Rock said, "Forget whether Hollywood is black enough. A better question is, 'Is Hollywood Mexican enough?'"

In January of this year, when the Oscar nominees were announced for films released in 2017, African Americans were amply represented and several new milestones had been established. For example, for the first time in the Academy's history, two black men were nominated for the Best Actor award: Denzel Washington for his performance in *Roman J. Israel, Esq.* and Daniel Kaluuya for his role in *Get Out*.

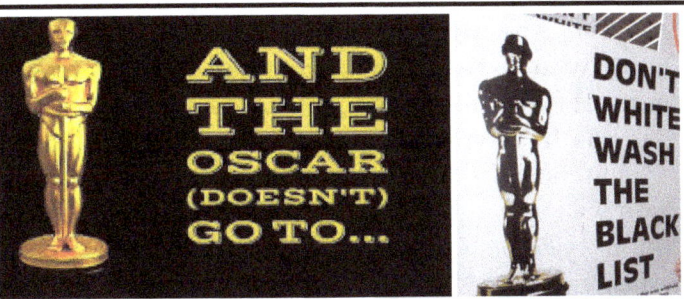

Jordan Peele is the African American screenwriter and director of *Get Out*, a film that made history when it received a trifecta of Oscar nominations (Best Picture, Best Director, and Best Original Screenplay) for a film defined as "an assault on the smugness of white liberalism."

Another group under-represented as players in the movie industry (older actresses) staged a kind of comeback, too: Eight of the ten Oscar-nominated actresses for 2017 were over 40, and all of them played characters you wouldn't want to cross. More and more women are demanding better and pithier roles in the film industry, and more and more of them refuse to tolerate even a hint of sexual harassment. Also, to an increasing degree, women behind the camera are being recognized as well: Greta Gerwig became the fifth woman in film history to receive a Best Director nod for her brilliant work on *Lady Bird.*

OscarsSoWhite has been described as a hashtag that morphed into a social media phenomenon. It focuses on a movement inaugurated by April Reign in 2015 that drew attention (and sustained pressure) to the lack of racial diversity to the Oscar nominations, especially in the acting categories.

While progress has been made in the decade since its founding, the movement continues its advocacy for racial and ethnic diversity within the film industry

Although more diversified than Oscar nominees in

years past, one major segment of the population, the Latino community, is still relatively under-represented. The Mexican director, Guillermo Del Toro, carried a lone Latino banner into battle for his direction of the widely celebrated *The Shape of Water*, the story of a mute cleaning woman who falls in love with a Merman.

One out of every four people who attend a movie theater in the U.S. is Latino, a group that comprises 18 percent of the population. *[In contrast, 13.3 percent of the population defines itself as African American.]*

In the long and tormented history of Hollywood, only a few Latinos have emerged into super stardom, beginning with Ramon Novarro in his breakthrough performance as *Ben-Hur* in that film's 1925 silent version.

The biggest Latina star in U.S. entertainment history was the love goddess, Rita Hayworth. Born in Brooklyn, she was of Mexican ancestry. Anthony Quinn, who some fans incorrectly remember as Greek because of his brilliant performance as Zorba, emerged from South of the Border.

Only one Hispanic actor, José Ferrer, ever won an Oscar, taking the gold for *Cyrano de Bergerac* (1950). *[Despite many brilliant performances, no Latina has ever won a Best Actress Oscar.]*

Latinos can be equally talented behind the camera too, but they're rarely honored. A notable exception is Alejandro G. Iñárritu, who won the Best Director gold for his memorable insight into the anguish of show-biz with *Birdman* (2014), starring Michael Keaton, and for that grim evocation of vengeance on the American frontier, *The Revenant* (2015), starring Leonard DiCaprio.

Dream Works and Creative Artists are helping aspirants get a leg up on a Hollywood career by offering internships to women and people of color. Creative also manages careers for at least 100 Latino clients. One of them is Penelope Cruz, who won a Best Supporting Actress Oscar for her role in *Vicky Cristina Barcelona* (2009).

Two of Golden Age Hollywood's most bankable (and adored) actors were Latino...even if mainstream audiences didn't know it at the time: *Left photo:* **Anthony Quinn,** *Right photo:* **Rita Hayworth.**

Rivers of ink have been justifiably spilled to document the racial barriers faced by *left photo* **Lena Horne** and *right photo* **Dorothy Dandridge.**

Dandridge, in defiance of the color barrier, won an Oscar nomination for her performance in *Carmen Jones* (1954). With her is **Harry Belafonte.**

Dandridge became the first African American to be nominated for an Academy Award for Best Actress, but lost to **Grace Kelly** for *The Country Girl.*

During the next two years, new high-profile films will visibly feature Latino stars. Sony is prepping the release of a remake of the 2011 Mexican crime thriller *Miss Bala*, which includes a teeth-grinding role for a sensitive and empowered Latina. And insiders tell us that other Hollywood projects with strong Latino casts will soon be announced.

Alex Nogales, president of the National Hispanic Media Coalition, picked up the bullhorn. "Enough is enough," he said. "We Latinos are going to start protesting left and right. If that doesn't work, we'll pick one of the studios and launch a boycott. We will not be denied any longer."

April Reign, creator of the *Oscars So White* movement, asserted that her goal "is to promote a media culture where everyone can visit a theater and see themselves on the screen. America is becoming a more inclusive society and definitely browner. People who pay $15 to sit in a movie theater deserve to see their stories being told."

March 2010

ALEXANDER MCQUEEN
The Jack the Ripper of Fashion

Alexander McQueen

His death noose had hardly been removed by London police officers before filmmakers in Hollywood went to work on a documentary based on the short, turbulent life of British fashion renegade, Alexander McQueen.

At the age of 40, and at the apex of his career, he was found hanged in his multi-million pound London apartment, an apparent suicide. Pre-dawn transatlantic calls brought the tragic news to *fashionistas* in New York, who were launching "Fashion Week" collections for the coming autumn.

"Why did he kill himself?" asked supermodel and friend Naomi Campbell. "He had everything to live for." From the White House, First Lady Michelle Obama expressed her grief about the loss of her favorite designer.

One can only speculate as to why McQueen committed suicide. Major figures in his life had fallen away, including his beloved mother, Joyce, who had died on February 2, following a long illness. "She was the light of my life," McQueen told the press. Right before Joyce died, her son told her, "My greatest fear is dying before you." On the day of his suicide, he had been scheduled to attend her funeral.

Alexander McQueen *(center)* in Ibiza with his husband, **George Forsyth**, at their wedding in 2002. On the left is Forsyth's sister, **Belle**.

He'd experienced a series of losses, including that of his longtime mentor, Isabella Blow, an eccentric stylist herself, who committed suicide in 2007. His 2002 marriage on the island of Ibiza to filmmaker George Forsyth had ended in a break-up. In the aftermath of their split, he'd dated a porn star known only as "Mr. Stag." The fashion icon later fell in love with another man. Only days before he killed himself, he revealed that they'd broken up. "That bastard Aussie, a real cad, has gone back Down Under." McQueen said. "And I have his f----cking name tattooed on my arm."

Depicted above in a hat designed by Alexander McQueen is **Isabella Blow** (1958-2007) the British magazine editor and fashion-industry powerhouse who "discovered" him. Her penchant for headgear was so memorable that Princess Margaret once greeted her at a party with: "Good evening, Hat." Blow died at the age of 48 after a lifelong battle with depression.

She's acknowledged today as a central figure in one of British fashion's golden ages, a powerhouse who helped put 1990s London at the center of the creative world.

McQueen dropped out of school when he was 16. Bullies taunted him, calling him "McQueer." He went to work on London's Savile Row for tailors who catered to Prince Charles. In a suit intended for the Prince of Wales, McQueen famously stitched in the words, "I am a C*NT" into the lining of the jacket.

Alexander McQueen with his beloved mother, **Joyce**. He hung himself on the day scheduled for her funeral.

During the day, McQueen managed a dazzling career in fashion that was skyrocketing as he created clothes for everybody from Madonna to today's Lady Gaga. By night, his life was devoted to "sex, drugs, alcohol, and food."

As a means of launching his career as a designer, McQueen presented his daring designs on ravaged models who looked like they'd been physically abused. He was still carrying on that theme in 2009 when he presented his show, "The Highland Rape," his models appearing in clothing with their bodices ripped, their hair a mess. He was commenting on England's "rape" of Scotland.

As nod to Jack the Ripper, he sewed locks of human hair into the jackets he sold.

He introduced trousers for men called "bumsters," that barely covered their rear ends. That bold, brassy statement caught on. Today, every jeansmaker in the world creates low-hanging jeans (*décolletage* for the *derrière*?) that barely stays up. Even President Obama has criticized this trend. But the jeans continue to roll off assembly lines around the world.

Queen Elizabeth elevated McQueen to the rank of a Commander in the British Empire in 2003. He famously linked his efforts with the House of Givenchy in Paris, but soonafter denounced the designs of the company's founder as "irrelevant." He later formed a more suitable business bond with Gucci.

One of his latest trends involved accessorizing his models with platform shoes that evoke the hulls of ships.

At the time of his death, McQueen's foibles and eccentricities had been widely bruited around the circles of the terribly fashionable. A McQueen fashion show always carried its share of surprises. If preview audiences didn't like McQueen's design, he was known to moon them.

As the world learned about McQueen's untimely death, his designs were "flying off the racks" in New York, Milan, London, Paris, and Los Angeles.

Hollywood filmmakers should have no trouble preparing the story of his life. The outrageous designer was nothing if not cinematic.

His fashion shows, though troubling, were the most astonishing ever presented. As fashion editor Serena French commented on one of them: "The voyeurism was disturbing, like a Victorian mental-hospital cell, but with clothes. Suddenly, the walls of a glass box fell to reveal a tableau of a naked woman in a demonic mask with a breathing tube. It was bizarre. It was exquisite."

From Alexander McQueen's **Highland Rape Collection**, referencing the subjugation of Scotland by England.

As one cynic said about this *tableaux*, "it's the *haute monde's* view of a bonnie lass fleeing from her croft after being raped by a Redcoat."

THE BUMSTER: More politely designated as "ultra-low rise," MacQueen is said to have received his inspiration from the so-called "builder's bum" – when trousers are worn accidentally too low – yet the designer later said it was about elongating the female form. "It wasn't about showing the bum... To me, that part of the body – not so much the buttocks, but the bottom of the spine – that's the most erotic part of anyone's body, man or woman," the late McQueen told a fashion reporter at The Guardian after his first collection.

According to fashion historian Andrew Bolton, "I think what's interesting about McQueen is how he would harness the attitude in the street. He was very much about anarchy and about the anarchy of the British street, the anarchy of British music, and trying to, again, harness that into his clothes. **The bumster** was one of the garments that, very early on, would make his reputation as a *provocateur*."

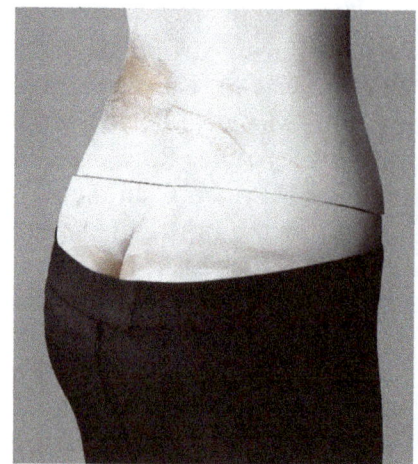
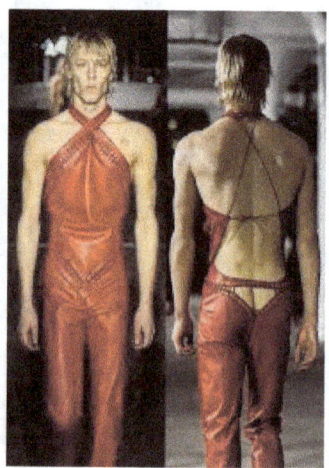

DINA MERRILL
The Heiress Who Grew Up at Mar-a-Lago

Gorgeous, charming, and when called for, stately

Two views of **Dina Merrill**, *right* with then-husband **Cliff Robertson**.

The world took little notice of Dina Merrill, age 93, who died on May 22, 2017, suffering from dementia. The rebellious heiress, who defied her parents to become an actress, grew up at Mar-a-Lago in Palm Beach, dubbed today "the Southern White House."

Between 1924 and 1927, the 126-room estate—part Mediterranean, part Arabian Nights—was constructed for $8 million by Dina's formidable mother, Marjorie Merriweather Post, owner of General Foods (*aka* "the Post Toasties heiress) and the wealthiest woman in America.

Born Nedenia Marjorie Hutton, the future Dina Merrill was the daughter of the multi-millionaire E. F. Hutton, Wall Street financier and one of the most influential men in America.

With parents like that, Dina grew up in a world of almost unimaginable luxury.

Dina often spent months aboard her father's yacht, the *Sea Cloud*, which was a floating palace, with such fixtures as fireplaces, a wine cellar, and a beauty parlor. She often helped to entertain the Duke and Duchess of Windsor, who were frequent guests.

Even as a girl, Dina showed a sharp eye for business. Her father gave her $50,000 to invest, and before she was 16, she had turned it into a million dollars. She urged her father to buy Birdseye Frozen Foods Company for $1.7 million, but he dismissed it a "a passing fad." When its value rose to $22 million, he listened to his daughter and purchased it.

He strongly opposed her wanting to be an actress, viewing it as a profession for "fallen women." She resisted, him and followed her heart. Hailed in Hollywood as "the new Grace Kelly," she ultimately made 100 films or teleplays.

Darwin Porter first met her in 1959, when he was the bureau chief of *The Miami Herald* in Key West. She had flown to the Florida Keys to film *Operation Petticoat* with Tony Curtis and

Four of the stars of the film *(Operation Petticoat, 1959)* on the Key West film set where **Darwin Porter** met **Dina Merrill** *(third from left)*.

Her cinematic colleagues included *(left to right)* **Cary Grant, Joan O'Brien,** and **Tony Curtis.**

Dina's imperious and formidable mother, **Marjorie Merriweather Post**, with her then-husband, Joe Daniels, during his stint as U.S. Ambassador to the Soviet Union. During his sojourn there, she amassed the most comprehensive collection of Imperial Russian art in the Western hemisphere.

Cary Grant, who had been married to her cousin, Woolworth heiress Barbara Hutton.

She was the epitome of charm, grace, and style, and was forever making the list of America's Best Dressed Women.

Over the years, he encountered her time and again at various charity events and premieres. Between 1966 and 1986, she was married to the Oscar-winning actor, Cliff Robertson. In the late 1960s and 70s, when he was often away shooting movies, she sometimes asked Darwin to escort her to various charity events. She had become a major-league philanthropist.

The last time he saw her was in the late 1970s when the late, great literary agent, Audrey Wood (famous for having launched the career of Tennessee Williams) asked him to escort her to see Dina appearing in an off-Broadway production of Tennessee's *Suddenly, Last Summer*. Katharine Hepburn had starred in the 1959 movie version, winning an Oscar nomination.

Over a late night supper in her lavish Manhattan apartment, Dina shared memories of her girlhood. None was more notable than when she'd flown to Moscow with her mother to be entertained by the Soviet dictator Josef Stalin. Post was buying up many art treasures seized by the Communists after the execution of the royal Romanoff family. He needed hard currency for war supplies.

Many of those treasures can be seen today at Hillwood, her former estate outside Washington, D.C., which is now a museum.

Dina was a liberal Republican, favoring pro-choice and women's health issues. When her mother died in 1973, she willed Mar-a-Lago to the National Park Service, hoping that it would be designated as a winter vacation retreat for U.S. Presidents. Jimmy Carter said, "Not for me."

When the government found it too costly to maintain, they gave it back to Dina and to Post's other two daughters.

They had a hard time getting rid of it, and kept lowering the price until Donald Trump purchased it in 1985 for only $7 million, one of the great real estate bargains of all time.

As the world knows, he turned it into a private club. When he became president, he raised the membership fee from $100,000 to $200,000.

For the most part, Dina remained silent about what happened to Mar-a-Lago. However, she did make one comment, as her mother's estate became a club: "A honeymoon haven for Michael Jackson and Elvis Presley's daughter. A setting for beauty pageants. A private club. Of course, Mother once hired performers from Ringling Brothers and Barnum & Bailey circuses to set up tents on her grounds for a charity event. But it's a different type of circus today."

Built in 1931 in Kiel, Germany, and originally named the **Hussar, The Sea Cloud** was the on-again, off-again vacation home of Dina Merrill.

Weighing 2492 gross tons, it was a-four-posted sailing barque and diesel-powered cruise ship that comfortably accommodated 64 guests, a crew of 60, and eventually, decades of history.

The dining room aboard the **Sea Cloud** during its ownership in the 1930s by Dina's formidable mother, Marjorie Merriweather Post.

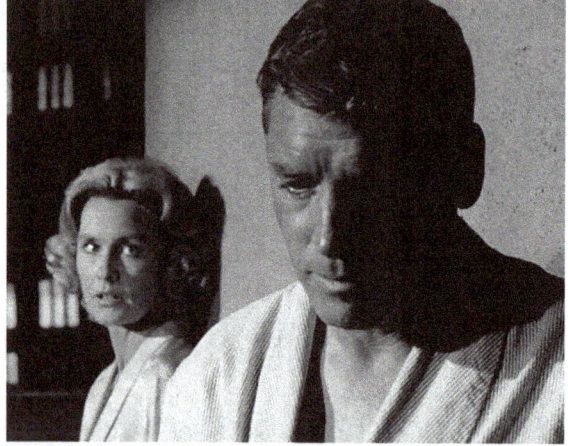

Dina Merrill with **Burt Lancaster** in *The Young Savages* (1961).

February 2008

MERV GRIFFIN

The Richest, Most Successful, and (until surpassed by Donald Trump) most notorious mogul in the history of America's entertainment industry.

Our budget was only $500 to provide a live entertainer to sing at the University of Miami's senior prom in the late 1950s. Young Darwin Porter, then president of that university's student body and editor of the school newspaper, put through a call to Merv Griffin's agent, who wanted $1,000 but settled for our $500.

In dire need of singing engagements, Merv was very available. His movie career at Warner Brothers had bombed—Doris Day failed to live up to her promise to make him her new leading man—and his days of singing with Freddy Martin's band were nostalgic memories even then. At the U of M dance, Merv sang his only hit record, a silly novelty tune called "I've Got a Lovely Bunch of Coconuts," a song he hated.

It appeared back then that Merv would join the array of dozens of other forgotten singers of the 50s, including Fabian. We underestimated him. Rising from the ashes of a show business career in the late 40s and 50s, he went on to become the most successful male entertainer and entrepreneur in show business history.

When he died of prostate cancer at the age of 82 in August of 2007, he left behind a billion-dollar empire. He created two of TV's most popular game shows, *Jeopardy!* and *Wheel of Fortune*, before becoming a big time player in the hotel and gambling business, challenging Donald Trump. After his early failures, he seemed to have the Midas touch. For example, he needed a little ditty for *Jeopardy!* to be played while the contestants were puzzling out the questions. In fifteen minutes, he wrote "*Think,*" which at the time of his death had earned him $85 million in royalties.

He won 17 Emmys in television, and his *The Merv Griffin Show* became one of the most successful in the medium. "I interviewed everybody," he claimed. "Only the Pope turned me down."

Like many closeted homosexual men of his day, Merv entered into a marriage, wedding Julann Wright in 1958, the union ending in divorce in 1976. The troubled marriage produced a son, Tony.

The first woman Merv ever seduced was Judy Garland during her

Decades before he became very rich and impossibly famous, here's "young and **early Merv**," during his Big Band Singer" era,.

This is how he appeared around the time **Darwin Porter** hired him as the singing entertainment for the senior prom at the University of Miami.

AGING DRAGONS

Although **Merv Griffin** and former First Lady **Nancy Reagan** had been friends since their shared days in show-biz, they became especially close after her exit from the White House. He had interviewed her (both with and without her husband) frequently during their respective heydays, and mutual friends described how she became, to some degree, emotionally dependent on him during her final years.

Published in 2009, Porter's biography of Merv elicited screams of outrage from his children and from his estate. One critic reviewed it with "*Darwin Porter tears the door off Merv Griffin's closet with gusto in this sizzling, massively researched bio.*"

tumultuous marriage to Sid Luft. But when he was young, trimmed down, and relatively handsome in the 1950s, he preferred such partners as Roddy McDowall, Rock Hudson, Guy Madison, and his all time idol, Errol Flynn.

As a teenager, Merv took the train from San Francisco to Los Angeles where he visited his Uncle Elmer. As he came into the living room, Merv encountered, a nude Errol Flynn sitting on the sofa wearing only a towel on his head. The swashbuckler marked the beginning of Merv's involvement with the most celebrated figures of his day. He befriended the rich and famous, ending with his dear friend and companion, Eva Gabor. She was the "arm candy" that he could parade out at public functions in an attempt to conceal his private life.

That secret life was spent behind closed doors with a string of boyfriends—most often paid companions—who ranged from one-night stands to more enduring relationships. He confided to his best male friend, Liberace, "I've never fallen in love." He could always count on Liberace to cheer him up, and the flamboyant piano player often "traded" boyfriends with Merv.

Show business insiders in both Los Angeles and New York knew for years that Merv was gay. Most of the public did not until he was more or less "outed" in two lawsuits, both filed in 1991. Charging sexual harassment, Denny Terrio, the host of *Dance Fever*, a show Merv created, sued him. A few months later, Brent Plott, a longtime bodyguard and companion, filed a $200 million palimony suit against Merv. Both suits were mysteriously dismissed, the terms of the settlement unknown.

Other than family, Merv's best friend of more than 50 years was the last celebrity to visit him in the hospital, where his cancer had spread to his bones, lungs, and liver. He had met the starlet, Nancy Davis, when she was having an affair with Clark Gable in 1947. Ronald Reagan, of course, lay in her future.

Accompanied by two secret service agents, Nancy appeared at Merv's deathbed to tell him, "You were my rock during Ronnie's final years. I just can't stand the thought of losing you too."

The next day, seeing that his father was in great pain and suffering terribly, and that there was no hope, son Tony made the most painful decision of his life. He ordered that a DNR notice be posted on his beloved father's bed. Do Not Resuscitate.

At 11pm, Merv, in a hoarse, raspy voice, whispered in Tony's ear: "You were my life."

Two hours later at 1am, he closed his eyes for the last time.

Even his detractors praised **Merv** for his "Midas Touch," in which silly jingles and brainless plots grabbed the public imagination of his era and became vastly profitable.

Here's one of the many daytime TV game shows Merv developed and (in some instances) copywrit, *Play Your Hunch* with (on the right) **Liz Gardner.**

Watched by millions, *The Merv Griffin Show* ran weekday afternoons nationwide for 21 years and won eleven Emmys. Sometimes it was controversial and cutting-edge.

More frequently, it was chummy, diverting, and jovial —-and always centered around *"HEEERE'S MERV"* (who emoted like everyone's hip and funniest uncle) and his "in the *zeitgeist* of the moment" guests.

But whereas Merv grew adept at getting the world's most famous people to spill their secrets on TV, he managed to keep his own closet of secrets tightly locked....until the publication of Darwin Porter's widely publicized *exposé*.

In his later life, at least in public, Merv often escorted **Eva Gabor** to public functions, in part because of a genuine affection, in part as a means of concealing his homosexual promiscuity.

Here's Eva in her most famous role, the ditzy and oh-so-charming urbanite whose TV character fled from Manhattan to pursue the country life in the hit TV sitcom *Green Acres*.

Eva was one of the three Gabor sisters ("the Bombshells from Budapest"), whose epic personal histories were later explored by Darwin Porter in another of his bios.

Odd Couples from the Cold War

WHEN MARILYN BONDED WITH NIKITA KHRUSHCHEV

TERRIFYING: *Left photo* Soviet leader **Nikita Khruschev** addresses, with "fire and brimstone" the United Nations during his "goodwill tour" of the U.S. in 1959.

Right photo: Crowds line the curbs of Des Moines, Iowa, greeting news of Khruschev's state visit with signs reading "THE ONLY GOOD COMMUNIST IS A DEAD ONE." Khruschchev, reacted to that and other news like a seasoned media pro., ultimately emerging as the star of the tour.

As we approach the 50th anniversary of the mysterious death (August 4, 1962) of Marilyn Monroe, her tragic life is being reviewed in movie houses, TV documentaries, plays, and books. In Darwin Porter's upcoming overview of the strange circumstances of her death, *Marilyn at Rainbow's End*, he came across a treasure trove of relatively unknown aspects of her intriguing life.

One of the most tantalizing stories is the afternoon she spent with Nikita Khrushchev— First Secretary of the Soviet Union's Communist Party—in September of 1959.

Spyros Skouras, head of 20th Century Fox, summoned Marilyn from New York to Los Angeles to be among the *glitterati* turning out to greet the Soviet chairman. On the morning of the luncheon, Marilyn arose in her hotel bungalow to prepare herself for the occasion, with a hair stylist, makeup artist, masseur, and dress designer who had created a black net outfit for her that was almost transparent in the bosom.

Marilyn, seated with a phalanx of studio executives, looking glorious despite having risen early to greet the Soviets.

Despite generations of geopolitical brinksmanship and saber-rattling, someone in Hollywood thought it might be wise to invite **the Soviet Premier** with his wife, **Nina** *(third from left)* to lunch. Thus evolved, with winks and grins,, the most bizarre PR event in the history of entertainment.

Potty-mouthed **Shirley MacLaine** *(2nd from left)* and "that Froggie Hoofer" **(Maurice Chevalier;** *far right) r*ound out the "improbable quartet" whose photos were flashed around the world.

Backing them up are the dancers and actors from the *Can-Can*, Fox's then-blockbuster in production. Cynics described it as a Belle Epoque tribute to naked buttocks and memories of love.

Arriving early at the luncheon (unusual for her), she kissed Frank Sinatra, chairman of the event. He was at Fox starring in the film, *Can-Can*, which Marilyn had turned down, her role going to Shirley MacLaine. At one point, Marilyn had wanted to marry Sinatra, but he ditched her for the dancer, Juliet Prowse, another star in the musical.

To greet Khrushchev, Marilyn lined up with such stars as Cary Grant, Rita Hayworth, Richard Burton, Gregory Peck, and Elizabeth Taylor with her husband, Eddie Fisher.

MacLaine cut in line in front of Marilyn. "How the hell are you, Khrush?" she asked. "I'm glad you're here. Welcome to our country. Later, I'm going to dance the can-can for you without pants."

Marilyn spotted Nina Khrushchev, and later described her to Sinatra, "I thought she was a bag woman who slipped in."

As Marilyn extended her hand to the Soviet dictator, he smiled and held it for a long time, slowing down the receiving line. Through a translator, he told her, "I insist you sit with me at the head table."

Sinatra would later tell Elizabeth Taylor, "When Nikita met Marilyn, the atmosphere oozed with sex with a capital S." A translator was kept busy.

Marilyn asked the chairman, "Have you seen anything in America you like?"

"Yes," he replied through the translator. "You.."

She giggled. "Anything else?"

"Yes, again. Those bumper stickers that proclaim BETTER RED THAN DEAD."

After the food was served, the can-can dancers in the film performed their naughty dance, ending with a finale where they raised their skirts to show their panties, at least those dancers who didn't want to display bare butt.

Although secretly excited, Khrushchev attacked the can-can as a display of blatant sexuality associated with decadent capitalism. He denounced the dance, claiming, "The face of mankind is prettier than its backside. The dance is lascivious, disgusting, and immoral."

Within two years of Marilyn's encounter with Khrushchev, relations between the US and USSR had deteriorated into open hostilities.

This photo above shows a US **P2V Neptune patrol plane** flying ostentatiously close to a **Soviet freighter** during the Cuban Missile Crisis of October, 1962.

Decades later, in his home in Key West, Frank E. Taylor, who in 1960 had produced Marilyn's final film, *The Misfits*, told me what transpired that afternoon at Fox. Taylor had been Marilyn's escort at the Fox luncheon.

"While we were filming *The Misfits* outside Reno, Marilyn one night claimed that "Khrushchev had invited her back to his suite," Taylor said. "Nina was off on a shopping expedition. Without being too graphic, Marilyn then described what happened when Khrushchev dismissed his security team. She claimed she did a striptease in front of him while he sat on a sofa in an ill-fitting business suit."

"Finally, he stood up in front of me, and I got his signal." Marilyn told Taylor. "I got down on bended nylon and did the dirty deed. It took all of six intense minutes."

When Khrushchev flew back to Moscow, he sent Marilyn an expensive present and invited her to visit Russia. "Nikita was the most fascinating man I've ever met except for Carl Sandburg," Marilyn told Taylor. "I could tell that he liked me the most of all the pretty girls at the luncheon."

Producer Frank Taylor—the source of Darwin Porter's anecdote about her "fling' with the Soviet Premier—works with Marilyn on the set of *The Misfits* in September of 1960.

That night in the Reno bar during her dialogue with Taylor, Marilyn added a caveat. "There's a problem with Nikita. He's got so many warts on his face. Who would want to be a communist with a president with all those warts? As for me, I'm voting for this handsome senator from Massachusetts who's going to run for president. He's the sexiest politician in America."

MYSTIC LADIES

October 2011

The Theft of a Portrait with a Smile that Enchanted the World
THE MONA LISA

The enigmatic most famous painting in the world **(the Mona Lisa, aka La Joconde)**, and *(illustration right)* the genius who crafted her, **Leonardo da Vinci** (1452-1519).

The story's been told before, but never better than in R.A. Scotti's new book, *Vanished Smile: The Mysterious Theft of the Mona Lisa*, which may become the subject of a TV special.

On the morning of Monday, August 21, 1911, at the Louvre Museum in Paris, the greatest art theft in history occurred. Leonardo da Vinci's acclaimed masterpiece, *La Joconde*, was removed from the wall and slipped out of the museum, which was closed that day. Even when the museum opened the following Tuesday, no one was particularly alarmed. As amazing as it seems, photographers were allowed to remove masterpieces from the Louvre, even the lady with the enigmatic smile, take the art to their studios, where they photographed the masterpieces before bringing them back to the Louvre.

By noon on that Tuesday, a police guard discovered the broken and discarded glass box and the frame that had encased the *Mona Lisa*. The painting had clearly been stolen.

Art superstar **Pablo Picasso** *(left)* and French poet **Guillaume Apollinaire** *(right)*, although guilty of trading in lesser (stolen) works of art, were ultimately absolved of guilt in the theft of the Mona Lisa.

The news made front pages around the world. After all, the *Mona Lisa* was more than a mere painting: Many art lovers viewed her as a real woman. She even received love letters, and one "jilted" lover had fatally shot himself in front of her mysterious eyes.

A French psychologist suggested the thefts might have been by a sexual psychopath, who would thrill at "mutilating, stabbing, and defiling" her.

When the Louvre reopened after a week's assessment of the damage, it drew the largest crowds in its history. Queues formed for blocks to view the empty space once occupied by the da Vinci masterpiece. Actually, the theft helped elevate the *Mona Lisa* into the legend it is today. Her enigmatic smile began to appear everywhere in reproduction, advertising everything from cigarettes to corsets.

Left photo The "glaringly empty" spot on the wall of the Louvre which had contained the Mona Lisa prior to its theft; and *Right photo:* a recent view of the everyday crush of visitors who have flocked to see it since its return.

The plot thickened after Pablo Picasso became the prime suspect. A bisexual Belgian, Honoré Gery, was arrested and, under heavy grilling, he admitted that he had stolen two ancient Iberian statuettes from the Louvre and had sold them to Picasso. At his studio in Montmartre, Picasso had used the heads as models for his 1907 depiction of a brothel, *Les Demoiselles d'Avignon,* the first painting to bear the mark of Cubism. With his friend, the poet Guillaume Apollinaire, who had once argued that the Louvre should be burned down, Picasso put the stolen statuettes in a suitcase and traveled miles across Paris to dump them in the River Seine. At the last minute, he decided he could not destroy such great ancient art.

Through Gery, the police were led to Apollinaire, who was arrested. Under questioning, he broke down and implicated Picasso in previous thefts of stolen Louvre art. From his responses to their questions, police concluded that he might also have purchased the *Mona Lisa*.

Arrested and brought to trial, Picasso lied, claiming, "I have never seen this man (Apollinaire) before." With no direct evidence tracing Picasso or Apollinaire to the theft of the *Mona Lisa,* they were both set free.

By December of 1912, the police had given up. The masterpiece seemed lost to history.

A breakthrough came eleven months later, on November 29, 1913, when Alfredo Geri, an antiques dealer in Florence, encountered a man who wanted to sell him the *Mona Lisa* for 500,000 lire. Ironically, the dealer's shop was just a short walk from the studio where da Vinci had painted his masterpiece 400 years previously.

Alerting the police, Geri entrapped, as part of a sting operation, a tiny man with a waxed mustache. The man turned out to be a 32-year-old Italian, Vincenzo Peruggia, a house painter-cum-glazier. He had worked briefly for the Louvre and had made the glass case which, until the painting's theft, had encased the Mona Lisa. Perrugia told Geri that he had kept the painting for two years in his tiny apartment in Paris, where she had rested on his kitchen table. "I fell in love with her," he admitted.

Geri followed Peruggia to his hotel room in Florence, where he did indeed have the treasure. The police moved in and arrested him. The *Mona Lisa* was recovered and soon after, returned to the Louvre. Diagnosed by a court psychologist as "mentally deficient," Perruggia had been partially motivated by an incorrect premise. He claimed he had wanted the *Mona Lisa* returned to its rightful home in Florence. Actually the painting had never belonged to or been directly associated with Italy at all. The French Renaissance king, François I, had paid Leonardo 4,000 gold crowns to paint the portrait from his base in a château in France's Loire Valley. For the "crime of the century," Peruggia served only seven months in prison.

Europe soon forgot about him and even the theft, as it plunged into the disaster known as World War I. Heavily guarded, the *Mona Lisa* hangs today in the Louvre. In the decades since the theft, only Jackie Kennedy had the influence to get her removed from her place in the Louvre and shipped across the ocean for an exhibition on another continent.

A breakthrough in Cubism: Pablo Picasso's *Les Demoiselles d'Avignon,* allegedly modeled after ancient Etruscan portrait busts stolen from the Louvre.

EVENTUALLY APPREHENDED: Vincenzo Peruggia, an Italian glazier and housepainter who had stolen and smuggled La Joconde, concealed under his coat, from its loosely supervised location in the Louvre.

The return, in 1914, of **La Joconde** to the Louvre. Paris, and the rest of Europe, with the outbreak of World War I that year, suddenly had a lot more than art to worry about that year.

August 2016

LADY LIBERTY IS NO LADY

A MYSTIC LADY IN TRANSITION

Lady Liberty under construction within the Paris studio of its creator, Frederick Auguste Bartholdi. The figure to the right is is the artist's mother, Augusta.

Lady Liberty in New York Harbor is 130 years old, her uplifted "lamp" symbolizing the hope and promise of America. As such, the Statue of Liberty has received bomb threats from would-be terrorists.

Recently, it has been revealed that the face of the venerable lady may not have been modeled on a lady after all. But a man! Investigative journalist Elizabeth Mitchell, in her book, *Liberty's Torch: The Great Adventure to Build the Statue of Liberty*, delivered a bombshell: For decades, it was believed that the quixotic and visionary French sculptor, Frederic August Bartholdi, had modeled the face of Liberty from his mother, Augusta. But during the course of her years-long investigation, Mitchell discovered that the iconic face was taken from his brother, Jean-Charles, who had been locked away in a mental asylum. He was mute, and Frederic would visit him once a week, sitting in silence studying his face. Comparisons of the few remaining photographs show that Liberty didn't look like Augusta at all. The mother had a much thinner nose, much thinner lips, and more steeply arched eyebrows. Instead, the face of the statue strongly resembled that of Jean-Charles.

Bartholdi may have used his brother's face, but, for the body, he was inspired by the curves of his paramour. According to myth, the 305-foot statue was a gift from the French government to the United States. Actually, it was not. Bartholdi raised money to erect the statue by charging the people of Paris admission to his workshop where the statue was being sculpted and manufactured. Originally, he had wanted it to represent the body of an Egyptian slave and to stand in Port Said, along the Mediterranean coast of Egypt, at the mouth of the Suez Canal.

Frederic-August Bartholdi

Master of art and political rhetoric

Bartholdi in his Paris studio. An early mock-up of the Statue of Liberty is visible on the left.

It was Bartholdi's friend, Edouard René de Laboulaye, a French jurist, poet, author, and anti-slavery activist, who persuaded the sculptor to dedicate the statue to the American concept of Liberty, as a protest against the autocratic French government. Laboulaye felt that democratic ideals had been suppressed during the reign (1852-1870) of Napoleon III.

Bartholdi took some strong persuading. A snobbish boor, he disliked America, labeling its people as "subpar."

The copper statue's green hue is a result of the metal's oxidation over the decades. The sculptor had wanted it to be covered with a thin sheathing of gold leaf, but he couldn't afford it.

For a while, it was likely that the statue might have gone to Boston or to Philadelphia. Then, New Yorkers were asked to pay for construction of the pedestal. Rich people refused, but newspaper magnate Joseph Pulitzer intervened and persuaded the working poor of the city to contribute whatever they could. One little office boy put up a nickel. Pulitzer raised $100,000, the equivalent of $2.3 million in today's currency.

Thomas Edison wanted to get in on the act. After introducing the phonograph in 1878, he tried to create a monumental disc, to be placed inside the statue, allowing Lady Liberty to deliver speeches in a voice loud enough to be heard all the way to Harlem.

At the dedication on October 28, 1886, the towering and robed neoclassical *Libertas*, the Roman goddess, was widely attacked in some American newspapers, who questioned if America was indeed "the land of the free." *The Cleveland* Gazette, an African American newspaper, called for the statue, torch and all, to be shoved into the ocean "until men of color were no longer being ku-kluxed or perhaps murdered."

On July 30, 1916, during World War I, German saboteurs set off an explosion at "Black Tom Island," immediately adjacent to Liberty Island and the site of a vast munitions depot supplying Allied forces fighting the Kaiser. The force of the explosion was equivalent to that of an earthquake, and was felt as far away as Philadelphia. Shrapnel pierced the statue, whose arm, based on safety reasons, has been closed to visitors ever since.

As author Mitchell so accurately claims, the riveting story behind the statue is one of "chicanery, rivalries, hustling, back-stabbings, lies, and disappointments."

So it was a bumpy path to glory before she (or he) could stand in the center of NY Harbor welcoming "your tired, your poor."

Lady Lib under construction in Paris.

Also by F.A. Bartholdi: Equally rich in national sentiment, here's a view of Bartholdi's rendering of **Vercingetorix,** the mythical French national hero and anti-Roman resistance fighter, in Place de la Jaude, in central France, at Clermont-Ferrand.

Briefly, at least, Bartholdi was almost as famous as the mammoth statue he created. Here's the cover of the June 13, 1885 edition of *The Illustrated Newspaper.*

July 2018

NAMATH
Broadway Joe's Historic Life Moves into Its Fourth Quarter

They called him football's version of Mick Jagger

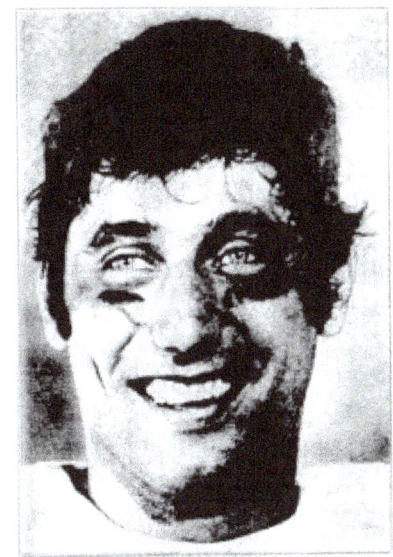

SUPERDUPER!

B'way Joe Jolts Colts By 16-7

Now a resident of Jupiter, Florida, Joe Namath—nicknamed "Broadway Joe"—has turned 75. He faces his "fourth quarter" with hope and optimism.

He told the press, "My plan is simple. I intend to live to be a hundred, and hopefully further. When I turned 50, this dude told me I was getting old. 'No, no, no,' I said. 'It's only halftime at 50.' You mention my latest birthday. I'm 75. That's the end of the third quarter, with the fourth just getting started.'"

The Hall of Fame quarterback speaks in a syrupy voice once called "a mix of Beaver Falls (PA), Tuscaloosa, and New York City." With his long hair and sideburns, he was football's Mick Jagger.

He admits, "Time flies by too fast, and I want to say to God, 'Hey, Man, can you please slow it down a bit?'"

In his heyday, Namath was a mammoth football celebrity and pop icon. He played for both the NFL and the AFL, spending most of his career as an AFL icon for that league's New York Jets during his career peak in the 1960s and '70s.

Superbowl III, January of 1969. His career breakthrough, the moment when Las Vegas betting pools REALLY turned in his favor.

Of Hungarian descent, he was born in Pennsylvania in 1943. The highlight of his career was his performance in the Jets' win 16-7 over the Baltimore Colts, "the greatest football team in history." That was at the Super Bowl III in January of 1969.

Namath's reputation extended far beyond being a football hero. Although no one ever accused him of being Laurence Olivier, he became an actor, starring with such sexpots as Ann-Margret in the 1970s "biker film," *C.C. and Company*. He also appeared on Broadway and was always popping up on television, including

Nobody didn't like **Broadway Joe.** Here he is, stadium-ready, as a superstar in fur.

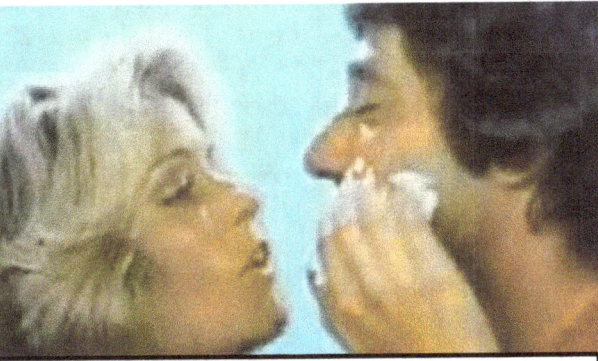

Early in **Farrah Fawcett's** spectacular career as an actress, model, and icon, she appeared in ads (aired during the Superbowl) removing **Noxema** shaving cream from the face of the then-reigning sports hero of America: **Joe Namath.** The commercial was a blowout success that took American living rooms by storm. "I'm so excited, I'm gonna get creamed," declared Namath, before Fawcett sensually slathered his face with the shave cream product. A critic later evaluated the ad as "A near-seamless blend of football slang and sexual innuendo."

Some said that the one-minute spot launched Farah Fawcett's career. Almost everyone found the ads charming and piquant—but not at all vulgar. Throughout the process of "taking it off," Joe remained bemused, charming, modest, and—always one of his best qualities—self-satirical.

frothy, good-natured appearances on *The Love Boat*.

Mostly because of his very hip ability to self-satirize, his commercials became some of the most popular ever aired, especially in 1974 when he shaved his legs and posed seductively for a Hanes Beautymist Pantyhose commercial. His shapely gams were hailed as "the most beautiful in football history." He also posed lathered up with Noxzema shaving cream, where he was shaved by the then-unknown Farrah Fawcett.

He became somewhat notorious for wearing floor-length fur coats. In November of 1971, he showed up at Shea Stadium in a stunning white fur coat crafted from coyote and Norwegian fur. The *New York Daily News* asserted that "The Namath fur attracted more attention than the game." It also inspired a massive upturn in fur sales for men.

Others ridiculed it as "a caveman coat" and denounced him for wearing fur, citing it "as disgusting and cruel."

Nonetheless, Blackglama Mink hired Namath to pose in fur for its ad campaign, adding him to a roster celebrities (including Judy Garland and Bette Davis) in *"What Becomes a Legend Most?"*.

Namath also earned a reputation as a major-league player in the boudoir, at least some of his sexual exploits "kicking off" within his bachelor penthouse in Manhattan beneath a mirrored ceiling. In a *Playboy* interview in 1969, he claimed that he had seduced at least 300 women. "I like my girls blonde and my Johnnie Walker Red." One of his companions was Raquel Welch, seen out on the town with him in a gown so low-cut you could see how she was sculpted.

For long periods of his life, he battled the bottle, including during the course of his 1984 marriage to an aspiring young actress, Deborah Mays. "I was 41 and she was 22 when she caught my last pass," he said.

The couple produced two children before divorcing in 2000. He became a grandfather when his sixteen-year-old daughter, Olivia, gave birth to a child.

"I've had my down times," he said, "like everybody else. But the rough times have been rare, since most of my life has been joyful and healthy, except I had to have both of my knees replaced. Perhaps the saddest thing is when I get together with my old teammates for a reunion. My buddies keep thinning out every year."

As a last request upon turning 75, Namath said, "I want my loyal fans to know I'm still in the game."

Namath, then and now: A superstar at any age, he cemented his legacy in 1969 when he spearheaded the underdog Jets win against the NFL's Baltimore Colts in 1969 during Superbowl III in one of the greatest sports upsets of all time.

Briefly, at least, **Namath** was the hottest actor and "the most psychoanalyzed-from-afar" celebrity in America. *On the left,* he appears on the cover of **Sports Illustrated** with **Ann-Margret** in a feature article about the biker drama *C.C. and Company* (1970). On the right, he's the focus of a psychological evaluation in the October, 1969 edition of *Esquire.*

June 2018

DEBBIE REYNOLDS & CARRIE FISHER

After Garland & Minnelli, they were the Greatest Mother-Daughter Act in Show-Biz

In the Beginning: Here's a spontaneous view of a scrappy, wryly funny mother-daughter team.

On the left is **Debbie** ("unsinkable Tammy," aka ""hard as nails and with more balls than any five guys I've ever known,") and her daughter, **Carrie Fisher** "one of the smartest, hippest chicks in Hollywood."

The most ardent fans of Debbie Reynolds and Carrie Fisher, two movie legends, like to think they are united in a galaxy far, far away. Both of them died within hours of each other in December of 2016.

Debbie still holds the record as the singing and dancing sensation of *Singin' in the Rain* (1952), hailed today as the greatest Hollywood musical ever made. Carrie earned her own kind of immortality when she starred in "my lifetime career" of playing Princess Leia with that "cinnamon bun hairdo" beginning with the first installment of *Star Wars* (1977).

The tragic lives and loves of these two stars live again in Blood Moon's latest Hollywood biography, *Carrie Fisher & Debbie Reynolds: Princess Leia and Unsinkable Tammy in Hell.* For the first time, their remarkable lives are revealed in detail with many hidden revelations.

They were remarkable survivors whose struggles evoke those of a heroine by Shakespeare. They faced a total of five failed marriages (three for Debbie, two for Carrie), bankruptcies, bipolar disorders, electroshock treatments, endless lawsuits, hopelessly doomed love affairs, and

Frequently at odds, but ferociously loyal, Debbie and Carrie evolved into one of the most-watched mother-daughter teams in show-biz.

The film that launched Debbie as a star was *Singin' in the Rain* (1952). One of her greatest scenes involved emerging as a "party favor" from a birthday cake *(see above).*

dreams that never came true. Through it all, both of them endured and kept their careers going at full blast.

Carrie was born to Debbie and Eddie Fisher, the pop crooner of the 1950s. Both "Debbie & Eddie" were hailed as "America's Sweethearts." A forest of trees in Canada were needed for the newsprint that described their glorious love affair that was all a sham.

Away on singing engagements, Eddie was almost never at home, indulging in a series of affairs.

His best friend, producer Mike Todd, the husband of Elizabeth Taylor, died in a plane crash in New Mexico in 1958. Fisher rushed to the side of his widow and never left. As he later told Debbie, "I love Elizabeth. I never loved you. I only married you because my fans would desert me if I walked out on America's Sweetheart."

Through it all, Debbie bounced back as the button-nosed, *boop-boopie-doo* girl, strutting her stuff and emoting as an unpretentious girl next door. She had found her lifetime schtick—that of a relentlessly upbeat show-stopper with plenty of spunk, humor, and razzmatazz. America gobbled it up.

That bouncy image was cemented in 1957 when she appeared as the country girl in *Tammy and the Bachelor*. Her recording of "Tammy" went gold, playing on jukeboxes across the land. For the rest of her life, wherever she appeared on stage, Debbie had to sing this song of a virginal innocent. She accurately predicted, "I'll be singing 'Tammy' on stage until I die."

"It was all an act," Carrie said. "Debbie was a hardened survivor who drank bat's blood for breakfast and smeared bug brains on her skin."

She was more in tune with her role in the 1964 *The Unsinkable Molly Brown*, which brought her an Oscar nod. It was the tale of the actual Molly Brown, heiress to a Colorado gold mining fortune who survived the sinking of the Titanic.

Along the way, Debbie fell in love with a number of men who didn't want to marry her or were already married: Glenn Ford, Robert Wagner (her first love), James Dean, Frank Sinatra, James Garner, and Gower Champion, among others.

She also married two more times, a show manufacturer and a real estate developer, both of whom went through their fortunes and hers as well. Debbie ended up getting booted out of her palatial home by the bank which held hefty mortgages.

"You've heard of Queen for a Day?" Debbie asked. "Well, I was Queen for a long weekend on two different occasions." She was referring to her affairs with the handsome young King Baudouin of Belgium and King Hussein of Jordan during their visits to Hollywood.

Baudouin told his handlers that Debbie Reynolds was his favorite movie star, and they arranged a visit for him to meet her on the set of It Started With a Kiss in 1959. The title of the film was apt. Evading his security forces, she ran away with him for a long weekend spent at Rock Hudson's villa in Malibu.

Their disappearance, although hidden from the press, caused much speculation among insiders. She later followed Baudouin to New York, where he bid her farewell and never returned. "There went my chance to become Queen of Belgium and First Lady of the Congo." (At the time, the Congo was a colony of Belgium.)

Back in Hollywood, she entertained another royal visitor, King Hussein of Jordan. She later claimed that her brief fling with him "was straight out of Arabian Nights." When he flew out of Hollywood, he too, would never return "There went my chance to become queen of the oldest dynasty in the Muslim world."

Carrie made her first screen appearance as a teenager in Shampoo (1975) opposite Warren Beatty. Her opening line on the screen was to ask him if he wanted to seduce her, although she used the "F" word. Apparently, he accepted her invitation off screen. She claimed he took her virginity, whether he did or not.

Debbie sent her daughter to London to study drama for a year, and it was here that she became enveloped in Mick Jagger's drugged-out world of the glitterati. She also entered into romances with two dazzling bisexual stars, Freddie Mercury and David Bowie.

Back in Hollywood, she made Star Wars in 1977 as Princess Leia. In New York, she was lured into the heavily drugged world of John Belushi, her doomed co-star in The Blues Brothers.

America was transfixed by the wreckage of Debbie's marriage to pop singer Eddie Fisher. *The upper photo* shows "**Debbie and Eddie**" with their newborn daughter, **Carrie**.

The *lower photo* shows **Elizabeth Taylor** in the late 1950s, during the peak of her notorious "Theft" of Eddie from the arms of Debbie.

In the notoriety that followed, it took years for "Bad Girl" Elizabeth to recover from the negative publicity she'd generated. Ironically, Elizabeth's (brief) marriage to Eddie morphed into a union that was just as unhappy as Debbie's had been.

In part because of the scandal brewing almost since her birth, Carrie was able to accu-rately say that she, almost more than any other child in show-biz, truly grew up in a glass cage.

She would go on to have two husbands of her own. The first was the singer and composer Paul Simon, and together, they crossed a "Bridge Over Troubled Water." Although the marriage ended, their affair continued for years.

When she married for the final time, it was to a top Hollywood talent agent, Bryan Lourd, which led to the birth of a daughter, actress Billie Lourd. One night, he informed her he was leaving her since he wanted "a husband of my own."

After that, all of Carrie's affairs were doomed to fail. Her two most big name seductions began when she was filming *Liberty* (1985) on the East Coast. There, she was introduced to Senator Chris Dodd of Connecticut, and they began a fling. After he introduced her to one of his best friends, Senator Teddy Kennedy of Boston, a brief romance followed. She said "Both of these men, at different times, ran for President of the United States. Each of them failed in that pursuit, and I failed, too, in not becoming First Lady of the United States."

Lost in a world of drugs and enduring electroshock therapies, Carrie broke with her mother and didn't speak to her for a decade. They finally reunited, living in separate but nearby homes within their enclosed compound in Los Angeles.

While she was in London to promote her latest book, *Princess Diarist*, Carrie made world headlines when she revealed her love affair with Harrison Ford, who had played Han Solo in *Star Wars*. Regrettably, the affair didn't last, as he was already married.

She flew back to Los Angeles but lapsed into a coma during the flight, dying on December 27, 2016. She was only sixty years old, and an autopsy revealed that she had traces of at least five recreational drugs in her system at the time of her death.

During her planning for her daughter's funeral, Debbie said, "My heart is broken."

In less than two days, Debbie herself was dead at the age of 84. Her career had spanned six and a half decades. "The shock of Carrie's death was more than my mother could take," said her son, Todd.

Many medical authorities came forth to proclaim that it is entirely possible to die of a broken heart.

***

One of Carrie's most durable (and enduring) roles derived from her portrayal of Princess Leia in the *Star Wars* franchise. As she aged, so did the character of Leia, which survived through galactic revolts and a changing times, measured, in sci-fi style, over the course of many light years. Here are two views of **Carrie Fisher**, who —in real life—proved almost as durable as Princess Leia herself.

CARRIE FISHER & DEBBIE REYNOLDS

Princess Leia & Unsinkable Tammy in Hell

ANOTHER OUTRAGEOUS TITLE IN BLOOD MOON'S BABYLON SERIES
DARWIN PORTER & DANFORTH PRINCE

Darwin Porter is the most visible and widely read author of celebrity biographies in America today. His most recent, co-authored with Danforth Prince, is *Carrie Fisher & Debbie Reynolds: Princess Leia and Unsinkable Tammy in Hell*, Biography/Rich & Famous, 6x9 Softcover, with photos. 630 pages. (ISBN 978-1-936003-57-0), the first comprehensive overview of this mother-daughter team ever published.

For more information about Porter's ongoing literary opus, click on www.BloodMoonProductions.com.

Celebrating 24 Years of PRINT, RADIO & WEB

Boomer Times
& Senior Life

 Google

Blast from the Recent Past

RADIO—IT'S FREE... LISTEN AND LEARN

Every Saturday from 5am to 8am, tune in to WSBR 740AM to listen to exciting, interesting and enlightening conversations with the best and brightest here in South Florida and throughout the country— And for more, tune in Sundays on WWNN 1470AM at 7am to 7:30am and 4:30pm to 5:00pm to hear host Anita Finley talk to other interesting guests.

JANE RUSSELL
"Even Christians Have Bosoms"

The world took little notice of the passing, on February 28, 2011, of the sultry, busty brunette, actress Jane Russell, who died of respiratory failure at her home in Santa Monica. She was 89.

Boys or young men growing up in the late 1940s and early 50s often had a picture of Jane tacked to their locker room door. It depicted her in a cleavage-revealing blouse falling off one shoulder, as she rested in a haystack holding a gun. The scene was from the most notorious A-list film of the 1940s, Howard Hughes' controversial *The Outlaw*, shot in 1941. Jane was cast as a sagebrush vixen, Rio McDonald, playing opposite an equally sexy Jack Buetel as Billy the Kid. The film provoked one of America's greatest censorship battles, with Hughes· eventually emerging triumphant.

Tons of newsprint centered on a specially engineered bra that Hughes had designed for his 38D leading lady. But Jane later claimed she tossed it in the wastepaper basket and wore her own support. Tame by today's standards, *The Outlaw* played for nine weeks in San Francisco in 1943, Hughes advertising it as "Two good reasons to go see this film." Then he put it in mothballs until a 1947 New York opening. It wasn't until 1950 that Florida residents got to see it.

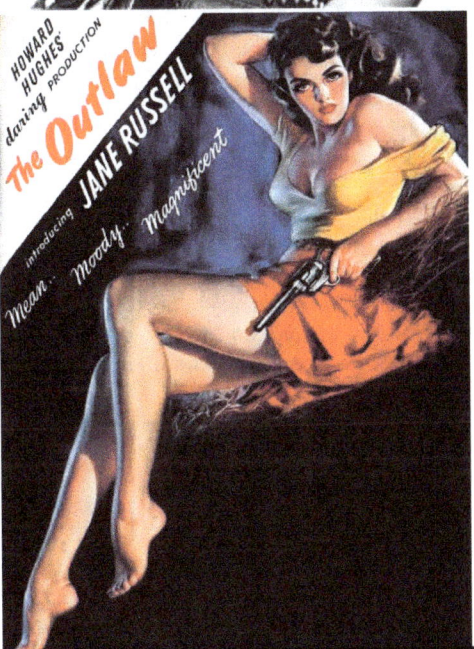

Two views of **Jane Russell,** an actress made famous by the mammary obsession of the industrial mogul, film producer and bi-sexual billionaire, Howard Hughes.

For most of her life, Jane was under contract to Hughes. Her most memorable film was the 1953 *Gentlemen Prefer Blondes*, in which she co-starred with Marilyn Monroe. The blonde bombshell just seemed to ooze femininity whereas Jane came off as brusquely butch. Although a great success, the movie marked Jane's decline. Her haystack picture came down from those locker walls to be replaced by MM's nude calendar.

Two views of Jane Russell with her co-star, Marilyn Monroe, in Jane's OTHER most famous film,, **Gentlemen Prefer Blondes.**

Frothy, witty, and fun, the "dissimilar" co-stars were marketed by the studio as "the (busty) blonde" and "the bustier brunette."

Even though Jane's career fizzled, she came back into the public spotlight in the 70s and 80s when she was the TV spokeswoman for Playtex bras, hawking them for "full-figured gals like me."

After a botched abortion in 1942 before she married her high school sweetheart, U.C.L.A. football player Bob Waterfield, Jane could never have any more children. She became an outspoken opponent of abortion and an advocate of adoption, founding the World Adoption International Fund in the 1950s. After nearly a quarter of a century of married life with Waterfield, she divorced him when she caught him "playing around." In 1968 she married actor Robert Barrett, who died three months later of a heart attack. In 1974 she wed a retired Air Force

"Hurry, full-figured gals."

Last 7 days of the Playtex 18 Hour Time-to-Save Sale.

Even after her career as a full-figured siren ended, Jane's phone kept ringing with calls from Madison Avenue—in her case as a busty icon of well-endowed women everywhere.

The sponsor was **Playtex**—specifically their line of **"18-hour, cross-your-heart"** brassières.

She was a hit. Sales soared, sustaining the by-then out-of-work actress for decades.

Cinematic embarrassments happened:

Here's Jane, stripping, teasing, and "**Looking for Trouble**" in **The French Line** (1953).

Lieutenant, John Calvin Peoples. After his death in 1999, she became an alcoholic for several years before rehabilitation. Robert Mitchum, Jane's sleepy-eyed, sardonic co-star in *His Kind of Woman* and *Macao*, once said, "Minnesota-born Ernestine Jane Geraldine Russell showed the world what a gal with a pair of knockers could do."

Although Jane slept with some of her leading men, notably Mitchum and Victor Mature, she later claimed "my longest running affair was with a living doll." By that, she meant God.

Unlike most Hollywood sex symbols such as Lana Turner, Jane spent most of her life as a devout Christian. "I'm a tee-totaling, mean-spirited right wing, narrow-minded, conservative Christian bigot, but not a racist," she said. "Bigotry just means I don't have an open mind."

Even though Jane and MM are gone, we suspect that some two-hundred years from now they will still be appearing in their classic duet, thrilling future audiences with their "Two Little Girls from Little Rock."

As one WWII veteran remembered, "Jane was not the girl next door. She was lust, desire, and everything good boys weren't supposed to dream about."

In summation of her life, she claimed that she always knew "if I could just hold tough a little longer, I'd find myself around one more dark corner, see one more spot of light and have one more drop of pure joy in this journey called life."

Older, wiser, and more demure:

Still photogenic, here's **Jane Russell** during her later years.

Giggly, charming, splotched with cement, and ready for their closeups

Here are **MM** and **Jane Russell** sinking their hands into cement in front of Graumann's Chinese Theater during the peak of their respective fame.

According to Marilyn, "Jane tried to convert me to religion, and I tried to introduce her to Freud."

Russell's most famous, most charming, and most enduring role: That of the brunette in *Gentlemen Prefer Blondes*. Film critics claim that unless the world comes to an end, this film will survive for centuries.

March 2013

Twin Sisters Offer Advice to the Lovelorn

DEAR ABBY

Tart-tongued Guidance for Millions

Dear Abby:
I am a housewife married to an advertising executive. Recently, my 13-year-old stepson raped me. Since then, he has repeated the act at least twice a day when his father is at work. I have fallen madly in love with the boy. What should I do?
Confused.

***

Dear Confused:
Divorce your husband, wait for the kid to grow up, then marry him.

Twin sisters **Pauline Phillips** (aka *Dear Abby,* left) and **Eppie Lederer** (aka *Ann Landers,* right) share a laugh in this later-in-life celebration of their reunion after years of feud-ing.

Although DEAR ABBY was the progenitor and first of the two advice columns, each of them rose to national prominence. based on wise advice from writers with high "emotional I.Q.s."

Although authored today by "replacement advisors," each of the columnist's advice columns is still alive and thriving.

That letter was among thousands of others sent to Pauline Phillips, who wrote a "Dear Abby" column under the pen name, Abigail Van Buren.

Newspaper editors in the late 1950s considered the letter too *risqué* and didn't run it as part of her column. Abigail sent a personal letter to "Confused" instead.

After battling Alzheimer's disease for years, Pauline Phillips (Dear Abby) died at the age of 94 on January 16, 2013.

In a touch of irony, Abigail was the identical twin of the world's other leading advice columnist, Esther Lederer, who wrote under the pen name of "Ann Landers." She died in 2002.

A script about them, with two strong roles for women, is currently being shopped around Hollywood studios. Several actresses have expressed a desire to play one or another of these two feuding sisters, who dressed and acted like movie stars themselves. As sisters, their sibling rivalry in media was equaled only by two of Hollywood's super stars, actresses Olivia de Havilland and Joan Fontaine, both in their mid-90s and still alive.

The identical twins were born on July 4, 1918 in Sioux City, Iowa, the daughters of an itinerant Russian chicken peddler. He later achieved the American dream by acquiring a string of movie houses.

Originally, the woman who became known as Abigail was nicknamed "Popo," and Esther (Ann) was called "Eppie." At an early age, both of them vowed to marry millionaires, and on the same day in 1939, they fulfilled that dream. Abigail married Morton Phillips, heir to a liquor

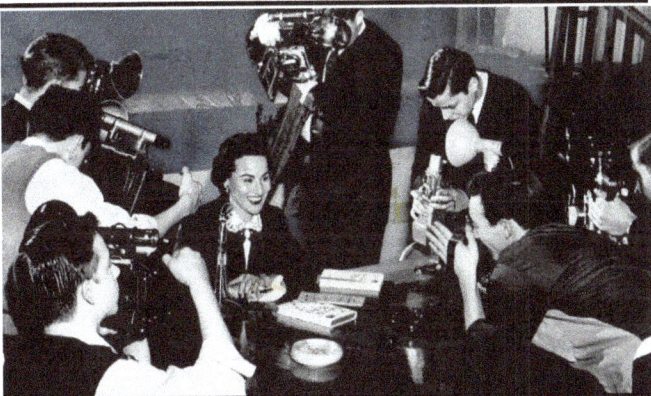

OKLAHOMA, 1960: High-school reporters flock around **Abigail Van Buren** during a press and PR trip she took to the Grain Belt. The 60s were probably the headiest peak of her early notoriety and fame.

Impossibly admired, impossibly famous: Here's **DEAR ABBY** at the White House with then-President **Ronald Reagan** in 1985.

fortune, and Ann married Jules Lederer, co-founder of Budget Rent-a-Car.

In Chicago in 1955, Ann became the first sister to write an advice column, becoming a sensation almost overnight. However, she made a big mistake. Overwhelmed with letters, she sent some of them to Abigail to help her concoct some answers.

A bored San Francisco housewife, "tired of mah-jongg," Abigail found she had an amazing talent for delivering tart, witty responses, though filled with common sense. She decided to write her own advice column.

Wearing a Dior dress, with her chauffeur-driven Cadillac parked around the corner, she approached an editor of a local newspaper. He tried her out and within an hour and a half, she was assigned a role as a columnist at $20 a week.

She, too, became an overnight success, an achievement which plunged her into a bitter life-long feud with Ann. Both fought for the same readers and the same syndication deals, and many newspapers carried both columns. In record time, both sisters were run in about 1,400 newspapers around the world, reaching 110 million readers. Letters arrived by the mailbag.

Their responses were similar, as they buried forever the self-image of weepy Victorian advice columnists. The sisters were called a "combination Groucho Marx and Damon Runyon." They gave salty, no-nonsense advice to "monster" in-laws, cheating spouses, pregnant teenagers, gays, sinning clergymen, unwed mothers, alcoholics, and those inclined to suicide. They often dished out tough love when needed, but had sympathy for human flaws and failings.

Ann was the more controversial, advocating Pro-choice and calling for the legalization of prostitution and homosexual acts. She often incurred outrage, as when she called Pope John Paul II "a Polack who hates women," and Joseph P. Kennedy "an anti-semite."

Even so, they became friends of famous, persons as diverse as Senator Hubert Humphrey, Dean Martin, and Jerry Lewis. Abigail was also a friend of the Catholic bishop, Fulton Sheen, though warning him, "You'll become a Jew like me before I'll become a Catholic."

So popular was Abby's advice that it spilled out in book formats too. Here, published in 1960, is one which morphed into a library of advice columns.

Culled from the illustration's (see above) fine print:

"**DEAR ABBY:** I'm 44 years old and would like to meet a man my age with no bad habits. ROSE."

"**DEAR ROSE**: So would I."

At her death, Ann requested that her column be discontinued. In contrast, Abigail's column since 1987 was assisted by, and since 2002, fully authored by, her daughter, Jeanne Phillips. Abigail's marriage to Mort Phillips lasted 73 years, until her death.

During their heyday, Ann and Abigail were the most widely read and most quoted women in the world, according to *Life* magazine.

Inspired by them, Debbie Reynolds carried on their tradition, with her weekly advice column, entitled "Dear Debbie," in *The Globe*. America's sweetheart of the 1950s, however, lacked the punch and fire of "Popo" and "Eppie."

A publisher is considering issuing a book of "Dear Abby" letters with responses never printed. Here's a typical one:

Dear Abby:

I'm a tall girl nearly six feet dating two men—one is 6'3", the other only 5'7". I'm sometimes ashamed to be seen with "Shorty," especially in my high heels. However, he has twice the endowment of my tall basketball player. Which one should I marry?
Perplexed.

Dear Perplexed:
"Shorty," of course.

August 2010

SARAH FERGUSON

"Grasping Black Sheep" of the House of Windsor

The scandal-scarred Sarah Ferguson, the disgraced Duchess of York, breezed into New York in late May of 2010 in her desperate quest to raise much-needed cash to deal with her ever-mounting debt. The tabloid press was cruel, labeling her "The Duchess of Pork."

When Fergie hinted that she might move permanently to America, the *New York Post* asked "If we pay you, will you go home?"

What's it all about, Fergie? A lavish lifestyle of champagne, caviar, chauffeured Bentleys, and chambermaids have left Fergie swimming in a sea of debt. Bad investments have left her drowning.

Caught drunk on tape, she fell for a tabloid scam to entrap her. On film, she is seen selling access to Prince Andrew, Britain's roving trade ambassador. The flame-haired flake thought she was dealing with an international tycoon. In reality, she was confronting a reporter for *News of the World*, a British tabloid.

For "unlimited access" to Andrew, she demanded $750,000, actually bagging $40,000 of it in cash on that ill-fated night. Access to royalty doesn't come cheap. At least, she didn't place the Queen on the auction block.

In the past when Fergie needed cash, she turned to America, making various deals, the most lucrative of which was as a spokesperson for Weight Watchers, which gave her $3 million. That deal ended in 2007.

She was seen in New York in May at Book Expo America, the nation's leading book fair, hawking her books for children which have had anemic sales. A spokesperson for Barnes & Noble claimed her recent scandals may actually increase book sales.

In part, Fergie is desperately poor because she agreed to accept only $20,000 annually in alimony from Prince Andrew, hardly enough to maintain a royal duchess.

A spy told us that anytime Fergie wants to cash in on her royal connection, revealing the deepest, darkest secrets of the House of Windsor, she could walk away with a cool $2 million from either of two of America's leading publishers.

To cement such a deal, she'd have to spill the beans about two major questions that have been repeatedly asked in British tabloids. First and foremost is the question, "Who is the father of Prince Andrew?" Secondly, is it true that her former husband—once known as "Randy Andy" in the tabloids—also has a fondness for "strapping lads" from Her Majesty's Royal Navy? Prince Edward, his younger brother, has long been rumored to be a homosexual, with charges that his marriage is a cover up. But Andrew, too, has come in for his share of similar rumors. Presumably Fergie knows the answers to both questions—and a lot more.

It has long been speculated that Prince Andrew was the lovechild of Queen Elizabeth and Henry George Reginald Molyneux Herbert (1924 – 2001), known variously as the 7th Earl of Carnarvon or Lord Porchester, her racing manager since 1969. As some House of Windsor biographies have claimed, the Queen became romantically involved with his lordship after she discovered that

Although today, **Fergie's wedding to Prince Andrew** seems only a dim memory, at the time, it was one of the biggest events on the royal (and international) calendar.

Many Brits were horrified by what they interpreted as a flagrant commercialization of the Royal Family by one of its disgraced ex-members.

Here are two of the dozens of tabloid *exposés* that further embarassed the Crown. On the left is a review of **Fergie's** involvement with Texan **Steve-Wyatt**. On the right is an overview of her affair with **John Bryan**. Its editors referred to its centerpiece as *"the toe-sucking photo that ruined the Duchess of York."*

her errant husband, Prince Philip, was carrying on a secret affair with her cousin, Princess Alexandra.

Andrew bears an uncanny resemblance to the late Lord Porchester, not only facially but in his chunky body, unlike his more slender siblings who look more like Prince Philip during his youth.

When Andrew was born, he was kept under wraps as no other royal baby has been before or since. Even when he was christened, official photographers were banned in what is normally a state occasion

Of course, it's long been known that the Queen's marriage to Prince Philip is an unromantic partnership. In fact, Philip was gone for months on one of his world tours during the time when the Queen might have become impregnated.

As one royal watcher said, "What's the big deal? Royals in Britain have been shagging around for centuries."

Fergie was married to the Queen's second son from 1986 to 1996. They have two children, Princess Beatrice of York, age 21, and Princess Eugenie of York, age 20. The two young women once were, respectively, fifth and sixth in line of succession to the British throne.

During her marriage to Andrew when he was away on naval duties, Fergie dated other men, including the Texas multi-millionaire Steve Wyatt. The marriage was all but over when *paparazzi* snapped photographs of Fergie on the French Riviera with an American financial manager, John Bryan. She was topless and was getting her toes sucked by Bryan.

Since 2008 the Duchess has lived with Prince Andrew in separate quarters at the Royal Lodge outside Windsor. The mansion once belonged to Andrew's grandmother Elizabeth, the Queen Mother.

Although still referred to as the Duchess of York, Fergie has lost her other titles—Her Royal Highness, Countless of Inverness, and Baroness Killyleagh.

Fergie is not a total sleazeball. She does turn down offers, including one from a member of the Saudi royal family to become the world's most expensive prostitute. At an intimate dinner with the Arab prince, he offered to pay off her millions of dollars of debt if she'd become his mistress.

She turned down the offer but suffered through a kiss. She claimed that "when those lips sprung forward and plastered themselves upon my mouth, it felt like extricating myself from a suction cup." She nicknamed the prince "Rupper Lips." For that kiss, from the lascivious prince in his flowing white robes, she made off with $70,000.

Fergie has turned down other far less repulsive offers, including a $1.46 million deal to model a pair of jeans from an American manufacturer; a free multi-million condo in New York if she'd claim she was a tenant; an offer of a million pounds to appear on stage in London with Peter O'Toole, playing the wild Queen Boadicea, the ancient queen of the Celts, who fought off the Romans.

"Even I have my limits of what I'll do for money," Fergie has proclaimed.

An independent filmmaker in Hollywood is preparing a movie script on the life of the Duchess, reportedly based in part on the Allan Starkie bio, *Fergie: Her Secret Life*.

But who will play Fergie? One of her (many) detractors vindictively suggested "Miss Piggy."

Royal Diversions, Royal Distractions

Upper photo: **Princess Elizabeth** (later **Queen Elizabeth II**) with her then-fiancé, Philip, during the heady days of their early nuptials.

Lower photo: At the races with **QEII** and the **7th Earl of Carnarvon** (*aka* **Lord Porchester**). Was he the biological father of Prince Andrew?

Sarah, Duchess of York Loses Patronage Role After Calling Jeffrey Epstein a 'Supreme Friend' in Leaked Email

Sarah Ferguson's embarassments continued deep into the 21st Century. In October of 2025, she was evicted from some of the charities she represented because of her 2011 endorsement of sex trafficker **Jeffrey Epstein**.

Where this one will end, no one—at least for now—knows.

The Queen's cousin, **Princess Alexandra**, depicted here in 1961, long rumored to have sustained a prolonged affair with Philip.

January 2022

GOD SAVE THE QUEEN

Queen Elizabeth II, who ascended the throne of Britain on February 6, 1952, will mark her Diamond Jubilee in February of 2022

The Jubilee will be followed by festivities associated with her birthday in June.

But inside the walls of Buckingham Palace, there is little to celebrate. A sense of crisis prevails, even more so than during the events of 1936 when Edward VIII abdicated the throne "to marry the woman I love."

Queen Elizabeth is 95 years old. She has been one of the most active monarchs in history, with a hard-won reputation for seemingly showing up everywhere. But no more.

According to leaked reports, and under the shroud of night, an ambulance recently carried the Queen to a hospital where she faced a battery of tests. According to unconfirmed reports that appeared in the London tabloids, she was diagnosed with an acute case of leukemia, among other ailments.

Her absence suddenly came to world attention, especially when she was a no-show at the COP26 climate change conference in Scotland., where she was to have been seated next to President Biden. Even before that, she caused speculation on November 14 when, for the first time, she didn't appear at the annual "Remembrance Sunday" celebration, a National Holiday honoring Britain's war dead.

Even worse, many of her scheduled events for early 2022 have been cancelled.

It is believed that she interprets her greatest challenge as the rescue of the monarchy from the constant battering it's taken from the press, much of it based on the cynical and foolhardy blunders of her children.

In December, Prince Charles' longtime chief aide, Michael Fawcett, made international headlines when he was implicated in a bribery scandal for helping steer a (reputedly undeserved) knighthood toward an oil-rich Saudi.

Currently, no Royal has caused the Queen more grief than her son, Prince Andrew, and her grandson, Prince Harry. Andrew is charged with raping the 17-year-old "sex slave" of disgraced financier and convicted sex offender

In 1947, after the ravages of World War II, **Princess Elizabeth (**later, **Queen Elizabeth II)** spent her 21st birthday in South Africa on a tour with her family.

During her time there, she delivered a speech via radio in which she made a commitment to serve the British Commonwealth. "I declare before you all that my whole life whether it be long or short shall be devoted to your service and the service of our great imperial family to which we all belong," she said.

In the years that followed, even her greatest detractors sometimes grudgingly agreed that, indeed, she kept her word.

Some historians have surmised that Elizabeth's deeply entrenched sense of royal protocols derived from her grandmother, **Mary of Teck**. She appears here with baby Elizabeth and her ferociously Imperial husband, **King/Emperor George V.**

Young Elizabeth is seen here in the early 1930s at Balmoral, riding home from church with the dowager empress widely viewed as one of the most frightening and scary royals in Europe.

Elizabeth with her father, the "reluctant King" **George VI** in the gardens of Windsor Castle. One of of the ironies of 20th-Century history is that her monarchy resulted from the bizarre, scandal-soaked abdication of George's dim-witted older brother, **Edward VIII** (later, the **Duke of Windsor**), who changed history in a fit of pique when he wasn't allowed by Winston Churchill and others "to marry the woman I love."

Jeffrey Epstein, who committed suicide in New York City's Metropolitan Correctional Center in 2019.

Andrew's defense has been to "deny, deny, deny." He has been relieved of Royal duties, and is said to be hiding at Balmoral Castle, the Scottish summer home of the Queen. He may be with his ex-wife, Sarah Ferguson, who has generated her own share of scandalous headlines.

Topping Andrew in the churning out of headlines has been the exiled Prince Harry and his American-born wife, Meghan, who now live in a $14 million mansion in Montecito, California. His attacks on the Royals have caused a bitter rift between Prince William, his older brother, and himself. Harry has accused the Royals of racism and of making Meghan suicidal.

According to the latest gossip, the Queen wants to draw up an agreement where, upon her death or resignation, Charles would become King until he was eighty. After that, he would step down from the throne in favor of his son (her grandson), William.

Charles was never popular with the British public and became even more unpopular after his divorce from Princess Diana. William, however, is very popular, even though a large percentage of the British population wants to eliminate the monarchy entirely.

Elizabeth is still mourning the death of her late husband, Prince Philip, who died in April of 2021 at the age of 99. As his former valet told the press, "Her Majesty did not demand sexual fidelity from him but insisted on loyalty."

Reportedly, among Philip's last words to Elizabeth were, "Lilibet *(his nickname for her)*, you and I have not been well served by our spoiled progeny. God Save the Queen, and the monarchy for generations to come."

***

Editor's Note: At the age of 96, Queen Elizabeth II died on September 8, 2022. At the time of her death, she had reigned for 70 years and 214 days, the longest of any monarch in British history. She also was the second-longest running monarch in history behind Louis XIV of France.

Elizabeth's coronation after the tragedies and heartbreaks of World War II, injected Europe and the world with new hope and a new sense of optimism. Here she is on the cover of the "coronation edition" of Italy's *Grazia* magazine in their edition of May 31, 1953. She was 25.

Pomp & Circumstance: Same Setup, Different Eras

Elizabeth gave confusing signals about the degree to which she either enjoyed or detested (or both) the pageantry that came with her *schtick*. Here she is at different stages of her monarchy, stable and consistent to the end.

Motherhood Wasn't Her Scene. *Do you blame her?*
(Above, left) Here are **Prince Philip** with **Elizabeth** and their two oldest children, **Charles** and **Anne**, in 1951.

September 2013
Celebrity & Fame in America

FANS VOTE ON WHOM THEY MOST WANT RESURRECTED FROM THE GRAVE

Today, it's easy to conduct a poll on just about anything. Take the bizarre, rather morbid poll just made by *60 Minutes* and the magazine *Vanity Fair*.

Poll respondents were asked, "Which dead celebrity would you want to bring back to life?"

Just so that Marilyn, Elvis, and JFK would not dominate the list, only celebrities who died between 1994 and today were included in the vote. Of the top seven, four were drug addicts.

Diana, the 36-year-old Princess of Wales, topped the list, garnering 35 percent of the vote. She died on August 31, 1997 in a car crash in a Paris tunnel, with carloads of *paparazzi* in hot pursuit.

First runner-up was Apple founder Steve Jobs (14 percent). The next four celebs on the list were drug addicts—Michael Jackson and Whitney Houston (tied at 11 percent each); actor Heath Ledger (9 percent); and grunge rocker Kurt Cobain (6 percent). The recently deceased star of Sopranos, James Gandolfini, landed at the bottom of the list at an unimpressive 3 percent.

Speculation about the death of Princess Di reached an alltime high this year. She's making headlines around the world, especially in Britain, where Scotland Yard reportedly has reopened an investigation into her untimely death.

After the car crash, she lived only a short time, dying in a hospital. But her boyfriend, Dodi Fayed, and the drunken driver of their Mercedes-Benz, Henri Paul, were pronounced dead at the scene. Di's bodyguard, Trevor Rees-Jones, survived, but had no memory of what happened.

Dodi's father, billionaire Mohamed al-Fayed, still claims that Di and his son were murdered. Most of the accounts point a finger at a former soldier, a member of an elite unit in the British military, along with two accomplices. The soldier is said to have flashed a light into the face of the driver, blinding him. Today, the soldier is said to be hiding out in Croatia on a forged passport. Obviously, if this is true, he was acting on orders from a higher authority. Speculation has even pointed to a member (or members) of the royal circle, but so far, no smoking gun has emerged.

The most serious accusations have been toward ruthless arms dealers who make millions selling weapons to terrorists and corrupt governments. Di's campaign against land mines, or so it is reported, made her a prime target.

The concept of **"Resurrection from the Grave"** is so fraught, and so complicated, that most scientists have consigned its conceptualization to artists and theologians. Until now.

Here's *Salvador Dali's* renowned surrealistic painting, **The Ascension of Christ.** Highly spiritual, it derived, the artist said, from a "cosmic dream" he'd had eight years before he painted it in 1958.

Who would most Americans want to see RESURRECTED FROM THE GRAVE, according to a recent poll?

With the full understanding that the answer (and the question, too) is as weird as anything America has been credited with recently producing, here's a short **"Rogues' Gallery" of Winners.**

High on the list is **Diana, Princess of Wales,** shown here in full dynastic drag before her death in 1997.

The *right-hand photo* shows her *inamorata* and companion in death, the Egyptian-born heir presumptive to Harrod's Department Store, **Dodi Fayyed.**

Steve Jobs, the charismatic pioneer of the personal computer revolution, died on October 5, 2011, age 56, of complications from pancreatic cancer. He'd undergone a liver transplant in 2009.

Prior to its release, the movie *Jobs* (2013), starring Ashton Kutcher, was envisioned as a hit, but failed at the box office. Critics claimed that the film did not navigate the passions, perfectionism, demons, desires, artistry, devilry, and obsessions of its subject. In a mock turtleneck and "mom jeans," Kutcher struggled valiantly in the role, but millions of Steve Jobs fans stayed away.

Since his death on June 25, 2005, Michael Jackson, age 50, never left the headlines. As he prepared for his comeback concert series, This Is It, the singer died of acute propofol intoxication after suffering cardiac arrest. The Los Angeles County Coroner ruled the death a homicide.

Jackson's personal physician, Conrad Murray, was convicted of involuntary manslaughter and was sentenced to four years in prison. He is scheduled for release this month (October, 2013).

Jackson continued to make headlines all summer, as his estate sued concert promoter AEG for billions, claiming that they failed to properly investigate the doctor and his record. AEG officials denied ever hiring him, maintaining it was Jackson himself who employed Murray.

Tied with Jackson by fans hoping for a "resurrection" was Whitney Houston, who died, age 48, on February 11, 2012. The most awarded singing star of all time, Houston was found unconscious and submerged in her bathtub at the Beverly Hilton Hotel. Before getting into the water, she'd consumed large amounts of cocaine.

An Australian, actor Heath Ledger, died in New York City, age 28, on January 22, 2008 from accidental intoxication from prescription drugs. He had just finished interpreting the role of "The Joker" in *The Dark Knight*, which became the biggest-grossing film of the year. Most of his millions went to his daughter, Matilda Rose Ledger, born to the actor's girlfriend, actress Michelle Williams, who had starred with him in the 2005 Brokeback Mountain.

Kurt Cobain, the lead singer of the American grunge band, Nirvana, was found dead at his home on April 8, 1994, apparently having committed suicide three days prior. A persistent drug addict, he may have shot himself with his own gun. But speculation continues to this day that he was murdered. His wife, singer Courtney Love, hired private detectives, but the issues associated with his death have never been resolved.

New Jersey born James Gandolfini scored a big hit as the troubled crime boss, Tony Soprano, on the TV series *The Sopranos*. In Rome, he was discovered on the bathroom floor of his hotel suite by his 13-year-old son, Michael. He was pronounced dead within 20 minutes of his arrival at a local hospital. Michael inherited the bulk of his father's $70 million estate.

Apple computer visionary & tech genius **Steve Jobs**.

Nirvana kingpin, musician **Kurt Cobain** on the cover of *Request* magazine. The frilly frock he's wearing, he said at the time, was an expression of his dislike of "toxic masculinity."

Other contenders for the (for now, at least, technically unfeasible) "honor" of being resurrected from the grave iinclude *(left to right)*: actor **Keith Ledger**, TV *(The Sopranos)* star **James Gandolfini** (depicted on the cover of *New Jersey* magazine); **Michael Jackson**; and **Whitney Houston**.

April 2021

WHO IS THE BIOLOGICAL FATHER OF PRINCE HARRY?

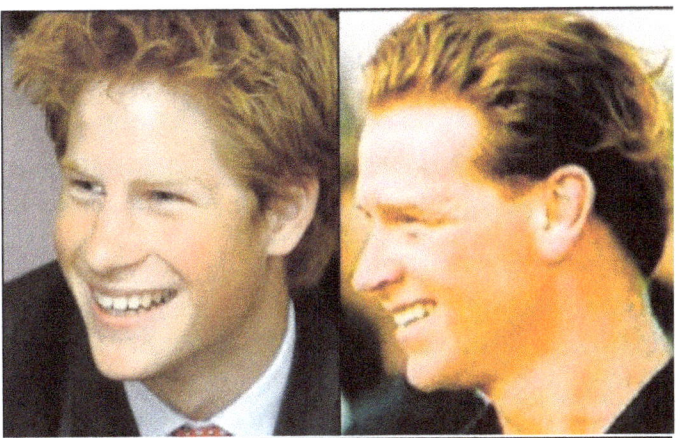

In addition to the excruciating embarrassment it caused everyone involved, many found the similarities between **Harry and Hewitt** "very very striking."

Millions of people around the world watched Oprah Winfrey's recent (March 2021) television interview with Meghan Markle (the Duchess of Sussex) and her Duke, Prince Harry.

The controversial interview sparked debates about racism in the Royal Family. Regrettably, throughout Britain, it also revived old, oft-repeated claims that the red-bearded Harry is not the biological son of Prince Charles.

Decades-old rumors about Harry's paternity were renewed, especially when he revealed to the world that Prince Charles no longer received his phone calls.

There is little doubt that the Queen, years ago, ordered DNA tests, and although officially, she has remained "Mum," she's (privately) aware of his true paternity. Harry doesn't look like Charles. Nor does he look like his blonde-haired (now balding) brother, Prince William, second in line (after Charles himself) to the throne.

Even her most devoted (i.e., quasi-fanatical) suppoters interpret some of Diana's self-destructive decisions as *naïve* and in some cases, stupid.

James Hewitt, hawking, in 1994, the second of two embarrassing tell-all *exposés* of his affair with Diana. Ironically, he was two-timing Diana with a simultaneous affair with a girlfriend named **Emma Stewardson**.

In 2003, *The Guardian* published an article that described Stewardson as "politely icy" about Princess Diana and "rather more heated about Hewitt," whom she and her family wished would "just shut up and go away."

But there's a roaring undercurrent in the U.K. about OTHER issues rekindled by Oprah's interview, even though CBS rigorously avoided mentioning them on camera:

When Princess Diana was at the peak of her beauty and sexuality, and as Prince Charles maritally "abandoned" her for *in flagrentes* with his then-mistress (Camilla), Diana went searching for love elsewhere. Prince Harry was born in 1984. Catalyzed by intense media pressure at the time, Buckingham Palace's ongoing "official" version informs us that Diana met, fell in love

When Hewitt's story hit the tabloids, it hit them hard. In the long run, everyone was a loser.

317

with and launched an affair with James Hewitt two years later. According to the official version, she fell in love with Hewitt one afternoon in 1986 while watching the dashing cavalry officer competing in a polo match.

Born in April of 1958 in Derry, Northern Ireland, Hewitt was red-haired and handsome, with a roving eye trained on the then-most-publicized young woman in the world.

From afar, Hewitt had always--the official version says--adored her. Numerous biographies have revealed that she was sexually attracted to him from the moment of introduction. Soon, their affair was in full swing, although at first, they had to be very secretive.

Their love and their long-lived sexual affair, as articulated—in print and on TV by the Princess herself-- is not in question: What has re-emerged in the wake of Oprah's interview, is controversy about the date of their first encounter.

Witnesses have come forth alleging that Diana actually met Hewitt sometime in 1983. Emma Stewardson, his girl friend at the time, alleged that he was "two-timing" her, and that he visited Highgrove, Charles' country home, at least nine months in advance of Harry's birth when the prince was away.

It is also alleged that Hewitt, before the birth of Harry, rented a room in West London as a secret meeting place, and that the Princess, in heavy disguise, went there time and time again for clandestine rendezvous.

Not only that, but many of Hewitt's colleagues in the Life Guards claimed that he boasted of his affair with Diana during its early stages, aka before the birth of Harry. The prominent Scottish journalist, Ross Benson, later wrote: Years after their affair, Diana, to her horror and to the horror of her in-laws at Buckingham Palace, learned that Hewitt was "more than boastful about how well he knew Diana."

Permeating the tabloid frenzy was a pervasive sense of sadness at the failure of an organization (the monarchy) that probably should have handled things better. But as one embittered wit pithily said in reference to its failures, **"You can do almost anything you want in life except control your children."**

Left to right in lower photo, above, **Diana, Charles**, and Charles' long-time mistress,

This was later "outed" and publicized in Simone Simmons' biography *Diana, The Last Word*, published in 2003. Ms. Simmons was a healer and a clairvoyant, who, during the last five years of Diana's life, became her confidante. Her book revealed that Diana admitted that with Hewitt, she experienced oral sex for the first time, and her first orgasm.

Diana claimed that "Jimmy treats me like a sex slave," and that she loved it. She lavished gifts on him, including a diamond tie pin, and form-fitting underwear "to show off his best hidden assets." She opened charge accounts in his name, later admitting, "He was bloody expensive."

Diana herself was embarrassingly indiscreet about her chronic unhappiness and her marital infidelities, confessing broadly to then-trusted friends who later betrayed her. Some of her indiscretions were expressed directly to members of the press.

For five years, their love affair flourished, although Diana admitted that outside the boudoir they had little in common, finding him as interesting as a knitting pattern. According to Simmons, as confided in her by Diana, "His head was in his trousers."

Deep into their affair, Diana confessed to being nosey and began to suspect that Hewitt was having affairs outside their boudoir in Kensington Palace. One night, she searched the pockets of his trousers and found the phone number of a woman who turned out to be one of his mistresses. When she confronted him, he angrily denied it: "How could I make love to you so forcefully, and for such extended periods, if I'm wasting my seed elsewhere?" he was rumored to have said at the time.

She hired detectives to follow him, and indeed, one of the men she employed turned up with some incriminating proof, some of which was photographic.

Gallantly, one of her "private dicks" told her, "Ma'am, I just don't understand. He's the luckiest man on the planet, and he turns elsewhere."

Hewitt later revealed to the British press that after Diana said farewell, he contemplated suicide. "I got into my car and loaded a few things," he said, "and then took the ferry across the Channel to France. I planned to shoot myself in transit. But at the last minute, my mother insisted on going along, too, and she may have saved my life."

During the course of their relationship, whenever Hewitt was away from her for any extended period, Diana wrote him passionate love letters. She later admitted to Simmons, "They were red hot, even pornographic, praising his lovemaking."

Later, she heard he was going to sell her letters to the highest bidder, and she knew at once she had to buy them herself. In a call to him, she learned that he wanted £250,000 for them, later doubling that price. She felt she had to pay it.

He wanted the cash-only transaction to take place in the resort of Benidorm on the eastern coast of Spain. With the banknotes stuffed in a large purse, she flew to Spain, wearing a wig and dark glasses. However, someone—perhaps Hewitt—alerted the press and paparazzi, and she was mobbed. Without retrieving the letters, she immediately returned to London on the next plane.

Much more information about these love letters later appeared in a tell-all book. Published in 1994, it was entitled *Princess in Love* by Ann Pasternak. [*Pasternak is a descendant of the early 20th-Century Russian writer Boris Pasternak, who had written the highly acclaimed novel,* Doctor Zhivago, *which was adapted into a box office hit in 1965.*]

After reading *Princess in Love*, Diana gave her own review: "I hope his cock shrivels up."

Diana read the book with heartbreak and in tears. According to those close to her, she felt a sense of the most awful betrayal—first from her husband, Charles, and now from her years-long lover, Hewitt.

She also had to face indelible rumors that Hewitt and Prince Harry looked alike, especially with their red hair. Around the time *Princess in Love* was released, a British tabloid published a picture of Harry, age 11, and Hewitt, age 11. They looked like identical twins.

In the aftermath of Hewitt's blackmail, fellow members of the British cavalry seemed somehow less gallant to royal fans, worldwide.

Hewitt, a Northern Irishman with a gift for polo, had been elevated to the rank of lieutenant in the British Army in 1980. Shortly after meeting Diana at a party, he had insinuated himself into her orbit by offering to give her riding lessons.

The Saga of James Hewitt quickly jumped from coverage in the tabloids to an audient of millions through streaming video.

In 2020, Season Four of Netflix's *The Crown* explored in teeth-grinding detail the tawdry progression of the Royal Infidelities.

Portraying **James Hewitt** was the multi-lingual Russian-German actor **Daniel Donsky** *(photos above)*.

Diana consistently denied that Hewitt was the father of Harry, saying he had been born two years before the debut of her affair, and that Harry's red hair derives from genetics associated with her own family, the Spencers. In fact, she sometimes referred to her growing boy as "My Little Spencer."

[*In Season Four of the recent hit TV series,* The Crown, *Hewitt is portrayed by actor Daniel Donskoy.*]

When Bill Clinton, then-U.S. President, was impeached, in part because of his affair with Monica Lewinsky, Diana wrote him a long letter, sharing his grief and referring to each of them as "fellow sufferers."

[*Unofficially, she gossiped with author Simone Simmons about the U.S. President, too: "I don't find him sexy at all. Perhaps that awful girl Monica did. I wonder what the Presidential willy looks like."*]

A reporter for the *New York Daily News* described the state of affairs like this: "Diana's former lover, James Hewitt, wrote a kiss-and-tell bio of her. He has suffered bad Karma ever since. His riding school has failed, and he was busted for alleged drug possession and tax evasion."

In 2009, after publicizing his affair with Diana in a relentless stream of tabloid reality TV shows, Hewitt opened a bar, the Polo Club, in Spain.

It was in Marbella, the "mobbed by British expats" resort along the southern coast of Spain. Positioned midway along that resort's "Golden Mile," it drew the rich and famous of international society until Hewitt closed it in 2013.

[Marbella, of course, had been chic long before Hewitt "discovered" it. In 1954, the Marbella Club opened, catering to an international coterie of movie stars, business tycoons, star athletes, and aristocrats, many with titles. Famous names like Bismarck, Rothschild, Thurn und Taxis, and Metternich patronized it regularly. At one point, the Marbella Club was run by Princess Marie-Louise of Prussia, the great-granddaughter of Kaiser Wilhelm II. Prince Rainier and Princess Grace were among the visitors, as was King Fahd of Saudi Arabia, who spent up to five million Euros a day here. Everyone from the Aga Khan IV to Julio Iglesias followed, as did exiled Cuban dictator Fulgencio Batista, who had escaped from Cuba after stealing $300 million from its Treasury.]

In collaboration with my co-author, Danforth Prince, we featured Hewitt's bar, The Polo Club, as a newsworthy rendezvous in our annual updates of Frommer's Guide to Spain and Frommer's Guide to the Costa del Sol.

It was obvious whenever he was there that Hewitt had evolved into a "babe magnet" of international notoriety. Night after night, chicly dressed women clustered around him. Although interpreted in many quarters as an unpatriotic "cad" for his revelations about Diana, he often behaved like an English gentleman full of charm and articulate grace, the kind of man a young woman could take home to meet her parents. It was obvious why Diana had found him so appealing. Charles, it was widely understood at the time, had moved into separate quarters shortly after their marriage.

At least some of **Darwin Porter's** "up close and personal" views of **James Hewitt** derive from frequent sightings of him (by then I.D.'d as "the ultimate British cad") at his club in Marbella, on Spain's Costa del Sol.

Darwin had reason to visit the club: It was part of his "beat" during his authorship of many editions of *Frommer's Spain*. It was also one of the most active and "happening" clubs on the Costa del Sol—until it folded after the nightclubbing public grew tired of Hewitt's *schtick*.

During its heyday, "comparison photos" of **Prince Harry** were prominently posted in the bar in close proximity to photos of **Hewitt** himself—an obvious reference to Hewitt's notoriety as the prince's probable (biological) father. Ironies (and embarassments) were rife. And in the end, everyone lost.

Hewitt admitted that he'd been dazzled by Diana's beauty and charm, but at first could hardly imagine that he, a commoner, had a chance to bed the Princess of Wales.

"It seemed to good to be true, but sometimes, dreams come true, though not often."

He seemed filled with a sense of male pride, secure in his appeal, his charm, and his masculinity. He once told friends that he had enough self-assurance to walk nude through a room filled with people.

He admitted he still has nightmares about Diana's tragic death in Paris. "But all in all, I can't complain. I was given five years with the most desirable woman on the planet."

WHATEVER HAPPENED TO JAMES HEWITT?

In July of 2004, he had trouble with the police when he was arrested drunk outside a diner in Fulham and charged with possession of cocaine. . Given a warning, he was released without being charged with drug possession. Local police also found a disassembled 16-bore shotgun at his home. As a result, he lost his firearm license.

In 2015, he suffered a stroke and ended up fighting for his life. At the end of June, he was released from the hospital and was in recovery. In 2021, he was reportedly working as a gardener. As of this writing, in 2025, he was still alive.

Darwin Porter

As a precocious nine-year-old, **Darwin Porter** began meeting entertainers through his mother, Hazel, a charismatic Southern girl whose husband had died in World War II. Migrating from the Depression-ravaged valleys of western North Carolina to Miami Beach during its most ebullient heyday, Hazel became a personal assistant to the vaudeville comedienne **Sophie Tucker**, the kind-hearted "Last of the Red Hot Mamas."

Loosely supervised by his mother, Darwin was regularly dazzled by the likes of **Judy Garland, Dinah Shore, Frank Sinatra, Ronald Reagan** (at the time near the end of his Hollywood gig), and **Marilyn Monroe**. Each of them made it a point, whenever they were in Miami (either on or off the record), to visit and pay their respects to "Miss Sophie."

At the University of Miami, Darwin edited the school newspaper, raising its revenues, through advertising and public events, to unheard-of new levels. He met and interviewed **Eleanor Roosevelt** and later invited her, as part of a sponsored event he crafted, to spend a day ("Eleanor Roosevelt Day") at the university, and to his delight, she accepted. Years later, in Manhattan, during her work as a human rights activist, he escorted her, at her request, to many public functions.

On another occasion, he invited **Lucille Ball and Desi Arnaz**, then at the pinnacle of their fame and popularity, to the University. On campus, after the photographers and fans departed, Lucille launched a bitter attack on her husband, accusing him of having had sex the previous night with two showgirls. Because of that and other upsets that unfolded that day, Darwin learned early in his life that Lucille Ball and Desi Arnaz were definitely not Ricky and Lucy Ricardo.

After his graduation, Darwin, in a graceful transition from his work as editor of the University's newspaper and his sponsorship by **Wilson Hicks** (Photo Editor and then Executive Editor of Life magazine) became a Bureau Chief of The Miami Herald (the youngest in that publication's history) assigned to its branch in Key West. At the time the island outpost was an avant-garde literary mecca and—thanks to the Cuban missile crisis—a flash point of the Cold War.

Key West had been the site of Harry S Truman's "Winter White House" and Truman returned a few months before his death for a final visit. He invited young Darwin for "early morning walks" where he used the young emissary of The Miami Herald to "set the record straight."

Through Truman, Darwin was introduced and later joined the staff of **Senator George Smathers** of Florida. Smathers' best friend was a young senator, **John F. Kennedy**. Through "Gorgeous George," as Smathers was known in the Senate, Darwin got to meet Jack and Jacqueline in Palm Beach. He later wrote two books about them—*The Kennedys, All the Gossip Unfit to Print*, and one of his all-time bestsellers, *Jacqueline Kennedy Onassis—A Life Beyond Her Wildest Dreams*. (A commemorative new edition was released in 2022 as *JKO: Her Tumultuous Life & Her Love Affairs*).

Buttressed by his status as *The Miami Herald*'s Key West Bureau Chief, Darwin met, interviewed, and often befriended **Tennessee Williams. Ernest Hemingway, Tallulah Bankhead, Gore Vidal, Truman Capote, Carson McCullers**, and a gaggle of other internationally famous writers and entertainers: **Cary Grant, Rock Hudson, Marlon Brando, Montgomery Clift, Susan Hayward, Warren Beatty, Christopher Isherwood, Anne Bancroft, Angela Lansbury,** and **William Inge**.

Eventually transferred to Manhattan, Darwin worked for a decade in television advertising with the producer and arts-industry socialite **Stanley Mills Haggart**. In addition to some speculative ventures associated with Marilyn Monroe, they also jointly produced TV commercials that included testimonials from **Joan Crawford** (then feverishly promoting Pepsi-Cola); **Ronald Reagan** (General Electric); and **Debbie Reynolds** (Singer sewing machines). Other personalities they promoted, each delivering televised sales pitches, included **Louis Armstrong, Lena Horne, Rosalind Russell, William Holden**, and **Arlene Dahl,** each of them hawking a commercial product.

Beginning in the early 1960s, Darwin joined forces with the then-fledgling **Arthur Frommer** organization, playing a key role in researching and writing more than 50 titles and defining the style and values that later emerged as the world's leading travel guidebooks, *The Frommer Guides.* Darwin's particular journalistic expertise on Europe, New England, California, and the Caribbean eventually propelled him into authorship of (depending on the era and whatever crises were brewing at the time), between 70 and 80% of their titles. Even during the research of his travel guides, he continued to interview show-biz celebrities, discussing their triumphs, feuds, and frustrations. At this point in their lives, many were retired and reclusive. Darwin either pursued them (sometimes though local tourist offices) or encountered them randomly as part of his extensive travels. **Ava Gardner, Lana Turner, Hedy Lamarr, Ingrid Bergman, Ethel Merman, Andy Warhol, Elizabeth Taylor, Marlene Dietrich, Bette Davis, Judy Garland,** and **Paul Newman** were particularly insightful.

Porter's biographies—at this writing, they number sixty-three— have won thirty first prize or "runner-up to first prize" awards at literary festivals in cities or regions which include New England, New York, Los Angeles, Hollywood, San Francisco, Florida, California, and Paris.

Darwin, also a magazine columnist, can be heard at regular intervals as a radio and podcast commentator, reviewing the ironies of celebrities, tabloid culture, politics, and scandal.

A resident of New York City, where he spent years within the social orbit of the Queen of Off-Broadway (the eccentric and very temperamental philanthropist, **Lucille Lortel),** Darwin is currently at work on a three-volume trilogy on the life of Clark Gable.

Danforth Prince

For years, Danforth Prince was one of the "Young Turks" of the post-millennium publishing industry. He's president and founder of Blood Moon Productions, a firm devoted to researching, salvaging, compiling, and marketing the oral histories of America's entertainment industry.

One of Prince's famous predecessors, the late **Lyle Stuart,** founder of **Barricade Press**, was self-described as "the last publisher in America with guts." Stuart once defined Prince as "one of his natural successors." In 1956, that then-novice maverick launched himself with $8,000 he'd won in a libel ludgment against gossip columnist **Walter Winchell**. It was Stuart who published **Linda Lovelace**'s two memoirs—*Ordeal* and *Out of Bondage.*

"I like to see someone following in my footsteps in the 21st Century," Stuart told Prince. "You publish scandalous biographies. I did, too. My books on J. Edgar Hoover, Jacqueline Kennedy Onassis, and Barbara Hutton stirred up beehives. You do, too."

Prince launched his career in journalism in the 1970s at the Paris Bureau of *The New York Times*. In the early '80s, he resigned to join Darwin Porter in the research, development, and publishing of various titles (including *Frommer's France* and *Frommer's Paris*) within **The Frommer Guides**. As a collaborative team, they reviewed the travel scenes of more than 50 nations for Simon & Schuster. Authoritative and comprehensive, the guides they spearheaded were perceived as indispensable "travel bibles" for millions of readers with recommendations (hotels, restaurants, shopping, nightlife, and "what to see and do" for the nations of Western Europe, the Caribbean, Bermuda, New England, The Bahamas, Georgia, the Carolinas, and California.

Prince, with Porter, is also the co-author of many celebrity biographies, each configured as a title within Blood Moon's Babylon series. These have included *Hollywood Babylon—It's Back; Hollywood Babylon Strikes Again; The Kennedys: All the Gossip Unfit to Print; Frank Sinatra, the Boudoir Singer,* and *Elizabeth Taylor, There is Nothing Like a Dame.*

Prince, in tandem with Porter, has also co-authored four books on film criticism, along with provocative "postmodern" biographies of, among many others, Lana Turner and Peter O'Toole. With Porter, he also co-authored *Pink Triangle: The Feuds and Private Lives of Tennessee Williams, Gore Vidal, Truman Capote, and Famous Members of their Entourages.*

Prince, a graduate of Hamilton College and a native of Easton and Bethlehem, Pennsylvania, is the president and founder (in 1996) of the Georgia Literary Association, and of the Porter and Prince Corporation. Founded in 1983, the Porter and Prince Corp. produced dozens of travel titles for both Prentice Hall and John Wiley & Sons. In 2011, he was named "Publisher of the Year" by a consortium of literary critics and marketers spearheaded by the J.M. Northern Media Group.

According to Prince, "Blood Moon provides the luxurious illusion that a reader is a perpetual guest at some gossipy dinner party populated with brilliant but occasionally self-delusional figures from bygone eras of the American Experience. Our success at salvaging, documenting, and articulating the (till now) orally transmitted histories of the Entertainment Industry—in ways that have never been seen before—is one of the most distinctive aspects of our backlist."

During the years he published in collaboration with the **National Book Network**, he electronically documented some of the controversies associated with his stewardship of Blood Moon. From that collaboration emerged more than fifty videotaped documentaries, book trailers, public speeches, and TV or radio interviews. Any of these can be watched, without charge, by performing a search for Đanforth Prince" on YouTube.com; checking him out on Facebook *[either "Danforth Prince" or "Blood Moon Productions]*, on Twitter (now X) (#BloodyandLunar); or by clicking on BloodMoonProductions.com.

During the rare moments when he isn't writing, editing, neurosing about, or promoting Blood Moon, he works out at a New York City gym, rescues stray animals, talks to strangers, and maintains the physical plant and gardens of his historic home in St. George, Staten Island.

Since 2004, under Danforth's stewardship, Blood Moon titles have been awarded dozens of nationally recognized literary prizes. They've included both silver and bronze medals from the IPPY (Independent Publishers Assn.) Awards, four nominations and two Honorable Mentions for BOOK OF THE YEAR from Forward Reviews; nominations from the Ben Franklin Awards; and Awards and Honorable Mentions from the New England, the Los Angeles, the Paris, the New York, the San Francisco, and the Hollywood Book Festivals. Two of its titles have been Grand Prize Winners for Best Summer Reading, as defined by the Beach Book Awards.